The Cold War at Home and Abroad

The Agony And The Ecstasy

THE COLD WAR AT HOME AND ABROAD

DOMESTIC POLITICS AND US FOREIGN POLICY SINCE 1945

EDITED BY
ANDREW L. JOHNS
AND
MITCHELL B. LERNER

UNIVERSITY PRESS OF KENTUCKY

Scholarly publisher for the Commonwealth,
serving Bellarmine University, Berea College, Centre College of Kentucky, Eastern Kentucky University, The Filson Historical Society, Georgetown College, Kentucky Historical Society, Kentucky State University, Morehead State University, Murray State University, Northern Kentucky University, Transylvania University, University of Kentucky, University of Louisville, and Western Kentucky University.

Editorial and Sales Offices: The University Press of Kentucky
663 South Limestone Street, Lexington, Kentucky 40508-4008
www.kentuckypress.com

Cataloging-in-Publication data is available from the Library of Congress.

ISBN 978-0-8131-7573-7 (hardcover : alk. paper)
ISBN 978-0-8131-7575-1 (pdf)
ISBN 978-0-8131-7574-4 (epub)

This book is printed on acid-free paper meeting the requirements of the American National Standard for Permanence in Paper for Printed Library Materials.

Manufactured in the United States of America.

Member of the Association of University Presses

Contents

Introduction

Janus, Tocqueville, and the World

The Nexus of Domestic Politics and US Foreign Policy

Andrew L. Johns

In late October 2011 President Barack Obama announced that the last US combat soldiers would leave Iraq by the end of the year, effectively ending a war that had cost more than 4,400 American lives and helped fuel Obama's meteoric rise to the White House. The timing of the president's statement, which came the day after the death of Libyan dictator Muammar Qaddafi and six months after US Navy SEALs killed Osama bin Laden in Pakistan, was not coincidental. As the *New York Times* observed, the combination of the removal of two key adversaries and the withdrawal of US troops "may help insulate him from Republican charges that he is weak on national security," a critical consideration as Obama geared up for his 2012 reelection campaign.[1] The decision to disengage from Iraq had been a long time coming. Understanding that delivering on his 2008 campaign promises would be crucial to securing a second term, Obama had declared on February 27, 2009, at the Marine Corps base at Camp Lejeune that combat forces would begin leaving Iraq on August 31, 2010, and the process would be completed by the end of 2011.

That domestic political calculations played a pivotal role in the timing of both announcements should not be a surprise to those who understand the nature and history of American politics and the country's engagement with the rest of the world. As Robert McMahon pointed out in 2005, the history of US foreign relations is inextricably linked to domestic politics because it is, "intrinsically, a Janus-faced field, one that looks both outward and inward for the wellsprings of America's behavior in the global arena."[2] Nearly two centuries earlier, Alexis de Tocqueville similarly observed that the American political system consistently exerts a profound effect on the country's international affairs. Democracies, he argued, tend to have "confused or erroneous ideas on external affairs, and decide questions of foreign policy on purely domestic considerations."[3] Although reductionist, Tocqueville's comment is instructive, particularly in the US context. Domestic determinants have always factored into the making and implementation of US foreign policy, even if the documentary evidence is sometimes lacking due to a reluctance on the part of policymakers to admit that they are, in fact, cognizant of and pay attention to them. This consciousness of what former national security adviser Walt W. Rostow referred to as the "Tocqueville Oscillation" between domestic politics and foreign policy underscores the significance of engaging this nexus for scholars of US foreign relations.[4] While any historical decision or action must be assessed based on a hierarchy of causation, domestic political considerations should be part of any balanced judgement of history, along with geostrategic, economic, cultural, ideological, and military perspectives.

Indeed, the nexus of foreign policy and domestic politics dates to the founding of the country (if not before, as the colonial era teemed with such interactions); there are countless examples throughout the course of American history that demonstrate the influence of these factors in the evolution of US foreign policy. George Washington's Farewell Address, for instance, not only advised against "entangling alliances" but also was specifically calculated to help John Adams win the White House in 1796. Partisan and intraparty divisions helped propel an unprepared and fractured United States into the War of 1812, trumping virtually all other considerations. Slavery and expansionism in the nineteenth century were inextricably linked, the rhetoric of Manifest Destiny notwithstanding. Domestic political concerns seriously limited Franklin Delano Roosevelt's efforts to assist the Allies prior to Pearl Harbor. And the long US involvement in Vietnam is replete with examples of domestic politics influencing decision-making. As Julian Zelizer wrote in *Arsenal of Democracy,* "it has proven difficult if not impossible to keep national security above the political fray" because US politicians "have been willing to use national security to distinguish themselves from their opponents."[5]

Nevertheless, for many historians of US foreign relations, domestic considerations do not factor into their analyses, despite the fact that scholars such as Jussi Hanhimäki have pointed out that "one simply cannot understand foreign policy and international relations without relating it to domestic contingencies and vice versa."[6] In fact, failing to do so verges on the ahistorical. Perhaps the most pointed critique along these lines came more than two decades ago from Ralph Levering, who noted that "emphasis on domestic factors is vital for understanding the making of U.S. foreign policy." Yet, he argued, "those scholars who seek to minimize the role of domestic politics . . . betray a gross misunderstanding of how the American political system actually works."[7] Levering's commentary should be understood in context. It came as the field of diplomatic history (or US foreign relations or international history, depending on one's definitional proclivities) was undergoing a renaissance of sorts. In response to a combination of external and internal criticism, many scholars increasingly focused on international and transnational perspectives, utilizing multiarchival and multilingual sources to a much greater degree and decentering the United States in their work. Concurrently, the field began to experience a "cultural turn" in the literature, which broadened the scope of inquiry as old questions were examined from new perspectives and with new methodologies. As a result, the state and foreign policy elites lost their privileged place in many studies. Moreover, traditional avenues of research that engaged the political aspects of the US role in the world were relegated to the margins of the field.[8]

These methodological and interpretive changes certainly silenced many of the criticisms of the field and revitalized the historiography. As Thomas Zeiler argued in a 2009 overview of recent literature on US foreign relations, the breadth and depth of the new scholarship had resulted "in the field's vigorous renovation" and helped reshape the study of American history.[9] Yet while Zeiler's article celebrated the vibrancy of the work being done on US foreign relations, and though he admitted that "rooting the field in international history risks losing sight of the Americanness that is the very character of US diplomatic history," he barely mentioned the relevance of domestic political factors, an oversight addressed by one of the responses to his essay.[10] Even the broader disciplinary trends Zeiler cited in the article that have been adopted by foreign relations scholars and are rooted in the domestic realm—race, gender, identity, culture—have obscured the political aspects of policymaking.

Despite the pendulum swing away from exploring this nexus, some scholars have continued to recognize the centrality of politics and have examined ways to integrate domestic considerations into the new paradigms. Melvin Small's *Democracy and Diplomacy* remains the seminal work on the relationship between politics and foreign policy, although it has become somewhat dated two decades after its publication.[11] Thomas Schwartz, in his 2008 presidential address to the Society for Historians of American Foreign Relations, reminded his audience that even with the emphasis on the international and transnational, "domestic partisan politics, the struggle for power at home, has played, and no doubt continues to play, a substantial role in the making and direction of American foreign policy."[12] And scholars such as Fredrik Logevall, Julian Zelizer, Steven Casey, Robert David Johnson, and myself have explored how these factors shape US foreign relations in both general and specific ways.[13]

But we should insert a caveat here. It would be easy to limit the definition of "domestic politics" to traditional conceptions of the phrase. Logevall's essay in the most recent edition of *Explaining the History of American Foreign Relations* does just that. He correctly and passionately argues for the inclusion of electoral considerations and partisan politics as a critical methodological approach that makes it possible for scholars to gain a more complete understanding of how US foreign policy is made and implemented.[14] And as Condoleezza Rice, national security adviser and secretary of state during the George W. Bush administration, noted in September 2007, "those who shape international affairs are best understood first as politicians and only later perhaps as statesmen. Understanding how leaders come to and stay in office is far more important to our grasp of major events in international politics than traditional ideas about the balance of power or polarity."[15] But what about other domestic political factors? Recent scholarship demonstrates clearly the inclusive and diverse nature of what should be considered "domestic factors," including gender, religion, human rights, immigration, regionalism, race, and ethnicity.[16] As Jason Parker notes, "If 'domestic politics' are considered this way, in their fullest dimensions—not just elections and campaigns but political culture and rhetoric, public and partisan opinion, and state policy, -power, and -institutions—then these very much deserve a place in our analyses."[17]

The authors of the essays that follow make clear that their interpretations of "domestic politics" measure up to Parker's notional definition and transcend traditional conceptions. As Mitchell Lerner trenchantly observes in the conclusion to this volume, these authors share a desire to bring together political and international history and reflect the growing methodological diversity that has transformed the field over the past twenty years. Yet they do so by incorporating domestic factors into their analyses rather than ignoring or marginalizing them. Moreover, the essays herein are linked by several central themes: the impact of nonelites on the shaping of US foreign policy; the degree of correlation between political language and evolving social values; the importance of place and its local context in shaping political values and, by extension, US foreign policy; and the conviction that domestic factors should be intrinsic to our overall conception of how the United States interacts with the rest of the world, and vice versa.

Appreciating the "Janus-faced" nature of US foreign relations—particularly in a contemporary era in which turmoil, controversy, and deep partisan divisions pervade the country's politics and directly influence decisions and actions, while also affecting how both allies and adversaries perceive US foreign policy—seems crucial to understanding how and why the United States acts on the global stage. The contributors to this volume examine a spectrum of diverse domestic factors and their influence on the history of US foreign relations since 1945, ranging from traditional conceptions such as elections and Congress's influence on policy to the role of religion and regionalism. In doing so, they highlight influences and ideas that expand our understanding of the history of US foreign relations and provide guidance and direction for contemporary observers of the US role in the world.

Notes

1. *New York Times,* October 22, 2011.

2. Robert J. McMahon, "Diplomatic History and Policy History: Finding Common Ground," *Journal of Policy History* 17, no. 1 (January 2005): 97.

3. Quoted in George Kennan, *American Diplomacy,* expanded ed. (Chicago: University of Chicago Press, 1984), 176.

4. Walt W. Rostow, "Domestic Determinants of U.S. Foreign Policy: The Tocqueville Oscillation," *Armed Forces Journal,* June 27, 1970, 16B.

5. Julian E. Zelizer, *Arsenal of Democracy: The Politics of National Security—From World War II to the War on Terror* (New York: Basic Books, 2009), 505.

6. Jussi M. Hanhimäki, "Global Visions and Parochial Politics: The Persistent Dilemma of the 'American Century,'" *Diplomatic History* 27, no. 4 (September 2003): 446.

7. Ralph B. Levering, "Is Domestic Politics Being Slighted as an Interpretive Framework?" *SHAFR Newsletter* 25, no. 1 (March 1994): 34–35.

8. On the "cultural turn," see, for example, M. Todd Bennett, "It 'Jes Grew': A Roadmap of the Cultural Turn in U.S. Foreign Relations History," *Passport: The Society for Historians of American Foreign Relations Review* 44, no. 3 (January 2014): 20–24.

9. Thomas W. Zeiler, "The Diplomatic History Bandwagon: A State of the Field," *Journal of American History* 95, no. 4 (March 2009): 1073.

10. Ibid., 1060; Fredrik Logevall, "Politics and Foreign Relations," *Journal of American History* 95, no. 4 (March 2009): 1074–78.

11. Melvin Small, *Democracy and Diplomacy: The Impact of Domestic Politics on U.S. Foreign Policy, 1789–1994* (Baltimore: Johns Hopkins University Press, 1996).

12. Thomas A. Schwartz, "'Henry, . . . Winning an Election Is Terribly Important': Partisan Politics in the History of U.S. Foreign Relations," *Diplomatic History* 33, no. 2 (April 2009): 173.

13. See, for example, Zelizer, *Arsenal of Democracy;* Campbell Craig and Fredrik Logevall, *America's Cold War: The Politics of Insecurity* (Cambridge, MA: Belknap Press, 2009); Steven Casey, *Selling the Korean War: Propaganda, Politics and Public Opinion, 1950–1953* (New York: Oxford University Press, 2008); Andrew L. Johns, *Vietnam's Second Front: Domestic Politics, the Republican Party, and the War* (Lexington: University Press of Kentucky, 2010); Robert David Johnson, *The Peace Progressives and American Foreign Relations* (Cambridge, MA: Harvard University Press, 1995); Robert E. Jenner, *FDR's Republicans: Domestic Political Realignment and American Foreign Policy* (Lanham, MD: Rowman and Littlefield, 2010); Andrew Johnstone and Andrew Priest, eds., *U.S. Presidential Elections and Foreign Policy: Candidates, Campaigns, and Global Politics from FDR to Bill Clinton* (Lexington: University Press of Kentucky, 2017); Gary Stone, *Elites for Peace: The Senate and the Vietnam War, 1964–1968* (Knoxville: University of Tennessee Press, 2007); Melvin Small, *At the Water's Edge: American Politics and the Vietnam War* (Chicago: Ivan R. Dee, 2005); Colin Dueck, *Hard Line: The Republican Party and U.S. Foreign Policy since World War II* (Princeton, NJ: Princeton University Press, 2010); Robert David Johnson, *Congress and the Cold War* (New York: Cambridge University Press, 2005).

14. Fredrik Logevall, "Domestic Politics," in *Explaining the History of American Foreign Relations,* 3rd ed., ed. Frank Costigliola and Michael J. Hogan (New York: Cambridge University Press, 2016), 151–67. It should be noted that this essay is new in the third edition; the first edition contained a general essay on public opin-

ion by Melvin Small, but the second edition did not include any methodological essay on the topic of domestic politics, broadly defined. See Melvin Small, "Public Opinion," in *Explaining the History of American Foreign Relations,* ed. Michael J. Hogan and Thomas G. Paterson (New York: Cambridge University Press, 1991), 165–76. Logevall and Kenneth Osgood made a similar point in an op-ed titled "Why Did We Stop Teaching Political History?" *New York Times,* August 29, 2016. They received a great deal of criticism for what many considered their narrow and limiting construction of the field. See also https://historians.org/publications-and-directories/perspectives-on-history/january-2017/political-history-an-exchange for a subsequent roundtable discussion on the merits and shortcomings of their argument.

15. *New York Times,* September 15, 2007.

16. Representative books include Andrew Preston, *Sword of the Spirit, Shield of Faith: Religion in American War and Diplomacy* (New York: Knopf, 2012); Mary Dudziak, *Cold War Civil Rights: Race and the Image of American Democracy* (Princeton, NJ: Princeton University Press, 2002); Sarah B. Snyder, *Human Rights Activism and the End of the Cold War: A Transnational History of the Helsinki Network* (New York: Cambridge University Press, 2011); and Joseph A. Fry, *The American South and the Vietnam War: Belligerence, Protest, and Agony in Dixie* (Lexington: University Press of Kentucky, 2015).

17. Jason Parker, "'On Such a Full Sea Are We Now Afloat': Politics and U.S. Foreign Relations across the Water's Edge," *Perspectives,* May 2011, https://www.historians.org/publications-and-directories/perspectives-on-history/may-2011/political-history-today/on-such-a-full-sea-are-we-now-afloat.

1

Fact Givers or Fact Makers?

The Dilemma of Information-Making in the State Department's Office of Public Affairs during the Truman Administration

Autumn Lass

In 2012 Congress updated the Smith-Mundt Act of 1948, which prohibited domestic propaganda, by passing House Resolution 5736, or the Smith-Mundt Modernization Act. It "authorized the domestic dissemination of information and material about the United States intended primarily for foreign audiences."[1] The act gave the Broadcasting Board of Governors (BBG), the agency responsible for broadcasting American messages to international audiences, access to the American public.[2] While the BBG's primary target remains international listeners, the agency can now seek to influence the American public as well. In its own FAQs page, the BBG addressed the question of whether its content is news or propaganda by stating that it presents "accurate and objective news and information" to the American people.[3] According to BBG spokeswoman Lynne Weil, the rationale behind the modernization of the Smith-Mundt Act of 1948 was to provide taxpayers with access to the messages the agency uses to champion the United States and to combat terrorism abroad.[4]

The revision of the Smith-Mundt Act did not create domestic political turmoil for Congress, the State Department, or the Obama administration. It received very little coverage in the national media and resulted in almost zero public outcry.[5] Why? The modernized version of the Smith-Mundt Act claims that the government provides the American people with access to accurate information on US foreign policy. It does not make propaganda—it releases news. Americans have become accustomed to this official description of state-sponsored information. This definition has been used for years to mask domestic propaganda. By looking at the history of this process, we can understand how the federal government has used "truth" and "news" as a way to influence the American people.[6] While the origins of this process date back to the Wilson administration, it was the Truman administration and the Department of State's Office of Public Affairs (PA) that relied solely on "news" and "truth" as their method of influencing the American people. Unlike early information institutions that used overt methods to pressure the public, the PA's sole purpose was to create an educated and supportive public through less conspicuous methods.

The PA's mission was to foster domestic support by teaching Americans about the "true" nature of the United States' place in the world and the administration's foreign policies. It provided Americans with the "facts" so that they could come to the "right" conclusions about Truman's foreign policies. The PA served as both teacher and persuader, and its dual nature made its job complicated. On the one hand, the PA was simply providing the American public with facts about Truman's foreign policies. On the other hand, those facts were meant to create domestic support for the president's policies. Not all facts would accomplish this goal—only a select few would do so. Therefore, the PA chose the "right" set of facts to teach Americans the "truth" about US foreign policy in order to win their support.

The PA's approach to disseminating information marked a turning point in twentieth-century domestic propaganda. Previously, the government had used high-pressure propaganda methods to sell foreign policy to the American public. During the Truman administration, the PA adopted low-pressure techniques or "soft-selling" strategies meant to covertly influence its audience.[7] "Soft-selling" propaganda was a clear alternative to tactics used by agencies such as the Committee for Public Information during World War I or the Office of Wartime Information during World War II—the sole purpose of which was to influence the American public with overt pressure. Even though these institutions used "truth" and "fact," their methods of dissemination included blatant pressure techniques such as posters, leaflets, and radio or film broadcasting. For example, the Committee for Public Information aggressively promoted World War I and Wilson's foreign policies to the American public through the use of Four-Minute Men; these speakers, working at behest of the Wilson administration, traveled throughout the United States publicly espousing Wilson's foreign policy agenda.[8] In contrast, the PA used less aggressive tactics—carefully selecting facts to influence its audience through banal presentations or third-party distributions—to subtly influence public opinion. It relied on the distribution of educational materials, publications, and relations with national organizations and the media to spread its truth to the American public. These types of soft-selling techniques were meant to allow the American people to believe that they were coming to their own conclusions.

The Office of Public Affairs frequently differentiated between "high-pressure" and "low-pressure" information techniques. For example, it considered the Voice of America, the overseas broadcasting arm of the State Department, a high-pressure operation because its information and tactics were clearly meant to influence. The PA described its own messages as "low-pressure" because it only provided Americans with information—it did not openly try to pressure or influence them. This difference was key to the PA, which equated high-pressure propaganda to "peddling wares or policies," while low-pressure propaganda allowed Americans to feel as though they had reached "their own conclusions."[9] This self-made distinction illustrates the complex identity of the Office of Public Affairs: it needed to have the *effect,* but could not have the *appearance,* of high-pressure propaganda.

This distinction between low- and high-pressure propaganda illustrates the link between public opinion and foreign policymaking. The PA needed to steer the public into supporting Truman's foreign policies without making them feel as if they had been coerced into that decision. Otherwise, it risked losing public support completely. The PA's job was to control and manage the relationship between the American public and foreign policy. It was crucial for the Truman administration's global agenda to have public consensus with regard to its foreign policies. If the public did not support Truman's global vision, it would be incredibly difficult for the administration to turn its global ambitions into realities.[10]

This essay examines how the Department of State's Office of Public Affairs defined its identity during the Truman administration. Was it just a fact giver, or was it also a fact maker for the administration? Could it be both? I analyze the PA's identity dilemma in two different situations. First, I examine how the PA grappled internally with its official and unofficial purpose. These internal debates demonstrate that even within the State Department there was confusion over the PA's domestic information program. Second, I illustrate how the PA's identity dilemma manifested in its "domestic publicity" tactics. It struggled to maintain its self-made distinction between simple information and propaganda when creating information programs for the public.[11] Finally, I argue that this identity dilemma sprang from the complex relationship between public opinion and foreign policy. The PA had to do its part in influencing public opinion because public consensus was so important to early Cold War policies. But it could not exert too much pressure for fear of being linked to the kind of domestic propaganda operations found in the Soviet Union. Dean Acheson aptly described the PA's information-making dilemma: "If we have a program for giving out information, we are *propagandizing.* If we don't give our information promptly and systematically we are cynically denying your right as citizens to know what is going on behind those musty old walls. Servicing the public with facts is apparently a dangerous business. The Department is damned if it does and it's damned if it doesn't."[12] Ultimately, the PA was damned. It struggled to accomplish its mission because it could not effectively manage that relationship between public opinion and foreign policy while attempting to balance its fact-giving and fact-making identities.

A Brief History of the Office of Public Affairs

The PA's origins can be traced back to 1943 when Undersecretary of State Edward Stettinius created the Office of Public Liaison to establish a relationship between the Department of State and the public.[13] By January 1944 the State Department had created a larger office called the Office of Public Information (OPI), which included the Public Liaison Office. The office had two basic tasks: study public opinion and give the public information about US foreign policy and the Department of State.[14] In its early days the OPI mostly utilized its relations with the press, organizing press meetings and issuing press releases regarding US foreign policy. However, in the fall of 1944 Secretary of State Cordell Hull fully embraced the notion of managing public opinion.[15] Hull began to look for ways to increase the State Department's interaction with the general public and utilize the American people's newfound interest in foreign policy.[16] To reflect this new direction, the OPI changed its name to the Office of Public Affairs.[17] This name change reflected the dilemma the PA would face throughout its stint as information maker for the Truman administration.[18] It needed to avoid any connection to propaganda or information-making while making it clear that the State Department was truly interested in connecting with the American public. Therefore, the office adopted the title "public affairs" as a way to free itself from the stigma of information-making while still emphasizing its new mission of public interaction.[19]

The Office of Public Affairs was officially "responsible for the formulation and coordination of policy and action concerning domestic informational aspects of foreign relations."[20] The new PA director, Francis Russell, argued that the Department of State needed to engage in a domestic information program to fulfill its duty of providing Americans with the "facts concerning international affairs and to explain current American foreign policies."[21] Its job was to create domestic support and manage that support to establish a public consensus for Truman's foreign policies. To measure its success and create consensus, the Public Studies Division within the PA polled the American public and worked with other major polling centers to gauge public reception. It worked constantly to provide detailed studies and reports about public opinion.[22] This information was then used to update and alter the PA's information programs to ensure that they were addressing specific public concerns. Russell explained that the PA operated as the "middleman" between the Department of State and the American public. He also firmly believed that Americans needed to "entrust to the State Department the discretion" to make the right decisions about what information it provided to the public about US foreign policy.[23] It was in these decisions about what to reveal to the American people and what to keep confidential that the PA crossed the line between being merely a "fact giver" and becoming a "fact maker."

Almost immediately, the new Office of Public Affairs was put to work creating and managing public opinion about US foreign policies. The

Cold War presented the Truman administration with a different challenge in winning public support. Because the Cold War did not originally appear to be a "life-or-death" type of conflict to the American people, the administration had to convince them to support the Cold War without an obvious reason for urgency.[24] Creating a consensus at home was pivotal for the Truman administration's ability to wage the Cold War and to win it, which was considered vital for world security and for the protection of American international interests.[25] It was the PA's responsibility to convince the American public of this. The relationship between the American public and policymakers only intensified as the Cold War continued; therefore, the PA's task of managing this volatile relationship only grew more important and more complicated.

Internal Debates over Identity

Francis Russell was asked later in life whether he was confident his work with the Office of Public Affairs had not crossed the propaganda line. He answered, "You couldn't be—different people inevitably would draw the line at different points. All I can say is that I was very much aware that this was an operation that could become an instrument of high-pressuring the American public, or misleading them. It could be a danger, there's no doubt about it."[26] This statement indicates that both Russell and the PA saw a difference between high-pressuring and low-pressuring the American public. High-pressuring the public involved the use of hard-sell propaganda tactics, which, according to Russell, was not what the PA was intended to do. Yet he could not say that the PA did not create domestic propaganda. Instead, Russell simply stated that whether the PA created information or propaganda depended on an individual's point of view. The difference between giving facts and making facts was often indistinguishable, which resulted in an identity dilemma within and without the PA. This dilemma first manifested in internal State Department debates on the nature of information provided by the PA.

In 1947, after Russell appeared before a congressional appropriations committee, Assistant Secretary of State for Public Affairs William Benton asked Russell why he had claimed that the PA served "the Department primarily, rather than the public." Appearing to be sarcastic, Benton asked, "If this is so, doesn't your office have a name that is deceptive and incorrect—why call it the Office of U.S. Public Affairs?" Benton cut to the heart of the issue when he asked Russell whether he was willing to "face up to your own concept of what you are supposed to do." Benton asked whether Russell's contention that the PA served primarily the State Department had been a way to ensure congressional funding. Instead of waiting for Russell's reply, Benton answered his own question by stating that Russell could not truly believe his primary informational responsibility was to the department because half of the PA's funds were "devoted to the public interest."[27] When Russell eventually responded, he explained that the committee had been given "misleading" information about the Office of Public Affairs and he was simply trying to set the record straight.[28]

Benton's line of questioning and Russell's response are both enlightening. Clearly, Benton believed that Russell had adjusted his definition of the PA's mission to secure more funding from Congress, but he was equally concerned about whether Russell actually believed that definition. Benton clearly wanted the PA to function as more than just a public opinion provider to the State Department. He wanted it to focus on information activities directed toward the public. Benton's questioning also indicates that both men had a specific understanding of the PA. It was obviously more complicated than just providing the public with facts about US foreign policy; otherwise, Russell would have admitted as much to Congress. Why else would Benton ask him, "Are you afraid to face up to your own concept of what you are supposed to do?" Finally, Russell's attempt to set the record straight included misleading Congress. He purposefully underplayed the PA's role with the public. This decision demonstrates that he understood that the PA's information mission was controversial enough that Congress might defund his office. Therefore, Russell claimed that the PA's primary responsibility was to provide State Department officials with information about the public. In this conversation, the PA's identity crisis is evident. Benton and Russell both understood what the functions of the PA were, but Russell was uncomfortable explaining those tasks to Congress for fear that they tended too closely to propaganda-making.

One of the best examples of internal discussions over the Office of Public Affairs involved the possible merger of overseas and domestic information-making offices. In the fall of 1949 Howland Sargeant, deputy assistant secretary of state for public affairs, combined the making of domestic and overseas information for a three-month trial period. The fusion was intended to create a comprehensive information guide for the assistant secretary of state for public affairs. This broad program was supposed to emphasize the commonalities in both programs, encourage cooperation between both branches, and create mutual solutions for all information-related problems.[29]

However, the merger personally offended PA director Russell. One of his major concerns was how the information would be presented to domestic audiences. He wondered whether the information programs would constitute a "positive enumeration of information policy objectives" or whether they would "consist primarily of specific injunctions as to what should be stressed, omitted, slanted, or emphasized."[30] Russell believed that domestic information programs should provide positive descriptions of foreign policies and should not be a collection of instructions from the overseas branch telling the PA what to include in its own program. Once again, this highlights Russell's complicated view of the PA's mission by differentiating between positive portrayals of American foreign policy and stressed or slanted information. The former was acceptable; the latter was not. Yet the difference between the two was very small. Russell believed that accentuating positive facts would bring about public support, while omitting, slanting, or emphasizing certain information would amount to overtly manipulating the truth. These "overt" attempts at manipulation were where Russell apparently drew the intellectual distinction between "fact" and "information."

Most important, Russell worried that if the foreign information branch took over domestic information programs, Congress and the American people would have ample evidence to argue that the PA was attempting to "sell" ideas to the public. He feared that blending foreign information programs with domestic ones would give the "false impression that the Department is carrying on a high pressure propaganda effort against the American public," which would hurt the PA's image and possibly lead to its defunding by Congress.[31] Russell was concerned that if the domestic campaigns were taken over by the overseas division, it would further obscure an already blurry line.[32] Therefore, the PA insisted that it alone should have control over domestic information programs and that clear distinctions should be made and kept between foreign and domestic programs.

Russell's fears were confirmed in the fall of 1949 when the entire Formosa information policy paper was leaked to the public.[33] This paper explained both the overseas and the domestic information strategies for selling US policies in the region. When the paper was leaked, Congress and the media accused the State Department of using the Office of Public Affairs to disseminate domestic propaganda. Russell used the incident to illustrate how dangerous it was to merge the domestic and overseas branches. He explained that the leak of the Formosa paper gave the false impression that the PA was "engaging in a high pressure, manipulated propaganda effort with the American people."[34] Russell's comments illustrate that he believed the merger endangered the domestic component of the State Department's information activities because it linked the PA with high-pressure propaganda. After the brief merger, the trial was considered a failure, and the overseas and domestic information programs were kept separate.[35]

The debate over the temporary blending of domestic and international information demonstrates that State Department officials could never completely differentiate between overseas and domestic information. The PA's identity was questioned and often directly connected with overseas propaganda by those working within the Department of State. Some State Department officials, particularly those working in the office of the assistant secretary for public affairs, believed there was no need for two different offices creating information themes for the promotion of US foreign policy, as there was minimal difference between their approaches. If domestic and overseas information were as different as Russell proclaimed, there would have been no calls to consolidate the branches and no instances of conflation within the State Department. It was this image of similarity that Russell worked desperately to dispel. But no matter how hard he tried to avoid the appearance of propaganda-making, he was never able to fully convince those within the State Department that the PA's messages were intended only to inform and not to influence the American public. One of the main reasons he failed to make this distinction was that the PA did cross the line and attempt to influence public opinion—it just used subtler methods than the overseas propaganda program.

These State Department debates over the PA also illustrate how closely US public opinion and foreign policy were linked. Those working within the State Department readily accepted the importance of domestic public opinion in the formation and execution of US foreign policy. While the techniques and strategies for influencing the public were clearly up for debate with the State Department, the decision to mold the public's opinion had already been made. It was the PA's job to navigate and control the relationship between US foreign policy and public opinion. While the PA constantly struggled to determine which role—fact giver or fact maker—would achieve its goal of creating domestic support, it never doubted that its mission to shape public opinion was important to the development and execution of US foreign policy.

Domestic Publicity Strategies

The Office of Public Affairs' dilemma was visible not only in internal debates but also in its strategies to disseminate messages to the American public. "Domestic publicity" was the PA's formal name for the low-pressure tactics it used on the US public, and it consisted of two prongs: information and education.[36] The term "domestic publicity" was an interesting choice. On the surface, it describes the PA's information activities as nothing more than publicity campaigns. However, a closer analysis of the distribution methods and mediums it employed makes it clear that the mission was not just to publicize information about foreign policy; it was to convince Americans, through the presentation of "facts," to support Truman's foreign policies. The phrase "domestic publicity" worked as a safeguard, keeping the PA's activities from being perceived as high-pressure propaganda techniques. The information it supplied was simply publicity, not propaganda. Characterizing its activities as "publicity" provided a formal cloak for the PA's low-pressure propaganda techniques. These techniques could not be overt, so as to avoid the appearance of propaganda, but they needed to be successful enough to influence public opinion. Therefore, the PA's identity dilemma was evident in its domestic publicity activities.

One of the main mediums the PA used to meet its informational responsibilities and spread the "facts" of foreign policy was publications. In its publications the PA claimed to provide strictly facts, not interpretations. Use of the printed word was incredibly appealing to the PA, and Assistant Secretary Sargeant heralded the value of publications.[37] The printed word was permanent; it could be studied, reread, and passed on to others. It was a medium by which the PA could simplify complex foreign policies. Therefore, it relied heavily on publications to perform its informational duty.[38]

The PA's Division of Publications was primarily responsible for creating published materials.[39] Publications were broken down into four major groups, two of which were specifically used to influence public opinion on foreign policy.[40] Group II targeted the general public, emphasized "long-range goals and public education," and included graphic primers, story pamphlets, and foreign affairs outlines. These publications were written in "simple, non-technical" language. Their overall purpose was to give a "few sharp impressions that will stay in the mind of the type of reader who is impatient with complex explanations." Unlike the other types of publications, they included illustrations and presented information through story-like writing. Whereas group II targeted the general public, group III publications were geared toward the "informed minority and middleman groups."[41] These publications were used to influence and manipulate the messages organizations provided to their members about US foreign policy. All of the PA's publications presented facts on US foreign policy in ways that were meant to be appealing and applicable to the targeted audience.

Of all its publications, the graphic primers of group II best illustrate the thin line the PA walked between providing facts and making propaganda. General pamphlets were easy to understand, featured graphics and pictures, and defended and simplified complex policies of the emerging Cold War.[42] Two of the best examples were *Our Foreign Policy* and *Let Freedom Ring*. Both pamphlets presented versions of the "truth" that were specifically meant to create domestic support for Truman's foreign policies. They also demonstrate the PA's identity dilemma because the publications were intended to both provide "facts" about US foreign policy and persuade Americans to support those policies.

Originally published in 1950, *Our Foreign Policy* provided altruistic and positive explanations of American foreign policy.[43] It portrayed US foreign policy through the lens of American exceptionalism, with slanted motives and favorable outcomes for the United States. According to the pamphlet, the United States' main foreign policy objective was stopping the spread of a "totalitarian nation"—identified as the Soviet Union.[44] Throughout the pamphlet the PA described Soviet motives as malicious, while crediting the United States with benevolent global intentions. Following the pamphlet's logic, if one of the foundations of US policy was to protect freedom, and if its current policy was to stop the spread of totalitarianism, how could the United States not stand against the Soviet Union? By connecting the United States' overall foreign policy mission directly to the Soviet Union, the pamphlet perpetuated the notion that at its foundations, the Cold War was simply about protecting global freedom. According to the pamphlet, US policies consisted of three broad goals: national security, economic prosperity, and world peace. Using these broad categories, the pamphlet justified each major US foreign policy as a necessary tool to defeat the spread of international communism, secure economic prosperity, and promote world peace. The pamphlet contended that global security, economic success, and peace were dependent on the United States' international actions.

Let Freedom Ring: The Struggle for a Peaceful World was published in 1952.[45] Its overarching message was that the United States was engaged in an age-old battle to protect the globe from tyranny. While *Our Foreign Policy* placed its roots in the Revolutionary War, *Let Freedom Ring* traced the origins of American foreign policy to the battle between the ancient Greeks and Romans.[46] The pamphlet used polarizing and extreme examples such as the Dark Ages, English knights, and the Magna Carta to trace the history of the bitter fight between oppression and freedom, ultimately arguing that freedom's first real sustained victory was actually the American Revolution.[47] *Let Freedom Ring* painted the Cold War as an extension of a conflict that had been raging since the beginning of democracy. Whereas *Our Foreign Policy* was primarily an enumeration of all the positive components of US foreign policy, *Let Freedom Ring* justified that policy based on the claim that the Soviet Union was the antithesis of freedom and morality. The pamphlet concluded, "Historically man's evolution has been *away* from tyranny and *toward* freedom . . . hence the society which favors and encourages this process is inevitably the way of the future."[48] By presenting the Cold War as the continuation of a historical struggle between freedom and tyranny, and by using only negative descriptors of the Soviet Union, the pamphlet advocated for stronger foreign policies through negative terms, rather than through positive portrayals of American motives.

When taken together, the pamphlets provide insight into how the PA used "facts" to sell the Cold War to the general public. It combined simplification and positive portrayals of American policies with negative depictions of the Soviet Union and its international motives to sell Americans on Truman's foreign policy agenda. Graphic pamphlets were simple in their analysis, used clearly contrasting historical references, and linked all of Truman's foreign policies to the threat of the Soviet Union. The graphic pamphlets were considered the most successful publications for teaching the public because they supposedly provided simple truths about US foreign policy.[49]

The other component of the PA's domestic publicity strategy involved its work with national organizations and interest groups. It too illustrates the fine line the PA walked between informing and influencing the American public and demonstrates the nexus between foreign policy and public opinion. The PA's Public Liaison Division was considered the most influential and important division specifically because it worked with national organizations to reach and influence the public's understanding of foreign policy. Working through civic organizations not only gave the PA access to more Americans; it also created a gray area in which the PA could operate. The Public Liaison Division explained to organizations why policies were important, knowing that these organizations would convey those messages to their members. The PA purposefully used liaison activities to create a buffer zone between itself and the American people.

Officially created during World War II, the Division of Public Liaison was intended to construct a two-way relationship between the American public and the Department of State and to promote better understanding between them. However, according to Andrew Johnstone, that two-way relationship quickly deteriorated with the start of the Cold War. Replacing the two-way relationship was a "state-heavy one-sided relationship," and the division suddenly "found itself treading a fine line between information and propaganda—between engaging the public on the one hand and selling its policies on the other."[50] During the Truman administration, the PA wanted to exploit the liaison relationship to "focus public attention on those areas to which policy officers attached particular significance at any one time."[51] In other words, the Public Liaison Division used its relationships with organizations to emphasize policies that were of particular importance to the administration. The PA hoped to create long-term support for Truman's policies by actively promoting certain policies to certain national organizations.

Working with private organizations afforded the PA access to the American public in a less conspicuous fashion. In 1946 Russell explained his vision for the Public Liaison Division, recommending that it take the middle ground between "passivity" and "high-pressuring" techniques. If these were the two extremes, Russell believed the "third way" was to educate national organizations, which in turn would take that information and convey it to their members. Russell argued that the "liaison operation should at all times give the impression to the organizations, magazines, feature writers, editors, newspapers, etc., that the State Department is doing everything humanly possible to give them the information that they so urgently desire." It was important to stress that national organizations sought out this information, because doing so protected the Public Liaison Division's middleman image. Russell also warned that the appearance of "high-pressure liaison" must be avoided because the organizations would resent "being used as instruments of a selling campaign," and they might lose all interest in the program. He believed organizations and the public were more likely to support foreign policies if "they feel that they do it as a result of their own convictions and initiative," rather than feeling as if "the Department is pushing or using them."[52] According to Russell, the State Department was not forcing its information on organizations; instead, organizations actively sought that information, and the State Department was more than willing to comply.

Russell's motivation for the incorporation of private groups is enlightening. On the surface, he believed that organizations' memberships would give the State Department access to more of the American public. The Public Liaison Division could use national organizations and their national memberships to circulate the PA's published materials and promote its messages across the country. According to Russell, "there was an economy of effort working chiefly through national organizations" because their officers were in "the unique position to present the story of U.S. foreign policy" to their members.[53] For Russell, working with national organizations created additional avenues for the PA to reach as many Americans as possible. But his reasons for using private organizations ran deeper than just sheer circulation. To ensure that the American people believed they were coming to their own conclusions, it was imperative that the PA's selling strategies appeared to be merely educational, for two reasons. First, Russell was hyperaware that the Public Liaison Division's work with organizations could be construed as propaganda, so he went to great lengths to ensure that it not push organizations too hard to adopt certain opinions. Even then, as he readily admitted to Secretary Benton, the division sometimes crossed the line. Second, Russell believed that in order to create domestic support that would last throughout the Truman administration, Americans needed to sincerely believe in Cold War policies. To Russell, this meant convincing Americans that they had come to their own conclusions about Truman's policies. The division could not use overt pressure tactics but had to rely on subtler techniques of influencing opinion. Therefore, its job was to teach organizations' leaders why these policies were vital to American international success and security. Then, once convinced, the leadership would persuade the members.

The Public Liaison Division did not walk the line between information and propaganda; rather, under Russell, its role was intentionally developed to operate in the gray area of domestic information. In fact, Russell was aware that the division often crossed the line and became too aggressive in its tactics. He admitted that organizations sometimes believed they were being "marshaled rather than served," but he argued that the division always quickly remedied those situations.[54] Nevertheless, Russell believed that the Public Liaison Division was the most ambitious and potentially successful division within the PA. It could provide the American people with information that served the interests of both the public and the State Department. The overarching goal of this new, more active division was to secure public support for Cold War foreign policies without making the American people feel as if the State Department were "pushing or using them."[55] To do this, the Public Liaison Division used a variety of tactics to exploit its relationship with national organizations.[56] For example, it arranged and hosted conferences for national organizations. These conferences served as large educational meetings where various members of the State Department participated in roundtables and question-and-answer periods about US foreign policy. One of the largest and most successful conferences took place in June 1947, and participants consisted of those groups that had shown a "continuing interest in international affairs and which carry on educational programs in this field."[57] Interest in foreign policy and a willingness to carry out educational programs highlighted the general approach of the PA. It wanted to work with groups that were interested in foreign affairs, embraced the PA's version of the truth, and educated their members and the masses about foreign policy.

The June 1947 conference included participants from 240 groups representing farming; labor; business; women's, veterans', educational, religious, and professional organizations; universities; and other government agencies. Some of the more prominent groups in attendance included the Council on Foreign Relations, National Council of Women in the United States, National Association for the Advancement of Colored People (NAACP), Boy Scouts of America, American Legion, Woodrow Wilson Foundation, Brookings Institute, and Foreign Policy Association.[58] Each group sent one or two high-ranking representatives to the conference, individuals who could then take back what they learned and incorporate it into the group's own educational program. The conference featured presentations by high-ranking State Department officers such as George Marshall, Dean Acheson, Dean Rusk, and Francis Russell. There were four major topics: political foundations of peace, Congress and American foreign policy, economic foundations of peace, and cultural foundations of peace.[59] Using these themes, the conference attempted to sell the Truman administration's global vision for the United States to these organizations, in the hope that attendees would then sell it to the American public.[60]

The conference's panel discussions and question-and-answer periods were all "off the record" so that participants would feel more comfortable asking questions and making comments.[61] However, the off-the-record aspect of the conference also benefited the Public Liaison Division. By not keeping transcripts of the discussions, the division had more freedom in what information it presented to national organizations and how it did so. This also prevented any of its methods or information from later being used against the PA. The Public Liaison Division orchestrated several other larger conferences, as well as some regional conferences. On the whole, these conferences provided the State Department and the PA with the opportunity to meet face-to-face with the leaders of national organizations and teach them about Truman's foreign policy agenda.

The Office of Public Affairs used hundreds of national organizations to influence the American people, but the Foreign Policy Association (FPA) was one of the most influential groups it worked with.[62] The FPA focused exclusively on foreign relations and on educating the public. Founded in 1918, it was originally called the League of Free Nations Association, and it grew out of support for Woodrow Wilson's League of Nations.[63] Over the next two decades, the FPA evolved into an organization that sought to promote US foreign policy agendas and policies to the masses.[64] Its self-ascribed mission was "to help the people of the United States understand the problems of American foreign policy," making it the ideal organization for the Public Liaison Division to target during the Truman administration.[65] The FPA emphasized foreign affairs and education related to the United States' role in the world.[66]

The Public Liaison Division encouraged the FPA to publish articles in its Headline Series (one of the FPA's premier educational series) because they were presented in "a popular style" similar to that of the *Our Foreign Policy* and *Let Freedom Ring* pamphlets created by the Division of Publications.[67] In 1947 Margaret Carter, chief of the Public Liaison Division, asked the FPA to publish a variety of articles on current foreign policy issues. In particular, Carter wanted the FPA to publish "Who Makes Our Foreign Policy?" and she requested that the FPA emphasize "the role of the individual citizen" in foreign policy making.[68] Carter's conversation with Thomas Ford, the chief editor for the FPA, illustrates the influence the PA had over FPA publications. At the end of their conversation, Carter noted that the FPA "appreciates from us any suggestions on areas of public interest and concern."[69] The Public Liaison Division frequently provided the FPA with lists of important foreign policy topics, and the FPA was more than willing to work those topics into its educational publications and programs.

The Public Liaison Division's sway over the FPA can also be seen in several off-the-record meetings at which various members of the State Department met with the FPA leadership to discuss US policies more "directly."[70] These meetings demonstrate that the State Department actively tried to influence the knowledge and understanding of civic organizations, and it often did so in private meetings to avoid any unsavory propaganda-making accusations by Congress or the media.

The Foreign Policy Association–Public Liaison Division relationship perfectly illustrates the work of the latter. The FPA was invited to all the division's conferences, accepted suggestions and requests with regard to what topics should be featured in its publications, and met with State Department officials to gain private information and explanations of US foreign policy. This relationship serves as an excellent example of how the Public Liaison Division approached the management of national organizations. The PA actively strove to influence the messages civic organizations disseminated to their members and the masses. It purposefully created and cultivated relationships with these organizations as a way to control their internal messages and opinions. The Public Liaison Division did this through its conferences, the personal relationships it fostered with group leaders and members of the press, the guest lecturers it sent to group meetings, and the educational materials it provided for groups' members. In all instances, the division's purpose was to manage the messages of these nonstate actors as much as possible. Although national organizations were not the only tool used to teach Americans about Truman's foreign policies, they offered a more assertive but less conspicuous method of influencing the public.

Domestic publicity strategies, both informational and educational, created either state-sanctioned "truth" through the Division of Publications' educational materials or third-party propaganda through the Public Liaison Division's activities with national organizations. This approach allowed the PA to cover all its bases, using a variety of avenues to influence public opinion. Whether through its publications or its liaison activities, the PA strove to present the "facts" on US foreign policy in ways that would be easy to understand, ensure domestic support, and not look like propaganda.

Similar to the Broadcasting Board of Governors' defense of its own domestic activities in 2013, President Truman defended the Office of Public Affairs in 1951: "Far from being a propaganda operation as some of its opponents have charged, the State Department's public liaison activities are a service operation set up to fill the legitimate requests of our people for information about foreign affairs."[71] He argued that the PA was merely a fact-giving entity, not a propaganda machine for his administration. Truman claimed that the PA simply "suppl[ied] the American people with factual information on the nature of the world situation and this Nation's part it in."[72] He insisted that the PA did not make propaganda; it just offered the facts. Truman and State Department officials such as Francis Russell may have convinced themselves that the PA was simply involved in the fact-giving business, but in reality, it was in the fact-making business. Its domestic information programs had the same goals as the State Department's foreign information propaganda. To the Department of State, the American public was just another audience that needed to be educated about the truths of US foreign policy. It was the PA's job to steer the American people into supporting US foreign policy during the Cold War. What Russell saw as attempts to "inform" were most certainly attempts to "influence" the American public. The information choices the PA made, the wording it chose, the policies it stressed or minimized, and the facts it provided or omitted were all conscious decisions. These decisions were part of an elaborate operation by the State Department to teach the American people what it wanted them to know about US foreign policy. Fact-making, not fact-giving, lay at the heart of the PA's mission.[73]

The Office of Public Affairs' mission and its identity crisis demonstrate the delicate relationship that exists between the public and foreign policy in the United States. In a democratic system, public opinion is vital to enacting successful foreign policy because the public plays such an important role in the election of officials and the implementation of international agendas. Therefore, ensuring that the public supports foreign policy is a critical component of the government's attempt to craft foreign policy.[74] Yet a democratic system also limits the methods the government can use to manage and control public opinion, especially on foreign policy issues.[75] Noam Chomsky argues that a democratic state must have popular consent when crafting policy, and he claims that in a democracy, the state must manage, control, and shape the public's opinions and understandings through various forms of propaganda. Its efforts cannot be blatant attempts to influence the public; instead, it must appear that the government is fulfilling its role as information provider.[76] Thomas Bailey contends that "in a dictatorship the masses must be deceived; in a democracy, they must be educated."[77] Similarly, Melvin Small argues that "all democratic societies confront the problem of how to explain complicated foreign policy problems. . . . Unless the message is simple and exaggerated, allegedly short-sighted citizens might reject the costs and sacrifices demanded of them to achieve some obscure long-term goal."[78] Essentially, foreign policy is too complicated for the public to understand, and people cannot feel as if they are being overtly pressured to support or approve such policies. Therefore, they must believe they have come to that knowledge and formed that opinion on their own.

Managing the relationship between public opinion and US foreign policy is exactly what the Office of Public Affairs was tasked to do during the Truman administration. It specifically created domestic information programs that simplified the complicated foreign policies of the Cold War in order to maintain long-term support for Truman's agenda. The PA's mission illustrates the influence of public opinion on foreign policy because creating domestic support for foreign policy was its sole job. Yet the PA had to do so in ways that did not push the public too hard, thus creating an identity dilemma for it. It was to be both teacher and persuader of the American public. It constantly struggled to maintain a balance between fact giver and fact maker, while ensuring that it was subtly successful at influencing public opinion. Throughout the Truman administration the State Department attempted to control and manage public opinion about US foreign policy through the Office of Public Affairs, and the PA's identity dilemma shows how truly important that task was. Ultimately, the PA never overcame its identity dilemma. It was constantly plagued by criticism that it was either not doing enough or doing too much to influence public opinion.

The Office of Public Affairs did not believe it was deceiving the public, but it deceived itself into thinking its techniques were different from the State Department's overseas propaganda campaigns. Both were attempts to manage and control the minds of their intended audiences. Both audiences' opinions, domestic and international, were crucial to the Truman administration's international success. The PA's identity dilemma resulted not because its mission was unclear but because it was hesitant to admit that it created propaganda for the American public. Instead, it held on to the notion that it was solely a fact provider for the American public, ignoring the fact that the State Department itself had already argued that "the best propaganda in the world is truth."[79]

Notes

1. H. R. 5736, Smith-Mundt Modernization Act of 2012, https://www.congress.gov/bill/112th-congress/house-bill/5736 (accessed November 22, 2015). The act was passed as part of the larger 2013 National Defense Authorization Act and went into effect in the summer of 2013.

2. The Broadcasting Board of Governors is the federal agency that was given control and oversight of US international broadcasting in 1999. It oversees propa-

ganda agencies such as the Voice of America, Office of Cuba Broadcasting, Radio Free Europe/Liberty, Radio Free Asia, and Middle East Broadcasting Networks. See History tab at Broadcasting Board of Governors homepage, http://www.bbg.gov/about-the-agency/history/ (accessed November 22, 2015).

3. See Smith-Mundt tab at Broadcasting Board of Governors homepage, http://www.bbg.gov/about-the-agency/history/ (accessed November 22, 2015).

4. John Hudson, "U.S. Repeals Propaganda Ban, Spreads Government-Made News to Americans," *Foreign Policy,* July 14, 2013, http://foreignpolicy.com/2013/07/14/u-s-repeals-propaganda-ban-spreads-government-made-news-to-americans/ (accessed November 22, 2015).

5. Michael Kelly of the *San Francisco Chronicle* argued that the law was a "strategic move in influencing U.S. public perception in regards to the Global War on Terror." John Hudson of *Foreign Policy* contended that the resolution would be "an unleashing of thousands of hours per week of government funded radio and TV programs for domestic U.S. consumption." Kelly argued that repealing the Smith-Mundt Act "appears to serve this purpose by allowing for the American public to be a target audience of U.S. government–funded information campaigns." According to Hudson, while the BBG is "no Pravda . . . it does advance U.S. interests in more subtle ways." See Michael Kelly, "U.S. Government–Funded Domestic Propaganda Has Officially Hit the Airwaves," *San Francisco Chronicle,* July 16, 2013, http://www.sfgate.com/technology/businessinsider/article/US-Government-Funded-Domestic-Propaganda-Has-4668001.php (accessed November 22, 2015); Hudson, "U.S. Repeals Propaganda Ban."

6. For purposes of this essay, when words are placed in quotation marks it is to illustrate that the Office of Public Affairs' use of these terms was sometimes questionable. The information the PA considered true, factual, and right was always judged first by its ability to promote foreign policy and secure domestic support.

7. Susan Brewer defines this type of propaganda as "overt propaganda." She argues that "overt propaganda comes from a known source and is understood to be based in facts. . . . To rally Americans around the flag, officials have manipulated facts, exaggeration, and misinformation. The primary purpose, after all, is not to inform, but to persuade." Brewer applies her definition to US wartime propaganda, and her work examines how US officials have used facts and "truth" to rally Americans around messages of patriotism to convince them to support war. However, Brewer's definition can and should be applied to the government's use of facts to persuade Americans outside of wartime, as well as to presidents' use of "truth" to garner domestic support for their foreign policy agendas. Brewer specifically addresses the Truman administration's use of "fact" to sell the Korean War and create domestic support for the president's limited war to contain communism in Asia. See Susan Brewer, *Why America Fights: Patriotism and War Propaganda from the Philippines to Iraq* (New York: Oxford University Press, 2009), 7.

8. For the Committee for Public Information's domestic propaganda operation, see Alan Axelrod, *Selling the Great War: The Making of American Propaganda*

(New York: Palgrave Macmillan, 2009); Christopher Capozzola, *Uncle Sam Wants You: World War I and the Making of the Modern American Citizen* (Oxford: Oxford University Press, 2010).

9. Office memorandum from Francis Russell to William Benton, July 17, 1946, 3, OPI-1946 file, box 3, entry 586, Record Group (RG) 59, General Records of the Department of State, National Archives and Records Administration, College Park, MD (NARA).

10. Robert Beisner, *Dean Acheson: A Life in the Cold War* (New York: Oxford University Press, 2006), 248.

11. "Your Memorandum to S/P—Mr. Davies on December 16 Concerning Domestic Publicity Problems Relating to the Marshall Plan," December 17, 1947, European Reconstruction, 1947–1949 file, box 3, entry A1530, RG 59, General Records of the Department of State, NARA.

12. Release of statement by Undersecretary of State Dean Acheson, November 27, 1945, Publicity & Propaganda, 1945–1951 file, box 8, entry 1530A-1, RG 59, General Records of the Department of State, NARA.

13. John S. Dickey Oral History, 34, Truman Library, Independence, MO, http://www.trumanlibrary.org/oralhist/dickeyjs.htm (accessed November 5, 2014).

14. The Office of Public Information included four major divisions: Division of Public Liaison, Division of Historical Policy Research, Division of Publications, and Division of Public Studies. Each division had its own mission. The Division of Public Liaison's mission was to create relationships with outside organizations such as civic education groups and the national media in order to educate Americans about US foreign policy. The Division of Historical Policy Research conducted research into American policies that provided the foundations for domestic information programs. The Division of Publications supervised the official publications of the State Department. The Division of Public Studies focused solely on public opinion, gauging how the public understood policies and which policies were supported, criticized, or misunderstood. Its role in the OPI was incredibly important because it helped the Historical Policy Research and Publications Divisions determine which topics needed to be addressed in domestic information programs. Each of the four divisions had its own chief who answered directly to the director of the OPI. The director of the OPI was in charge of steering attention toward certain policies and problems.

15. Andrew Johnstone, "Creating a 'Democratic Foreign Policy': The State Department's Division of Public Liaison and Public Opinion, 1944–1953," *Diplomatic History* 35, no. 3 (June 2011): 489.

16. See "Seminar on the Truman Doctrine with Ambassador Francis Russell," Fletcher School at Tufts University, April 1974, 1–2. See also Francis Russell Oral History, July 13, 1973, 4–6, Truman Library, https://www.trumanlibrary.org/oralhist/russellf.htm (accessed November 5, 2014).

17. In August 1945 Executive Order 9608 dismantled the Office of Wartime Information and transferred all remaining information services to the Depart-

ment of State, which then expanded the operations of the Office of Public Information. See Executive Order 9608, http://www.presidency.ucsb.edu/ws/?pid=60671 (accessed October 24, 2014). Executive Order 9608 did not mention the fate of the domestic branch of the Office of Wartime Information.

18. Johnstone, "Creating a 'Democratic Foreign Policy,'" 489. Johnstone argues that renaming the OPI the Office of Public Affairs illustrates the change in the office's mission. He claims that "affairs" was used to emphasize the creation of "a two-way street and interaction between the State Department and the public."

19. In an internal department memorandum, arguments for the name change were explained. Avoiding words too closely associated with propaganda was clearly the number-one objective for changing the OPI's name. The detailed discussion illustrates the changing nature, scope, and mission of the OPI. See "Letter about Name Changing to William Benton from Francis Russell," October 2, 1946, 1, PA—Organization and Procedure file, box 21, entry 1587F, Office of the Assistant Secretary for Public Affairs, Subject Files, 1946–1953, RG 59, General Records of the Department of State, NARA.

20. "Draft Order by Management Planning and OPI in Regards to the OPA," July 1, 1946, 1, attached in a letter from Francis Russell to William Benton, July 12, 1946, PA—Organization and Procedure file, box 21, entry 1587F, RG 59, General Records of the Department of State, NARA.

21. "The Office of Public Affairs," *PA Week News,* September 16, 1946, 1, PA/PL Aims & Philosophy file, box 7, entry 1530, RG 59, General Records of the Department of State, NARA. One of the most important reasons for the success of the Office of Public Affairs was the naming of Francis Russell as its director—a position he held from 1945 to 1952. Under Russell's direction, the PA was the most active and influential it would ever be in the creation and dissemination of domestic information. Throughout his time at the PA, Russell worked to expand, protect, and promote the office. Without Russell's determination to actively use the PA as a teacher, it would have remained merely a manager of public relations.

22. Francis Russell to William Benton, "Office of Public Information Descriptions," July 12, 1946, PA—Organization and Procedure file, box 21, entry 1587, RG 59, General Records of the Department of State, NARA; office memorandum from Shepard Jones to Francis Russell, March 4, 1947, PA—Program Planning file, ibid.

23. Russell to Benton, "Office of Public Information Descriptions," 4, 5.

24. Melvyn Leffler, *A Preponderance of Power: National Security, the Truman Administration, and the Cold War* (Stanford, CA: Stanford University Press, 1992), 146.

25. Kenneth Osgood, *Total Cold War: Eisenhower's Secret Propaganda Battle at Home and Abroad* (Lawrence: University Press of Kansas, 2006), 2–3.

26. Russell Oral History, 18.

27. Memorandum from William Benton to Francis Russell, March 10, 1947, 1–2, Francis Russell January–May 1947 file, entry 1241-A1, RG 59, General Records of the Department of State, NARA.

28. Memorandum from Francis Russell to William Benton, March 19, 1947,

Francis Russell January–May 1947 file, entry 1241-A1, RG 59, General Records of the Department of State, NARA.

29. "Relationship of PA and P/POL," memorandum from James Swihart and Walter Schwinn to Howland Sargeant, November 4, 1949, 1–2, P/POL file, box 3, entry 568, RG 59, General Records of the Department of State, NARA.

30. Office memorandum from Francis Russell to Howland Sargeant, December 20, 1949, 1, P/POL file, box 3, entry 568, RG 59, General Records of the Department of State, NARA.

31. Ibid., 3.

32. Office memorandum from Francis Russell to Mrs. Curran, March 8, 1950, P/POL file, box 3, entry 568, RG 59, General Records of the Department of State, NARA.

33. "Leak of Information: Policy Information Paper on Formosa," January 3, 1950, Deputy Assistant Secretary of State for Public Affairs 1947–1950 file, box 4, Howland Sargeant Files, Truman Library.

34. Office memorandum from Francis Russell to Howland Sargeant, January 27, 1950, 1, Records of Assistant Secretary of State for Public Affairs, 1945–1950 file, box 3, entry 568, RG 59, General Records of the Department of State, NARA.

35. Walter Schwinn, director of the P/POL (Public Affairs Policy Advisory Staff), explained that the differences between the overseas and domestic operations kept the merger from going smoothly. Schwinn believed the various information bureaus were confused about the difference between "classified overseas propaganda guidance" and "public affairs information." He argued that the differences in the two divisions' missions lay at the heart of the failure, noting that the primary concern of foreign information programs was to influence overseas audiences, while domestic information programs were responsible for "interpreting foreign policy to the U.S. public." What is striking about Schwinn's admission is that his explanation of the difference between domestic and overseas programs clearly shows that both were intended to have the best possible effect on their audiences and to build support for American foreign policies. According to Schwinn, the State Department was "responsible for interpreting foreign policy to the U.S. public," but it did not "attempt to influence U.S. attitudes as it must with influence with foreign attitudes." See "Responsibilities of P/POL," office memorandum from Walter Schwinn to Howland Sargeant, January 31, 1950, 1, Records of Assistant Secretary of State for Public Affairs 1945–1950 file, box 3, entry 568, RG 59, General Records of the Department of State, NARA.

36. "Your Memorandum to S/P—Mr. Davies on December 16 Concerning Domestic Publicity Problems Relating to the Marshall Plan."

37. "Draft Outline of Remarks by Howland Sargeant on Behalf of the Secretary of State before the Consultative Meeting on Publications," February 10, 1950, 2, Consultative Meeting 1950 file, box 138, entry 1587U, RG 59, General Records of the Department of State, NARA.

38. Margaret Carter to Francis Russell, "Preliminary Report by the PL Study Group," March 17, 1949, 1, PA/PL Aims & Philosophy, box 13, entry 568, RG 59, General Records of the Department of State, NARA.

39. "PA's Information Activities," memorandum from J. W. Swihart to Howland Sargeant, September 10, 1947, 2, PA-FHR-1947 file, box 3, entry 568, RG 59, General Records of Department of State, NARA.

40. "Types of Written Materials: Definitions for More Common Forms of Informational Writing," undated, 2, Miscellaneous PB Memos, 1947–1952 file, box 1, entry 1587-U, RG 59, General Records of the Department of State: Bureau of Public Affairs, Public Services Division, NARA.

41. Ibid., 6–7.

42. Division of Publications, "Summary Report of Consultative Conference on Publications," February 10, 1950, Consultative Meeting 1950 file, box 138, entry 1587U, RG 59, General Records of the Department of State, NARA.

43. *Our Foreign Policy,* Department of State Publication 3972, General Foreign Policy Series 26, September 1950, 1950 file, box 1, Papers of Harry Barnard, Truman Library. The 1952 pamphlet used the same themes and organization; the only major difference between the two versions was an updated explanation of specific policies. See *Our Foreign Policy,* Department of State Publication 4466, General Foreign Policy Series 56, March 1952, S 1.17:34–S 1.71:116, box S306, RG 287, Publications of the Federal Government: State Department, NARA.

44. *Our Foreign Policy* (1950), 7–8. It explained that this was just an extension of its World War II policy and justified the global expansion of the United States by claiming it had always been the United States' responsibility to protect freedom and peace. The totalitarian nation was portrayed as an octopus extending its tentacles while clutching a sickle, giving the reader the clear impression that the new threat was the Soviet Union.

45. *Let Freedom Ring: The Struggle for a Peaceful World,* General Foreign Policy Series 67, November 1952, Division of Publications: Office of Public Affairs file, box 306, entry S1.71, RG 287, Publications of the Federal Government: State Department, NARA.

46. Ibid., 3.

47. Ibid., 10.

48. Ibid., 95–96.

49. "PB Publication Display Program," memorandum from Elinor Bodds to Mr. Thompson, December 12, 1951, 1, 1951–1950 file, box 138, entry 1587, RG 59, General Records of the Department of State, NARA. According to the memorandum, the supply of *Our Foreign Policy* had nearly been exhausted.

50. Johnstone, "Creating a 'Democratic Foreign Policy,'" 486.

51. "Some Aspects of the Department's Domestic Information Program," 4, Domestic Information Program file, Correspondence/Subject Files 1945–1950, box 13, entry 568, Records of the Assistant Secretary of State for Public Affairs, RG 59, General Records of the Department of State, NARA.

52. Office memorandum from Francis H. Russell to William Benton, July 17, 1946, 2–3, OPI-FHR 1946 file, box 3, entry 568, RG 59, General Records of the Department of State, NARA.

53. Francis Russell to Howland Sargeant, "Department's Relationship with Religious Organizations," June 12, 1950, 1, Liaison Activities file, box 1, entry 5052, RG 59, General Records of Department of State, NARA.

54. Office memorandum from Francis Russell to William Benton, July 17, 1946, 4, Records of the Assistant Secretary of State for Public Affairs, 1945–1950 file, box 3, entry 568, RG 59, General Records of the Department of State, NARA.

55. Ibid.

56. "The Department of State and the American Public: Division of Publication," PL-1, January 1950, Foreign Policy Statements file, box 110, entry 1587-R, RG 59, General Records of the Department of State, NARA.

57. "Conference for National Organization," press release no. 367, Department of State, April 30, 1947, PA-FHR-1947 file, box 3, entry 568, RG 59, General Records of the Department of State, NARA.

58. For a full list of attendees, see "Attendance at Meeting of American Foreign Policy," June 4–6, 1947, box 3, entry 568, RG 59, General Records of the Department of State, NARA.

59. "Meetings on American Foreign Policy Program," hosted by the Office of Public Affairs, June 4–6, 1947, PA-FHR-1947 file, box 3, entry 568, RG 59, General Records of Department of State, NARA.

60. For each major topic, there were several brief panels that addressed specific issues. The political foundations of peace session featured panels on the United States' role in the United Nations, the status of American foreign policy, and the United States' relationship with different geographic regions. The Congress and American foreign policy session included statements from representatives of both the Senate and House Committees on Foreign Relations. The economic foundations of peace panel explained how US foreign economic policies helped secure international peace and prosperity. The cultural foundations of peace session explained how international programs encouraged cultural cooperation and included panels on how to increase citizen participation.

61. "Meetings on American Foreign Policy Program," 9.

62. "Untitled Departmental Memorandum," May 19, 1944, PA/PL Administrative file, box 1, entry 5052, RG 59, General Records of the Department of State, NARA. The Foreign Policy Association was used as an example of one of the earliest groups the Public Liaison Division worked with in 1944. The writing staff of the FPA was already contacting the Office of Public Information and the Public Liaison Division about publication topics, and the FPA sought speakers to attend its meetings.

63. The Foreign Policy Association's roots in promoting the League of Nations, combined with its emphasis on the United States' place in the world, made it the ideal candidate for the Truman administration to use to promote its foreign policy agenda.

64. "A Brief History of the Foreign Policy Association," *Foreign Policy Organization Bulletin* 1, 1–2, Services and Special Programs 1953 file, box 40, part II, FPA Records, Wisconsin Historical Society, Madison. In 1921 the organization officially changed its name to Foreign Policy Association. Also see http://www.fpa.org/about/ (accessed July 24, 2015).

65. "Brief History of the Foreign Policy Association," 2.

66. "National Leaders Write for 30th Anniversary," November 5, 1948, 1–2, Associate Records: Membership, Publicity, and Reports 1948–1952 file, box 73, part I, FPA Records, Wisconsin Historical Society. In fact, writing to congratulate the FPA on its thirty-year anniversary, both President Truman and Secretary of State George C. Marshall commended it for helping citizens understand the importance of US foreign policy.

67. "The Headline Series," memorandum of conversation between Margaret Carter and Thomas Ford, December 17, 1946, Foreign Policy Association folder, box 110, entry 1587R, RG 59, General Records of the Department of State, NARA.

68. Ibid.

69. Ibid, 2.

70. Charles Bohlen, off-the-record meeting, "Current Aspects of U.S. Foreign Policy," April 20, 1948, 1, Off-the-Record Meetings with the State Department 1948 file, box 95, part II, FPA Records, Wisconsin Historical Society.

71. Letter from Harry S. Truman to Senator Pat McCarran, September 24, 1951, 1, box 69, WHCF:OF, OF20-U Misc., Truman Papers, Truman Library.

72. Ibid.

73. Nancy Bernhard aptly describes this decision by claiming that PA officers "embellished the truth in order to save it, but they seem to have forgotten that they did so." Nancy E. Bernhard, *U.S. Television News and Cold War Propaganda, 1947–1960* (Cambridge: Cambridge University Press, 1999), 93. See also Nancy Bernhard, "Clearer Than Truth: Public Affairs Television and the State Department's Domestic Information Campaigns, 1947–1952," *Diplomatic History* 21, no. 4 (Fall 1997): 545–567.

74. Alexis de Tocqueville, *Democracy in America,* available online at http://www.gutenberg.org/files/815/815-h/815-h.htm (accessed February 20, 2015). Chapter 13 specifically discusses the relationship of democracy and foreign policy. Tocqueville argues that "foreign politics demand scarcely any of those qualities which a democracy possesses; and they require, on contrary, the perfect use of almost all those facilities in which it is deficient." In addition, democracies have the propensity "to obey the impulse of passion rather than the suggestions of prudence." For Tocqueville, the democracy that must obey the will of the people limits foreign politics because the people make their decisions based on emotion rather than knowledge.

75. Melvin Small, *Democracy and Diplomacy: The Impact of Domestic Politics on U.S. Foreign Policy, 1789–1994* (Baltimore: John Hopkins University Press, 1996).

76. Noam Chomsky, *Media Control: Spectacular Achievements of Propaganda* (New York: Seven Stories Press, 2002), 10.

77. Thomas Bailey, *The Man in the Street: The Impact of American Public Opinion on Foreign Policy* (New York: Macmillan, 1948), 2.

78. Small, *Democracy and Diplomacy,* 85.

79. "Our International Information Policy," *Department of State Bulletin* 13 (December 16, 1945): 950.

2

From Hawk to Dawk

Congressman Melvin Laird and the Vietnam War, 1952–1968

David L. Prentice

From 1952 to 1968, Americans witnessed the continued expansion of their nation's commitment to the noncommunist Republic of Vietnam. The 1960s began with about 900 military personnel in South Vietnam, but by the end of 1968, more than half a million American soldiers were on the ground in Southeast Asia.[1] Few men and women foresaw this development, but then again, before the war became an American conflict, very few people paid much attention to events in Indochina.

Melvin Laird stood in stark contrast to this public apathy, and his pronouncements on Vietnam before 1969 shed light on the escalation of the US war in Vietnam, the American search for an exit from that conflict, and the political calculations that influenced both decisions. Until his appointment as Richard Nixon's secretary of defense, Laird was a leading Republican politician from Wisconsin who served in the House from 1953 to 1969. Representative Laird took great interest in foreign affairs and advocated a tough stand on communism, but he proved most zealous when attacking his political opponents. He castigated Presidents John F. Kennedy and Lyndon B. Johnson for failing to do more to contain communism in Southeast Asia. His militant rhetoric and incessant demands that the Democratic White House begin bombing and mining North

Vietnam earned him a reputation as a decided hawk in the early and mid-1960s. But along with his persistent commitment to South Vietnam and faith in American firepower, Laird harbored an aversion to US troop deployments in Asia. Johnson's war was not the war Laird wanted, but he accepted it as a necessary Cold War struggle. As large numbers of US soldiers did little to stabilize South Vietnam, Laird grew increasingly pessimistic about the chances of success in Indochina. This pessimism, along with the prospect of Republican gains in the 1968 election, would shift Laird away from escalation toward a strategy that would remove American soldiers while preserving South Vietnam. By the time he became secretary of defense, Laird was no longer a hawk. As his longtime assistant William Baroody noted, "Laird was neither a dove nor a hawk but a dawk."[2]

The historiography of the Vietnam War has focused on the evolving views of other key congressional politicians, but historians have overlooked Melvin Laird.[3] This oversight is unfortunate because Laird's progression from militant hawk to pessimist was a path many hawks took as they changed their views on and prescriptions for the war while remaining committed to South Vietnam. Moreover, Laird was a hawk with significant influence. He shaped 1960s GOP politics, led Republican pro-war efforts, and framed his party's position on the conflict. Indeed, as a popular Wisconsin politician from a safe congressional district, Laird could act as his party's political attack dog. In galvanizing the Right, he would restrict President Johnson's political freedom to maneuver at home while pushing him to escalate the war. His contemporaries appreciated his influence. President Johnson reminded his advisers that Laird was the "ablest Republican in the House, [the] meanest Republican in the House, [and the] most partisan." Johnson and his advisers also agreed that Laird was "*very* smart." Given his travails with the congressman, LBJ would know. Longtime CBS political correspondent Bob Schieffer concluded that Laird "was with the possible exception of Lyndon Johnson, the best politician I ever knew, certainly one of the wisest."[4]

Laird's actions, rhetoric, and proposed policies demonstrate the confluence of politics and foreign policy. Historian Thomas Schwartz aptly wrote, "Professional politicians are, almost by their very definition, ambitious people seeking office for individual recognition, career advancement, and the power to affect their societies. No matter how often they might speak of public service, it is naïve not to recognize the more selfish drives in their nature. Such individuals are not likely to forget domestic politics when they are weighing foreign policy alternatives."[5] And Laird was a politician par excellence. He anticipated the growing military and political crisis in Southeast Asia and deftly positioned himself and his party to benefit from the Democrats' dilemmas there. Laird's actions and rhetoric demonstrated how congressional leaders can play politics with foreign crises, especially when their party is out of power. Yet he was also a man of principles and ideas who advocated his own solutions to the crises in Southeast Asia, even when they were out of step with the opinions of most Americans. His convictions delineated the range of policies he could accept, while his partisanship and ambition sharpened his attacks on Democratic presidents and their foreign policies.[6]

Privately, Laird understood the political and military agonies of a war in Vietnam. Publicly, he demanded that his political rivals adopt his strategy wholesale or accept the blame for losing South Vietnam. In this way, he remained true to his principles, even as he made hard choices appear simple and laid the foundation for future political success.

The Pragmatic Politician from Marshfield, 1922–1960

Born on September 1, 1922, Melvin Laird—or "Bom," as his family affectionately called him—grew up in Marshfield, Wisconsin, in a family that was well acquainted with politics. His maternal grandfather had been lieutenant governor. His father, Melvin R. Laird Sr., served as a state senator from 1941 to 1946, and Laird Jr. often spoke on his father's behalf in campaigns. His mother was active in politics through community organizations and the Republican Party. At home and later at college, Laird learned the art of politics, but the Second World War interrupted this civilian life.[7] Like millions from his generation, he enlisted. He joined the US Navy in 1942 and served in the Pacific on the USS *Maddox*.[8] A Japanese kamikaze attack on the *Maddox* killed eight and critically injured Laird. He returned home with shrapnel in his body, a Purple Heart, and firsthand experience that would temper his hawkishness as a politician and a policymaker.[9]

After the war, Laird got involved in politics. His father died unexpectedly in 1946, leaving his state senate seat open. Laird's outgoing personality made a career in politics a natural choice for him, and he won the election to fill the vacancy. At age twenty-four, he became the youngest state senator in Wisconsin's history. After six years in the state senate, Laird ran for Congress in Wisconsin's Seventh Congressional District and won. With Dwight Eisenhower entering the White House and the GOP controlling both houses of Congress, 1953 was a good year for an up-and-coming Republican to enter Congress.[10]

As a young representative, Laird understood the domestic limits of US foreign policy. His war experience and injuries made him wary of military intervention, but so did local political realities. Wisconsin's Seventh Congressional District, "The Heart of America's Dairyland," had favored neutrality before Pearl Harbor. The Second World War and the early Cold War shifted public opinion away from isolationism, but Laird understood that support for US global responsibility represented a cautious internationalism at best. To his constituents, the price of butter mattered far more than sending guns to far-off Turkey. The legacies of war and politics gave Laird two firm convictions: policymakers should commit US soldiers only as a last resort, and the American people speak through their congressional representatives.[11]

While the views of his constituents delineated an acceptable foreign policy, they did not curtail Laird's interest in international affairs. As a member of the Defense Appropriations Subcommittee, Laird made frequent pronouncements on foreign policy and worked with other prominent Republicans to develop a partisan (and at times bipartisan) consensus on these issues. But in keeping with his district's agricultural and domestic concerns, he also acted as a cost-cutter on defense and foreign aid appropriations, even though President Eisenhower considered the latter vital to his Cold War foreign policy. Despite this disagreement over foreign aid, Eisenhower and Laird generally agreed on America's Cold War strategy. Both appreciated that the American people would not endure the deployment of soldiers to fight limited wars in the Third World. Instead, Eisenhower emphasized foreign aid to strengthen those nations, psychological and covert operations to discourage or thwart internal subversion, and the use of America's strategic air, sea, and nuclear power to deter outright Soviet and Chinese aggression. Laird would look back on Eisenhower's 1950s as a period of successful diplomacy.[12]

In particular, Laird's interpretation of Eisenhower's handling of the conflicts in Korea and Indochina would shape his outlook on 1960s Vietnam. For Laird, the Korean War demonstrated that Americans could not stomach limited wars for long. Rather than try to meet the communists man-for-man on the ground, the United States should use its preponderant air and naval strength to target the sanctuaries, industrial cities, and logistics that made communist insurgencies and military offensives possible. Like other 1960s hawks, Laird inflated Eisenhower's role in ending the Korean War, concluding that the president had achieved peace by threatening to destroy the enemy. Laird later wrote, "How was the Korean War finally ended? When the Chinese Communists did not join in a truce, the United States warned she would bomb north of the Yalu, might blockade the Chinese coast, might use tactical atomic weapons, and would aim at winning a united Korea." The Korean War affirmed Laird's faith in American airpower, even as it reinforced his aversion to committing US troops abroad, especially in Asia, as domestically unsustainable.[13]

Hence, Laird endorsed President Eisenhower's rejection of American intervention in Vietnam to bolster the French in the First Indochina War. He firmly stated on May 7, 1954, "Indochina is no place for American soldiers to fight." Though militant cold warriors would fault Eisenhower for failing to back the French sufficiently and prevent the division of Vietnam, Laird interpreted events there as another Eisenhower success. Without a legitimate nationalist government in Vietnam supported by its own army, America had few options, especially as the Vietminh insurgents presented few industrial and military targets susceptible to US airpower and coercive diplomacy. Subsequently, both men hoped the newly formed South Vietnamese government could become a capable anticommunist proxy. Laird backed Eisenhower, arguing that the president had made the strategically and politically smart choice.[14]

Eisenhower's coercive diplomacy avoided another major conflict and seemingly held the line on communism's advance in the Third World. Eisenhower was fortunate that America's enemies were not as aggressive or as strong as they would be in the 1960s. In most of the major crises of the 1950s, the Soviet Union and China stood down rather than press the challenge. As historians Campbell Craig and Fredrik Logevall aptly noted, "That's the beauty of a winning bluff: no one gets to see your cards." Without seeing the opposing hand, Republicans bragged in 1960, Eisenhower "got us out of Korea and he kept us out of Vietnam."

Laird agreed. His wartime experience and political instincts, along with the perceived lessons of Korea and Indochina, all confirmed Eisenhower's wisdom.[15]

But Laird's position on Korea and Indochina, as well as his skepticism of foreign aid programs, demonstrated that he was far from the strident Cold War and Vietnam hawk he would become in the 1960s. Whereas other Republicans such as Richard Nixon were adamant about America's need to stand firm in places like Vietnam in 1954, Laird was quiet. Laird's transformation into one of the foremost Republican hawks would follow Kennedy's 1961 inauguration, indicating that partisanship was the crucial ingredient for this change.

Laird, Laos, and the Politics of Foreign Crises, 1961–1963

In spite of Laird's praise, as the Eisenhower administration ended, Southeast Asia was at a tipping point. Pro-American forces in Laos were on the retreat. Cambodia embraced Cold War neutrality. The Republic of Vietnam faced a rapidly growing insurgency. Yet, with a Democrat entering the White House, Laird sought to turn foreign setbacks into political gains.

Laird emerged in the early 1960s as one of the most vocal and ardent anticommunist Republicans. His speeches and publications increasingly demanded that President Kennedy do more not just to contain communism but to roll it back worldwide. And when JFK appeared to falter on foreign affairs, Laird pounced. In tandem with the rising conservative faction within the Republican Party, Laird's congressional standing rose as he made a name for himself as a shrewd foreign policy hawk.

Laird was an ambitious and pragmatic politician from a state that had been a bastion of less ideological, midwestern Republicanism. Though fiscally conservative, he was relatively moderate on civil rights and backed federal funding for medical research. By embracing the language of militant anticommunism, he could move toward the conservative wing of the party, act as a bridge to party liberals and moderates, and attack Democrats on foreign policy rather than risk alienating Wisconsin voters on domestic issues. Senator Jacob Javits (R-NY) characterized his colleague as a politician who was "quite conservative . . . but essentially he's a pragmatist. He's a man who's going not to try to talk about it, but do it." Results (measured in political success and the national interest), not ideology, mattered. Sensing the rise of the Republican Right, Laird tacked in their direction in the early 1960s, and his first book established his credentials as a militant anticommunist.[16]

In *A House Divided,* Laird depicted the Cold War as a civilizational and spiritual war against communism, and he ruled out peaceful coexistence.[17] He argued that rather than focusing on surviving the Cold War, policymakers should find ways to win it. Laird believed they should consider every strategic and tactical alternative, including the option of a nuclear first strike on the Soviet Union. Laird believed Americans could sustain the will necessary to maintain strategic superiority and, as opportunities arose, roll back communism, "fighting, winning, and recovering" lost territory. He boldly closed his book, "We have the means to roll it back. We must—and we shall!"[18]

Despite this confidence, Laird was anxious about wars of national liberation between communist proxies and the United States. He believed America must not allow these conflicts to distract it from its overall objective of defeating communism. Instead, the United States should continue to maintain nuclear superiority while relying on threats and asymmetrical responses to deter guerrilla wars. Hence, Laird's grand strategy emphasized the use of American air, naval, and nuclear weaponry. The commitment of US soldiers would be a measure of last resort. For insurgencies, the United States should use local forces and, if necessary, US air and naval power. When Democrats failed to adopt his firm stand or employ his prescriptions to Cold War crises, he would deride them for weakness and join with others to coordinate partisan attacks.[19]

Laird and Richard Nixon, who was down but not out after losing to Kennedy in 1960, saw a mutual advantage in working together to expose Kennedy's foreign policy weaknesses. In an April 11, 1961, letter, Nixon appealed to Laird for advice on how to criticize the Kennedy administration. Laird replied on May 1 that, "somehow or other, we must find a means of dramatizing to the American public the difficulty which the new President has in making big decisions and in standing by these decisions once they have been made." Every international crisis, every perceived Kennedy blunder or concession, provided an opportunity for political gain.[20]

In particular, Laos had all the makings of an international crisis tinged with political peril. Formerly part of French Indochina, the small landlocked nation ran along North and South Vietnam's western borders. When France formally withdrew in the mid-1950s, the Eisenhower administration stepped in to defend Laos. The United States provided pro-Western forces with aid and initiated a right-wing coup in pursuit of this objective. As neutralist and anti-American forces gained ground in Laos, President Eisenhower considered intervening militarily, but with time running out on his administration, he left that decision to his successor.[21]

Whereas Eisenhower saw Laos as vital to the success of US efforts in Indochina and rejected any neutralization agreement, President Kennedy disagreed. JFK considered the Lao people weak pacifists who were incapable of defeating the determined communists, and the Laotian geography would make any US military intervention difficult. Furthermore, the Bay of Pigs fiasco shook Kennedy's faith in his military advisers, making him reluctant to accept their advice on Laos. Finally, the pessimistic assessment of other Western leaders confirmed Kennedy's doubts. By the end of April 1961, the president had opted for a diplomatic solution to the Laotian predicament. Neutralization became America's aim in Laos.[22]

While the majority of congressional representatives and Americans supported President Kennedy's decision, Laird saw Laos's neutralization both as a significant Cold War defeat and as a chance to attack the Democrats' record on foreign relations. Delivering on his promise to Nixon, in May 1961 he charged that because of JFK's inaction, "Laos slipped away from a pro-Western position and is today undergoing the transformation into a 'neutrality' which smacks of communist sympathy." Laird argued that the proposed neutralization of Laos, coupled with the administration's failure to salvage the Bay of Pigs invasion, had weakened American credibility and emboldened Soviet leaders to keep testing US resolve. He predicted that America might find itself "fighting a series of limited wars since we have indicated, by word and by deed, that we prefer limited war to all-out retaliation." His protestations had little effect. On July 23, 1962, the Geneva conference settled the neutralization of Laos by creating a coalition government that included communist groups.[23]

But Laird continued to make Laos a political issue. In a 1962 campaign address he declared that, as a Republican representative, he was trying to be "objective, fair and responsible," but Kennedy's foreign policy "has already cost us Cuba, Laos and probably all of Southeast Asia." Laird continued, "I am firmly convinced that President Kennedy needs more Republicans in Congress to help him, in spite of himself, to wage a meaningful battle against Communism."[24]

Beyond partisanship, Laird considered Laos critical to the defense of South Vietnam. He asserted that the agreement "was a Communist victory as decisive as Dien Bien Phu"—the dramatic 1954 battle that symbolized French failure in the First Vietnam War.[25] Laos's strategic significance stemmed from the fact that the Ho Chi Minh Trail ran through its territory. Laird explained in *A House Divided* that since Laos's mountains held the geographic choke points necessary to keep the North Vietnamese from sweeping south down the trail, neutralization prevented US-backed forces from stopping the incursions there. He concluded that through either ineptitude or cowardice, JFK had handed Laos over to the enemy so that "the net effect of this agreement on Laos will be the intensification of war in Southeast Asia and a weakening of the confidence of free Asians in the value of close cooperation with the United States."[26]

Kennedy and his advisers appreciated the delicate political and strategic calculus, and they sought to mitigate the impact of Laos's neutralization on South Vietnamese security and American politics. Kennedy recognized how narrow his 1960 victory had been and feared that foreign setbacks could precipitate a political backlash from the Right, hurting his reelection chances. So for every step JFK took away from Laos, he took a step toward a closer commitment to the Republic of Vietnam. But so did his Republican challengers.[27]

Laird demanded that Kennedy stand firm in South Vietnam, and he offered a strategy for defeating communism in that troubled region. Laird's solution involved an offensive strategy that accounted for physical terrain rather than territorial boundaries, improved the South Vietnamese military, and played to America's strengths in the air and at sea. He called for a firm defense of South Vietnam achieved by training and equipping South Vietnamese soldiers to fight and win the guerrilla war with the National Liberation Front (NLF). As their military strength grew, the South Vietnamese could launch a counteroffensive against insurgent sanctuaries, "recognizing no borders" and perhaps invading North Vietnam with the help of the US Navy. The United States could also draw soldiers from the South East Asian Treaty Organization's members and use them to secure the mountain passes in Laos and North Vietnam, stopping the flow of men and material. Laird believed that North Vietnam's centers of industry and logistics, Hanoi and Haiphong, were uniquely vulnerable to American air and naval power and that policymakers should not hold back against them. His only caveat to this military escalation involved the use of US troops: Asia remained no place for an American land war. Overall, the Laotian settlement did not make the job impossible, only more difficult.[28]

In a 1963 article appearing in the *Saturday Evening Post,* Laird underscored this gloomy prognosis. He wrote that Kennedy's "timid" foreign policy has "set the stage really for a future dilemma in which we will have to abandon all of Southeast Asia or fight a dirty war." Believing that Third World conflicts were nothing more than "Soviet-dictated ping-pong games," Laird urged policymakers to deter further aggression by threatening to escalate these conflicts on US terms. He wrote that Kennedy should give Hanoi an "ultimatum" that North Vietnam would face "invasion" if it did not stop infiltrating Laos and South Vietnam. Given the disparity of power, the communists would stop their aggression, he believed, if America made a clear, credible stand.[29]

The War He Wanted and the War He Accepted, 1964–1965

After the assassination of John F. Kennedy in November 1963, Representative Laird continued to be a leading hawk, demanding that Kennedy's successor, Lyndon Johnson, use American airpower to halt communist aggression and save the Republic of Vietnam. Speaking before Wisconsin Republicans on March 2, 1964, Laird asserted, "Either we abandon [South Vietnam], and therefore all Southeast Asia, to Communism; or we enlarge our own commitment of material and supplies, and carry the war to North Vietnam."[30] Laird favored the latter and wanted a war to save South Vietnam, but he made it known that he intended for others to do the fighting. In both public statements and classified congressional briefings, Laird suggested that the Johnson administration supplement South Vietnamese forces with soldiers from other nations rather than Americans. He thought that US air and naval power combined with local manpower would suffice. Halfway measures (other than his own), he warned, would either concede Southeast Asia or produce a protracted war that could last a decade or more. He pressed the president to escalate the conflict, bomb North Vietnam, and invade the North with regional forces "so the war does not drag on for 10 years."[31]

Laird emphasized the use of American airpower and indigenous defense, but President Johnson took the war in a different direction. Even as LBJ began to adopt his bombing policies, Laird derided him for doing too little. Meanwhile, Laird opposed Johnson's deployment of US forces. Beyond Americanization, Laird disagreed with the president on the value of negotiating with North Vietnam. He doubted talks could bring peace with honor. As the president sent more and more US troops to South Vietnam and offered the prospect of negotiations, Laird's frustration grew. Nevertheless, he chose Johnson's war over losing Vietnam.

All the while, Laird's political calculations sharpened his militant rhetoric, providing a blueprint for how to play politics with foreign policy. Laird pitched alternatives in all-or-nothing dichotomies, with his preferred policy—all-out bombing—providing the illusion of victory without the sacrifice of US soldiers. Thus, he could attack Johnson for not going far enough in the politically popular bombing campaigns and for going too far on the politically dangerous deployment of troops. The wily Republican also sought to anticipate Johnson's policies and then head him off by publicly announcing them as fact or condemning any possible diplomatic compromise as abandonment. Of course, when the president chose escalation, Laird praised him for belatedly accepting Republican advice. President Johnson faced grim choices on Vietnam in 1964–1965, but as Laird sought to exploit the Democratic president's situation for partisan gain, he made hard choices even more difficult.

Laird's hawkish rhetoric and election-year politics proved to be a volatile mixture that created a firestorm at the White House by early June 1964. In a May 31 radio interview Laird stated, "The administration plans to prepare to move into North Viet Nam. . . . I have felt [for some time] that we should be prepared to move into North Viet Nam. . . . And I am happy to say that the administration takes the same position."[32] In part, this declaration of the administration's presumed plans was a typical Laird gambit. He intended to force Democratic officials to either confirm policies he was on the record as supporting or deny the plan and thus open themselves up to credibility problems should they alter course later. To prod LBJ, Laird gave a June 1 congressional speech that further criticized the administration's foreign policy. Laird argued that events in Laos bore out his predictions, implying that if Kennedy had taken his advice, disaster might have been avoided. Laird urged Johnson to change his Southeast Asian policies before the rest of Indochina fell, imperiling US national security.[33]

President Johnson was sensitive to congressional pressure to escalate the war and already feared an aggressive attack from the Right should he fail in Vietnam. Laird's statements confirmed this threat. Just a few days before Laird spoke, Johnson lamented to Senator Richard Russell, "Well, they'd impeach a President though that would run out, wouldn't they? . . . Everybody I talk to says you got to go in . . . including all the Republicans. . . . And I don't know how in the hell you're gonna get out unless they tell you to get out."[34] Despite national security adviser McGeorge Bundy's assurances that Laird was "too small" to worry about, Laird's statements upset the president.[35] On June 2 the president implicitly addressed Laird's accusations at a morning news conference. When asked if the administration was planning to expand the war, President Johnson replied, "I know of no plans that have been made to that effect." Johnson also rebuffed Laird's criticisms as he declared, "America keeps her word," and he claimed that his administration saw Vietnam as part of the larger struggle for freedom.[36]

Laird had goaded LBJ into reaffirming America's commitment to Vietnam. Although the two men shared the same objective there, they differed on the means, scale, and timing.[37] The Johnson administration had spent much of the spring planning covert operations and air attacks against North Vietnam. Even as the president stated that he knew of no plans to attack North Vietnam, his top officials were in Honolulu considering that alternative.[38] Although the president had not yet made a decision, he was moving in that direction. He did not want to reveal these deliberations because of their potential volatility in the 1964 election, as well as his fear that doing so would turn congressional attention away from social reform. Laird's speeches hinted at the political problems that awaited LBJ if he suddenly changed course or failed in Vietnam. Laird and other Republican hawks wanted Johnson to escalate the war, but they would not hesitate to attack his credibility or his policies. Win, lose, or draw in Vietnam, Republican hawks hoped to capitalize on Johnson's dilemma.[39]

The Republican Party faced its own problems as moderate New York governor Nelson Rockefeller and conservative Arizona senator Barry Goldwater battled for their party's presidential nomination. The mid-July 1964 Republican National Convention in San Francisco promised to be an acrimonious affair. Yet Laird recognized that a hawkish stance on foreign affairs would reunite most Republicans.

Laird chose the task of drafting the platform to both ameliorate tensions and aggrandize his political power. Political commentators Stephen Hess and David Broder noted that by "choosing the platform committee as his arena, [Laird] sought power and gained it."[40] Laird believed his greatest challenges were predicting the actions of an administration "racked with the disease of indecision" and making party factions cognizant of how close they were on most top issues. To marry these sides, Laird recruited Rockefeller adviser Henry Kissinger to help write the foreign policy sections of the plank.[41] Laird's draft affirmed that the "overriding foreign policy goal must be victory over Communism," while Kissinger argued that the United States must live up to its word and resist "aggression wherever and whenever it occurs." The final platform retained this bellicosity. If elected, Goldwater would work to defeat communism and advance freedom. The platform made America's commitment clear: "We will move decisively to assure victory in South Vietnam."[42]

Laird and Goldwater were out of step with the country, though. At the time of the 1964 GOP convention, the majority of Americans, including many Republicans, were either against escalation or apathetic toward the crisis in South Vietnam. Republican doves were numerous and outspoken. Newspaper editorial writers favoring de-escalation not only outnumbered their pro-escalation counterparts but were more vocal as well. For its part, Congress largely abdicated its role in shaping US policy on Vietnam, instead offering uncritical support for whatever path LBJ chose. Historian Fredrik Logevall accurately assessed the situation: "For most Americans, Vietnam remained a place and an issue of which they knew little and cared less." Thus, the conservative Republicans' preference for immediate escalation was contrary to the wishes of most Americans.[43]

The August 2, 1964, North Vietnamese attack on the USS *Maddox* in the Gulf of Tonkin and the supposed second attack two days later altered the domestic mood.[44] President Johnson authorized US air strikes against North Vietnam and proposed a congressional resolution that would empower him to expand the war. As Laird rose to support the resolution on August 7, he commended the president for bombing North Vietnam but argued that Johnson's policy of "measured response" was inadequate for the task. He reminded Congress, "The war in Vietnam goes on. We still face a grim choice. . . . The land war remains. And we still have a policy to develop." He urged the president to widen the war and "take whatever steps are necessary to win the war . . . within a reasonable period of time." Laird's appeals had little effect; Americans gave Johnson their support both on Vietnam and at the ballot box. Johnson won the election by a landslide.[45]

After the disastrous 1964 election, Laird had his work cut out for him in reconstituting the Republican Party, and he urged fellow Republicans to join him in this effort rather than hunting for "scapegoats" or "bickering." Democratic gains in Congress and Johnson's big win left Republican moderates and conservatives blaming each other for this outcome.[46] This division only hardened in the House as Laird and his close friend Gerald Ford (R-MI) initiated an internal coup against senior Republican leadership. Ford came out as House minority leader, and Laird became chairman of the Republican Conference, a position he used to consolidate his political power in the House by controlling appointments and organizing Republicans on the issues. They hoped the emerging war in Vietnam could prove the Democrats' political weakness and help rebuild the GOP.[47]

Laird's prescriptions remained simple, but they established his party's record of offering what Americans wanted (and Johnson was unable to provide)—a quick, decisive victory in Vietnam. In February 1965 Laird demanded that the president "pull out completely or go all out and go in to win."[48] Laird argued that if LBJ chose not to withdraw from Southeast Asia, the United States should use its air and naval power against communist forces in the region, an alternative then favored by only 18 percent of Americans.[49] Laird went on to make it clear that his vision of escalation did not entail the use of US ground troops. Reacting to events in South Vietnam and politics at home, President Johnson changed the nature of America's commitment to South Vietnam in early 1965, though not in the manner Laird desired.

The February 7, 1965, NLF attack on the US army base at Pleiku in the central highlands of South Vietnam catalyzed Johnson's escalation of the war. Having concluded that it could not allow South Vietnam to fall without first taking military action, the Johnson administration chose to institute a gradual bombing campaign against North Vietnam. Pleiku was the pretext for this action.[50]

Hawkish Republican leaders intensified their pressure on LBJ to continue escalating the war. On February 17 Laird and other Republicans in the House and Senate issued a joint statement endorsing Johnson's recent air strikes against North Vietnam. They wrote, "If we have any difference with the President in this respect, it is the belief these measures might have been used more frequently since the Bay of Tonkin decision last August and an even stronger policy formulated in the meantime." The Democratic administrations' 1962 Geneva settlement on Laos and 1964 bombing of North Vietnam had failed to bring peace to Indochina. These congressional Republicans maintained that events had proved them right and had demonstrated that "agreements can only fail when the Communists negotiate only for domination and we negotiate only for peace." So long as North Vietnamese soldiers infiltrated into South Vietnam, "there can be no negotiations." If the United States desired a negotiated settlement, it might as well pull out of South Vietnam.[51]

A month later President Johnson made a negotiated settlement his stated goal. In his April 7 "Peace without Conquest" address at Johns Hopkins University, Johnson declared, "We will never be second in the search for such a peaceful settlement in Viet-Nam. . . . And we remain ready, with this purpose, for unconditional discussions." The president conditioned such negotiations on the continued independence of South Vietnam, but his rhetoric ruffled the feathers of outspoken hawks. Yet Johnson's true position was closer to that of those who favored a wider war.[52]

Without question, LBJ agreed with Laird on the value of South Vietnam in terms of credibility, Cold War strategy, and domestic politics, but he faced the reality of a rapidly deteriorating situation. There were no easy answers, and unlike his opponents, Johnson could not offer up simple platitudes and political attacks. Building up the South Vietnamese military with US advisers and aid had failed. An all-out bombing of North Vietnam would invite criticism at home and abroad and risk provoking Soviet or Chinese intervention. Sending in large numbers of American soldiers seemed to be the only answer, but as LBJ lamented to Secretary of Defense

Robert McNamara, "*What human being knows* [how many men that will take]?" Johnson rationalized that he was not trying to get out or end the war with troops, simply "trying to hold what we *got.* And . . . we're losing, at the rate we're going. . . . When [the South Vietnamese] can't resist it and they're overrun, why, we got to carry in men to help them." Meanwhile, the Johns Hopkins speech and the prospect of negotiations were attempts to defuse criticism of his escalation of the war. Weighing the Cold War risks and domestic costs, LBJ chose to escalate the air and ground war gradually rather than adopting the Republicans' all-out approach. Vietnam defied simple solutions, but this path seemed to minimize the political and military perils while offering the hope of victory.[53]

In principle and in rhetoric, Laird adamantly opposed Johnson's Americanization of the conflict. When Johnson expanded the bombing, Laird praised him for adopting part of the Republican hawks' prescriptions, but he demanded that the president escalate the air and naval campaign against North Vietnam without sending more US ground troops. In a July 25 televised interview on ABC's *Issues and Answers,* Laird reaffirmed his faith that an escalated air campaign against significant North Vietnamese targets and a naval blockade of North Vietnam would preclude the need for more US ground forces in South Vietnam. He proclaimed that President Johnson should expend American bombs rather than American lives to achieve a negotiated settlement. But like other Americans, Laird could only express his "hope that we will not drift into a major land war in Southeast Asia."[54]

This criticism needled the president, but he needed Laird's support. With the Democratic Party increasingly divided over the war, Johnson needed pro-war Republicans for his foreign agenda, even as he needed antiwar Democrats to advance his domestic programs. Privately, LBJ groused to Ford, "I think you ought to get a muzzle on Laird and make him quit telling me that I can't have ground troops I need to protect my own airplanes. Because I can't bomb like he wants to if the goddamned Vietcong are destroying my airplanes on the ground." But, Johnson continued, "would you consider letting me trade [antiwar Democratic senator Wayne] Morse to you for Laird?" Due to the nation's partisan alignment, Johnson could only wish that some of the war's strongest supporters were not in the opposition party.[55]

Johnson's Vietnam policies similarly put Republican hawks in a difficult position. They had frequently pressed for a bipartisan foreign policy and a wider war. Although he had rejected their plans for escalation, the president had the same overall objective: the preservation of a non-Communist South Vietnam. They could either support the president's Americanization of the conflict or appear to have abandoned South Vietnam. Republican leadership chose the former alternative but they did not do so enthusiastically. As Laird often pointed out during Johnson's Americanization of the war, "*Support* for a policy is not necessarily synonymous with enthusiastic approval of that policy."[56]

"I Am . . . a Pessimist," 1966–1967

Melvin Laird harbored no illusions of a quick end to the conflict, and from late 1965 to 1967 he grew more pessimistic about the prospects of preserving South Vietnam. He feared that LBJ had embroiled the United States in an endless Asian land war without a clear strategy to attain "victory over Communism." In a moment of candor he said, "So far as Vietnam is concerned, I am genuinely and deeply apprehensive about the corner into which the President has painted himself." His late 1965 demands for more air strikes as well as a declaration of war to force President Johnson to lay out his aims and strategy led Wisconsin's Democratic Party chair to label Laird the "head of the war hawks."[57] Yet that title became less and less appropriate as the war wore on.[58]

After Democrats made such accusations, Laird responded, "I am keeping the Republicans quiet on the issue [of an expanded war]. It is ridiculous to talk about military victory in Southeast Asia."[59] The Johnson administration had chosen a ground war, and Laird, like most members of Congress, felt politically compelled to finance American troops that were already in the field. He recognized that President Johnson had rejected his counsel and that public sentiment could turn against further escalation. He stopped calling for an escalated air and naval campaign. From late 1965 to 1967 Laird stood by the Republic of Vietnam, but his pessimism grew as the war continued and Johnson sought a negotiated settlement that might fail to ensure South Vietnam's survival. While urging Johnson to stay the course, Laird's speeches grew somber as he feared a hasty settlement would result in a communist takeover. By 1968, he was no longer a hawk but a pessimist looking for a way out of Vietnam.[60]

Having failed to persuade the president to adopt his tactics, Laird spent much of 1966 pressuring the Johnson administration to avoid an overall objective that permitted a coalition government in South Vietnam. On March 1, 1966, Laird told Congress, "If a coalition government including Communist representation is acceptable to the President—as it is to many influential members of his party, all the fighting in South Vietnam—all the sacrifices—all the bloodshed—make no sense, and they should be no further prolonged." Laird was not against communists who came to power via free elections, although he believed it would be several years before South Vietnam could hold meaningful elections. Instead, Laird opposed a negotiated settlement that gave communists a stake in a coalition government. He believed the inclusion of communists would give them the means to gain complete power through terror and subversion; consequently, "South Vietnam will go the way of the satellite nations of Eastern Europe and of Laos." An honorable peace, he believed, should guarantee the Republic of Vietnam's political survival.[61]

Peace with honor should also enable the Republic of Vietnam's military survival, and the conclusions of the October 1966 Manila conference between America and its allies in Vietnam discouraged Laird. The conference's key agreement was that there would be a complete withdrawal of foreign allied forces six months after North Vietnamese soldiers left South Vietnam. Laird disagreed with this proposed timetable for the mutual withdrawal of American and North Vietnamese forces. The South Vietnamese needed more time and more US assistance than a swift, negotiated exit would allow. According to Laird, a six-month American exit would return South Vietnam to the anarchic state of 1964, and he urged Johnson to renounce the timetable. Laird's opposition to a compromise settlement put him at odds with a majority of Americans. More than 60 percent of respondents told Gallup pollsters they were more likely to vote for a congressional candidate who advocated a compromise settlement, but Laird's stand was consistent with his principles.[62] His criticisms solidified his position that any such settlement was a sell-out, so perhaps he traded immediate approval for long-term political gain.[63]

Coming in the midst of the 1966 midterm election campaign, the Manila conference invited partisan criticism of the Democrats' handling of the conflict. Even as he pledged to keep Vietnam out of politics, Laird accused the Johnson administration of deciding war policy "with an eye for domestic political considerations." Laird and his Republican Conference's white paper on Vietnam brought this charge front and center. Republicans argued that LBJ freely chose to commit US ground forces to Southeast Asia and that none of the obligations made by previous administrations required him to take this action. Referring to the tract, Laird stated that it "sets forth the deception practiced by the Democratic spokesmen during the 1964 [and] . . . 1966 election period[s] by withholding information concerning the costs of the war and the planned escalation of the war within the next year."[64] After chronicling what they considered Johnson's errors in Vietnam, the Republicans concluded, "Administration policy has prevented Communist conquest of South Vietnam. However, peace or victory or stability there are still remote."[65]

In contrast to the optimistic reports coming out of the White House and Pentagon in 1967, Laird's pessimism grew, and he muted his calls for escalation. With US soldiers doing the bulk of the fighting and dying in Vietnam, Laird held out little hope that South Vietnam could survive America's exit, even with the withdrawal of North Vietnamese regulars. He stated, "I cannot believe that the South Vietnamese are ready today, or will be ready within the short space of a year or so, to act successfully against a rejuvenated Vietcong unhampered by American involvement in support of the South Vietnamese." Furthermore, Laird believed that the opportunity to employ America's full air and naval power against North Vietnam had passed and that the start of serious negotiations was only a matter of time. On a trip back to Wisconsin in March, Laird told his constituents that he saw "no real chance for a U.S. military victory in Vietnam." Back home, he also met with close friends who had lost fathers, husbands, brothers, and sons in Vietnam. Johnson's war of limits and unclear objectives was maddening as public support fell and dissent quickened. Reflecting on this grim situation in July 1967, Laird declared, "I am neither a 'hawk' nor a 'dove' on Vietnam but rather a pessimist."[66]

Laird's search for an exit from Vietnam had begun. He had noted in the 1966 Republican white paper on Vietnam, "The urgent immediate question facing the nation is how to end this war more speedily and at smaller cost while safeguarding the independence and freedom of South Vietnam." Even five more years of this "limitless war" would be excruciating for US soldiers, American society, and South Vietnam. Laird observed that the political and military situation was improving in South Vietnam, but the administration needed to adopt a strategy that emphasized and accelerated this process. Once South Vietnamese forces could handle the insurgency, the president could negotiate the mutual withdrawal of American and North Vietnamese forces. By late 1967, Laird had developed the rationale for Vietnamization—strengthening the South Vietnamese so that American forces could return home. His anticommunist convictions, emphasis on indigenous self-defense, and antipathy toward a phony settlement undergirded this policy. But with Gallup reporting that more than 70 percent of Americans favored such a plan, his political instincts confirmed that this approach was the best way forward.[67]

In autumn 1967 Representative Laird was looking forward to the 1968 election. Republicans feared the Democrats would play politics with the war by getting a breakthrough settlement during the presidential campaign, but uncertainty over White House plans and the trajectory of public opinion made identifying a politically safe position difficult. Politically, escalation was losing its appeal, and Laird concluded that campaigning as the peace party was the surest ticket to electoral victory. To that end, Laird restrained Republican hawks from criticizing Democratic doves. When Robert Kennedy spoke of a possible coalition government, Laird warned his peers, "Don't hit Bobby on this one. He may come out smelling like a rose." Yet he also began to build a dossier of past Democratic statements condemning talks with the NLF, just in case the administration sought a compromise settlement in the election year. It was unlikely that a dove would win the Republican nomination, but the successful candidate would need maximum flexibility on the war to tack with the American political and Vietnamese diplomatic winds during the general election campaign. So long as the Republican candidate appeared more dovish than the Democrat, Laird thought the GOP had a good chance of winning the election. Laird concluded that de-Americanization through progressive US troop withdrawals based on South Vietnamese improvement was the only sound political and military way forward. It also offered Republican hawks and doves a way out of Vietnam that included a chance of peace with honor. He would work with the Nixon campaign and the 1968 Republican platform to ensure that this became the GOP's position on the war.[68]

After years of being rebuffed by Democratic administrations, Laird abandoned his call for immediate and decisive air and naval escalation, but he had not given up on South Vietnam. By 1968, Laird was much more pessimistic than the young Wisconsin congressman who had championed decisive American intervention in the early 1960s. The Laotian settlement, the Americanization of the war, President Johnson's apparent willingness to settle for a coalition government, and the possibility of the outright abandonment of South Vietnam all shook his faith in a positive outcome to the Vietnam War. Yet Laird still sought a magic formula that could win US elections and preserve South Vietnam.

Magic Formulas

Throughout the 1960s, Melvin Laird sought to use foreign crises in Southeast Asia to criticize Democratic presidents and score political points for Republican candidates. Laird's 1960s hawkishness was a marked departure from his relative Cold War pragmatism during the 1950s, indicating that his newfound zeal had as much to do with the Democratic occupants of the White House as with an objective appraisal of events. Yet Laird was consistent in his proposed solutions to Third World crises: avoid another American land war in Asia by punishing communist aggression with decisive US firepower.

Driven by the hawks on one hand and by frustration on the other, President Lyndon Johnson had greatly expanded and escalated the air campaign against North Vietnam. He increasingly removed restrictions on bombing Hanoi and Haiphong, but the hawks demanded more, even as they criticized the president for sending troops to South Vietnam. As journalist Walter Lippmann observed, Laird and his fellow Republican hawks had set "a trap for the President," knowing that the deteriorating situation in Indochina would compel him to escalate the war or abandon the area. When he did adopt escalation, Laird charged that it was "too little, too late." Of course, had Johnson somehow reached an agreement with Hanoi on South Vietnamese neutrality, Laird would have pounced on the president for condemning the South Vietnamese people to communist servitude.[69]

Sincere as it was, Laird's faith in American airpower was, as Lippmann put it, a "magic formula . . . to bomb North Vietnam from the air and keep the GIs out of the foxholes." The solution was simple to understand, and it gave the public what it wanted most of all—"a formula for victory." Laird never had to explain how this policy would compel North Vietnam's capitulation or save South Vietnam, but as James Reston pointed out, it was "a clever political argument," since Laird "has figured out how to embarrass the President no matter what happens." Indeed, as the war became an Americanized stalemate, Laird reminded the public that events had proved Kennedy and Johnson wrong. If only they had taken his advice, the stalemate in Vietnam with its daily toll in American blood could have been avoided.[70]

Over the course of his career as a congressman and as secretary of defense, Laird provided Americans with not one magic formula but two.[71] His Vietnamization of US troop withdrawals predicated on South Vietnamese improvement gave the public, a Republican president, and pessimistic former hawks the hope that the Republic of Vietnam could survive even as the United States gradually accepted the domestic and military limits of its power. Unlike his first magic formula, Vietnamization proved to be a political winner.[72] Laird reflected, "Vietnam elected Nixon twice. According to all the polls, Nixon won the 1968 and 1972 elections because of the War."[73] In both campaigns, Laird's program of US troop withdrawal was front and center. In that way, the representative who had done so much to galvanize the nation into backing a war in Vietnam became responsible for the manner of its conclusion. Bob Schieffer, who became the CBS Pentagon correspondent when Laird became secretary of defense, observed, "Mel Laird was the former congressman who knew what it meant back in the district when the coffins started arriving. And it was Laird, who I think had as much to do as anyone would with bringing the war to a much quicker conclusion."[74]

Notes

1. George Herring, *America's Longest War: The United States and Vietnam, 1950–1975,* 4th ed. (New York: McGraw-Hill, 2002), 182.

2. William Baroody, interview with James Reichley, n.d., folder "Ford White House: Baroody, William," box 1, A. James Reichley Interview Transcripts (1967), 1977–81, Gerald Ford Library, Ann Arbor, MI (hereafter GFL).

3. For instance, see Randall Bennett Woods, *J. William Fulbright, Vietnam, and the Search for a Cold War Foreign Policy* (New York: Cambridge University Press, 1998); Joseph Fry, *Debating Vietnam: Fulbright, Stennis, and Their Senate Hearings* (New York: Rowman and Littlefield, 2006); Randall Woods, ed., *Vietnam*

and the American Political Tradition: The Politics of Dissent (New York: Cambridge University Press, 2003).

4. Notes of meeting, George Elsey, December 9, 1968, #177, "Van de Mark transcripts [2]," box 1, George Elsey Papers, Lyndon B. Johnson Presidential Library, Austin, TX (hereafter LBJPL) (emphasis in original); Bob Schieffer, "Why Mel Laird Is Worried about Afghanistan," August 15, 2010, http://www.cbsnews.com/news/why-mel-laird-is-worried-about-afghanistan/ (accessed May 29, 2015).

5. Thomas Schwartz, "'Henry, . . . Winning an Election Is Terribly Important': Partisan Politics in the History of U.S. Foreign Relations," *Diplomatic History* 33, no. 2 (April 2009): 177.

6. I am indebted to H. T. Dickinson for my understanding that "political agents act and think"—principles and self-interest together inspire political action. See H. T. Dickinson, *Liberty and Property: Political Ideology in Eighteenth-Century Britain* (New York: Holmes and Meier, 1977).

7. Helen Laird, *A Mind of Her Own: Helen Connor Laird and Family, 1888–1982* (Madison: University of Wisconsin Press, 2006), 207; Lawrence Kestenbaum, "Index to Politicians: Laird," *Political Graveyard,* http://politicalgraveyard.com/bio/laird.html (accessed August 9, 2013).

8. This is the same USS *Maddox* (DD-731) that was later involved in the Gulf of Tonkin incident.

9. Laird, *Mind of Her Own,* 239–52; Dale Van Atta, *With Honor: Melvin Laird in War, Peace, and Politics* (Madison: University of Wisconsin Press, 2008), 7–8.

10. Laird, *Mind of Her Own,* 281, 341; William McNitt, "Melvin R. Laird Biographical Summary" and "Introduction," http://www.fordlibrarymuseum.gov/library/guides/findingaid/Laird,_Melvin_-_Papers.asp (accessed August 9, 2013); Van Atta, *With Honor,* 26.

11. James Reichley, *Conservatives in an Age of Change: The Nixon and Ford Administrations* (Washington, DC: Brookings Institution, 1981), 109–10; Ralph Smuckler, "The Region of Isolationism," *American Political Science Review* 47, no. 2 (June 1953): 393–94.

12. Van Atta, *With Honor,* 38–42. On Eisenhower's foreign policy in the Third World, see Chester J. Pach Jr., "Thinking Globally and Acting Locally" in *The Eisenhower Administration, the Third World, and the Globalization of the Cold War,* ed. Kathryn Statler and Andrew Johns (Lanham, MD: Rowman and Littlefield, 2006).

13. Melvin Laird, *A House Divided: America's Strategy Gap* (Chicago: Henry Regnery, 1962), 61, 63, 93.

14. Van Atta, *With Honor,* 43–44; Laird, *House Divided,* 93–97.

15. Van Atta, *With Honor,* 43; Campbell Craig and Fredrik Logevall, *America's Cold War: The Politics of Insecurity* (Cambridge, MA: Belknap Press, 2009), 152–53.

16. Mary Brennan, "A Step in the 'Right' Direction: Conservative Republicans and the Election of 1960," *Presidential Studies Quarterly* 22, no. 1 (Winter 1992): 73–87; Reichley, *Conservatives in an Age of Change,* 22–26, 66; Javits transcript,

Today Show, December 12, 1968, #2a, "Nixon, Hon. Richard M.," box 15, Clark Clifford Papers, LBJPL.

17. Senator Barry Goldwater's speechwriter, Karl Hess, provided editorial assistance for the book. The Henry Regnery Company printed 8,000 copies of *A House Divided* in 1962, though not all of them would sell. Significant book sales (and a second printing of 10,000 copies) would not come until Nixon named Laird his secretary of defense. Sales information is from James Wieghart, "Laird's Book Seen Sure Fuel for Foes," *Milwaukee Sentinel,* December 19, 1968.

18. Laird, *House Divided,* 7–8, 34, 50–51, 83, 143, 175–79.

19. Ibid., 27–28, 38–39, 61, 93–94, 134.

20. Nixon to Laird, April 11, 1961, and Laird to Nixon, May 1, 1961, Richard Nixon Presidential Library and Museum, Yorba Linda, CA.

21. Herring, *America's Longest War,* 47, 85–86; Richard Filipink, *Dwight Eisenhower and American Foreign Policy during the 1960s: An American Lion in Winter* (New York: Lexington Books, 2015), 5–7, 25–29.

22. Seth Jacobs, "'No Place to Fight a War': Laos and the Evolution of U.S. Policy toward Vietnam, 1954–1963" in *Making Sense of the Vietnam Wars: Local, National, and Transnational Perspectives,* ed. Mark Philip Bradley and Marilyn B. Young (New York: Oxford University Press, 2008), 47–48, 54–59; Robert Mann, *A Grand Delusion: America's Descent into Vietnam* (New York: Basic Books, 2001), 230; Herring, *America's Longest War,* 93–94; Fredrik Logevall, *Choosing War: The Lost Chance for Peace and the Escalation of War in Vietnam* (Berkeley: University of California Press, 1999), 23–25.

23. Henry Scheele, "Response to the Kennedy Administration: The Joint Senate-House Republican Leadership Press Conferences," *Presidential Studies Quarterly* 19, no. 4 (Fall 1989): 830–31; Melvin Laird, speech, "Foreign Policy," folder "Speeches-ca 5/61-Foreign Policy," box A15, Laird Papers, GFL.

24. Melvin Laird, "Foreign Policy as Campaign Issue," folder "Campaign Statements, 1962," box A4, Laird Papers, GFL.

25. Melvin Laird, speech on Laos, 87th Cong., 2nd sess., *Congressional Record* 108, pt. 13 (August 27, 1962): 17712.

26. Laird, *House Divided,* 104–6; Laird to Dean Rusk, 87th Cong., 2nd sess., *Congressional Record* 108, pt. 12 (August 13, 1962): 16274.

27. Jacobs, "No Place to Fight," 62; Andrew Johns, *Vietnam's Second Front: Domestic Politics, the Republican Party, and the War* (Lexington: University Press of Kentucky, 2010), 16, 25, 40.

28. Laird, *House Divided,* 53, 96–97, 102–11, 177.

29. Melvin Laird, "Peace without War?" folder "Articles—*Saturday Evening Post* article 'Peace w/o War?' 1963 (1)," box A2, Laird Papers, GFL.

30. "Laird Says Johnson Flunks Domestic and Foreign Tests," speech before Taylor County Republican Dinner, March 2, 1964, folder "Press Releases—Issued," box A12, Laird Papers, GFL.

31. "McNamara Tries to Blame Congress for S. Viet Nam Situation, Laird

Declares," *Sheboygan Press,* March 9, 1964; "Briefing on South Vietnam," May 21, 1964, folder "Vietnamese War," box 37, Baroody Papers, GFL; Laird, statement, June 1, 1964, folder "Vietnam," box 10, ibid.

32. "Laird Says U.S. Will Extend War," *Madison Capital Times,* June 1, 1964.

33. Press release, June 1, 1964, folder "Vietnam," box 10, Baroody Papers, GFL.

34. Michael Beschloss, *Taking Charge: The Johnson White House Tapes, 1963–1964* (New York: Simon and Schuster, 1997), 368–69.

35. McGeorge Bundy quoted in ibid., 379.

36. "The President's News Conference," June 2, 1964, in John Woolley and Gerhard Peters, American Presidency Project, http://www.presidency.ucsb.edu/ws/?pid=26286 (accessed May 31, 2015).

37. See Mitchell Lerner, "Vietnam and the 1964 Election: A Defense of Lyndon Johnson," *Presidential Studies Quarterly* 25, no. 4 (Fall 1995): 751–66.

38. Beschloss, *Taking Charge,* 380.

39. Herring, *America's Longest War,* 139, 141; Mann, *Grand Delusion,* 332; Johns, *Vietnam's Second Front,* 43–48, 51–57; Melvin Laird, "Leadership in Foreign Policy," *Mosinee Times,* June 18, 1964.

40. Stephen Hess and David S. Broder, *The Republican Establishment: The Present and Future of the G.O.P.* (New York: Harper and Row, 1967), 29.

41. Laird had long been an admirer of Kissinger and had even asked him to contribute a chapter to his 1963 work *The Conservative Papers.* See Van Atta, *With Honor,* 63–64.

42. Laird, "Leadership in Foreign Policy"; statement, *News from Republican Citizens,* June 18, 1964, folder "Critical Issues Council," box 8, Baroody Papers, GFL; Laird, statement ca. summer 1964, folder "Vietnam," box 10, ibid.; memo, "Foreign Policy General," 1964, folder 124, box 16, Subseries 2 National Political Campaigns, Series J1 Politics—NYC Office, RG 4 NAR Personal, Rockefeller Family Archives, Rockefeller Archive Center, Sleepy Hollow, NY; "Republican Party Platform of 1964," July 13, 1964, in Woolley and Peters, American Presidency Project, http://www.presidency.ucsb.edu/ws/?pid=25840 (accessed August 9, 2013).

43. Mann, *Grand Delusion,* 306; Andrew Johns, "Doves among Hawks: Republican Opposition to the Vietnam War, 1964–1968," *Peace and Change* 31 (October 2006): 587–89; Logevall, *Choosing War,* 134–36.

44. Edwin Moise's "Tonkin Gulf in Historical Perspective," *Passport* 45, no. 2 (September 2014): 46–50, provides a good overview of the Tonkin incident.

45. Melvin Laird, speech on Gulf of Tonkin incident, 88th Cong., 2nd sess., *Congressional Record* 110, pt. 14 (August 4, 1964): 17889; Laird, draft of Tonkin resolution speech, ca. August 7, 1964, folder "Speeches—ca. August 1964, Gulf of Tonkin Resolution," box A16, Laird Papers, GFL; Laird, speech on Gulf of Tonkin Resolution, 88th Cong., 2nd sess., *Congressional Record* 110, pt. 14 (August 7, 1964): 18548.

46. After the election, Democrats held approximately two-thirds of the House and Senate seats, along with two-thirds of the state governorships.

47. Press release, "Laird Calls for Moratorium on Party Bickering," November 11, 1964, folder "Press Releases—Issued," box A12, Laird Papers, GFL; Henry Scheele, "Prelude to the Presidency: An Examination of the Gerald R. Ford–Charles A. Halleck House Minority Leadership Contest," *Presidential Studies Quarterly* 25, no. 4 (Fall 1995): 767–85; Terry Dietz, *Republicans and Vietnam, 1961–1968* (New York: Greenwood Press, 1986), 74, 77, 84, 87; Johns, *Vietnam's Second Front,* 74; "Can Republicans Make a Comeback?" *US News and World Report,* January 18, 1965.

48. "'Pull Out or Fight in Viet Nam,' Says Melvin Laird," *Shawano Leader,* February 2, 1965.

49. Harris polls quoted in Logevall, *Choosing War,* 282.

50. Herring, *America's Longest War,* 152–54.

51. "Statement by the Joint Senate-House Republican Leadership," February 17, 1965, folder "Vietnam 1965, 66, 68," box D9, Ford Congressional Papers, GFL; Melvin Laird, speech on "Republican Opportunity and Responsibility in 89th Congress," March 1, 1965, folder "Credibility Gap—Johnson Administration and Public Misinformation," box A6, Laird Papers, GFL.

52. Lyndon Johnson, "Address at Johns Hopkins University: 'Peace without Conquest,'" April 7, 1964, in Woolley and Peters, American Presidency Project, http://www.presidency.ucsb.edu/ws/?pid=26877 (accessed August 9, 2013).

53. Michael Beschloss, *Reaching for Glory: Lyndon Johnson's Secret White House Tapes, 1964–1965* (New York: Touchstone, 2002), 352–53.

54. Melvin Laird, speech on "The Vietnam Situation" and reprint of *Today Show* transcript, June 17, 1965, 89th Cong., 1st sess., *Congressional Record* 111, pt. 10 (June 21, 1965): 13651–52; Laird, statement, July 16, 1965, folder "Vietnam War, '65," box 7, Baroody Papers, GFL; transcript, *ABC's Issues and Answers,* July 25, 1965, ibid.

55. Beschloss, *Reaching for Glory,* 362. For Johnson's political difficulties, see Johns, *Vietnam's Second Front,* 104–8, 132.

56. Melvin Laird, "Remarks for World Affairs Council," October 1, 1965, folder "Speeches—10/1/1965—World Affairs Council," box A16, Laird Papers, GFL (emphasis in original).

57. "Hanson Calls Laird Chief 'War Hawk,'" *Madison Capital Times,* November 22, 1965.

58. Laird, "Remarks for World Affairs Council"; Laird, "In Washington: Are We at War in Vietnam?" January 31, 1966, folder "Vietnam, 1964–1968 (1)," box A39, Laird Papers, GFL.

59. "Laird Sheds 'Hawk' Feathers," *Capital Times* (Madison, WI), June 27, 1966.

60. Melvin Laird, "Your Washington Office Report," May 30, 1966, folder "Vietnam: Progress and Policy (2)," box D118, Ford Congressional Papers, GFL; Mann, *Grand Delusion,* 436.

61. Melvin Laird, speech before Congress, March 1, 1966, folder "Credibility Gap—Johnson Administration and Public Misinformation," box A6, Laird Papers,

GFL; reprint of *Face the Nation* transcript, March 13, 1966, 89th Cong., 2nd sess., *Congressional Record* 112, pt. 5 (March 15, 1966): 5835.

62. Gallup poll, "Vietnam," November 21, 1965, and April 1, 1966, in *The Gallup Poll: 1959–1971* (Wilmington, DE: Scholarly Resources, 1971), 1998–99.

63. Lyndon Johnson, "Remarks Recorded for Broadcast to the American People, Following the Manila Conference," October 27, 1966, in Woolley and Peters, American Presidency Project, http://www.presidency.ucsb.edu/ws/?pid=27963 (accessed August 9, 2013).

64. Associated Press, "GOP's Laird Sees Bigger War after Nov. 8," *Washington Post,* September 21, 1966, 20.

65. Melvin Laird, interview with the press, ca. March 1966, folder "Press Materials," box A12, Laird Papers, GFL; Republican Conference, "Vietnam: Some Neglected Aspects of the Historical Record," folder "Vietnam White Papers, 1965–1967 (2)," box D2, ibid.; Andrew Johns, "Achilles' Heel: The Vietnam War and George Romney's Bid for the Presidency, 1967 to 1968," *Michigan Historical Review* 26, no. 1 (Spring 2000): 3–5; Johns, *Vietnam's Second Front,* 112, 120 127.

66. Laird to Johnson, February 9, 1967, folder "Misc.," box D1, Laird Papers, GFL; Laird, speech on "U.S. Trade Policy—Wars of National Liberation," February 16, 1967, 90th Cong., 1st sess., *Congressional Record* 113, pt. 3 (February 17, 1967): A720; press release, July 8, 1967, folder "Laird, Mel," box D55, Ford Congressional Papers, GFL; Laird, speech on "Proposal for Reciprocal Graduated Deescalation of the War in Vietnam," July 17, 1967, 90th Cong., 1st sess., *Congressional Record* 113, pt. 14 (July 17, 1967): 19052–54; Van Atta, *With Honor,* 117–19.

67. Republican Conference, "Vietnam: Some Neglected Aspects of the Historical Record"; Laird, "Proposal for Reciprocal Graduated Deescalation of the War in Vietnam," 19052–54; Laird, "Remarks for World Affairs Council"; Rowland Evans and Robert Novak, "The GOP 'Peace' Party," *Washington Post,* August 14, 1967, A15; Gallup poll, "Vietnam," September 20 and October 29, 1967, in *The Gallup Poll,* 2080, 2087–88.

68. Rowland Evans and Robert Novak, "House GOP Schism Puts Laird at Head of Pragmatic Minority," *Washington Post,* October 18, 1967, p. A17; Rowland Evans and Robert Novak, "GOP Is Prepared to Counterattack Any Vietnamese Approach to NLF," *Washington Post,* September 7, 1967, A21; David Broder, "GOP Role in Vietnam Debate Can Result in 'New Look' Policy," *Washington Post,* October 3, 1967, A17.

69. Walter Lippmann, "The Hard Lesson," *Newsweek,* July 19, 1965, 15; Laird quoted in press Q/A, ca. March 1966, folder "Press Materials," box A12, Laird Papers, GFL.

70. Lippmann, "Hard Lesson"; James Reston, "The Politics of Vietnam," *New York Times,* June 16, 1965, 42.

71. In the wake of Vietnam, many Americans and politicians would embrace Laird's magic formulas: first, that air strikes, cruise missiles, and drones can accomplish US aims without a significant loss of blood and treasure (or political popular-

ity); second, that well-equipped local forces can replace American troops. Laird and Nixon's creation of an all-volunteer force would further distance Americans from the costs and reality of modern warfare.

72. Aside from Laird's personal political standing, which remained high in his district, it is difficult to see how his political strategy of attacking the White House and demanding escalation succeeded (beyond uniting Republican Cold War hawks). The 1964 election was a rout, and in 1966 Republican candidates generally sidestepped the war. Perhaps it worked not in a single election cycle but over the course of years and decades by defining the presumed legacy, lessons, and lost opportunities of the war. From 1961 to 1965 Laird laid the groundwork for the conservative, revisionist critique of the war as he attacked Kennedy's agreement on Laos and Johnson's limited war. Laird demanded that Johnson "pull out completely or go all out and go in to win." He was among the loudest in arguing that the full might of American power had been held back and that when it was finally deployed it was too little, too late. Laird would also contribute to revisionism regarding the war's end: that Vietnamization would have worked had Congress not cut the funding or restricted the bombing. Hence, Laird was seminal in the formation of the first (1961–1965) and second (1968–1975) lost victory myths. On the origins of revisionism, see Mark Atwood Lawrence, "Too Late or Too Soon? Debating the Withdrawal from Vietnam in the Age of Iraq," *Diplomatic History* 34, no. 3 (June 2010): 589–600.

73. Excerpt of letter from Laird to Henry Kissinger, sent to the author April 2, 2007 (in author's possession).

74. Bob Schieffer, interview by Richard Norton Smith, April 30, 2009, GFL, http://geraldrfordfoundation.org/centennial/oralhistory/wp-content/uploads/2013/05/Bob-Schieffer.pdf (accessed May 29, 2015).

3

Senator Henry "Scoop" Jackson and the Intersection between Domestic Politics and Foreign Relations in the Postwar Era

Christopher Foss

Near the end of 1968, as the United States was in the midst of the Vietnam War, Senator Henry Jackson, a Democrat from Washington State, was in a bind. Incoming Republican president Richard Nixon wanted Jackson to become secretary of defense. Jackson had serious doubts, however, about the position, which he detailed to outgoing president Lyndon Johnson in a December 1 telephone conversation that intimately shows the connections between domestic politics and the United States' foreign policymaking concerns.

Though Jackson fretted that a job change could be upsetting to his family, politics was clearly foremost on his mind. He noted that Republican governor Daniel Evans could name a Republican replacement for his Senate seat until a special election could be held.[1] Jackson would be politically damaged if the perception was that he "just got out and turned the seat over to a Republican. . . . That would make my task more difficult for [Nixon] in dealing with the Democratic side." But Johnson pushed Jackson to accept Nixon's offer. "I think it's a great tribute to you," Johnson said. "You could do the job as well as few men could do it . . . [and] you would have the satisfaction of probably saving your country." Addressing Jackson's domestic concerns, Johnson said, "I'd try to work it out where I could name my successor," but he largely downplayed domestic political concerns as a legitimate consideration for Jackson. "I'd be very disappointed in a Democrat that didn't throw his hat in the air" when presented with such an opportunity, Johnson said, dismissing Jackson's contention that perhaps he could do better as a senator in terms of Vietnam. "I can tell you now that you can't," Johnson said. In the Pentagon, Johnson contended, "you've got a lot more goodies to work with."[2]

Ultimately, however, Johnson was a lame-duck president almost a decade removed from his own Senate career. He lacked Jackson's sense of the Senate's importance for both his regional and national ambitions. Jackson rejected Nixon's offer, and in the years to come he would obtain greater national prestige than Johnson probably thought possible in 1968. Jackson positioned himself for runs at the presidency in 1972 and 1976, and major legislation he sponsored, such as the National Environmental Protection Act and authorization for the deployment of defensive antiballistic missiles—both of which he pushed through Congress in 1969—probably played a role in his decision. The telephone conversation with Johnson also shows that Jackson was concerned with home-state politics. Their conversation demonstrates the effect domestic politics has on US foreign policymaking from the standpoint of a senator concerned about his credibility among fellow Democrats in the Senate but also fearing the consequences for his home region should he give up his seat to a Republican. As a member of the majority party in Congress for most of his career, Jackson did much to help his home state. This essay highlights Jackson's use of his foreign affairs expertise to tackle local issues.

Henry Jackson was one of the towering figures of post–World War II US foreign policy in the Senate and arguably the most important politician in the history of the state of Washington. This essay argues that domestic politics and US foreign policy intersected during Jackson's career, not just with regard to electorally minded decisions, such as his rejection of the secretary of defense position, but also in terms of his ability to win military dollars for his constituents and to improve the region's economy through liberalization of international trade.

Jackson is best known for increasing the volume of anticommunist, anti-Soviet rhetoric during the Cold War. He supported arms control only if the Soviet Union reciprocated, arguing that Moscow generally failed to do so. Jackson was a staunch supporter of the Vietnam War, abandoning his support only near the end, when the war had become highly unpopular with the American public. Throughout his career, Jackson was wedded to the cause of US engagement with the world, successfully pushing enhanced US relations with many countries over the years, particularly with Cold War allies. Jackson was an influential foreign affairs counselor to each US president, regardless of party, from John F. Kennedy to Ronald Reagan, a major factor in his ability to wield influence in Washington, DC. This essay focuses, however, on the variety of ways in which Jackson's foreign policies benefited his home-state constituents. Jackson brought home funds for military installations, particularly for the Hanford Nuclear Reservation, and expanded the presence of the US Navy in Puget Sound. He also served his constituents by working to expand the region's trade abroad, particularly to China.

This essay challenges the notion that domestic politics and regional differences rarely matter to foreign relations historians.[3] It follows on the heels of Joseph Fry's call for greater attention to "domestic regionalism" in understanding US foreign policy.[4] But Fry ignores the Pacific Northwest, despite its geographic proximity to East Asian powers such as China and Japan, its growing and increasingly ethnically diverse population, and the role of politicians like Jackson in shaping regional connections with the world.

Few works on US foreign relations have dealt directly with the Pacific Northwest, defined here as the states of Oregon and Washington.[5] Many books about the Cold War touch upon the views of northwestern senators and congressmen, but they rarely provide any clues as to how regional forces shaped the work of these individuals.[6] A small but growing literature on Congress and US foreign relations discusses northwestern senators, particularly Vietnam-era politicians such as Senators Mark Hatfield, Wayne Morse, and Jackson, but it does not focus on any of these individuals or on the Northwest at great length.[7] During the Cold War, however, regional politicians mediated the process whereby national policies that increased defense spending and legislative processes that gradually liberalized American trade and immigration laws affected states and regions. Politicians conversely affected the growth of defense spending and international trade in working for their home states and regions. Few were more successful at using their positions as ombudsmen for their constituents than Jackson.

Jackson always had strong ties to Washington, from the beginning of his life until he died of a heart attack in his home city of Everett on September 1, 1983. Elected to Congress in 1940 at just twenty-eight years old, Jackson was popular throughout his career; he was reelected to the House of Representatives five times, followed by six terms in the Senate, often winning by huge margins. Contemporaries regarded Jackson as studious and hardworking in his committees and in his attempts to help his constituents. Although his correspondence offers few glimpses into the senator's innermost thoughts, newspaper accounts and speeches found in Jackson's archives at the University of Washington reveal his legislative and behind-the-scenes accomplishments for both the Pacific Northwest and the nation. This essay first summarizes Jackson's foreign policy stature and his positions at the national level before moving on to its main discussion of the senator's use of defense dollars and the effects of his stance on trade at the regional level. As will be shown here, Jackson's hawkishness, for which he was nationally known, had strong support among his Washington constituents.

At the height of his power in the Senate, Jackson reflected that he first became a committed internationalist upon learning of the Buchenwald concentration camp in Nazi Germany after World War II. To avert a recurrence of the death camps, Jackson hoped the United States would take an active role overseas. As a young congressman, he was an early supporter of the United Nations and later became a staunch defender of the North Atlantic Treaty Organization and other more traditional military and economic alliances.[8] In Jackson's initial Senate campaign in 1952 against incumbent right-winger Harry Cain, he adopted a national security–oriented, extreme anticommunist position to win. Jackson was reluctant to take such a position, however, seeing it as more of a survival strategy in a year that Republicans took control of both Congress and the presidency.[9] Nevertheless, the senator would maintain this hardline anticommunism, whether it was fashionable or unpopular, throughout his career.

Well-versed in matters of national defense from his 1949 posting to the Joint Congressional Committee on Atomic Energy, Jackson assumed positions on the Senate Armed Services and Government Operations Committees, which made him a regional—as well as a national—voice on national security issues for the remainder of his career. His knowledge of defense matters quickly pushed him to the forefront, particularly when the October 1957 launch of the Soviet satellite *Sputnik* sparked fears of a technology gap between the United States and the Soviet Union. Days after the launch, Jackson said the Soviets had scored a "double victory" against America, although he stressed that with scientific and technological advances, the United States could catch up to the Soviets in the space race.[10] He slammed the US Bureau of the Budget for slashing millions of dollars from a program designed to develop nuclear rocket propulsion fuel to launch American rockets into outer space.[11] According to biographer Robert Kaufman, by 1960, Jackson had also "prevailed on a reluctant naval establishment that wanted more conventional warships, and a president who wanted fewer ships, to increase from four to nine the number of Polaris submarine platforms slated for early deployment."[12]

Jackson's foreign policy hawkishness had its critics. Journalist Walter Lippmann criticized Jackson when he hesitated to back the limited nuclear test ban treaty in 1963, arguing that his assumptions about the treaty were "drawn not from the deliberations of the Administration but . . . out of the more naïve letters which come to him in his mail and by the popular talk which he hears around him."[13] Given the hysterical tone of some of Jackson's correspondence, Lippmann may have had a point. One constituent called the Kennedy administration's 1963 proposal to sell wheat to the Soviets a "sell-out" and said he would "rather roast in HELL a thousand times from an Atomic Holocaust—THAN SELL OUR HERITAGE FOR '30 PIECES OF SILVER.'"[14] But other constituents were less hawkish. In February 1966 the *Seattle Post Intelligencer* published a column critical of Jackson's pro–Vietnam War rhetoric. In letters to the editor responding to the column, one constituent called Jackson "recklessly generous with other people's lives" and "just another politician who has lost touch with the common people and the basic realities of life."[15] In 1968, during the hostage crisis involving the USS *Pueblo* off the North Korean coast, another constituent blasted Jackson for suggesting that tactical nuclear weapons could be used against Pyongyang if negotiations failed to free the hostages, observing that such remarks could make ordinary citizens think the employment of nuclear weapons was reasonable.[16]

In general, however, regional and national constituents supported Jackson's leadership on these issues. He won his reelection campaigns by wide margins and influenced the national discourse on major policy issues, most notably arms control, the environment, and human rights. During the 1970s and early 1980s the senator was an important player in the passage of numerous pieces of legislation, including the National Environmental Policy Act of 1970 and the Trade Act of 1974. The latter contained his namesake Jackson-Vanik amendment, a provision that aimed to prevent the United States from conferring most-favored-nation trading status on countries that restricted emigration, particularly the Soviet Union. Late in his career, Jackson was the first chair of the Senate Energy Committee, and he used his prominent spot on the Armed Services Committee to help turn national opinion against passage of the second round of strategic arms limitation talks with the Soviets.

Historians have emphasized this national work on environmental, energy, and national security policy. But by examining the intersection of Jackson, Washington State, and US foreign policy, it becomes clear that Jackson was more than just a defense and energy wonk. When one considers foreign policy more broadly, beyond the realm of national security, it is clear that Jackson influenced the Cold War in general and, by bringing the Cold War to Washington, transformed his home state.

From his earliest days in Congress, Jackson worked to keep military bases open in Washington. He was generally praised for his efforts: as early as his first year in the Senate, the *Seattle Times* applauded Jackson for resisting the Eisenhower administration's push to lower the military budget.[17] There were dissenting voices: a church pastor in Tacoma slammed Jackson in 1956 for his position on defense spending, arguing that the senator thought "a step up of arms production will gain you voting support in a constituency that lives largely by producing machines of war" and adding, "I pray God that your constituents will see that this road of living high on war industries is the road to ultimate ruin."[18] But letters like these were few and far between, as national security concerns combined with a strong desire for the inflow of federal defense dollars to Washington.

Jackson's domestic liberalism and defense hawkishness translated into defense outlays for his home state. His support for big government stemmed largely from his political need to obtain defense contracts for airplane manufacturer Boeing, the shipyards in and around Puget Sound, and the Hanford Nuclear Reservation in southeastern Washington. While on the Joint Atomic Energy Committee, Jackson spent decades boosting for peaceful nuclear energy, largely because it benefited the workers at Hanford and the economies of nearby cities.[19] During the early 1970s, as Jackson reached the height of his influence, he helped increase federal outlays to Washington State from $3.4 billion in 1970 to $5 billion in 1972. The state's rank in Defense Department spending improved from eighteenth to twelfth, in NASA spending from twenty-sixth to nineteenth, and in Interior Department spending from sixth to second.[20] A survey by Capitol Hill News Service in 1970 ranked Jackson first among his peers in effectiveness at obtaining federal help for his constituents. Jackson's ability to bring home federal bacon pleased liberals, and his defense toughness enabled him to garner conservative votes as well. This combination allowed him to stay in office while other liberal Democrats were defeated as the Republican Party gained strength near the end of Jackson's life.[21]

Jackson is most often remembered for his work on behalf of Boeing, but he was arguably more obsessed with obtaining federal funding for the Hanford Nuclear Reservation. The senator favored nuclear power because of its role in national security and in creating energy for everyday usage by his constituents. As early as 1951, Jackson told his colleagues that the United States "should produce as many nuclear weapons as it could possibly afford, and do so as quickly as possible."[22] Jackson was so enthusiastic about nuclear power that he occasionally handed out cans of irradiated bacon to visitors to his office.[23] His brash display of nuclear cheerleading aside, Jackson's enthusiasm was clearly seen in his lobbying for Hanford, which continued despite cutbacks to the country's nuclear program. Overall, the federal government poured $2 billion into Hanford, even though all but one of its nine reactors had been shut down by the time of Jackson's death, a tribute to his effectiveness in maintaining federal outlays for the reservation.[24]

Jackson's effectiveness in obtaining appropriations for Hanford was largely attributable to his committee assignments. In 1949, when Jackson joined the Joint Atomic Energy Committee, he announced the "immediate start" of a $25 million expansion of Hanford's plutonium production plant.[25] In 1951, with US troops in Korea and a growing possibility that atomic weapons would be used in the conflict, Jackson announced that another $25 million would go into Hanford construction to keep "on top of stockpiling" plutonium. He said the project promised 7,000 new jobs during April and May 1951, 6,000 of which would remain until "mid-

1952."[26] Once he became a senator, Jackson criticized the new Eisenhower administration's proposals for reduced defense spending, while also supporting the armed forces that defended Hanford. When a constituent wrote to Jackson in 1956 claiming that there would be troop cuts at Hanford, Jackson contacted the Pentagon's chief legislative liaison, Colonel Edward N. Hathaway, who reassured the senator that despite a 10 percent reduction that year, new personnel were still being hired to staff the reservation's military camp. The cuts were so negligible that neither Hanford nor the Tri-Cities area would be dramatically impacted.[27]

Jackson also became a proponent of peaceful nuclear energy. In a 1951 speech in Spokane, Jackson argued that Hanford could be used to generate electricity for the Pacific Northwest. He argued that since the temperature of the Columbia River had already been raised several degrees as a by-product of its use to cool Hanford's nuclear fission piles, that water could generate steam to create electricity "to light cities, irrigate deserts, propel surface vehicles and commercial aircraft."[28] In 1957 Jackson told the *Bremerton Sun,* "We can have our atomic cake and eat it too," arguing that "atomic weapons are both a sword and a plowshare." Plutonium, unlike conventional military technology, was valuable because it would never become obsolete and could be used for both defense and civilian purposes.[29] In 1958 the *Oregonian* endorsed Jackson's $145 million plan for a dual reactor that would produce plutonium and electricity for the Bonneville Power Administration, the government agency supervising hydroelectric dams and other power facilities on the Columbia River. The paper supported the proposal because, it argued, the "N Reactor" would put the United States on equal footing with the Soviet Union and Great Britain as they constructed their own dual reactors and because "every addition of low cost power to the federal system which can be offered to industrial customers on long-term contracts helps to bolster the Northwest's economy." The N Reactor, said the *Oregonian,* "means jobs, profits, taxes and money in the bank."[30]

Jackson's interest in Hanford was driven not just by personal interest but also by lobbying on the part of Sam Volpentest, a Democratic booster and resident of the nearby Tri-Cities. Biographer C. Mark Smith argues that Volpentest was largely responsible for maintaining federal engagement in the Hanford–Tri-Cities area. According to Smith, "[Volpentest] and the management of the *Tri-City Herald* promoted the project with the knowledge that it would result in a major infusion of new federal money into the community. Funds for the N Reactor were appropriated in January 1958 and construction began shortly thereafter."[31]

In 1961 the N Reactor suffered a setback when the House of Representatives defeated an amendment for appropriations for the project. The Kennedy administration had requested $95 million to build the Hanford plant, but the Republican opposition called it a "public-power" encroachment on the free market. Some provincial GOP representatives also argued that the project would pull industry away from other regions and send it to the Northwest. Jackson retorted that the vote was a "victory for the private utility and coal industry. The losers were the American people."[32] Jackson tried to restore funding in the Senate, but he faced opposition during a floor debate on appropriations for the Atomic Energy Commission (AEC). Iowa Republican Bourke Hickenlooper contended, "There has been not one argument advanced by . . . the Senator from Washington that the operation of this electrical facility . . . will contribute a single provable benefit to the advancement of the art of atomic energy or to the art of the production of power."[33] Jackson countered with a national security argument, stating that the N Reactor "will manufacture fissionable material urgently needed for the defense of the free world." In disputing Hickenlooper's contention that there would be no provable benefit in terms of power production, Jackson argued, "The new production reactor will generate enormous amounts of energy—in the form of heat," which could either be "squandered into the atmosphere or dissipated into the Columbia River" or "transformed into steam, and thence into electricity for lighting homes and running factories." He also noted that the project had the backing of the AEC, General Electric (Hanford's main contractor), the Federal Power Commission, and the Bonneville Power Administration.[34]

Jackson's viewpoint ultimately carried the day, and much of the funding was later restored by a Senate-House conference. But Volpentest and Glenn Lee, editor of the *Tri-City Herald,* realized they might not be able to withstand congressional opposition to Hanford indefinitely unless the project was privatized to some degree. In 1962 they went to Jackson with their concerns, and the senator responded by pushing for a congressional investigation. The AEC published the Slaton Report, which was noncommittal in terms of future obligations to Hanford. Jackson connected

Volpentest and Lee with Washington, DC, lobbyist and attorney Fred Warren, who helped them form the Tri-City Nuclear Industrial Council to attract more atomic energy–related companies to the area.[35]

Jackson organized a fact-finding trip with top officials from General Electric (GE) and the AEC and John Pastore, chairman of the Joint Atomic Energy Committee. Jackson and AEC head Glenn Seaborg arranged for Volpentest to have top-level contacts with AEC and GE for the first time. Jackson also spearheaded the creation of three task forces: one to ramp up private investment at Hanford, another to push NASA and the Defense Department to invest more heavily in existing facilities at Hanford, and a third to have the AEC determine whether these facilities could be used by other public and private interests. Volpentest called Jackson the "father of diversification" in appreciation of his work to provide both public- and private-sector contacts. According to Smith, "the breakthroughs served as a major morale booster for a community that very badly needed one."[36]

Hanford was a key nexus between Jackson's domestic politics and US nuclear energy policy. Jackson often solicited Volpentest because he was a big booster for the Democratic Party in a conservative part of Washington State. At the end of one reelection campaign, Jackson told Volpentest, "Words are an inadequate means of expressing to you my deep appreciation. . . . When it comes to getting something done, I know I can always depend on you."[37] In return, "when 'Hanford problems require[d] attention,'" Volpentest might call Jackson's Senate office "up to three or four times a day."[38] In 1965 Jackson ensured that the shutdown of Hanford's aging reactors—which would trim $13 million from the federal budget but cost 2,000 jobs—would be spread over several years to give economic diversification time to succeed. Jackson got a post office mail processing plant opened in the Tri-Cities area to alleviate the fallout from the budget cut.[39] When General Electric left Hanford in 1965, Jackson helped recruit new businesses to the area.[40] His office put out releases emphasizing the Tri-Cities as a new frontier for private enterprise, being careful to gloss over GE's departure. Volpentest boosted the area's pro-business climate, its good weather, and his direct access to Jackson as selling points for new clients.[41] In 1967 the Joint Atomic Energy Committee approved construction of a nuclear reactor capable of regenerating its own fuel as it produced power. Jackson touted this project as the single largest government contribution to Hanford's diversification.[42] When Jackson got Jersey

Nuclear Company to develop a nuclear fuel rod reprocessing facility in 1970, Volpentest boasted, "This is going to be the nuclear energy capital of the world."[43]

By 1971, however, all the Hanford reactors had been shuttered except for the N Reactor, which was nearly shut down in February amid budget cuts by the Office of Management and Budget.[44] When Volpentest informed Jackson of the shutdown, the senator allegedly turned white, started shaking, and asked, "What the hell have they done?"[45] Warning that the closure of Hanford would impoverish southeastern Washington, Jackson convened emergency hearings with officials from the Atomic Energy Commission, ultimately working with the AEC and the Nixon administration to get the N Reactor back online.[46] Just two days after the N Reactor shutdown was reversed, however, an anonymous Nixon administration official told the *New York Times* that the plant was "unreliable and a possible safety hazard," as well as "a sloppy engineering job." The official argued that the reactor was subject to "frequent" breakdowns and thus had been only partially active in 1970. In a sign of future trouble for Hanford and the people of southeastern Washington, the official noted that 80 million gallons of radioactive liquid waste stored underground needed to be "managed."[47]

Thanks to Jackson's efforts, however, the N Reactor stayed online until 1987.[48] In 1981 Jackson helped put $14.7 million in appropriations into a bill aimed at getting Hanford invested in fusion-power technology.[49] In August 1983 Jackson helped obtain $750 million in appropriations for the construction of a facility that would refine plutonium-using lasers, employing 400 Washingtonians.[50] Three years after Jackson's death, Hanford still employed 14,000 of the 100,000-strong workforce in the Tri-Cities. Despite the subsequent closure of the N Reactor and the disclosure of massive environmental contamination in the area, cleanup efforts at Hanford have led to new employment opportunities for Washingtonians in the post-Jackson years. The continued existence of the Tri-Cities metropolitan area arguably owes much to Jackson's long interest in that part of Washington State.

Although Jackson's work to obtain federal funds for Hanford is better known, he also obtained appropriations for US Navy installations in western Washington's Puget Sound. At a Jackson tribute in 2012, Everett mayor Ray Stephanson praised the senator for playing an "instrumental role" in the creation of naval stations and bases at Everett, Whidbey Island, Kitsap (formerly naval bases Bremerton and Bangor), and the Madigan Army Medical Center.[51]

In the 1960s and 1970s Jackson obtained funding for Washington naval installations while resisting cutback attempts by the Pentagon. In 1962 he sought $13 million for the construction of a Polaris missile assembly center.[52] The *Bremerton Sun* remarked that Jackson "won his battle despite severe pressure from the 'sunshine' boys who wanted this installation in California." The *Sun* noted that the funds would boost the local economy by doubling employment in Bremerton and greater Kitsap County.[53] "I don't know of any area in the country that has a brighter potential in contributing to the national security," Jackson said, citing its naval ammunition depot, Polaris missile facility, and naval torpedo station, as well as the renovation of the nearby Puget Sound naval shipyard to refurbish nuclear-powered ships.[54]

According to Jackson, only the Puget Sound and Pearl Harbor naval shipyards escaped employment cutbacks in President Johnson's 1965 budget.[55] Jackson, meanwhile, boasted of the importance of the base at Bangor once nuclear submarines began docking there in 1965. Missile loading and ship overhaul, he said, would double its workforce from 500 to 1,000 and add "tens of thousands of square miles to our defense base." The fleet of Polaris missile ships, he said, "is the equivalent of free world bases a few hundred miles from Moscow and Vladivostok."[56] That year Jackson obtained $11.7 million for the construction of military bases in Washington, including $3.7 million for Whidbey Island naval air station.[57] In 1971 Jackson announced that Whidbey would receive EA-6 "Supertruder" aircraft. Nine squadrons with 1,500 men would be based at Whidbey, a rare increase amid military cutbacks. Eleven million dollars would be appropriated to construct new facilities to house the squadrons, including a jet engine test facility, sewage treatment plant, reserve air hangar, and training buildings.[58]

Jackson's move in the mid-1970s to make Bangor the home of the Pacific Fleet's new Trident nuclear missiles stirred up controversy. He cut a deal with the Nixon administration—which favored the Trident program: in exchange for his support, the Tridents would go to Bangor, pumping $550 million in construction money alone into Washington's economy. Jackson told the Senate that Tridents were necessary because preexisting submarines were becoming obsolete. Jackson tried to convince undecided senators by having them meet his friend and influential nuclear advocate Admiral Hyman Rickover. Ultimately the Trident vote narrowly carried in the Senate, and the interests of both the Pentagon and Washington State military boosters were served.[59]

After protecting Puget Sound from the cutbacks of the 1970s, Jackson announced in October 1982 that the US Navy would base part of the Pacific Fleet out of Puget Sound, resulting in the creation of 4,000 new civilian jobs.[60] The senator would not live to see the fruits of this effort, but part of the Pacific Fleet is still based there. Overall, between Hanford and the Puget Sound naval bases, Jackson showed dexterity and flaunted his political power in the pursuit of national security and defense dollars for his home state.

In terms of defense spending, Jackson is also well known for his assistance to Boeing, a major defense contractor. But Boeing also built and exported commercial airplanes abroad, and it was just one of many Washington companies that Jackson aided in expanding its international trade. Jackson once told a constituent, "I am opposed to measures which would have the effect of restricting free international trade. There are exceptions, however, particularly where foreign countries set up restraints on trade. However, the best interests of our state and country are served by tearing down trade barriers on a reciprocal basis, not in creating new ones."[61] These were the essentials of Jackson's position on international trade throughout his career.

Jackson's stance on trade remained consistent. In early 1953 he represented R. J. Darling of Pacific Coast Lumber and Shingles in a successful protest against duties on timber imports imposed by the Netherlands and Belgium.[62] Jackson's correspondence with the Foreign Operations Administration (FOA) in 1955 indicates a number of successful attempts to assist constituents: for instance, Jackson helped Walton Lumber Company in Everett obtain Export-Import Bank funding for lumbering operations in Chile.[63] With regard to the state's mining industry, Jackson's protests to the FOA regarding a slowdown in coal purchases led to a promise that the state could submit a bid to export coal to South Korea.[64] Jackson was cautious, however, with regard to some regional industries, telling the Yakima Fruit Growers Association in 1955 that he was generally in favor of lowering trade barriers but wanted to do so gradually, and not at the expense of domestic producers.[65] To a concerned resident of the Tri-Cities, Jackson iterated that he did not want tariffs lowered on industries that contributed to national defense.[66] To that end, he supported an amendment to an extension of the Reciprocal Trade Agreement to aid national security–related industries in free-trade injury claims.[67]

Big Washington industries were normally pro-trade and often called on Jackson for help in expanding their markets. In 1963 Jackson wrote to Undersecretary of State George Ball that the region's apple farmers had poor access to France. France prohibited imports of US apples unless they were of the "Extra" or "Fancy" quality, which the farmers believed was meant to exclude nearly all imports.[68] Ball replied that the French claimed that lowering their standards would result in a glut of apples, and they had no need for imports because of sufficient domestic supply.[69] Jackson would not let the issue drop. He wrote to special representative for trade negotiations Christian Herter, who promised the US embassy would negotiate with Paris; in addition, the government would file a complaint with the Organization for Economic Cooperation and Development about "irregular entry dates" for Washington pears exported to West Germany and Belgium, which constituted unfair trade practices. The correspondence ended with a follow-up from Herter indicating that the State Department had made only minor headway in negotiations with Paris.[70] Despite the mixed outcome, the exchange showed Jackson's tenaciousness on the issue.

Another example of Jackson's Pacific Northwest trade boosterism had clear connections to his interest in both national security and Israel. In 1969 the *Seattle Times* reported that the US Navy planned to scrap defective ships built by the Tacoma Boat Building Company. According to the *Times,* the company and Jackson were "secretly attempting to sell some of the jinxed ships to Israel." Three of these ships had been "plagued by prolonged overhauls and constant repairs," while four others remained in a San Diego yard because of defects. Jackson admitted the attempted sale to reporters and then "hurried into his office"; subsequently he was "unavailable in person or by phone to answer queries about the proposed sale."[71]

Was Jackson trying to dump the ships on an unsuspecting ally? Nonsense, he said the next day. "The Israelis don't buy a pig in a poke," Jackson said. "Have you ever known the Israelis to buy a loser?"[72] The *Times* corroborated Jackson's view of events, reporting that the US Navy denied it was trying to jettison the boats. "The Pentagon is worried about a 1963 directive prohibiting [the] introduction of major arms systems into the Middle East,'" Jackson told the *Times*. "But this is hardly a new weapons system. . . . Those boats would be very helpful in protecting the coast of Israel."[73] In all, the patrol boat episode portrays Jackson as a canny politician who worked to prioritize the Tacoma company's trade interests and the national security of an ally.

Human rights, long a part of Jackson's domestic New Deal–style liberalism, played a role in his thinking when it came to trade restrictions he *did* support. In July 1974 Jackson announced that his Government Operations Subcommittee on Investigations would investigate whether the United States had sold to eastern European countries any technology "that could be used to tighten totalitarian control over minorities and dissenting individuals," such as "print analyzers, stress evaluators [and] holographic identification cards."[74] In 1983 Jackson cosponsored a resolution calling for clothing imports to constitute no more than 25 percent of the total US apparel market. Jackson argued that in addition to being designed to save the US textile industry from "extinction," this was a human rights–based move. The resolution's authors claimed that unemployment in the textile industry was higher than the US average and that most jobs were held by women and minorities.[75]

In conjunction with his efforts to expand international trade, Jackson became a major proponent of strengthening relations between the United States and China. Biographer Robert Kaufman argues that this was one of Jackson's few career missteps, contending he supported China strategically while downplaying Beijing's human rights violations.[76] If Jackson did so, it may have been for sentimental reasons. As Kaufman notes, Jackson "admired, and at times romanticized, the Chinese . . . for their emphasis on hard work, strong families, and education, the very qualities he admired most about his own Norwegian background. His positive image of China stemmed largely from the mesmerizing novels of Pearl Buck, which engrossed a generation of Americans, particularly residents of the West Coast."[77] That generation of families included Jackson's wife; her grandfather had been a "missionary professor" at Soochow University in China, and her mother had been born in Soochow.[78] Jackson had personal reasons, then, to foster a strong bond between the United States and China. He also, however, hoped to forge stronger bonds between Washington State and China.

Jackson had long seen China as a linchpin of American strategy and a contributor to world stability. Ever the realist, however, he agreed with President Truman's decision not to send US troops to aid Chiang Kai-shek's Nationalist government against the communists at the end of the Chinese civil war in 1949.[79] In 1950 he wrote: "It is important that we not be diverted into a long war of attrition with the Chinese. It would be nothing short of colossal stupidity to be successfully maneuvered by the Russians into an impossible war with our friends and allies, the Chinese people, leaving the real antagonist, Russia, free to continue to build up their strength."[80] This highlights another of Jackson's major concerns in terms of US-China relations: he hoped that friendship with the Chinese would strategically damage the Soviet Union.

When Chiang fled to Taiwan, Jackson, like many other Americans, saw his regime as representing the real China. He opposed recognition of the communist People's Republic of China (PRC) for decades. In 1956 Jackson joined a group of senators—including Republican anticommunist demagogue Joseph McCarthy—to oppose the loosening of trade restrictions on the PRC.[81] Even then, however, he was pressured by locals who were aware of the market potential on the Chinese mainland. In 1957 Thomas Kerr, president of Kerr Grain Corporation in Portland, Oregon, wrote to Jackson, urging the resumption of flour and wheat exports to China and asking for protection for regional exporters like himself. He complained that the Eisenhower administration paid little attention to northwestern exporters when they asked for relief from the embargo on trade with China.[82] Kerr told Jackson the United States needed a more "realistic" policy on China trade.[83] Meanwhile, D. L. Sancrant, a Port Townsend, Washington, constituent, argued that the United States should play a constructive role in the evolution of China. Using language later echoed by Jackson, Sancrant contended that industrial development was taking place in China, and whether Americans liked it or not, the PRC was gaining acceptance from other Asian and European nations. If the US-China trade embargo ended, Sancrant said, "the results, in years to come, might well be a volume of commerce between the United States and China the like[s] of which we have never before known with any other nation."[84]

Jackson also received plenty of anti-PRC mail. For instance, in 1957 the China Club of Seattle opposed the Senate Interstate and Foreign

Commerce Committee's explorations into ending the embargo.[85] Jackson continued to be against improved relations with China and grew more hawkish toward the communist regime in the 1960s. In 1960 Jackson's Government Operations Subcommittee reported that China had become a "giant on the march" whose existence could not be ignored any longer.[86] In a 1963 press release he warned that Beijing would soon have a full arsenal of nuclear weapons and that China was joining the arms race.[87] Later that year Jackson criticized Canada and Australia for not joining the US grain embargo against China.[88] In a March 1967 speech he warned that the United States could not underestimate the PRC because Beijing wanted the West "eradicated" from East Asia, noting that "to know Red China is to fear its ambitions."[89] In a speech to Seattle Democrats in 1969 Jackson reportedly "got carried away" while talking about China's military and the need to keep US defenses strong against an attack. According to biographer Peter Ognibene, "reaching for a metaphor to emphasize his point, he raised his voice and loudly declaimed, 'We can't afford to have any *chinks* in our armor!'"[90]

Even aside from that (possibly) slip-of-the-tongue racial epithet, Jackson seemed unlikely to champion improved relations with Beijing in the 1970s. Yet by 1969 he favored an opening with China because he saw the Chinese as inherently different from the Soviets; specifically, he believed they were more trustworthy deal makers.[91] As he later recalled, "It seemed that ongoing Chinese trends—coupled with a demonstrable growth in Soviet conventional and strategic power—suggested the appropriateness of a new American approach to China. I advocated then that we attempt to get our relations with China on a less-rigid footing.[92] Meeting with the Puget Sound League of Women Voters in April, Jackson said, "It is important to keep in touch with the Chinese," and he expressed the hope that both Chinas could be in the United Nations.[93] In November Jackson pushed for better relations through "the exchange of journalists and scientists, regularizing communications links, [and] lowering trade barriers."[94] The existence of a local imperative was obvious. He told the Seattle Rotary Club, "In the Pacific Northwest, we have always felt close ties to the countries of the Western Pacific. Our economic and cultural relationships have special significance."[95]

In February 1973, after President Nixon's 1972 visit to China, Jackson recommended that the United States recognize the PRC.[96] He also called for the official severing of diplomatic ties with Taiwan, but he believed the United States should leave a mission there and continue to fulfill its treaty commitments to Taipei.[97] Jackson explained his rationale in a May 1973 article he wrote for the *New Leader*, contending that the long-standing difficulties between the United States and China were overshadowed by those that had emerged between the Soviet Union and China since the late 1960s. He called for China to allow more people-to-people exchanges and warned that since China was not a democracy, the United States needed to establish more relationships with Beijing to better understand its political systems. He contended, "The Chinese will respect us the more if we approach Sino-American relations with a certain amount of our own Yankee reserve."[98]

Jackson received angry correspondence after taking that stand on China and after supporting a bill introduced in April 1973 by Senator J. William Fulbright to move the US embassy from Taipei to Beijing. One writer called the bill a "monstrosity which seems to have been designed to circumvent" the US Constitution. She called the mainland Chinese "the most vicious outspoken and determined enemies of our country anywhere in the world" and accused Chinese diplomats of coming to the United States with "satchels full of homegrown heroin." She slammed Jackson as a "puppet" of Nixon and asked God to bring Jackson back to his senses before it was too late.[99] A somewhat more tempered letter asked Jackson to stop Nixon from recognizing the PRC because of its human rights violations, but the writer also called communist Chinese leaders "murderers" and expressed concern that China would "flood" the United States with heroin.[100] The fear of heroin was a recurring theme in Jackson's correspondence at this time. A husband and wife wrote that the Fulbright bill "leaves the door wide open, enabling the Red Chinese to distribute their dope without being checked," and they worried that the communist leaders wanted to enslave Americans.[101] Another writer was concerned that the Fulbright bill "will turn loose into our Country countless agents of the Red Chinese Regime, with immunity to our laws and with many other privileges that even our own citizens do not enjoy."[102] Some constituents demanded that Jackson work to pull the United States out of the UN because it had admitted the PRC and expelled Taiwan.[103] Jackson, for his part, replied that although some aspects of the UN needed to be reevaluated, the United States must stay in. Ducking the China controversy altogether, he contended that backing out would harm the UN's work to improve child care and health worldwide.[104]

Jackson ignored this vituperative correspondence and oversaw a dramatic thaw in US-Chinese relations. In 1974 he led a congressional delegation on a trip to China—the first of four for Jackson. He had fifteen hours of "substantive discussions with Chinese leaders," including the first of many meetings with future premier Deng Xiaoping.[105] In a statement to the press Jackson observed that "there are many areas in which American interests parallel those of the Chinese." In terms of economic relations, he reported that "trade with China is evolving on a solid commercial basis." In the future, Jackson contended, "the U.S.-China relationship must be strengthened by moving beyond contacts between a limited number of personalities to a more institutionalized process and a far wider range of exchanges and other relationships. This is in our own interest, and it is in the interest of world stability and peace, especially as China moves ahead to become a nuclear and industrial power."[106]

Jackson pushed for the extension of most-favored-nation (MFN) trading status to China while simultaneously trying to deny such status to the Soviet Union through an amendment to a trade bill working its way through Congress. Responding to those concerned that China—like the Soviet Union—violated the so-called Jackson-Vanik amendment because it barred the emigration of refugees, Jackson said the issue needed to be dealt with in the future. Since no more than 100 people were trying to leave China, he believed it was not a major issue compared with the Soviet situation.[107] Improving US-Chinese relations seemed to be a bigger priority than human rights issues.

When Jackson returned from his second trip to China in 1978, he thought the United States had not given "sufficient priority" to the bilateral relationship. "We should immediately move towards increased and more substantial consultation with the Chinese in areas where we have parallel interests," Jackson contended. "The lack of normalized relations makes working together on these common concerns more difficult and we should seek to resolve with the Chinese the outstanding issues that stand in the way of full normalization." Jackson encouraged China to send delegations to learn more about US petroleum-refining technology, including to his home state of Washington. "I suggested . . . that they send a delegation of hydroelectric experts to visit the hydroelectric production and long-range transmission facilities of the Pacific Northwest," Jackson said, to learn how to develop China's "vast hydroelectric potential."[108]

Jackson concluded that Chinese leaders wanted agreements that allowed them to purchase "petroleum technology" from US energy companies. "The Chinese appear to be convinced that American petroleum technology is superior to that available anywhere else in the world," he said.[109] In a *New York Times* op-ed Jackson wrote, "China's leaders think their oil reserves may be as large as, or larger than, the reserves of the United States." Jackson noted that in 1974 he had urged China to develop its reserves and that the next step was to help China develop its offshore oil exploration by allowing Beijing to buy oil technology and services.[110]

Despite these and other benefits of normalized relations, opposition ran high even in Jackson's home state after the United States officially transferred diplomatic relations from Taiwan to China on January 1, 1979. One letter called for Jackson to "stop" President Carter from recognizing China.[111] Another constituent was convinced that just as British prime minister Neville Chamberlain had ceded the Sudetenland to Adolf Hitler's Nazi Germany in 1938, the United States had abandoned Taiwan to communism. The writer contended that "nothing will convince the American people that we needed trade relations as badly as they needed us as a counterbalance to Moscow."[112] A more moderate constituent wanted a US-China relationship, but not at the expense of ending formal ties with Taiwan.[113] Jackson told his constituents that he favored normalization "on terms that would not jeopardize peace and stability in the region, including Taiwan." He contended, "America has a significant stake in a strong, independent China which can hold its own in the world and work with us where our interests run parallel."[114]

During the normalization debate, Jackson arranged for Deng Xiaoping to visit Seattle in February 1979, near the end of his first visit to the United States. Based on the itinerary, it seems clear that the major aim of Deng's visit was to drum up trade between Washington State and China. On February 3 Jackson and other members of the Washington congressional delegation greeted Deng's party; notably, they were joined by Boeing chairman T. A. Wilson and United Airlines CEO Edward Carlson. On February 4 Deng and his delegation toured the Port of Seattle in the morning and then attended a luncheon with Washington businessmen. Later Deng and Jackson toured a Boeing 747 plant and met with Boeing president Malcolm Stamper. Deng dined with local businessmen that night and met the next morning with newspaper editors and publishers before leaving Seattle.[115]

During the February 4 luncheon Jackson remarked to Deng, "It has been my good fortune to know you as a personal friend," and he observed that Deng had rekindled "the affection the Chinese and American people have always shared." Because China and the Pacific Northwest shared the Pacific Ocean, he said, they "have always understood the enormous potential that lies in cooperation between our two nations." He claimed that "the first steps have now been taken along a path that will lead increasingly to a realization of that potential. And we in the Northwest are eager to play our full part in bringing it about." According to Jackson, Zhou Enlai had said that agriculture, industry, science and technology, and defense were the four fields essential for China to modernize by the year 2000. "Here in the Northwest we pioneer in all four fields," Jackson touted.[116]

Reaction to Deng's visit was mostly positive. The front page of the *Oregonian* featured Deng and Jackson shaking hands, although the banner story noted that fifty "Maoist demonstrators" had chanted "Death! Death! Death to [Deng]! Long live Mao-tse Tung!" and had been joined by other anti-Deng demonstrators in Seattle's university district while the Secret Service guarded the delegation's hotel. Nevertheless, Jackson contended that "the attitude of our people here is that they want to help China." He told the press that the Port of Seattle would "offer the Chinese a group of experts who can go over and help them modernize their own port facilities," and he said he had extended an invitation for Chinese engineers and hydropower officials to tour dams in the Northwest.[117] Between the "bear hug" he received from Jackson and his "elegant" dinner with local leaders, Deng and his delegation were pleased with their visit and believed their reception in Seattle had been warmer than on earlier stops in the United States.[118] In his airport departure speech, Deng told the crowd, "The Pacific, instead of being a barrier, should henceforth serve as a link."[119]

The most-favored-nation issue still had to be worked out. In May 1979 the *New York Times* reported that "Jackson and the Administration are satisfied that the Chinese will have no problem in qualifying for trade preferences under Jackson-Vanik." During his Seattle visit, Deng had told

Jackson that, if he wished, he "would have one million Chinese in Seattle Monday morning," and the senator had replied, "You'll have no trouble with me."[120] Upon arriving in China for his third summit in August, Jackson said he believed China should be granted MFN status after the Senate approved a US-China trade treaty signed on July 7. Under the treaty, China would get access to Export-Import Bank credits and face only minimal trade tariffs.[121] On August 25 Jackson held a two-and-a-half-hour meeting with Deng and then told the press that China was upset with the Carter administration for holding up the treaty. The administration claimed it wanted to conclude a similar agreement with Moscow before sending the China treaty to Congress for approval, but Jackson felt China should not be held to the Soviet standard because China had complied with the Jackson-Vanik amendment tying trade to emigration. On October 23 Carter finally submitted the trade agreement to Congress, and it passed in January 1980.[122]

Jackson and his constituents worked to open China to Washington State businesspeople even before the passage of the trade treaty. A variety of constituents sought Jackson's assistance. In December 1978 Paul H. Symbol, senior vice president of a professional services company in Seattle specializing in engineering, design, architecture, and environmental sciences, contacted Jackson and requested information regarding China's "technological requirements."[123] Jackson sent Symbol a background briefing paper from the State Department and recommended that he contact the Office of PRC Affairs, Bureau of East-West Trade in Washington, DC, for further information. Jackson gave Symbol the office phone number as well as contact information for the China National Technical Import Corporation and the China Council for Promotion of International Trade in Beijing.[124] In January 1979 the Washington Council on International Trade received assistance from Jackson's office in launching a trade trip scheduled for mid-May.[125]

Jackson also helped natural resources and agricultural trade interests. One constituent wrote to Jackson for assistance in starting negotiations with the Chinese to import down. Jackson provided him with the contact information for the China National Native Produce and Animal By-Products Import and Export Corporation.[126] Jackson also assisted the head of Icicle Seafoods in Seattle by sending him a State Department package on traveling to China, where he hoped to make contacts to export seafood.[127]

The senator sent the head of Seattle-based New England Seafood a *Doing Business with China* pamphlet from the US Commerce Department and suggested that he cable the Chinese Export Commodities Fair in Guangzhou to obtain an invitation to the trade fair there.[128]

On the agricultural front, Jackson received a letter in January 1979 from George E. Sage, president of Sage Electronics in Redmond, Washington, who was hoping to obtain an audience with Deng during his Seattle trip and discuss his company's electronic controls for crop irrigation equipment. "I believe it would be advantageous to acquaint the Deputy Premier . . . and the Chinese representatives with our capabilities and advanced technical knowledge of electronic irrigation control rather than have them find out later that they have purchased outdated and less reliable electro mechanical controls," Sage wrote. Jackson directed him to contact the China National Machinery Import and Export Corporation and provided Sage with background about the corporation. Sage later replied that the information from Jackson and his staff had been "very helpful," and he attached a booklet his company had presented to Deng—presumably a contact Jackson had facilitated.[129]

Jackson also helped arrange trade missions to China from Washington State. On January 24, 1979, James B. Scroggs, president of the Seattle Chamber of Commerce, wrote to Wang Yao Ting, president of the China Council for the Promotion of International Trade, asking the council to receive a trade delegation. On August 2 Scroggs wrote to Wang that he was "pleased" to hear the chamber had been approved for a ten-day trade mission in December 1979 or January 1980, but he asked for a delay until later in 1980, noting that the US holiday season might make it difficult to put together a high-caliber trade mission at that time.[130] On September 24 Holt W. Webster from the Chamber of Commerce wrote to Jackson, thanking him for passing on their request to foreign policy adviser Dorothy Fosdick, who had passed it on to the China Council, which had then granted the chamber's request for postponement of the trade mission.[131]

Correspondence indicates that Jackson got business exchanges to come to Washington State as well. In a March 1979 letter to the Chinese vice minister of agriculture, Donald E. Swanson, mayor of the city of Moses Lake, let him know that the city council had voted to allow Chinese agricultural leaders to visit.[132] Don Beckley, president of Business Consultants of Central Washington, had wanted the vice minister to bring a group from China to learn about "agriculturally oriented problems" in the region.[133] In April Jackson wrote to Beckley that he was "on the right track" and told him he wanted to stay informed, implying there may have been some personal involvement by the senator.[134]

Jackson also dealt with Washington-China shipping concerns. In April Jackson hosted the "first PRC flagship to call at [a] U.S. port." The docking of the *Liu Lin Hai* honored an agreement between Washington company Lykes and the China Ocean Shipping Company signed in February.[135] Jackson helped lift restrictions on the shipping of Washington apples to China, helping exporters such as Cathay Imports, which thanked Jackson personally for his assistance.[136] In September the director of operations and facilities at the Port of Seattle sent Jackson a telegram enclosing an agreement between the Seattle and Shanghai "establishing [a] friendship-port relationship."[137] Jackson also received a letter from Richard Ford, executive director of the Port of Seattle, thanking him for his efforts in facilitating the Shanghai-Seattle relationship. Ford did not specify what Jackson did, but he mentioned that the Chinese had acknowledged the senator as a friend during negotiations to establish the relationship.[138]

Along with trade relations, Jackson also worked to build the China study program at the University of Washington. In February 1980 he helped organize a symposium on Chinese modernization sponsored by the university's School of International Studies (SIS).[139] Luminaries in attendance included academics, trade lobbyists, and representatives of shipping interests already involved in China-Washington trade. In his opening remarks, Jackson reiterated that "we in the Pacific Northwest have a special relationship with China." He contended that "the trade we now have with China, the amount moving across the Pacific, far exceeds that moving across the Atlantic. And, of course, Seattle has a special interest, inasmuch as Seattle is the sister city of Shanghai." He also observed that "foreign policy, more and more, plays a critical role in domestic policy." Comparing the Pacific Northwest, and the United States more broadly, to the British Empire, Jackson said the nation was dependent on foreign policy "for our salvation" because of the nature of global markets. At a dinner speech to symposium attendees, Jackson argued for the provision of "technology" for "economic modernization" to help the US balance-of-payments deficit, and he said the United States and China needed to deepen their good relations in the area of economic, science, and cultural exchange. Furthermore, he said, "I believe our relations with China are now mature enough for each side to raise tough issues with the other, confident that this will not disrupt that candid relationship."[140]

Jackson later wrote to SIS director Kenneth Pyle, expressing his opinion that the symposium "came off with flying colors!" The senator predicted, "There should be all kinds of interesting repercussions of our meeting in both intellectual and more worldly circles."[141] George Taylor, president of the Washington Council on International Trade, wrote to Jackson that it was "probably the first time in the history of the University that a United States Senator has given so much time and support to an enterprise sponsored by a combination of the University and a community organization. Quite frankly, I think the show was spectacular. . . . You paid a tremendous compliment to the University of Washington and to the Council on International Trade by making this such an outstanding event."[142]

Even before the symposium, records show that Jackson was working to bolster China-related programming at the SIS. During the winter of 1979, he successfully solicited a $5,000 donation to the SIS from Harold S. Shefelman, an attorney in Seattle and his former law school professor.[143] Jackson also contributed his own speech honoraria to the SIS; in February and March he sent Pyle a series of $1,000 checks reflecting his earnings from speeches given to the United Jewish Appeal, American Stock Exchange, Talmudical Academy of Central New Jersey, and Environmental Industry Council.[144] In March Pyle thanked Jackson for his contributions and said the senator had given "the China faculty a great boost" by praising them during Deng's visit to Seattle earlier in the year, noting that "it was widely quoted in the newspapers and helped give us the visibility we need."[145]

Jackson was also a founding ex-officio member of the Washington State China Relations Council (WSCRC) in 1979 and as it gained strength in the early 1980s. This group of academics, government officials, and businesspeople dedicated to improving trade and cultural ties between Washington and China officially incorporated on August 6, 1979, six months after Deng's Seattle visit.[146] Jackson warned eager trade boosters that "because our two nations have been out of contact for a long time and have different historical backgrounds, development of mutually useful relationships will not happen automatically." He nevertheless praised the group, noting that improved relations with China "will take care, patience, good communication and organization. The Washington State China Relations Council should provide those key ingredients."[147] Notable members of the council eventually included Microsoft, the Ports of Seattle and Tacoma, Boeing, various law firms, Northwest Airlines, US Bank, Starbucks, and most major Washington universities.[148] The last annual report the WSCRC produced before Jackson's death discussed the group's work to establish a sister-state relationship between Washington and China's Sichuan Province in October 1982. It also noted that the sale of forest products to China increased in 1982, and late in the year China had bought Boeing 737s and 747s. It touted a broadening of scientific, cultural, and trade relations and noted that the number of member organizations had increased from forty-seven in January 1981 to eighty-four by January 1983.[149]

Jackson continued to work to improve US-China and Washington-China relations in the early 1980s. When President Ronald Reagan caused a crisis by hinting at broadening of relations with Taiwan, Jackson worked to defuse the situation. In July 1982 he told the CBS news program *Face the Nation* that the Reagan administration "would be making a serious mistake" if it allowed additional arms sales to Taiwan, warning that China might be incensed enough to deal in arms with the Soviet Union: "We could wake up one morning and find another 1939 Hitler-Stalin pact with a new group in power in China."[150] The crisis passed, but it was clear that Jackson's adherence to the policy of officially dealing only with Beijing was unwavering, despite Reagan's early flirtations with Taiwan.

Jackson also worked to ensure that China continued to receive most-favored-nation status with the United States. In August 1982 he testified before the Senate Finance Committee's international trade subcommittee with regard to extending China's waiver from the Jackson-Vanik amendment. "The Chinese-American relationship has come a long way, and it is today comprehensive and complex," Jackson told the committee. "China's leaders explicitly recognize shared and parallel interests with us, and our NATO allies, and Japan." Jackson reiterated his desire for a strong China, arguing that helping China develop industrially was in the national interest. In "strongly" advocating for MFN renewal for China and a Jackson-

Vanik waiver, he noted that in previous years, this status had "laid the basis for the significant increase of trade and financial ties between our two countries, with substantial mutual benefits," including putting US firms in "a better position to compete with firms from other nations." China provided assurances, Jackson said, that it would liberalize emigration practices, and he contended that the United States had issued 6,920 immigrant visas to Chinese in 1981 and more than 15,000 nonimmigrant visas.[151]

With the Jackson-Vanik waiver granted and MFN status extended, Jackson could continue his work to support his home state's interests in China. In late 1982 he helped the WSCRC secure Ji Chaozhu, the minister counselor at the Chinese embassy in Washington, DC, as the speaker for its annual meeting in January 1983. Jackson wrote to WSCRC president Stanley Barer, expressing his regret that Senate responsibilities would prevent him from attending the meeting, but he praised Ji as an old friend, a great man, and a good conversationalist.[152] Jackson continued to work to aid Washington-China trade interests right up until his death. In a pamphlet issued by the Washington Council on International Trade in 1983, Jackson stated, "The Pacific Northwest has long understood the great potential of trade between the United States and countries of the Pacific Rim, including China. Thanks to the pioneering work of the Washington Council on International Trade, important steps to realize this potential have already been taken." The pamphlet noted that $19.7 billion in exports and imports had moved through Washington in 1980 and that international trade—including with China—was responsible for one in five jobs in the state.[153]

Shortly before embarking on his fourth and final trip to China, Jackson reiterated the importance of relations between Washington State and China in a speech to the Friendly Ports Seminar in Seattle, which included representatives from the ports of Seattle; Kobe, Japan; and Tianjin and Shanghai, China. As he had done so often before, Jackson observed that "we in the Pacific Northwest share a common bond with our guests that goes beyond an economic interest in ports and shipping. We share a great ocean and a way of life that living by the sea brings." Growing up in the Puget Sound city of Everett, Jackson recalled spending "countless hours" at the docks watching as goods were unloaded, giving him a "lifelong appreciation" for marine and shipyard work. "One of the things I learned at that early age was the importance of trade to my community's economy," Jackson said. "Thousands of people had jobs—not just those working on the waterfront—but also the people who made goods for export and the ones who sold products that had been imported from abroad." He said the importance of trade among Pacific Rim nations "cannot be overstated. To the Pacific Northwest, the world is our marketplace and trade is our economic lifeblood." Noting a growing protectionist mood in response to fears that Japan and China were on the verge of subverting US economic hegemony, Jackson said, "As seductive as protectionist policies sound, I cringe every time I hear them because of the harmful effect such measures would have on our own state economy."[154] Trade benefited Washington State, and keeping that pipeline open would be a key part of the overall approach taken by Jackson's successors in Congress with regard to US-China relations.

After returning from his August 1983 trip to China, Jackson died of a heart attack in Everett on September 1. A posthumously published delegation report submitted to the Senate Armed Services Committee noted that the senator had met with Deng Xiaoping and toured northeastern China cities. "His influence on our Nation's China policy during the past decade would be difficult to overestimate," the report noted. "Less known is the impact he had on the Executive Branch." Jackson successfully pushed Secretary of Defense Caspar Weinberger and Secretary of State George Shultz to visit China in 1983, and he convinced President Ronald Reagan to send a letter to China in August 1983 reaffirming the US-PRC relationship. Jackson also encouraged the visits of Chinese premier Zhao Ziyang and foreign minister Wu Xuequin to the United States, which took place after his death.[155]

The appendix of the report contained a transcript of a press conference Jackson held at the US embassy in Beijing on August 27, 1983. "My major finding is that both sides must intensify their consultations, both on matters of common strategic concern and at the bilateral level as well," Jackson told reporters. "The opportunity is now present to expand our relations." Jackson said he was pleased with the willingness of Deng and Reagan to pursue major improvements in relations, and he pointed out that he had personally reassured China's leaders that, despite Reagan's 1980 call to Taiwan, the president was committed to a policy that recognized Beijing as the sole representative of China.

In relation to trade issues—so crucial in the Pacific Northwest—a reporter pointed out that US-China trade had dropped "sharply." Jackson replied that a wheat and corn trade deal was on the table and noted that China had committed to buy 6 million tons of wheat in 1983 but had bought only 2.6 million so far. He acknowledged that China was having a "bumper crop" of wheat but noted that if it could export wheat and corn, it should have cash to buy more US goods. In a tongue-in-cheek reference to Boeing, Jackson said, "While I don't want to get too parochial about my own state—maybe [the Chinese could buy] airplanes."[156] The senator's easy-mannered response indicated that, despite this trade hiccup, he was not overly concerned about the Washington State–China relationship in the long run.

Jackson remarked that he had invited Deng to stay with him at his house in Everett on his next US visit and that Deng was seriously considering the offer.[157] They never got the chance. But US-China trade relations continued to burgeon in the decades after Jackson's death, despite the difficulties in the two countries' strategic relationship and concerns over China's human rights record. Clearly, that legacy, important to both Jackson's national record and the renewal of US relations with mainland China, had a lot to do with Jackson's desire to strengthen his constituents' economic ties with the largest populace in the Pacific Rim.

"If you seek Scoop Jackson's monument," conservative commentator George Will said at Jackson's birthday centennial in 2012, "look around and see what you do not see. You do not see the Soviet Union. You do not see the Iron Curtain. What you do see are nations restored to their full vitality in eastern Europe, you see the free movement of goods and peoples across Europe, and not least of all you see a preserved, vital state of Israel."[158] As Will's remarks demonstrate, national commentators continue to ignore Jackson's essential contributions to the economic transformation of Washington State. At home, Jackson was not just the senator from Boeing, although he did help the company position itself as a major player in the aerospace industry. Jackson also helped small companies seeking loans to do business abroad, and he kept the military presence in Washington State strong.

While Jackson is a figure alternately beloved and loathed by the Left and the Right, by New Dealers and free-market conservatives, and by economic developers and environmentalists, there is no doubt that he made an indelible impact on the region and the world by connecting his home state to global issues and international affairs. Jackson's long-term legacy is complicated, particularly by the environmental issues that plagued Hanford. However, Jackson's power and home-state interests dramatically affected US naval deployments, federal defense spending, international trade, and US-China relations in ways that continue to shape the region today. Jackson will be remembered for his opposition to arms control and his support of major environmental and human rights legislation, but this broad look at his record suggests that Jackson's political history is much richer when considering the intersection of domestic politics, regional interests, and US foreign policy.

Notes

1. Ironically, Jackson's death in 1983 caused this very circumstance, when Republican Governor John Spellman chose ex–Republican governor Daniel Evans to temporarily fill Jackson's vacant seat. Evans went on to win a special election later that year to fill out the remainder of Jackson's term.

2. Recording of telephone conversation between Lyndon B. Johnson and Henry M. Jackson, December 1, 1968, citation no. 13801, tape WH6812.01, program no. 1, and citation no. 13802, tape WH6812.01, program no. 2.

3. C. Campbell Craig and Fredrik Logevall, *America's Cold War: The Politics of Insecurity* (Cambridge, MA: Belknap Press, 2009).

4. Joseph A. Fry, "Place Matters: Domestic Regionalism and the Formation of American Foreign Policy," *Diplomatic History* 36, no. 3 (June 2012): 451–82; Patty Limerick, "Fencing in the Past," *Diplomatic History* 36, no. 3 (June 2012): 505–10.

5. Oregon and Washington constitute the common denominator in every definition of the "Pacific Northwest"; some also include part or all of Alaska, British Columbia, Idaho, western Montana, or northern California.

6. For example, see Robert D. Schulzinger, *A Time for War: The United States and Vietnam, 1941–1975* (New York: Oxford University Press, 1997); Robert Dallek, *Flawed Giant: Lyndon Johnson and His Times* (New York: Oxford University Press, 1998); Fredrik Logevall, *Choosing War: The Lost Chance for Peace and the Escalation of War in Vietnam* (Berkeley: University of California Press, 1999); David E. Settje, *Faith & War: How Christians Debated the Cold and Vietnam Wars* (New York: New York University Press, 2011).

7. See Melvin Small, *Democracy and Diplomacy: The Impact of Domestic Politics on U.S. Foreign Policy, 1789–1994* (Baltimore: Johns Hopkins University Press, 1996); Robert David Johnson, *Congress and the Cold War* (New York: Cambridge University Press, 2006); Julian E. Zelizer, *Arsenal of Democracy: The Politics of National Security from World War II to the War on Terrorism* (New York:

Basic Books, 2010); Andrew L. Johns, *Vietnam's Second Front: Domestic Politics, the Republican Party, and the War* (Lexington: University Press of Kentucky, 2010); Larry Blomstedt, *Truman, Congress, and Korea: The Politics of America's First Undeclared War* (Lexington: University Press of Kentucky, 2016); Kenneth Kolander, "Phantom Peace: Henry 'Scoop' Jackson, J. William Fulbright, and Military Sales to Israel," *Diplomatic History* 41, no. 3 (June 2017): 567–93.

8. Jeffrey Bloodworth, *Losing the Center: The Decline of American Liberalism, 1968–1992* (Lexington: University Press of Kentucky, 2013), 102.

9. Shelby Scates, *Warren G. Magnuson and the Shaping of Twentieth-Century America* (Seattle: University of Washington Press, 1997), 165.

10. "Jackson Says Russians Scored Double Victory," *Walla Walla Union Bulletin,* October 24, 1957.

11. "Russ May Have Atomic Propulsion," *Columbia Basin News,* November 5, 1957.

12. Robert G. Kaufman, *Henry Jackson: A Life in Politics* (Seattle: University of Washington Press, 2000), 93.

13. Walter Lippmann, "Sen. Jackson's Objections to Test Ban Treaty Naïve," *Baltimore News Post,* August 7, 1963.

14. John McKliget to Henry M. Jackson (hereafter HMJ), November 1, 1963, Henry M. Jackson Papers, University of Washington Special Collections (hereafter HMJ Papers), accession 3560–3, box 204, folder 1.

15. "Voice of the People," *Seattle Post Intelligencer,* February 19, 1966.

16. Kurt A. C. Minnich, "Nuclear Weapons," *Everett Herald,* February 20, 1968.

17. Marquis Childs, "Defense Cuts May Impair Security," *Seattle Times,* April 6, 1953.

18. Harold J. Bass to HMJ, June 27, 1956, HMJ Papers, accession 3560–003, box 120, folder 5.

19. Kaufman, *Henry Jackson,* 53.

20. Peter Ognibene, *Scoop: The Life and Politics of Henry M. Jackson* (New York: Stein and Day, 1975), 102.

21. Kaufman, *Henry Jackson,* 112.

22. C. Mark Smith, *Community Godfather: How Sam Volpentest Helped Shape the History of Hanford and the Tri-Cities* (Richland, WA: Etcetera Press, 2013), 148.

23. John Sinclair Petifer Robson, "Henry Jackson, the Jackson-Vanik Amendment and Détente: Ideology, Ideas, and United States Foreign Policy in the Nixon Era" (PhD diss., University of Texas at Austin, 1989), 204.

24. Ognibene, *Scoop,* 51.

25. "AEC to Spend Millions in Hanford Expansion," *Oregonian,* October 19, 1949.

26. "Millions Due for Hanford," *Oregonian,* March 3, 1951.

27. Edward N. Hathaway to HMJ, May 2, 1956, HMJ Papers, accession 3560–3, box 22, folder 27.

28. "Atomic Plant Waste Seen," *Oregonian,* June 19, 1951.

29. Henry Jackson, "New Hanford Reactor Would Give Double Value to Our Atomic Outlay," *Bremerton Sun,* September 5, 1957.

30. "Atom Power Breakthrough," *Oregonian,* June 26, 1958.

31. Smith, *Community Godfather,* 93.

32. John W. Finney, "Atom Power Plan Rejected in House," *New York Times,* July 14, 1961.

33. *Congressional Record,* July 18, 1961, 87th Congress, 1st session, 12845.

34. Ibid., 12854.

35. Smith, *Community Godfather,* 103–4.

36. Ibid., 109.

37. Ibid., 143.

38. Ibid., 161.

39. Ibid., 169–70.

40. For example, Jackson was successful in recruiting the Batelle Memorial Institute to operate AEC laboratory facilities at Hanford; see "Pact Signed for Hanford," *Oregonian,* January 1, 1965.

41. Smith, *Community Godfather,* 175.

42. "$80 Million Test Reactor Approved for Hanford," *Oregonian,* June 16, 1967.

43. Smith, *Community Godfather,* 181.

44. Leverett Richards, "Forces Rally against Reactor Close," *Oregonian,* February 2, 1971.

45. Leverett Richards, "Closure of Hanford N-Reactor Held Threat to U.S. Security," *Oregonian,* February 4, 1971.

46. Elsie Carper, "Dismantling Is Stopped at Hanford," *Washington Post,* February 5, 1971.

47. Philip Shabecoff, "Reactor on Coast Called a Hazard," *New York Times,* February 7, 1971.

48. Smith, *Community Godfather,* 182.

49. "Fusion at Hanford," *Tri-City Herald,* June 15, 1981.

50. "Plutonium Refinement Plan Revealed for Hanford Site," *Oregonian,* August 5, 1983.

51. "Senator Henry M. Jackson Centennial Celebration," YouTube video, 1:30:00, posted by "TheCityofEverett," August 6, 2012, https://www.youtube.com/watch?v=lusZLHl-UUI.

52. HMJ to R. L. Busch, January 26, 1962, HMJ Papers, accession 3560–3, box 85, folder 2.

53. "The Bangor Expansion Is a Tribute to Senator Jackson," *Bremerton Sun,* January. 15, 1962.

54. "Cuba Is Serious but Just a 'Speck,' Jackson Says," *Bremerton Sun,* November 3, 1962.

55. "Bremerton Yard Escapes Navy Cutbacks," *Seattle Times,* March 20, 1964.

56. "Senator Says A-Subs to Dock at Bangor Soon," *Tacoma News-Tribune,* February 10, 1964.

57. "Senate Committee Okays Whidbey Construction," *Bellingham Herald,* June 21, 1965.

58. "Statement by Senator Henry M. Jackson, Oak Harbor, Washington," January 29, 1971, HMJ Papers, accession 3560–5, box 236, folder 34.

59. Ognibene, *Scoop,* 162–65.

60. Martin Heerwald, "Navy Plans New Home for Ships," *Oregonian,* October. 14, 1982.

61. HMJ to James Huntley, December 15, 1967, HMJ Papers, accession 3560–4, box 168, folder 10.

62. R. J. Darling to HMJ, April 7, 1953, HMJ Papers, accession 3560–3, box 14, folder 24.

63. HMJ to Walter Wilkes, March 17, 1955, HMJ Papers, accession 3560–3, box 19, folder 30.

64. R. W. Clark to HMJ, June 16, 1955, ibid.

65. HMJ to Charles B. Stoll, January 27, 1955, HMJ Papers, accession 3560–3, box 116, folder 25.

66. HMJ to Alice G. Rigdon, February 14, 1955, ibid.

67. HMJ to John Trunk, May 3, 1955, HMJ Papers, accession 3560–3, box 116, folder 29.

68. HMJ to George Ball, January 23, 1963, HMJ Papers, accession 3560–3, box 97, folder 8.

69. Ball to HMJ, February 4, 1963, ibid.

70. HMJ to Christian Herter, April 16, 1963; Herter to HMJ, May 3 and July 29, 1963, ibid.

71. Vera Glaser and Malvina Stephenson, "TFX-Style Flop Feared: Navy May Junk Seven Tacoma-Based Ships," *Seattle Times,* June 13, 1969.

72. "'Israel Won't Buy Pig in a Poke,'" *Seattle Post-Intelligencer,* June 14, 1969.

73. Svein Gilje, "'Flop' Denied: Dozen Countries Interested in Buying Tacoma Gunboats," *Seattle Times,* June 14, 1969.

74. "Jackson Response to Ziegler Comment on Sale of Surveillance Equipment to Soviets," July 15, 1974, HMJ Papers, accession 3560–5, box 260, folder 129.

75. "S. Res. 122," April 26, 1983, HMJ Papers, accession 3560–5, box 231, folder 27.

76. Kaufman, *Henry Jackson,* 7.

77. Ibid., 36.

78. "Senator Jackson Announces Peking Trip," June 12, 1974, HMJ Papers, accession 3560–6, box 10, folder 142.

79. Kaufman, *Henry Jackson,* 59.

80. Ibid., 60.

81. Guangqiu Xu, *Congress and the U.S.-China Relationship, 1949–1979* (Akron, OH: University of Akron Press, 2007), 155–56.

82. Thomas Kerr to Wayne Morse, June 7, 1957, HMJ Papers, accession 3560–3, box 131, folder 8.

83. Thomas Kerr to HMJ, June 20, 1957, ibid.

84. D. L. Sancrant to HMJ, June 8, 1957, ibid.

85. China Club of Seattle to HMJ, June 20, 1957, HMJ Papers, accession 3560–3, box 131, folder 9.

86. Xu, *Congress and the U.S.-China Relationship,* 165–66.

87. "From the Office of Senator Henry M. Jackson," July 10, 1963, HMJ Papers, accession 3560–3, box 232, folder 59.

88. "Jackson Warns against Overrating Grain Export," *Pomeroy East Washingtonian,* September 26, 1963.

89. Speech, "The Importance of Vietnam," HMJ Papers, accession 3560–4, box 232, folder 5.

90. Ognibene, *Scoop,* 105.

91. Robson, "Henry Jackson, the Jackson-Vanik Amendment and Détente," 218.

92. "Prospects for United States–China Relations," *New Leader,* May 31, 1973, HMJ Papers, accession 3560–6, box 10, folder 48.

93. Q&A with Puget Sound League of Women Voters, April 8, 1969, HMJ Papers, accession 3560–6, box 7, folder 9.

94. Xu, *Congress and the U.S.-China Relationship,* 263.

95. Speech, "New Directions in the Pacific Area," November 5, 1969, HMJ Papers, accession 3560–4, box 233, folder 52.

96. Xu, *Congress and the U.S.-China Relationship,* 263.

97. "Senator Jackson Calls on U.S. to Recognize Peking Promptly," *New York Times,* February 5, 1973.

98. "Prospects for United States–China Relations."

99. Mrs. R. F. Wolf to HMJ, June 15, 1973, HMJ Papers, accession 3560–4, box 112, folder 13.

100. Elmore Anderson to HMJ, June 18, 1973, ibid.

101. Robert E. and Marguerite K. Hamlin to HMJ, June 30, 1973, ibid.

102. Bettie Chappell to HMJ, July 2, 1973, ibid.

103. Mr. and Mrs. John MacDonald to HMJ, August 3, 1973, HMJ Papers, accession 3560–4, box 107, folder 10.

104. HMJ to Mr. and Mrs. John MacDonald, August 10, 1973, ibid.

105. "On Return from the People's Republic of China," July 8, 1974, HMJ Papers, accession 3560–6, box 10, folder 157.

106. Henry Jackson, "On Ties with Moscow, Peking," *New York Times,* July 28, 1974.

107. "Draft from Press Conference of July 8, 1974," HMJ Papers, accession 3560–4, box 10, folder 158.

108. "Press Conference Statement, Feb. 22, 1978," HMJ Papers, accession 3560–4, box 245, folder 55.

109. "Jackson Says China Wants U.S. Oil Skill," *New York Times,* February 23, 1978.

110. Henry Jackson, "The Geopolitics of China's Oil," *New York Times,* March 25, 1978.

111. Jerald Woodall to HMJ, January 19, 1979, HMJ Papers, accession 3560–4, box, 184, folder 45.

112. John Corley to HMJ, February 6, 1979, ibid.

113. James Botz to HMJ, February 7, 1979, ibid.

114. HMJ constituent mailer, March 7, 1979, ibid.

115. "The Official Visit of Vice-Premier Deng Xiaoping to Seattle, Washington, February 3–5, 1979," HMJ Papers, accession 3560–4, box 246, folder 17.

116. "Remarks of Senator Henry M. Jackson, Luncheon Honoring Vice Premier Deng Xiaoping, Washington Plaza Hotel, Seattle, Washington, February 4, 1979," ibid.

117. Dick Thomas, "Chilly Seattle Greets Teng Warmly," *Oregonian,* February 4, 1979.

118. Wendy Liu, *Connecting Washington and China: The Story of the Washington State China Relations Council* (New York: iUniverse, 2005), 5, 8.

119. Stephen H. Dunphy, "Visit Sparked Close Business Ties to State," *Seattle Times,* February 19, 1997.

120. Leonard Silk, "Doing Business with Peking," *New York Times,* May 30, 1979.

121. "Jackson, on China Visit, Supports Trade Accord," *New York Times,* August 8, 1979.

122. Xu, *Congress and the U.S.-China Relationship,* 364, n. 141.

123. Paul Symbol to HMJ, December 20, 1978, HMJ Papers, accession 3560–4, box 80, folder 22.

124. HMJ to Paul Symbol, January 23, 1979, ibid.

125. H. Dewayne Kreager to HMJ, January 12, 1979, ibid.

126. Jim Berry to HMJ, February 12, 1979; HMJ to Jim Berry, February 23, 1979, ibid.

127. HMJ to Larry Hill, March 2, 1979, ibid.

128. HMJ to C. R. Rogers, March 5, 1979, ibid.

129. George Sage to HMJ, January 15, 1979; HMJ to George Sage, January 25, 1979; George Sage to HMJ, June 14, 1979, HMJ Papers, accession 3560–4, box 80, folder 21.

130. James Scroggs to Wang Yao Ting, January 24 and August 2, 1979, ibid.

131. Holt W. Webster to HMJ, September 24, 1979, ibid.

132. Donald Swanson to Chinese Vice Minister of Agriculture, March 28, 1979, ibid.

133. Don Beckley to Chinese Vice Minister of Agriculture, January 10, 1979, ibid.

134. HMJ to Don Beckley, April 2, 1979, ibid.

135. Bob Nichols to HMJ, April 12, 1979, ibid.

136. Eddie Eng to HMJ, September 26, 1979, ibid.

137. Glenn Lansing to HMJ, September 26, 1979, ibid.

138. Richard Ford to HMJ, October 2, 1979, ibid.

139. After Jackson's death, the school was renamed the Henry M. Jackson School of International Studies.

140. "China's Modernization: Problems and Prospects, Symposium, Sponsored by the School of International Studies, University of Washington; Saturday, February 9, 1980," HMJ Papers, accession 3560–6, box 28, folder 37.

141. HMJ to Kenneth Pyle, February 18, 1980, HMJ Papers, accession 3560–4, box 246, folder 59.

142. George Taylor to HMJ, February 11, 1980, ibid.

143. HMJ to Harold Shefelman, January 29, 1979, ibid.

144. HMJ to Kenneth Pyle, February 16, March 1 and 20, 1979, ibid.

145. Pyle to HMJ, March 7, 1979, ibid.

146. Liu, *Connecting Washington and China,* 4.

147. Press release, Washington State China Relations Council, undated (ca. 1980), HMJ Papers, accession 3560–6, box 35, folder 4.

148. Liu, *Connecting Washington and China,* 224–28.

149. "Washington State China Relations Council Highlights of 1982," HMJ Papers, accession 3560–6, box 35, folder 4.

150. "Taiwan Arms Sales Criticized," *New York Times,* July 19, 1982.

151. "Jackson-Vanik Waiver Authority Extension—Romania, Hungary, China; Testimony by Senator Henry M. Jackson, Subcommittee on International Trade, Senate Finance Committee, August 10, 1982," HMJ Papers, accession 3560–6, box 18, folder 24.

152. HMJ to Stanley Barer, January 25, 1983, ibid.

153. "International Trade: Washington's Strength & Its Future," undated (ca. 1983), HMJ Papers, accession 3560–4, box 316, folder 10.

154. "Present Challenges to the World Economic System," May 31, 1983, HMJ Papers, accession 3560–4, box 355, folder 7.

155. *The China Policy of Senator Henry M. Jackson: Staff Report to the Committee on Armed Services, United States Senate, December 1983* (Washington, DC: US Government Printing Office, 1983), 1–7, HMJ Papers, accession 3560–6, box 28, folder 37.

156. Ibid., 13.

157. Ibid.

158. "Senator Henry M. Jackson Centennial Celebration," YouTube video.

4

Religious Pluralism, Domestic Politics, and the Emerging Jewish-Evangelical Coalition on Israel, 1960–1980

Daniel G. Hummel

In 1970 *Newsweek* dubbed Rabbi Marc H. Tanenbaum the "Apostle to the Gentiles."[1] Throughout the previous decade, Tanenbaum had ascended into the national spotlight as the director of interreligious affairs for the American Jewish Committee (AJC), the so-called dean of American Jewish organizations at midcentury.[2] As the *Newsweek* headline made clear, Tanenbaum was best known for improving relations between Christians and Jews. For Tanenbaum, this encompassed not only the classic definition of Jewish philosopher Martin Buber—open and honest dialogue as part of authentic relationships—but also more deliberate efforts to reform Christian anti-Judaism in everything from liturgies to textbooks to making Christians more receptive to Jewish perspectives on Israel.

Tanenbaum played a decisive role in shaping American Jewish engagement with the Christian world in the 1960s, especially in pioneering its interreligious shift toward evangelicals. At the beginning of the decade, Tanenbaum capitalized on monumental developments in the Christian world. This included advising the Catholic Church in its Second Vatican Council (1962–1965), which resulted in major theological reforms, including a declaration rejecting antisemitism and redefining the Catholic Church's relationship to Jews. Tanenbaum also advised large Protestant organizations, such as the World Council of Churches, as they articulated the condemnation of Christian anti-Judaism. By 1967, Tanenbaum's work seemed to show the potential of Jewish-Christian cooperation to reform Christian thinking. However, the June 1967 war between Israel and five Arab states revealed its limits. Most Christian organizations, including the World Council of Churches, resisted Jewish appeals to publicly support Israel before and after the war. Jewish observers wrote of the "silence of the churches" and wondered whether the relationships Tanenbaum and others had cultivated amounted to anything substantial when it really counted. Tanenbaum's response was not to abandon Jewish-Christian efforts but to focus on the issue of Israel. This facilitated Tanenbaum's courtship of a group of Christians that most other Jews had sworn off: American evangelicals, who were already gaining public and political attention in the late 1960s.[3]

Evidence of Tanenbaum's approach was apparent even in the 1970 *Newsweek* article, which dedicated much of its analysis to Tanenbaum's appearance at a political rally, "Honor America Day," on July 4, 1970, in Washington DC. This event was sponsored and organized by supporters of President Richard Nixon, and although Tanenbaum was no friend of Nixon, he was a new friend of Billy Graham, the foremost representative of American evangelicals and a staunch Nixon supporter. Tanenbaum explained to *Newsweek,* "I went to Washington with some ambivalence. But I felt that the risk of possibly being identified with the right wing in America was worth it. Billy Graham has been a stalwart friend of Israel in every crisis and I felt a moral obligation to reciprocate his support."[4] The relationship between Tanenbaum and Graham expanded to form the basis of a powerful political coalition between Jews and evangelicals promoting American support for Israel. This coalition was both interreligious, including Jews and Christians, and bipartisan, including liberal Jews and conservative evangelicals.

In this setting, interreligious dialogue was a means to a political end.[5] It was also part of a profound transformation in the United States' relationship to Israel. While domestic lobbying for Israel was historically the purview of American Jewish organizations, by the end of the 1970s, it would become a core issue of grassroots evangelical activism pursued by a dizzying array of single-issue organizations.[6] By the twenty-first century, Christian Zionist groups such as Christians United for Israel could claim membership in the millions, vastly outnumbering Jewish pro-Israel groups.[7] Today, the "Israel lobby," made up of both Jewish and Christian Zionist organizations and individuals seeking to influence American policy toward Israel, argues for increased financial and military aid to Israel and increased resources to fight terrorism, and it defends Israel's reluctance to accelerate peace negotiations with Palestinians.[8]

Historians and political scientists have offered a number of explanations for the rise of the Israel lobby in postwar America, from demographic change to the rise of the religious Right to more focused explanations of Israeli and American Jewish realpolitik.[9] These explanations miss the institutional, religious, and domestic political factors in the 1960s and 1970s that sparked the first structured Jewish-evangelical cooperation at the elite level of both communities. From 1960 to 1980, elite cooperation centered on the relationship between Marc H. Tanenbaum and the foremost evangelical spokesperson in the world at the time, Billy Graham.

The Tanenbaum-Graham relationship presents a new explanation for the development of the domestic Jewish-evangelical coalition in support of Israel. The bipartisan, interreligious origins of Tanenbaum and Graham's relationship emphasize the role of religion in the domestic politics of the 1970s and the connection between religious concerns and domestic and foreign policy issues. In short, the theological and religious differences separating evangelicals and Jews were the most substantial barriers to consolidating the political agreement of both communities to support the state of Israel. The way that Tanenbaum and Graham circumvented these barriers had profound consequences for the emergence of the Israel lobby and the US-Israel relationship. In the 1970s evangelicals engaged the issue of Israel with the help of American Jews, a top-down process led by key figures that included Tanenbaum and Graham. Although rank-and-file evangelicals and American Jews did not immediately follow their leaders, Tanenbaum and Graham helped lay the foundation for the modern bipartisan support of Israel. Understanding the lobby as a religious coalition with a distinctive set of political positions that united its disparate elements provides a more complete picture of perhaps the most influential political lobby shaping American foreign relations, and it is a key factor in explaining the "special relationship" between the United States and Israel.

Background: Tanenbaum and Graham

Tanenbaum and Graham both emerged as national personalities in the postwar period, although Tanenbaum was a less recognizable figure and more passionate about the American landscape of interreligious relations. By the time they formally met in 1969, American political and cultural patterns had created a new basis for forging personal and political relationships.

Born to Jewish immigrant parents in Baltimore in 1925, Marc H. Tanenbaum developed an early interest in the intersection of religion and politics.[10] His training at Yeshiva University and the Jewish Theological Seminary reflected these interests. In 1952 he became the director of the Synagogue Council of America, an organization that coordinated the actions of Reform, Orthodox, and (his own) Conservative Jewish communities. During his time at the council, Tanenbaum established personal friendships with Christian leaders that forwarded both the religious and political interests of the American Jewish community. In the 1950s he befriended Martin Luther King Jr., Catholic televangelist Bishop Fulton Sheen, and Greek Orthodox Archbishop Iakovos, among others. However, by 1961, Tanenbaum grew disillusioned with the Synagogue Council's lackluster embrace of religious dialogue due to internal dissension among Jewish groups.

On the cusp of joining the American Jewish Committee in 1961, Tanenbaum saw dialogue as a tool to shift American attitudes toward Jews. Most Americans were Christians, and Christian denominations and religious organizations held important sway over their members' attitudes. Interreligious dialogue was one way to reform Americans' basic orientation toward the Jewish people. In this sense, Tanenbaum's desire for engagement was not much different from that of many Reform and Conservative Jews involved in other issues ranging from civil rights to antisemitism. American Jews worked for the eradication of social and religious prejudices through collective action. The American Jewish Committee's long-standing emphasis on "human relations" and combating prejudice overlapped and helped inform Tanenbaum's focus on interreligious relations.[11]

For Tanenbaum, engagement with Christians was a pragmatic necessity and a religious imperative. He was committed to the transformative power of dialogue, arguing that interreligious encounters provided the best opportunity for Jews and Christians to understand each other.[12] More cautious views toward dialogue were common in much of the American Jewish community, reflecting long-standing disagreements over Judaism's relationship to Christianity and America's predominantly Christian culture. Concerns over assimilation have always been paramount in the American Jewish experience, but there were also theological issues at play. How much did Jewish belief and history actually share with Christianity? Was it the Jews' role to stand apart or to engage with Christians, especially in light of modern antisemitism and the Holocaust? These questions divided the organized Jewish community and made Tanenbaum stand out as someone who was particularly optimistic about the potential of dialogue.

In the early 1960s Tanenbaum's pursuit of interreligious dialogue was not especially related to the state of Israel. Thorny questions of Jewish-Christian theological differences, as well as efforts to fight Christian anti-Judaism and to advance civil and human rights, were of greater concern to postwar American Jews. The AJC mirrored these priorities. The organization was engaged in a wide spectrum of global issues, including human rights, humanitarian relief, and emigration rights for Soviet Jews. Like much of the American Jewish community, Tanenbaum praised the establishment of Israel in 1948, but he expressed no particular concern about Israel and its status among American Christians until after the June 1967 war. In the 1960s improving Jewish-Christian relations was part of the broader matrix of Jewish liberalism that emphasized humanitarianism, religious pluralism, and dialogue.[13]

That same matrix—indeed, the interreligious impulse—was initially absent in the conservative evangelical culture of Billy Graham's youth.[14] Born in 1918 into a conservative Presbyterian household, Graham's early life typified the cultural isolation of American evangelicalism from American Judaism.[15] Graham's knowledge of Judaism as a young minister was minimal. He viewed Jews as God's chosen people but believed they were also in need of conversion. Raised as a fundamentalist, he subscribed to the basic theological positions of premillennial dispensationalism, a popular theology that regarded the "regathering" of the people of Israel in

Palestine as a sign of Christ's imminent second coming. Crucially, dispensationalists believed there was a permanent separation between "Israel" and the "Church"—between Jews and Christians—which meant that each group had a special role to play in God's plans. Unlike historic Christian teachings (including those by the Catholic Church and other Protestant denominations in the twentieth century), dispensationalists taught that Jews remained chosen by God even after they collectively refused to acknowledge Jesus as the messiah. For most other Christians, the designation "Israel" had been appropriated by Christians, leaving Jews bereft of God's favor or promises. Dispensationalists, however, maintained that God still had work to do through the "seed of Abraham." Graham would transform this theology into a type of pluralism to help him understand and justify new levels of engagement with American Jews.[16]

Graham's contact with American Jews diverged radically from that of most evangelicals after his meteoric rise during the 1950s. In the Los Angeles crusade of 1949 Graham gained media coverage from news magnates such as William Randolph Hearst and Henry Luce, who also wished for a spiritual revival to energize American society at the onset of the Cold War. Graham subsequently met American Jewish leaders. As the leading Protestant voice in America, he soon found himself at the center of the ecumenical and interfaith pressures then pervasive in an American society with a declining acceptance of antisemitism and a new emphasis on Judeo-Christian values.[17] On top of these broader cultural pressures, Graham engaged in public dialogue largely as a response to gains in Jewish-Christian relations won by liberal Protestant, Catholic, and Jewish organizations in the early and mid-1960s.

As these brief biographies of Graham and Tanenbaum illustrate, the line between interreligious relations and domestic politics blurred as both figures entered the prime of their careers. In a rapidly changing environment of increased religious pluralism, interreligious coalitions had powerful political saliency, though they were inhibited by enduring religious prejudices and a lack of interpersonal or organizational connections.

First Contact

In the late 1960s Tanenbaum, the AJC's director of interreligious affairs, and Graham, the interreligious neophyte, assumed a type of mentor-mentee relationship when it came to Jewish-Christian relations. Tanenbaum's deep thinking and planning informed Graham's orientation to the Jewish world—for Graham, just one part of a complex global agenda for his evangelistic ministries. Graham could not dedicate most of his time to improving Jewish-Christian relations; Tanenbaum, however, made courting Graham one of his primary objectives. This personal dynamic at the beginning of the Jewish-evangelical dialogue, as much as any other factor, shaped how the Jewish-evangelical coalition to support Israel emerged.

In addition to the Tanenbaum-Graham relationship, social, cultural, and political barriers that had historically separated Jews and evangelicals began to erode. In the latter half of the 1960s American Jews began to realize the potential political influence of national evangelical figures like Graham who were not tied to any specific denomination but commanded a vast following of Americans.[18] According to one political profile cowritten in 1972 (a critical election year) by Tanenbaum's associate in the AJC, Gerald S. Strober, Graham was representative of "31,000,000 conservative Protestants in America" and "Middle America." It noted that Graham "today stands in the closest proximity to the Presidency, to the majority of the nation's Protestants, and to the great center of America's social and political life." Strober urged readers to see Graham as the spiritual leader of America's "silent majority" and as a conduit to reach American voters by means other than party politics. Graham personified the "mood of Middle America"—that is, skeptical of large government structures and the rapid changes in American society—but he was also "ahead of his constituency" on domestic issues that mattered to American Jews, especially race relations and bipartisanship (Graham had been "friends with two Democrat[ic] presidents" before Nixon).[19]

Tanenbaum, Strober, and the AJC believed that a combination of evangelical beliefs and centrist politics (in the Nixon era) could bridge the gap between American Jews and evangelicals. Their position on dialogue was optimistic and would be helped along by international events in 1967.[20] The June 5–10, 1967, war between Israel and five Arab states reshaped American Jewish evaluations of Christians and drastically altered the balance of power in the Middle East. Reacting to an Egyptian blockade of the Straits of Tiran and the mobilization of Arab armies, the Israeli military launched a preemptive strike on the morning of June 5 that decimated the Egyptian and Jordanian air forces. In less than a week, Israeli forces cut through Arab armies to occupy the Sinai Peninsula, West Bank, Gaza Strip, East Jerusalem, and Golan Heights.

The tense lead-up to the war in May 1967 did not initially provoke major Christian reactions. Indeed, as American Jews like Tanenbaum later remembered it, "the Christian silence" in the face of a possible "second holocaust" was deafening.[21] Adding to Jewish anxieties, mainline (more liberal nonevangelical) Christian organizations began to criticize Israel after the war. Unfortunately for Tanenbaum, his existing Christian dialogue partners—the National Council of Churches, the World Council of Churches, and the Vatican—were part of this new criticism of Israel. These organizations intensified their attention on the Arab-Israeli conflict and increasingly identified with the plight of Palestinian refugees. The Israeli government's annexation of East Jerusalem in late June received special condemnation from internationalists (including the Vatican and Arab Christians) that wanted the entire city under United Nations control.[22]

By 1969, the relationship between Tanenbaum and his old Christian partners had been frayed. With rising disapproval of Israel; the deaths of major interreligious figures such as Abraham Joshua Heschel, Martin Luther King Jr., and Reinhold Niebuhr; and the fragmentation of the Democratic Party coalition, Jewish-Christian dialogue as it had been constituted in the early 1960s began to fall apart. For Tanenbaum, the June 1967 war elevated Christian theological support for the Jewish state as one of the dialogue's central concerns. At the same time, Zionism's close integration into the matrix of American political liberalism weakened. Like American Jewish Zionism more broadly, which, according to historian Michael Staub, was "sharp and narrow" in the late 1960s and was focused primarily on Israel's survival, Jewish-Christian engagement increasingly centered on Israel. Staub writes that by the 1970s, the once fluid and internally diverse ideological commitments of American Zionists had thinned out; Israel "stood alone at the center of Zionist concerns."[23]

Evangelicals became attractive partners in this narrower dialogue. They had overwhelmingly celebrated Israel's victory as both a military and a moral success.[24] Moreover, many dispensationalists saw the war's outcome as divinely ordained. In light of this outpouring of support for Israel, Tanenbaum and the AJC came to see evangelicals as more promising Christian dialogue partners for the future. The pivot was rapid—

so fast, in fact, that Tanenbaum had to explain it to outside observers. "Before the six-day war," he told reporters in 1970, "about 85 percent of the American Jewish Committee's interfaith efforts had been directed to Catholics, and most of the remainder to Protestants. About 40 percent of the committee's efforts this year [are] going to Evangelical Protestants."[25] This reallocation involved new efforts to expand the official dialogue to include Southern Baptist seminaries and the Evangelical Theological Society, as well as outreach with evangelicals located in Israel.

As a first step with Graham, the AJC planned a public meeting to "introduce" the two communities to each other.[26] In February 1969 Strober met with Graham's personal assistant to nail down a specific date. Over the course of the next four months, the AJC and Graham's organization meticulously planned a ninety-minute gathering with dozens of Jewish leaders in New York City to coincide with the first Baptist-Jewish Scholar's Conference, also sponsored by the AJC. Graham was not only the most visible evangelical in the United States but also a Southern Baptist who urged his denomination—the largest in the American South—to reach out to Jewish organizations. When Graham and Jewish leaders met in June, they discussed numerous issues ranging from "Israel and the Middle East" to "the relationship between American Jews and the Evangelical Protestant community" to "Proselytism, Conversion, Theology of the people of God," and "Church and State."[27] The mix of domestic, international, and theological issues reflected the broader concerns of both Graham and the AJC, but any collaborative effort would first need to address religious concerns and domestic political issues.

This meeting was important because both sides became familiar with the other's domestic, international, and religious priorities. Moreover, Graham impressed his Jewish audience on a personal level. He appeared to be a reasonable Christian who was concerned about Israel and interreligious relations. Tanenbaum flattered him by stating, "You elicited an unprecedented warmth, cordiality, and respect for your position . . . you helped overcome a number of misconceptions and strengthened the bonds of fellowship between our peoples."[28] Strober likewise admired Graham's "sincerity, warmth and grasp of issues of common concern."[29] Rabbi Ronald Kronish, future founder of the Interreligious Coordinating Committee in Israel, admitted that he had entered the meeting possessing an "image of the man as a wild and raving fundamentalist" but left with these prejudices "severely shattered." Graham's demeanor, Kronish observed, "was not loud and pompous, as one might expect." In an informal setting, Graham gave the impression of a "powerful, yet extremely sensitive human being, who expressed an unusual love for Israel and the Jewish people."[30]

Graham had many religious and political motivations to attend the meeting. He cited verses from Deuteronomy and Ezekiel to illustrate his belief that the Jews remained God's chosen people. He recalled Jesus's own Jewish background and the roots of Christianity in Judaism. He also "mentioned his positive feeling for the State of Israel" and noted that "his daughter and son-in-law had committed their lives to Israel and will be working on a Moshav [farming community]" in the coming year. These personal ties to Israel impressed Tanenbaum, who offered the services of the AJC's office in Israel to Graham's daughter. Graham also "said that all Christians are guilty as far as Jewish experience is concerned and he also ask[ed] forgiveness of the Jewish community as a Christian." Graham then elaborated on his political connections with the Israeli and American political leadership. Recounting a recent "two hour meeting with Golda Meir," Graham explained to his Jewish audience that his concern for Christian missionaries in Arab states precluded him from speaking out more publicly in support of Israel. He assured the Jewish leaders that privately he was completely supportive of Israel and was in constant conversation with President Nixon, who was "extremely sympathetic" to Israel.[31]

Graham's performance was indicative of an evolving electoral dynamic between the political issue of Israel and American religious pluralism. By emphasizing Israel and defending Nixon's record in the Middle East, Graham helped position Nixon as the pro-Israel candidate in his 1972 reelection bid. In that race, a number of Jewish intellectuals and leaders hesitated to support the Democratic nominee, George McGovern, in part because of his foreign policy views.[32] Leaders like Graham, who had developed these new contacts with Jews during Nixon's first term, spread the word that, for the first time, a Republican president was more supportive of Israel than a Democratic candidate. Graham's work seems to have been a contributing force to Nixon's massive success in the 1972 election. Both evangelicals (84 percent) and Jews (35 percent) increased their support for Nixon in 1972, and outlets such as the *Jewish Telegraph Agency* cited Israel as a major issue for Jewish voters.[33] Besides Ronald Reagan, who garnered 39 percent of the Jewish vote in 1980, Nixon's 1972 performance was the best by a Republican candidate since 1956 (when Nixon was the vice presidential candidate under Dwight Eisenhower). As a political surrogate for Nixon, Graham was uniquely suited for laying the groundwork for this interreligious coalition building.

In religious terms, Graham's appreciation of Jewish history and culture was dependent on a multilayered discourse about the current state of Jewish-Christian relations. The tie that bound Graham to his Jewish listeners in 1969 was a shared interest in cultivating a new understanding of Israel in a Christian context. Graham's ability to intuit this connection laid the groundwork for a more expansive dialogue and political collaboration through the next decade.

The Problem of Missions

American Jewish goodwill, which Graham had won during the late 1960s through his willingness to meet with Jewish leaders, express support for Israel, and engage in interreligious dialogue, helped temper a dramatic decline in domestic Jewish-evangelical relations in 1972–1973. Beginning in early 1972 American evangelical leaders planned one of their most ambitious campaigns in the United States. Titled "Key 73," this was a national effort to "Call the Continent to Christ in 1973," as its official slogan explained. This effort indicated that, at least among much of the leadership of American evangelicalism, interreligious dialogue continued to take a backseat to evangelism.[34] Graham and evangelical organizations initially contributed to Key 73, but they were forced into an uncomfortable and increasingly untenable conflict between their efforts at dialogue and the missionary impulse of Key 73.[35] The starkly different sentiments in the new Tanenbaum-Graham relationship and the two men's larger communities illustrated the exceptional nature of their relationship and extent to which they had moved beyond their communities.

For Graham, who both held on to a traditional understanding of Christian conversion and sought new respectability and influence in the areas of politics and interreligious relations, Key 73 proved especially harrowing. One of Key 73's most visible controversies was its approach to the American Jewish community. In the campaign's official handbook, Jews won the dubious distinction of being the only ethnic or religious community explicitly targeted for evangelization.[36] More broadly, Key 73 participants included Jewish mission agencies such as the Hebrew Christian Alliance and a new organization, Jews for Jesus.[37] Both were bitter adversaries of American Jewish organizations. The AJC and the Anti-Defamation League (ADL) interpreted Key 73's efforts at "Sharing Messiah with Jewish People"—another slogan of the campaign—as antisemitic and harmful to Jewish-Christian relations. To many Jews, Key 73 reinforced the wide chasm in religious and political views that separated American Judaism and American evangelicalism.

Graham played a key role in bridging the rifts that opened between evangelical and Jewish leaders over Key 73. Strober had a private conversation with Graham in November 1973, and he reported to Tanenbaum that better relations with the American Jewish community "is the only issue in which he [Graham] plays an advocate's role with his friends." Repeating his common refrain, Graham "concluded [the conversation] by saying as a Christian he owed everything to the Jewish people."[38] Graham had weighed in earlier in the year when, after hours of consultation with Tanenbaum and Strober at his home in Monticello, North Carolina, he decided to release a public statement clarifying his views on Key 73 and Jewish missions. In a February press release Graham affirmed his evangelistic concern "for all men" but denounced evangelistic "gimmicks, coercion, and intimidation" and condemned "overbearing witness to seek conversions" as "zeal without knowledge," a reference to Proverbs 19:2.[39] This language closely mirrored that of Jewish organizational literature warning against Key 73.

Given his concern for "Christian-Jewish relations," Graham also addressed the theological relationship between the two faiths, introducing a new dimension to the reshaping of American evangelical thinking by the Tanenbaum-Graham relationship. Graham explained, "Along with most Evangelical Christians I believe God has always had a special relationship with the Jewish people, as St. Paul suggests in the book of Romans. In light of that I have never felt called to direct my evangelistic efforts to Jews or any other particular group." In Romans 9–11, Paul articulates his conflicted relationship with the Jews of his day, at once praising their legacy but also criticizing their rejection of his new Christ-centered message. Paul elevates the nation of "Israel," the physical descendants of Abraham, over other non-Christian peoples of the day, writing, "Theirs is the adoption to sonship; theirs the divine glory, the covenants, the receiving of the law, the temple worship and the promises. Theirs are the patriarchs, and from them is traced the human ancestry of the Messiah, who is God over all, forever praised" (Romans 9:4–5). Graham, basing his statement on these verses, called for a new Christian appreciation of the Jewish people's role in God's plans.[40] In more political terms, Graham's statement urged Jews and evangelicals to look past theological differences and focus on shared principles that united Judeo-Christian culture. This included support for the state of Israel.

Tanenbaum was predictably enthusiastic about Graham's public statement and the direction of his theology. The process of counseling Graham had stimulated Tanenbaum's hopes for broad-based evangelical theological reform. "I cannot begin to find words adequate to express my deep personal pleasure of the several conversations we have had the past few days," Tanenbaum wrote to Graham the day after the press release. "I came away from our conversation persuaded that you have the capacity to make a historic contribution to the clarification of relationships between Christians and Jews in our century."[41] More broadly, Tanenbaum explained, "Christian leaders, including Evangelical leaders, have a valid theological alternative . . . namely, that the Covenant of Sinai is permanent, and that Christianity must see itself not in terms of substitution, but rather in terms of being a complimentary Covenant to the Covenant of Israel."[42] This "dual covenant" theology flatly contradicted Graham's stated evangelical beliefs of the need for salvation through Christ. Graham's position became confusing to both evangelical and Jewish critics, and he was forced to deny to curious reporters that he had adopted a dual covenant approach.[43]

Both Tanenbaum and Graham wanted to advance Jewish-evangelical relations, though in different directions. Graham was focused on messaging, language, and persuasion, as were many of his public efforts. As a centrist, he invariably sought positions that aligned with a majority of evangelicals, many of whom were feeling the new societal pressures of increasing religious pluralism. Graham staked out a middle ground that simultaneously affirmed evangelical theological convictions and the intense desire for interreligious relations and partnership. Tanenbaum, in contrast, focused on showing his fellow Jews that evangelical change was possible. Key 73 may have signaled a low point in Jewish-evangelical relations, but Tanenbaum argued that the "positive results" of more vocal support for Israel were "unquestionably the fruit of years of Jewish-Christian dialogue."[44] The promise of theological reform, even among American Christianity's most conservative communities, was an article of faith for Tanenbaum and other Jews committed to dialogue. This theological reform could lead to new opportunities for political cooperation. In Tanenbaum's eyes, Graham's support for Israel outweighed his "right-wing" label and his complicated association with missions. His close association with Nixon and the new cultural influence of "born-again Christians" pointed to the growing significance of evangelicals in American politics.

Thus, for Tanenbaum and Graham, the process of aligning domestic political cooperation and US support for Israel came to a head in 1973. Both obstacles and successes had shaped the relationship since its beginning in 1969. Key 73 and ongoing Jewish-evangelical tension over Jewish missions had transformed into a coup for Tanenbaum, who could cite Graham's moderating language as tangible progress in interreligious relations. Moreover, Graham's rejection of missions specifically targeting Jews did not alienate him from the evangelical world. The tides of evangelical thinking about Jews seemed to be shifting. The major political differences between conservative evangelicals and liberal Jews still made the two communities political opponents, but the unifying role played by support for Israel was a reservoir of untapped potential. While that potential continued to grow through the 1970s, the dislocation of Graham and Tanenbaum from the center of the new Jewish-evangelical relationship would also transform these nascent achievements into larger and more permanent political successes.

Graham's Retreat, Evangelicalism's Advance

In October 1973 Egypt's attack on Israel on the holy day of Yom Kippur surprised Israelis and stunned Americans. With the help of a massive American airlift, Israel eventually recovered from early losses, but the war left a lasting impression on the state and its supporters. The state of Israel's security was not nearly as strong as Jews and evangelicals had believed after 1967. In assessing Christians' response to the war, the AJC concluded similarly that evangelicals were becoming the only dependable segment of Christianity to support Israel. In a 1974 report the AJC lamented the organizational responses of the National Council of Churches and World Council of Churches. Outspoken critics such as Father Daniel Berrigan (Catholic), who gave a speech describing Israel as "a criminal Jewish community," were especially worrisome. Conversely, supportive statements came from Billy Graham, evangelical leader Arnold T. Olson, and Southern Baptist clergy in particular. One major difference from 1967, the report noted, was that Jews were no longer surprised by the diversity of Christian reactions. "In the intervening years, Jewish religious and communal leaders had learned, to a great extent, who were Israel's staunch supporters within the Christian community, who were her friendly critics, who were indifferent, who were hostile, and who were prepared to see Israel go down the drain in order to pacify her enemies." This confirmed American Jewish convictions that evangelicals, who rooted their support for Israel in theological arguments, were more valuable than mainline Protestants and Catholics in generating domestic political support for Israel. Subsequent developments through the 1970s—the rise of international terrorism, the collapse of Israel Labor and the rise of Likud, the Camp David peace process—would further cement this conviction.[45]

Yet by the mid-1970s, American Jewish attention was shifting from Graham to a new generation of pro-Israel evangelicals, many of whom built on the theological and rhetorical moves Graham had developed in the previous decade. By the late 1970s, Graham began to take a more measured approach to Middle East politics, weighing his statements on the region against his many other projects and evangelistic campaigns. When Graham received the AJC's first National Interreligious Award in 1977 (largely orchestrated by Tanenbaum), the differences between Graham and Tanenbaum over evangelical support for Israel came to the surface. Graham's acceptance speech, which highlighted his own story of Christian conversion and his subsequent realization of Christians' mistreatment of Jews, mentioned Israel only once, in a brief passage gesturing to the need to "pray for the peace of Jerusalem" and pointing to Isaiah 25:12, which prophesied that Israel, Egypt, and Syria would one day "live together in permanent peace."[46] Tanenbaum's comments on an early draft of Graham's speech reveal his preference for a speech dedicated largely to articulating evangelical support for Israel. Tanenbaum wrote back to Graham and sent two large inserts for the speech—one explaining the widespread support for Israel among evangelicals, and the other condemning

PLO terrorism. Graham ultimately modified his speech to include a statement of support for Israel's right to exist, but he did not incorporate most Tanenbaum's suggestions. One historian concluded, "Reverend Graham failed to deliver evangelical Christianity's unwavering support for the state of Israel."[47] This judgment goes too far, but it does highlight the diminishing role Graham would play in Jewish-evangelical relations after the mid-1970s.

The reasons for Graham's decreasing interest in the Middle East were many, but few were as serious as his defense of President Nixon throughout the Watergate scandal.[48] In the aftermath of the president's resignation, Graham sought to regain the more bipartisan image he had forged in the 1950s and 1960s. He would never again wed his political and evangelistic projects so explicitly, although he would remain the "pastor to the president" for decades. His retreat from politics helped pave the way for a new crop of evangelicals who did not carry the same baggage and were interested in influencing policy. As part of the emerging religious Right, these pro-Israel evangelicals combined support for Israel with criticism of "secular humanist" judges, feminism, homosexuality, and liberalism. Graham's critiques of the religious Right revealed a split between the evangelical establishment and the new, more ideological conservative leadership. The religious Right, an umbrella term for resurgent right-wing political groups made up of fundamentalist, evangelical, Catholic, Mormon, and other religious traditionalists in the late 1970s, had as its primary objective the election of conservative candidates in local and national politics.[49]

Graham had no interest in joining the political program of the religious Right. In fact, he disagreed with Jerry Falwell, the leader of its largest organization, the Moral Majority, on a number of issues, including nuclear nonproliferation (Graham was for it), closer relations between evangelicals and right-wing donors (Graham was against it), and closely identifying "the Kingdom of God with the American way of life" (Graham recanted his prior intimations and charged Falwell with conflating the two). "It would be unfortunate if people got the impression all evangelists belong to that group," Graham said in 1981, in reference to the Moral Majority. "The majority do not. I don't wish to be identified with them."[50]

Like Graham, American Jews reviled many of the religious Right's policy prescriptions, but also its more bombastic rhetoric and controversial remarks about Jews. When Bailey Smith, the Southern Baptist Convention's president, stated at a 1980 political rally that, "with all due respect to those dear people, my friend God Almighty does not hear the prayer of a Jew," American Jewish leaders, including Tanenbaum, denounced the religious Right.[51] When Falwell made jokes about Jewish moneymaking, he was forced to apologize to American Jews.[52] Yet even as American Jewish leaders lamented the rightward turn represented by the leadership shift from Graham to Falwell, the pro-Israel ties forged between evangelicals and Jews in the 1970s remained intact. In 1980, for example, Arnold T. Olson, who had been active in Christian Zionist circles since the 1950s, continued to be a primary evangelical spokesman at interreligious pro-Israel rallies.[53] This type of collaboration continued in the midst of tensions over the religious Right.

By the 1980s, Falwell and the Moral Majority, with its aggressive support for Ronald Reagan, had come to define the political expression of American evangelicalism, and with it, the new political relationship between evangelicals and American Jews on the issue of Israel. The religious Right's combative positions and language alienated evangelicals like Graham, whose support for Israel had come from a reassessment of Jewish-Christian relations. However, the Moral Majority's own staunch support for Israel also depended on the "middle way" approach Graham had pioneered, which rejected, or at least limited, aggressive Jewish mission tactics and celebrated the overlapping history and religious values of Judeo-Christianity.

Through the 1970s, the Tanenbaum-Graham relationship had drawn American Jews and evangelicals closer together in their shared support of Israel, creating the basis for a new bipartisan Zionism. As the evangelical community became more involved in right-wing politics, it left Graham behind but carried on this Zionism that Tanenbaum and Graham had helped forge. This pro-Israel orientation, inherited by the Moral Majority and the broader religious Right, retained little of the interreligious context of the 1960s that had fueled Tanenbaum and Graham. Instead, the religious Right's Christian Zionism was integrated into the rest of its political agenda and the rightward drift of American politics in the 1980s.

While Falwell and the religious Right remained on the American Jewish radar as dependable supporters of Israel, they also alienated American Jews who reacted to Falwell's more conservative political positions and controversial remarks. Yet, below the surface of disagreements about domestic policy, the religious Right and American Jewish organizations continued to build on developments from the 1970s. The new Israeli leadership, elected in 1977 with Menachem Begin's right-wing Likud party, played no small part in sustaining the momentum. As a trusted intermediary and object of support for both American Jewish organizational leaders and the religious Right, Begin was able to coordinate both communities' efforts to solidify US-Israeli relations.[54]

Thus, even with his demurral of political leadership, Graham left evangelicals an important legacy. He never reconciled his new positions on Jewish missions and his evangelical beliefs. Despite the confusion this may have caused his theology, Graham's position had a powerful rhetorical influence on religious Right activists and American Jews. The connections Graham forged, and that other evangelicals tapped into, papered over apparent contradictions in both his and Falwell's relationship with American Jews. For example, Graham remained close friends with Israeli and American Jewish leaders and continued to visit Israel, even as he uttered antisemitic remarks in his recorded conversations with President Nixon.[55] This paradoxical position reveals the conflicting influences of domestic and international interests on Jewish and evangelical relations. Yet these contradictions also expose the rapid changes in evangelical thinking on Jewish-Christian relations and Israel since the 1970s. The Tanenbaum-Graham relationship was both a microcosm and a cause of this shift.

The success of the Tanenbaum-Graham partnership elucidates the "narrowed and sharpened" basis for Jewish-evangelical engagement in the 1970s, a basis that would have been inconceivable without the influences of interreligious dialogue and the June 1967 war or Tanenbaum's choices in the AJC. After 1970 Israel was, in Tanenbaum's words, a "kind of Rorschach test" for interreligious encounters. The consequences of this narrowing would be monumental for both evangelicals and Jews. The interreligious scene was transformed to include the fastest growing and most politically conservative elements of American Protestantism, which would lay the foundation for the modern Christian Zionist movement and provide the basis for the bipartisan political coalition to support Israel. For Jews, the narrowing of Jewish-Christian relations was also transformative. Tanenbaum, for example, worried about the fate of religious pluralism in America with the rise of the religious Right, even as he encouraged evangelicals to become more politically engaged. This tension complicated a late-twentieth-century dialogue that was already fraught with difficulties. But it also highlighted the interreligious, bipartisan consensus that had emerged over support for Israel.

The pro-Israel coalition between Jews and evangelicals as it stands today traces its origins to the Tanenbaum-Graham relationship, which was based on a separate set of assumptions. American politics has increasingly polarized into liberal and conservative camps since the late 1960s, which makes the success of a bipartisan, interreligious relationship all the more remarkable. To fully grapple with the US-Israel relationship, historians need to account for the changing motives and justifications for interreligious cooperation between Jews and evangelicals in light of domestic politics.

Notes

1. "Apostle to the Gentiles," *Newsweek,* November 9, 1970, 53.

2. The designation is touted on the AJC's website and promotional material; see http://www.ajc.org/site/c.7°JILSPwFfJSG/b.8467183/k.DEB1/About_AJC.htm. See also Ari Goldman, "Jewish Group Faces Reorganization: A 'Top-to-Bottom Review' to Decide What Areas Will Be Cut," *New York Times,* February 13, 1990, A20.

3. On the growing influence of evangelicals in national politics in the postwar period, see Darren Dochuk, *From Bible Belt to Sunbelt: Plain-Folk Religion, Grassroots Politics, and the Rise of Evangelical Conservatism* (New York: W. W. Norton, 2011); Steven P. Miller, *The Age of Evangelicalism: America's Born-Again Years* (Oxford: Oxford University Press, 2014).

4. "Apostle to the Gentiles," 53.

5. For a history of interreligious dialogue fostering political cooperation in other contexts, see Kevin M. Schultz, *Tri-Faith America: How Catholics and Jews Held Postwar America to Its Protestant Promise* (New York: Oxford University Press, 2011).

6. See, for example, Gary Dorrien, "Evangelical Ironies: Theology, Politics, and Israel," in *Uneasy Allies? Evangelical and Jewish Relations,* ed. Alan Mittleman, Byron Johnson, and Nancy Isserman (Lanham, MD: Lexington Books, 2007), 103–26.

7. See www.cufi.org. On contemporary Christian Zionists' activism, see Faydra L. Shapiro, "'Thank You Israel, for Supporting America': The Transnational Flow of Christian Zionist Resources," *Identities* (2012): 1–16.

8. See, for example, John J. Mearsheimer and Stephen M. Walt, *The Israel Lobby and U.S. Foreign Policy* (New York: Farrar, Straus and Giroux, 2007). Mearsheimer and Walt went so far as to blame the lobby for masterminding the US invasion of

Iraq in 2003, a claim that was heavily challenged; see, for example, Dov Waxman, "From Jerusalem to Baghdad? Israel and the War in Iraq," *International Studies Perspectives* 10, no. 1 (2009): 1–17. For a more skeptical interpretation of the influence of the lobby, see Dov Waxman, *Trouble in the Tribe: The American Jewish Conflict over Israel* (Princeton, NJ: Princeton University Press, 2016), 147–73. On the special role historians ascribe to domestic lobbying in the US-Israel relationship, see, for example, Caitlin Carenen, *The Fervent Embrace: Liberal Protestants, Evangelicals, and Israel* (New York: New York University Press, 2012); Irvine H Anderson, *Biblical Interpretation and Middle East Policy: The Promised Land, America, and Israel, 1917–2002* (Gainesville: University Press of Florida, 2005); David Schoenbaum, *The United States and the State of Israel* (New York: Oxford University Press, 1993).

9. A wide range of research and punditry has been directed toward the Israel lobby or, as it is sometimes called, the "Jewish lobby." The latter term is a misnomer, especially since the 1990s, as most members of lobby groups are Christian Zionists. On the Israel lobby, see Mearsheimer and Walt, *Israel Lobby;* J. J. Goldberg, *Jewish Power: Inside the American Jewish Establishment* (New York: Basic Books, 1997), 197–227; A. F. K. Organski, *The $36 Billion Bargain: Strategy and Politics in U.S. Assistance to Israel* (New York: Columbia University Press, 1990); Edward Tivnan, *The Lobby: Jewish Political Power and American Foreign Policy* (New York: Touchstone Books, 1987). To various degrees, these authors cite the lobby's power over US policy in the Middle East. The lobby plays an important role in domestic debates about US policy and is notable for its prominence relative to the size and strength of Israel versus that of other American allies such as Great Britain, Japan, and Germany.

10. For biographical information, see Judith Herschcopf Banki and Eugene Joseph Fisher, eds., *A Prophet for Our Time: An Anthology of the Writings of Rabbi Marc H. Tanenbaum* (New York: Fordham University Press, 2002), xix–xxix.

11. See Marianne Rachel Sanua, *Let Us Prove Strong: The American Jewish Committee, 1945–2006* (Waltham, MA: Brandeis University Press, 2007), 67–98.

12. See Lila Corwin Berman, *Speaking of Jews: Rabbis, Intellectuals, and the Creation of an American Public Identity* (Berkeley: University of California Press, 2009), 45–60.

13. See Michael N. Barnett, *The Star and the Stripes: A History of the Foreign Policies of American Jews* (Princeton, NJ: Princeton University Press, 2016), 121–54.

14. On this culture, see George M. Marsden, *Fundamentalism and American Culture,* 2nd ed. (Cambridge: Oxford University Press, 2006). On the more reformist vein of fundamentalism that Graham led beginning in the 1940s, see George M. Marsden, *Reforming Fundamentalism: Fuller Seminary and the New Evangelicalism* (Grand Rapids, MI: W. B. Eerdmans, 1987).

15. For biographical details, see Grant Wacker, *America's Pastor: Billy Graham and the Shaping of a Nation* (Cambridge, MA: Belknap Press, 2014), 5–10.

16. On dispensationalism and support for Israel, see Paul S. Boyer, *When Time Shall Be No More: Prophecy Belief in Modern American Culture* (Cambridge, MA:

Belknap Press, 1994); Timothy P. Weber, *On the Road to Armageddon: How Evangelicals Became Israel's Best Friend* (Grand Rapids, MI: Baker Academic, 2005); Yaakov Ariel, *An Unusual Relationship: Evangelical Christians and Jews* (New York: New York University Press, 2013).

17. The two defining works that reframed American religious pluralism during the postwar period were Will Herberg, *Protestant, Catholic, Jew: An Essay in American Religious Sociology* (New York: Doubleday, 1955), and Robert N. Bellah, "Civil Religion in America," *Daedalus* 96, no. 1 (1967): 1–21. Both recast the role of Jews in American society, but in separate ways. For the differences, see Ronit Y. Stahl, "A Jewish America and a Protestant Civil Religion: Will Herberg, Robert Bellah, and Mid-Twentieth Century American Religion," *Religions* 6, no. 2 (2015): 434–50.

18. For the increasing influence of parachurch organizations in the postwar period, see Robert Wuthnow, *The Restructuring of American Religion: Society and Faith since World War II* (Princeton, NJ: Princeton University Press, 1988), 173–91.

19. Lowell D. Streiker and Gerald S. Strober, *Religion and the New Majority: Billy Graham, Middle America, and the Politics of the 70s* (New York: Association Press, 1972), 80, 39, 61.

20. For a survey of diverse Jewish perspectives on Jewish-Christian dialogue during this period and immediately after, see Frank Talmage, ed., *Disputation and Dialogue: Readings in the Jewish-Christian Encounter* (New York: Ktav Publishing House, 1975).

21. See Marc H. Tanenbaum, "Israel's Hour of Need and the Jewish-Christian Dialogue," *Conservative Judaism* 22, no. 4 (1968): 1–18; Solomon S. Bernards, "Arab-Israel Crisis and the American Christian Response," *Lutheran Quarterly* 20, no. 3 (1968): 260–75.

22. Michael Dumper, *The Politics of Jerusalem since 1967* (New York: Columbia University Press, 1997), 38–52.

23. Michael E. Staub, *Torn at the Roots: The Crisis of Jewish Liberalism in Postwar America* (New York: Columbia University Press, 2002), 48.

24. See Carenen, *Fervent Embrace,* 141–45; Weber, *On the Road to Armageddon,* 179–86.

25. Tanenbaum quoted in Paul L. Montgomery, "A Dialogue of Faiths at Seton Hall," *New York Times,* October 29, 1970, 45.

26. Gerald Strober to Marc Tanenbaum, February 5, 1969, box 21, folder 1, Marc H. Tanenbaum Collection, American Jewish Archives, Cincinnati, OH (hereafter MHT).

27. Strober to Tanenbaum, "Program for the Billy Graham Meeting," June 9, 1969, ibid.

28. Tanenbaum to Billy Graham, June 23, 1969, ibid.

29. Strober to Robert Ferm, June 24, 1969, ibid.

30. Ronald Kronish to AJC, June 1969, ibid. Kronish associated Graham's formal demeanor to that of his crusade rallies—the "Billy Graham of TV and Madison Square Garden"—which did not appeal to most American Jews.

31. Ibid.

32. See Justin Vaïsse, *Neoconservatism: The Biography of a Movement* (Cambridge, MA: Belknap Press, 2010), 63. Vaïsse documents the emerging neoconservative sensibility among many New York intellectuals.

33. For Jewish voting in 1972, see http://www.jta.org/1972/11/09/archive/jewish-vote-triples-for-nixon-jewish-majority-goes-for-mcgovern. In 1968 evangelicals voted for Nixon at a rate of 69 percent, while Jews did so at 17 percent. For evangelicals, see Daniel K. Williams, "Richard Nixon's Religious Right," in *The Right Side of the Sixties,* ed. Laura Jane Gifford and Daniel K. Williams (London: Palgrave Macmillan, 2012), 141–58.

34. Key 73 garnered support from more than 150 denominations and Christian organizations, including mainline Protestant denominations and Catholic dioceses.

35. For background on Key 73, see Yaakov Ariel, *Evangelizing the Chosen People* (Chapel Hill: University of North Carolina Press, 2000), 265–66; David A. Rausch, *Communities in Conflict: Evangelicals and Jews* (Philadelphia: Trinity Press International, 1991), 111–21.

36. Deane A. Kemper, "Another Look Back at Key 73: A Response to Carl Henry," *Reformed Journal* 25, no. 1 (January 1, 1975): 17.

37. On Jews for Jesus, see Yaakov Ariel, "Counterculture and Mission: Jews for Jesus and the Vietnam Era Missionary Campaigns, 1970–1975," *Religion and American Culture* 9, no. 2 (1999): 233–57.

38. Gerald Strober to Marc Tanenbaum, November 5, 1973, box 24, folder 1, MHT.

39. "Statement by Billy Graham," February 28, 1973, ibid. See also Billy Graham, "Billy Graham on Key 73," *Christianity Today,* March 16, 1973, 625.

40. By the time of Graham's statement in 1973, Romans 9–11 had already become a key text in Jewish-Christian relations. It was cited in the Vatican II document *Nostra Aetate* and had received voluminous treatment from theologians.

41. Marc Tanenbaum to Billy Graham, March 1, 1973, box 24, folder 1, MHT.

42. "Press Conference for Rabbi Marc Tanenbaum," transcript, January 23, 1973, box 18, folder 1, MHT.

43. On Graham's denial of dual covenant theology, see the blistering criticism of Tanenbaum and Graham in Rabbi C. J. Teichman, "Gratitude to Billy Graham, Jew Court Uncle Jakeism," letter to the editor, *Jewish Post and Opinion,* March 30, 1973.

44. Marc Tanenbaum to NJCRAC Program Plan, 1973–74, April 20, 1973, box 96, folder 2, MHT.

45. Judith Herschcopf Banki, *Christian Responses to the Yom Kippur War: Implications for Christian-Jewish Relations* (New York: American Jewish Committee, 1974). On the growing affinity between American Jews and evangelicals in the late 1970s, see Carenen, *Fervent Embrace,* 161–88.

46. Billy Graham, draft of speech, September 26, 1977, http://americanjewisharchives.org/media/podcasts/2008/millerAaron.pdf.

47. Aaron Miller, "The (False) Start of Jewish Evangelical Relations," 2008, podcast recording, http://americanjewisharchives.org/catalog/Record/vtls000027625.

48. See Steven P. Miller, *Billy Graham and the Rise of the Republican South* (Philadelphia: University of Pennsylvania Press, 2009), 182–95; Wacker, *America's Pastor,* 212–13.

49. For a history of the religious Right, see Daniel Williams, *God's Own Party: The Making of the Christian Right* (New York: Oxford University Press, 2010).

50. Marguerite Michaels, "Billy Graham: America Is Not God's Only Kingdom," *Parade,* February 1, 1981, 6.

51. "Baptist Leader Criticized for Statement About Jews," *New York Times,* September 18, 1980, A18.

52. Martin Schram, "Jerry Falwell Vows Amity with Israel," *Washington Post,* September 2, 1981, A1, A15. Falwell reportedly said that a Jew "can make more money accidently than you can on purpose."

53. "Olson Gives Statement of Hope Supporting Israel," *Evangelical Beacon,* December 1, 1980, 2.

54. See, for example, Colin Shindler, "Likud and the Christian Dispensationalists: A Symbiotic Relationship," *Israel Studies* 5, no. 1 (2000): 153–82.

55. See, for example, James Warren, "Graham, Nixon Anti-Semitism on Tape," *Chicago Tribune,* March 1, 2002, http://articles.chicagotribune.com/2002-03-01/news/0203010267_1_billy-graham-story-2-minute-gap-president-richard-nixon/2.

5

Subtraction by Addition

The Nixon Administration and the Domestic Politics of Arms Control

Henry R. Maar III

The 1968 presidential election came at one of the most tumultuous times in American history. In 1968 alone, the war in Vietnam claimed the lives of nearly 15,000 soldiers while another 30,000 young men received draft notices every month. The war highlighted the racial and financial disparities that existed in society, as a disproportionate number of poor and black individuals were both drafted and killed. In the streets of Chicago, outrage over the war sparked a police riot during the 1968 Democratic National Convention. As this and other riots sapped the already divided antiwar movement of energy, the presidential race of 1968 lurched forward.

With growing opposition to the war, both major candidates in 1968 were forced to address questions about de-escalation and exit from Vietnam. Vice president and Democratic Party presidential nominee Hubert Humphrey told antiwar crowds that the United States could begin withdrawing from Vietnam toward the end of 1968. Within twenty-four hours, however, both Secretary of State Dean Rusk and President Lyndon Johnson repudiated Humphrey's remarks. Republican nominee Richard Nixon promised an "honorable end to the war in Vietnam." The statement was deliberately vague. In reality, Nixon surreptitiously relayed a message that a better peace deal could be obtained under his administration. With the subsequent collapse of the Paris Peace Accords, the Humphrey campaign was denied the chance to end the war, and the fighting in Vietnam raged on. Although Nixon won the Electoral College vote by a wide margin, he squeaked out victory in the popular vote by less than 1 percent. Nixon would inherit the disastrous war in Vietnam, and with it, a society more divided than at any point since the Civil War a century earlier.[1]

As the incoming Nixon administration searched for both a solution to the Vietnam quagmire and a respite from the war and domestic unrest, the administration embraced détente: the lessening of tensions with the Soviet Union. At its core, détente offered a "mechanism for domestic fortification," as historian Jeremi Suri explains. Détente offered the illusion of a de-escalated Cold War and of an arms race that was under control. Arms control agreements such as the Strategic Arms Limitation Treaty and the Antiballistic Missile Treaty appeared to place limits on nuclear weapons while surrounding arms control in a haze of acronyms and technical jargon.[2]

This essay demonstrates the links between arms control summitry, national security, and domestic politics during the Nixon administration from 1968 to 1974. I argue here that in spite of the pageantry of superpower summit meetings and arms control treaties, the Nixon administration was more concerned with domestic politics than with the arms race. The Nixon administration used these displays to rally public opinion around an embattled administration, suppress peace activism, and create the illusion of a de-escalating Cold War. As a result of its insincere arms control diplomacy, the Nixon administration set the foreground for the arms race of the 1980s.

Vietnam, Arms Control, and the Nixon-Kissinger Grand Design

On the campaign trail in 1968 Nixon pledged that, if elected, he would seek "meaningful arms control agreements," adding that a "dampening of the arms race would provide both resources and time" to address "pressing domestic problems" such as the "age-old problems of hunger, disease and poverty." At the top of the agenda for the Nixon administration, however, was not arms control or these "age-old problems" but extraction from Vietnam. A quick withdrawal would have meant admitting defeat, and Nixon feared being the first president to both lose a war and preside over America's loss of prestige and credibility throughout the world. To ameliorate these concerns, he would pursue a "grand design." As part of this plan, the president rationalized that the phased withdrawal of troops from Vietnam, the end of the draft, and a renewed emphasis on arms control could undercut antiwar fervor and strengthen his political standing. Thus, to extricate the United States from the Vietnam morass, to exploit the recent split in the communist bloc between China and the Soviet Union, and to co-opt the antiwar sentiment, Nixon pursued détente.[3]

To help navigate the rapids of foreign policy, Nixon would rely on his national security adviser, Dr. Henry Kissinger. The head of Harvard's International Seminar and Defense Studies programs, Kissinger was widely regarded as a specialist in defense and European affairs and was an occasional consultant for several government agencies. Nixon and Kissinger, however, were not close allies. It was, as Suri writes, "a marriage of convenience, filled with all the suspicion, hostility, and jealousy that accompanies these dysfunctional alliances."[4]

With Kissinger, Nixon would run White House foreign policy as it pertained to the Soviet Union; all other major positions relevant to foreign policy would be filled with yes-men or those with little experience in the realm of diplomacy. For secretary of state, Nixon nominated William Rogers, the former attorney general from the Eisenhower administration. Rogers, a well-connected Republican lawyer, knew little about foreign relations, making him unlikely to interfere in Nixon and Kissinger's deliberations. Likewise, to lead the Arms Control and Disarmament Agency (ACDA), Nixon appointed Gerard C. Smith. Although Smith had been a special assistant for atomic affairs to Secretary of State John Foster Dulles during the Eisenhower administration, he was appointed to ACDA not because of his knowledge of nuclear weapons but because of his ability to get along with the military. Thus, as Raymond Garthoff observes, Nixon and Kissinger considered Smith "safe and malleable."[5]

When it came to arms control, neither Nixon nor Kissinger thought it was worth pursuing as an end on its own. Although China had recently developed—and tested—a nuclear weapon, and although the growth of the Soviet arsenal placed it nearly on a par with US weaponry, Nixon and Kissinger remained unconcerned about nuclear proliferation. Indeed, while publicly championing the 1969 Nuclear Nonproliferation Treaty, Nixon and Kissinger privately resented it and deliberately made "no efforts" to enforce it. The treaty, like détente itself, was merely a way to placate domestic critics.[6]

A Marriage Forged in Hell: ABMs and MIRVs

Despite Nixon and Kissinger's indifference to arms control, the issue was forced on them as new advances in missile technology had the potential to send the arms race spiraling upward. Multiple independently targetable reentry vehicles, or MIRVs, were the culmination of a decade of enhancements in missile technology. A MIRVed missile allowed multiple miniature warheads on a single missile, with each warhead capable of being both fired separately and aimed at different targets. This technology created several advantages for the United States, including the potential for a first strike. In the event of a nuclear exchange in which the United States launched its missiles first and targeted Soviet missile silos, a first strike could destroy much of the Soviet arsenal and thus limit or entirely negate a retaliation strike.

Proponents of MIRV argued for its necessity to counter another emerging controversial technology: the antiballistic missile (ABM) defense system. Since the *Sputnik* shock of 1957, the United States had been working simultaneously on miniaturizing warheads (culminating in MIRVs) and developing ABM systems. While the US Air Force was at the forefront of MIRV technology, the US Army took the lead on ABMs, experimenting with the Nike antiaircraft missiles in an effort to intercept and destroy incoming warheads. These experiments resulted in the Nike-Zeus ABM prototype by the early 1960s. But in early 1963 Secretary of Defense Robert McNamara canceled the Nike-Zeus ABM, concluding it would be both expensive and incapable of defending against a Soviet threat by the end of the decade.

ABM proponents, however, did not give up. One year later the Soviet Union deployed an ABM system around Moscow, and China tested its first nuclear weapon. Soon the Joint Chiefs of Staff were pressuring McNamara for a new ABM system, the Nike-X. The Nike-X would feature a new generation of advanced radars and computers to track incoming warheads. It also featured two new missiles: a large one dubbed Spartan and a smaller one called Sprint. In theory, the Spartan missiles would be used to intercept warheads before they reentered the earth's atmosphere; any warheads not destroyed by the Spartan missiles would then be destroyed at the last minute by the Sprints. But McNamara canceled the Nike-X as well, once again citing the expense of such a system and its inability to guarantee safety from an attack.[7]

To reconcile defense pressures and the limits of ABM technology, the Johnson administration opted for a compromise: a small deployment that could theoretically prevent an attack from a smaller nuclear arsenal (like China's), with the eventual capability of stopping a larger attack. In 1967, under pressure from Congress, McNamara reluctantly announced plans to deploy the Sentinel ABM system. The Sentinel was a scaled-down ABM based on the concept of Nike-X but consisting of only fifteen to twenty nuclear missiles in ten different locations.[8]

Although ABM systems had strong support in 1967, the political climate had changed by the time Nixon and Kissinger inherited the issue. Amid antiwar fervor, growing distrust of government, and concerns over defense spending, ABMs were in the crosshairs of Congress and were tied to opposition to the Vietnam War in the public realm. Opponents consisted of a diverse coalition of scientists, arms control advocates, peace activists, religious groups, and liberal political organizations. Anti-ABM forces lobbied Congress and informed the public about the issue, which was often perceived as too technical for the common man. Scientists lobbied against ABM systems, testified against them before Congress, conducted private briefings with senators, and mobilized grassroots opposition to ABM deployment with nonprofit organizations. Many of these scientists argued that an expanded ABM program would escalate the arms race. Furthermore, from a practical standpoint, they insisted that ABM systems simply did not work and never would.[9]

As Sentinel ABM construction went forward, public apathy turned into "massive public outcry" and "fear of 'bombs in the backyard,'" as Thomas Halstead reflected in the *Bulletin of the Atomic Scientists.* The development of a Sentinel site within a mile of downtown Seattle outraged residents. Anti-ABM forces there found an unlikely ally in Senator Henry "Scoop" Jackson, a Democrat from Washington State and an advocate of ABM systems. Under pressure from constituents, and with his own reelection campaign just over the horizon, Jackson helped persuade the army to move the Sentinel site from Fort Lawton (which the army promised the city it could use as a park) to Bainbridge Island across Puget Sound. But anti-ABM forces found another unexpected ally in hawkish Congressman Thomas Pelly (R-WA), whose district included Bainbridge Island. Pelly pressured the army to hold hearings on relocating the proposed Sentinel development site outside Washington altogether.[10]

Opposition to ABMs was also fomenting in Chicago. As the army was studying five potential Sentinel sites within the Chicago metropolitan region, five scientists from the Argonne National Laboratory formed the West Suburban Concerned Scientists to rally opposition. The scientists feared that an accident involving the system could devastate the entire region; furthermore, the Chicago metropolitan area would be a prime target in the event of a nuclear exchange. The army, however, chose to ignore public opinion and announced in December 1968 the deployment of Sentinel ABMs in the Chicago suburb of Libertyville. Within a week, local communities began to organize against the deployment of the Sentinels. A letter to the editor of the *Chicago Tribune* described the basing of a missile site in a Chicago suburb as "sickening" and asked, "Can we people of America do nothing to prevent the army from making decisions without regard for the average citizen?" In January 1969 the Northern Illinois Citizens against Anti-Ballistic Missiles filed a lawsuit in federal court seeking to block construction of the Sentinel site. Shortly thereafter, anti-ABM rallies were held, and more Chicago neighborhoods passed resolutions opposing the Sentinel.[11]

But, as historian Ernest Yanarella observes, grassroots organizing against the Sentinel was "perhaps most formidable and well organized" in Boston. In the surrounding communities of North Andover and Reading, the US Army had already started constructing Sentinel sites. The New England Citizens Committee on ABM was quickly formed to "oppose the deployment of the Sentinel system, and in particular its location in the greater Boston area." In the Reading High School auditorium, a public hearing on Sentinel construction "turned out to be less a staid public information event than an angry confrontation between fifteen hundred citizens and scientists and a handful of Army public relations specialists," writes historian Kelly Moore. For the army, the meeting was nothing short of "a public relations disaster."[12]

ABM opposition was not limited to Seattle, Chicago, and Boston; it was front-page news in Los Angeles, Denver, Detroit, and Honolulu as well. In communities across the nation, the army faced fierce opposition from residents who challenged the construction of Sentinel sites. "In order to pull the teeth of public criticism," Kissinger reflected, Nixon asked his deputy secretary of defense, David Packard, to chair an interagency review of the ABM program. Three days later, Secretary of Defense Melvin Laird ordered a halt to the Sentinel program, before completion of the review scheduled for the end of February.[13]

In the meantime, prominent Democratic senators attacked the Sentinel program. Massachusetts senator Edward Kennedy charged that the Nixon administration was only using the ABM review "to mollify critics." Former Minnesota senator Hubert Humphrey urged a halt to ABM deployment and proposed that the administration "begin as expeditiously as possible negotiation with the Soviet Union on the possible reduction of offensive and defensive strategic systems." Senator Albert Gore Sr.'s disarmament subcommittee heard testimony almost exclusively from opponents of the ABM. Congressional pressure to stop the ABM program was mounting.[14]

On March 14, 1969, Nixon announced that, after a "long study of all the options," his administration was going forward with a new ABM system: Safeguard. Unlike Sentinel, Safeguard would not be deployed near metropolitan communities; it would be located on twelve intercontinental ballistic missile (ICBM) sites, and the weapons would be protected with a "thick" defense that could withstand even a Soviet attack. Unannounced to the public, the Nixon administration was supporting an ABM system as a bargaining chip in the forthcoming arms control talks with the Soviets. Safeguard was also a way of co-opting anti-ABM sentiment. By moving ABMs to missile fields and away from the public, the administration could subvert the driving force behind domestic opposition to ABM construction.[15]

But the great ABM debate did not go away. With congressional opposition mounting against the Safeguard system, its proponents countered with their own lobbying organizations, the most prominent of which was the Committee to Maintain a Prudent Defense Policy. Though small, the committee had some big names from the Democratic Party establishment behind it. It was co-organized by Dean Acheson, Truman's secretary of state, and Paul Nitze, an illustrious diplomat who authored National

Security Council Report 68, which shaped America's containment strategy throughout the Cold War until the Nixon administration's embrace of détente. The committee also relied on the services of the lesser known Albert Wohlstetter, whose 1958 RAND study "The Delicate Balance of Terror" had sounded the alarm that the doctrine of mutual assured destruction was not enough to prevent nuclear war. Three of Wohlstetter's graduate students—Peter Wilson, Paul Wolfowitz, and Richard Perle—as well as Edward Luttwak, a classmate of Perle's at the London School of Economics, also worked with the committee. These men quickly became the primary advocates for Nixon's Safeguard ABM.[16]

When the Safeguard issue went to the Senate, it found its most ardent champion in Henry Jackson. Jackson had served in the Senate since 1953 and in the House of Representatives for twelve years prior to that. Although Jackson had a strong record on civil rights and labor, he was a hawk on foreign policy, earning him the nickname "the senator from Boeing." Even though Jackson had assisted anti-ABM efforts in Seattle, he still firmly believed in mutual assured destruction and viewed ABMs as a measure of security for the United States. Jackson distrusted the Soviet Union and saw the Cold War as a conflict in which the United States must prevail. Safeguard, Jackson believed, could pressure the Soviet Union into matching the United States in an arms race, leading to the bankrupting and eventual collapse of the Soviet system.[17]

The young graduate students Perle and Wolfowitz worked closely with Jackson on the ABM debate. Perle served directly on Jackson's staff, and Wolfowitz helped create charts demonstrating Soviet strength, which Jackson used to counter opposition in the Senate. Jackson had an aura surrounding him. As Wolfowitz recounted, when Jackson spoke on defense issues, it was "with such authority that . . . few members of the Senate were comfortable challenging him." Jackson understood how to apply the right amount of pressure on his colleagues and, equally important, when to apply such pressure. As a result of Jackson's efforts, Safeguard passed the Senate by one vote.[18]

In the shadow of the ABM quarrels, however, advances in MIRV technology continued apace. With the public and Congress focused on ABM systems, MIRVs quietly changed the dynamics of the entire arms race. *New York Times* journalist Robert Kleiman warned repeatedly that MIRVs were creating an arms race "far more difficult to control than the race in missile defenses which the U.S. has been trying to head off." Following Kleiman's lead, the *New York Times* editorialized in favor of delaying MIRV tests, prognosticating a foreboding future in the "MIRV era." Editorials against MIRV tests soon appeared in the *Washington Post,* the *Wall Street Journal,* and several other major national newspapers.[19]

The MIRV tests, however, went forward, leaving the *Times* to editorialize that "future generations" would "undoubtedly . . . look back with disbelief at the way the United States again has invented, publicized and tested a deadly new weapon, which, instead of improving American security, creates an added threat to it by putting the Soviet Union under pressure to produce the same weapon and aim it at the United States." In the *Bulletin of the Atomic Scientists,* David Ingles lamented that MIRVs were altering the course of the arms race from one that was tapering off to one that was spiraling "madly upward."[20]

The controversy over ABM and MIRV technology would plague the first year of the Nixon administration. According to historian Gregg Herken, because President Nixon was "notoriously uninterested in the technical details of arms control and modern weaponry," decisions about MIRV technology were made by national security adviser Kissinger. Although Kissinger wrote an influential book in 1957 entitled *Nuclear Weapons and Foreign Policy,* he knew "little about the complex technical issues of negotiating and verifying a nuclear arms ban," writes Seymour Hersh. Paul Nitze was highly critical of Kissinger's book and later said he hoped Kissinger was "listening to advisors more knowledgeable."[21]

To augment his own knowledge of nuclear weapons, Kissinger appointed a team composed of members of the President's Science Advisory Council headed by Paul Doty. A biochemist by training, Doty had carved out a second career as an expert on nuclear affairs dating back to his involvement with the Manhattan Project as a graduate student. In the Nixon administration, Doty headed what was informally called the "Doty group." Members of the group had regular meetings with Kissinger and made the implications of MIRV technology and arms control their primary concern.[22]

The development of MIRVs also faced internal opposition from ACDA and its director, Gerard Smith. As the second director in ACDA's history, Smith had inherited an agency that was "under funded, under staffed, and under represented in the Washington bureaucracy." A former aide of Smith's told Seymour Hersh that Nixon and Kissinger "probably figured ACDA was a throw-away job," and "they thought [Smith would] be easily managed." But Smith soon began to exert his independence, urging President Nixon to drop the demands for linkage and open arms control talks with the Soviets. In a June 1969 letter to Secretary of State Rogers, Smith pressed for a ban on MIRVs, arguing, "in the long run it is not in U.S. interests to see MIRVs enter U.S. and Soviet arsenals. Certainly it will bring increased instability." Nixon quickly became very distrustful of Smith.[23]

With the announcement of the opening of the Strategic Arms Limitation Talks (SALT), public opposition to MIRV technology reached its zenith. In a letter to the editor of the *New York Times,* Jay Orear, a professor of physics from Cornell, expressed the fear that unless the arms race was frozen, the world would lose its "best and perhaps last chance to halt a very dangerous and expensive arms race based on new technology." H. Stuart Hughes, chairman of the leading antinuclear organization SANE, wrote to Nixon and implored him to start negotiations with the Soviets to "reverse the arms race at a point when it threatens to multiply—perhaps beyond control—the number of deliverable warheads possessed by the United States and the Soviet Union." SANE urged both sides to agree to a bilateral moratorium "to prevent a calamitous escalation of the arms race."[24]

Political opposition was mounting, too. From the standpoint of SANE, the Senate was the "last line of defense against the Nixon Administration's plan to deploy MIRV's and expand the ABM system." SANE would find its anti-MIRV champion in Senator Edward Brooke (R-MA), the first African American popularly elected to the Senate. Brooke was a leading opponent of the Safeguard ABM system but became even more outspoken against MIRVs. He was convinced that the United States "should take the lead in proposing a halt to the arms race," for absent such a halt, "new technology would propel the arms race to new and infinite danger." In May 1969 Brooke appealed to Kissinger, warning that if MIRV tests went forward, "the genie would be out of the bottle."[25]

When the tests continued, Brooke, with bipartisan support from thirty-nine other senators, sponsored a resolution calling for a moratorium on future MIRV tests. But because some senators feared that a MIRV debate would divert attention from the ABM debate, the resolution sat in Senator Gore's subcommittee for months. Brooke pressed on. In October 1969 he called for a complete missile test ban, warning that MIRVs threatened "to erode one of the basic barriers to nuclear war"—the doctrine of mutual assured destruction—thus increasing the chances of a nuclear catastrophe.[26]

In March 1970, in testimony before the Senate Foreign Relations Committee, Secretary of the Air Force Robert Seamans accidentally announced that US nuclear forces would be MIRVed in June (his prepared testimony had apparently "slipped through" the Pentagon). Shortly thereafter, Brooke's resolution from the previous fall was finally picked up and adopted by the Senate Foreign Relations Committee, with broadened language to "urge a mutual suspension of deployment of all strategic weapons, offensive and defensive." Brooke seemed pleased by the changes, noting that the new language "offers clear support for a concerted effort to head off deployment of MIRV and other new strategic weapons." The resolution passed the Senate in April by a wide margin.[27]

Brooke continued to seek restraints on MIRV missiles. In August 1970 he introduced two amendments to a military procurement bill. The first asked the Pentagon to develop only a single warhead for the Minuteman III and Poseidon missiles to ensure that if MIRVs were banned during the SALT negotiations, it would not result in a "de facto reduction in U.S. strategic forces." The second amendment sought to limit the accuracy of MIRV warheads and, therefore, prohibit them from becoming potential first-strike weapons. Brooke's first amendment was adopted by a voice vote, but he withdrew the second amendment after failing to garner enough support. Although the Senate did not prohibit the accuracy of future MIRV warheads, it was now formally on the record as supporting a moratorium on MIRVs and ABM systems.[28]

Internally, the Doty group too expressed considerable opposition to the rush to develop MIRV missiles. In a memo dated June 2, 1969, Doty group members Jack Ruina and George Rathjens warned Kissinger that the strategic balance was in jeopardy primarily due to "MIRV development by the United States and possible MIRV development by the Soviet Union," bringing the arms race to the "point of no return." If the testing of MIRVs continued for even a few more weeks, they warned, "the United States might develop the weapon's accuracy to such a point that the Soviet Union could see it as a first-strike weapon." If the United States were capable of creating first-strike weapons, so was the Soviet Union, Ruina and Rathjens explained. If this happened, it would leave the United States "in the position of having its Minuteman land-based force—spread across the Western plains—under threat of an accurate Soviet MIRV attack."[29]

Despite opposition in the Senate and in the press, as well the Doty group's attempts to sway Kissinger against MIRVs, the system survived. The Nixon administration, like its predecessor, did not see MIRVs as an impediment to arms limitation talks. While the Doty group was never formally dissolved, it "simply faded out of existence," according to historian Ted Greenwood, and members believed that Kissinger had simply used them to "impart a false aura over the administration's deliberations on the ABM and MIRV." Although some officials in the State Department were eager for a showdown over MIRV, Secretary of State Rogers was not, believing that this was an issue for the Department of Defense, not State. ACDA too opposed the testing of MIRVs, although it shied away from a fight with the military. MIRV opponents were left hoping for a miracle—that the Soviets would press for a ban at the forthcoming SALT negotiations.[30]

The Illusion of Arms Control: SALT I

Negotiations finally commenced in Helsinki, Finland, in November 1969. From the outset, however, there were serious conflicts between Nixon's view of the talks and the negotiating team's view of them. Whereas the negotiating team did not want to link the talks to any outside proposals, Nixon emphatically wanted a linkage with other issues such as Vietnam. ACDA head Gerard Smith had been appointed chief negotiator, but Nixon pleaded with Paul Nitze to take a position on the SALT team and report any adverse developments directly to him. Nitze, however, agreed to join the SALT delegation only "as a member of Gerry Smith's team and not as someone reporting to someone else."[31]

With Nitze refusing to serve as Nixon's liaison on SALT, the administration had to find alternative means to maintain control over foreign policy and the arms control negotiations. Kissinger established a Verification Panel early in the SALT negotiations wherein senior diplomats representing the State Department, ACDA, Defense Department, Joint Chiefs of Staff, and attorney general met to discuss the issues surrounding treaty verification. Under Kissinger's control, however, the panel soon turned into the only senior-level body with an understanding of the SALT negotiations outside of the White House's National Security Council.[32]

Paralleling the establishment of the Verification Panel, President Nixon initiated back-channel negotiations with Soviet prime minister Alexei Kosygin, supplemented by secret meetings between Kissinger and Soviet ambassador Anatoly Dobrynin. These secretive measures cut both Secretary of State Rogers and the SALT bargaining team out of high-level verification discussions. Instead of relying on more competent American translators, Nixon relied on Soviet translators, eliminating the possibility that an American translator's notes could be shared with the other delegates. Less precise notes of discussions were taken by Kissinger's staff, but even these were not shared outside the White House. The result of this secrecy was the absence of any precise record of these high-level conversations, and as Nitze explained, both the SALT delegation and the Nixon White House were deprived of the expertise that could "fine-comb the relevant detail[s]."[33]

The SALT I negotiations consumed most of Nixon's first term in office. The two delegations quarreled over the classification of weapons, over language, and whether an agreement would include both offensive weapons (ICBMs) and defensive weapons (ABMs). By December 1970, after what the US delegation viewed as major concessions on its part, the talks appeared to be deadlocked, with the next meeting not scheduled until March 1971. But by then, an agreement was already being hammered out in private. In January 1971 Nixon and Kissinger seized the opportunity to jump in and "rescue" SALT. In secret back-channel negotiations between Kissinger and Dobrynin, Kissinger made it clear that Nixon was willing to settle for an ABM agreement, provided the negotiating teams continue to work on offensive limitations and a weapons freeze until a formal agreement could be reached. If Dobrynin agreed to these basics, Kissinger proposed that the two sides exchange letters, leaving the negotiators in Vienna to implement the deal.[34]

Although the Soviets proposed a limited ABM deployment around both Washington, DC, and Moscow, Nixon feared an ABM-only agreement would never pass Congress. A frustrated Nixon instructed Kissinger, "Just make any kind of damn deal. You know it doesn't make a god damn bit of difference. We're going to settle it anyway. Just drive the hardest deal you can." When Kissinger suggested that the administration might have to concede on a capital deployment, Nixon asked, "What about Scoop Jackson?" Kissinger bluntly replied, "He's only a Senator."[35]

As the negotiations resumed in Vienna, a *New York Times* editorial publicly criticized the Nixon administration, calling its strategy of seeking both an offensive weapons freeze and an ABM agreement "obstinate." Unconcerned, Nixon told Kissinger the real problem was that he doubted this "SALT thing" was "going to be that important." "I think it's basically what I'm placating the critics with," Nixon privately confessed. Far more important to Nixon than the substance of the agreement was the political theater of a summit meeting in Moscow—the first since Franklin D. Roosevelt had met with Joseph Stalin and Winston Churchill at Yalta during World War II. As Kissinger explained to Nixon, "The advantage of a summit, even if it gets a sort-of half-baked SALT agreement . . . [is] it would defuse people. They can't very well attack their President when he's getting ready for a summit meeting. . . . And that would get us a few months of . . . quiet around here."[36]

For Nixon, domestic politics was always at the forefront when it came to the SALT negotiations. In his private recordings, Nixon confided that the agreement "wasn't worth a damn" and called the negotiations "a bunch of shit." But with the pending Vietnam Veterans against the War rally producing headlines, Nixon confessed, "We could use something like this at this time."[37] American audiences would be susceptible to any agreement, he explained to Kissinger, "because the American people are so peace-loving, they think agreements solve everything." Therefore, if the administration could get an agreement for "political reasons" and carry the "peace issue" in 1972, it could "survive" the election and thereafter "lay the facts out before the American people and go all out . . . on defense."[38]

For these reasons, Nixon privately told deputy national security adviser Al Haig and presidential assistant Bob Haldeman that the SALT agreement was "the most important goddamn thing. It's more important than whether we have eternal aid to Vietnam, or combat troops, or anything else." Nixon's real worry was not the terms of the agreement but the timing. If he announced a SALT agreement at the wrong time, he would "confuse the hell" out of the American people, who viewed SALT as "not . . . directly related enough to Vietnam." But if he could secure a summit, it "would be enough," Nixon explained, because "people would think at the summit, you might talk about Vietnam." Haldeman responded, "A summit—a summit—people understand a summit. . . . People don't understand SALT." Nixon concurred, saying, "SALT is way over their heads. They haven't the slightest idea what SALT is. It's too goddamned complicated."[39]

Privately, Nixon and Kissinger worried that the Soviets would only agree to an ABM treaty, which would not pass the Senate. If the treaty failed in Congress, SALT was "dead. Absolutely dead," Nixon told Kissinger. Although the Soviets had been "tough customers," Kissinger was confident that a deal could be had, even threatening to cut off back-channel negotiations with Ambassador Dobrynin if they couldn't "settle a simple matter like a SALT exchange of letters."[40]

On May 20, 1971, President Nixon announced a "breakthrough" in the talks. Through negotiations conducted at the highest level, the two sides had reached an agreement to limit ABM systems, as well as "certain measures with respect to the limitation of offensive weapons." The announcement received near unanimous praise from both Congress and the public. Even SANE expressed cautious optimism about the pending agreement.[41] The use of private back channels to conduct negotiations led to problems, however. Lead SALT negotiator Smith and Secretary of State Rogers had been kept in the dark about the agreement until the day before the announced "breakthrough." This secrecy and lack of oversight resulted in Kissinger's agreeing to a freeze on ICBMs but not on submarine-launched ballistic missiles (SLBMs). Since the United States was not in a position to create new SLBMs, the Soviets were free to continue to build them during the five-year Interim Agreement—amounting to a major unilateral concession. This concession, along with questions over how to define a "heavy" missile, had to be worked out by the bargaining teams and would delay the onset of an agreement.[42]

On May 26, 1972, Nixon signed the Interim Agreement (SALT I) and the ABM Treaty in Moscow. The ABM Treaty limited both the United States and the Soviet Union to just two ABM deployments—one around the capital and the other to protect a missile field. In effect, the ABM Treaty prohibited the expansion of ABM systems on both sides. Unlike the ABM Treaty, however, SALT I was an agreement of finite duration. The five-year Interim Agreement froze US ICBMs at 1,054 and

Soviet ICBMs at 1,618. Under the agreement, the United States would be limited to 44 nuclear submarines and 710 SLBMs, while the Soviets were limited to 62 nuclear submarines and 950 SLBMs.[43]

On the surface, SALT I appeared to give the Soviets a major advantage in the arms race, providing them a quantitative edge in terms of both ICBMs and SLBMs. But as historian Anne Cahn explains, to obtain the numbers agreed to under SALT I, the Soviets were required to "deactivate 210 old, pre-1964 ballistic missiles, and the United States 54." The SALT I agreement also permitted the United States to keep nearly three times as many long-range bombers, in addition to thousands of missiles deployed in Europe. With American advantages in MIRV technology, US warheads were also on pace to outnumber their Soviet counterparts four to one by the time SALT I expired in 1977. "What the SALT I Treaty in effect did was to give the Soviets a numerical advantage in missiles, which was offset by the American technological and numerical lead in warheads," Cahn concludes.[44]

From the outset, the Nixon administration knew it faced "a critical problem in terms of avoiding a massive right-wing revolt on the SALT agreement," as Nixon wrote to Haig. "The deal we are making is in our best interests, but for a very practical reason that the right-wing will never understand—that we simply can't get from the Congress the additional funds needed to continue the arms race with the Soviet [Union] in either offensive or defensive arms." Nixon instructed Haig to head a small team that would "pick-off Senators and very important [right-wing] opinion makers . . . to mute their criticism when it comes in from Moscow."[45]

Nixon also instructed Haig's team to "have a talk with [Vice President Spiro] Agnew to get him on board" and to persuade prominent theoretical physicist Edward Teller to lobby on behalf of the administration. Haig's team was to approach its task in a "very hard-headed way," emphasizing that "the president is not being taken in and the military totally supports what we are doing." But the "most convincing argument" Haig could make to these individuals was "that the President is determined that we must go forward at the fastest pace possible with ULEs [undersea long-range missile systems], MIRV, B-1, and any missile system not covered by the agreement." This argument would help sell the agreement to the "more sensible hawks," but only if it could be done on "an individual basis before they get the announcement from Moscow and make up their minds and dig in against us." It was "no comfort" to Nixon that the agreement would receive praise from liberals, who would never support the administration. The hawks, Nixon concluded, were his "hard-core," and the administration "must do everything that we can to keep them from jumping ship."[46]

The most outspoken and important critic of both the ABM Treaty and SALT I was Senator Henry Jackson. Jackson attacked the ABM Treaty, claiming it would limit the United States' ability to stop a crippling Soviet first strike. Given his strong distrust of the Soviets, Jackson believed they had agreed to the treaty not out of a desire to maintain the threat of mutual assured destruction but to "constrain a program in which the United States enjoyed a technological advantage." Jackson's public criticisms of the ABM Treaty aside, he joined the majority in the Senate, which voted eighty-eight to two to approve it.[47]

On the heels of the ABM Treaty, Senator Jackson sought to amend SALT I so that all future arms control treaties with the Soviets would be based on numerical equality or "essential equivalence." Jackson's amendment was not run by either the State Department or ACDA, but it had the support of Senate Republicans. In private assurances, the Nixon administration surprisingly supported Jackson's amendment, even though, as Cahn writes, it was "a direct repudiation of the just-negotiated treaty." The Nixon administration was still indebted to Jackson for his support of the Safeguard ABM and its Vietnam policies. If conceding to Jackson's amendment would get his support for SALT I, then politically, it made good sense.[48]

But the administration soon came to regret appeasing Jackson. Kissinger later confessed that he had been so preoccupied with Vietnam that the implications of Jackson's amendment did not register with him. Attempting to downplay the significance of the amendment, Nixon's deputy press secretary Gerald Warren called it "consistent with our undertakings in Moscow." The equality amendment, however, was not the only concession the Nixon administration made to Jackson. A year later, Jackson would pressure Nixon for a purge of both ACDA and the SALT I negotiating team. Gerard Smith and 14 senior members of ACDA were ousted, and 50 of its 230 employees were let go; in addition, one-third of ACDA's budget was cut. ACDA's influence on arms control was severely diminished—by intent. Included in the SALT I purge was Raymond

Garthoff, a highly regarded State Department diplomat who was fluent in Russian. "Jackson and the hardliners knew what they were doing," Garthoff reflected in his memoirs: weakening the arms control establishment and making it not just harder but "ultimately impossible" for Henry Kissinger to "maneuver between hardline and softline alternatives."[49]

The ABM Treaty and SALT I were signed by both parties on October 3, 1972. Although Nixon called the agreements a "first step," SALT I had some serious if not fatal flaws. With no restrictions on MIRVs and Jackson's insistence on equality, the two sides could, in effect, build up their warheads. The absence of a MIRV ban was no accident. As Garthoff elaborates, the MIRV ban proposals Kissinger had given to the SALT negotiators were designed to fail, asking the Soviets for terms they would never agree to (such as on-site inspections). "It was almost as if there existed a silent conspiracy to make it look as though we were striving for a MIRV ban when in fact neither side was," Smith remembered. "Agreement on MIRVs," concludes Greenwood, "was not something that was barely missed at SALT I or that just kept eluding negotiators. Neither side really wanted such an agreement and neither side really tried to get one."[50]

Although the United States did not see an advantage in a MIRV ban, it was only a matter of time before the Soviets, with their larger ICBMs, developed the technology. Intelligence estimates pointed to Soviet MIRV acquisition by the mid-1970s, thus pushing the MIRV problem to a later date. But by mid-August 1973, Secretary of Defense James Schlesinger announced that the Soviets had successfully tested two MIRV rockets. The chances of controlling MIRV technology in the current arms limitation talks had "deteriorated sadly," Schlesinger told reporters. Although some in the State Department and ACDA opposed both MIRVing the warheads and testing them, they lacked the political power to push for a ban. Outside of ACDA circles and in the public realm, MIRV technology was never as much of a concern as ABM systems. In contrast to the "bitter fight over ABM," opposition to MIRV amounted to nothing more than "a minor skirmish."[51]

Publicly, Kissinger would express regret over not containing MIRVs. But this public regret, however sincere, was misleading, as Kissinger knew that a MIRV ban would severely affect the Pentagon and deny a national security advantage. With Soviet ICBMs having caught up and eclipsed US numbers by 1973, Kissinger viewed SALT I not as a means of controlling the nuclear arms race but as a way of allowing the United States to strengthen its strategic forces amidst congressional opposition and antiwar fervor.[52]

Following the conclusion of SALT I, détente appeared to be in full bloom, with President Nixon and Soviet general secretary Leonid Brezhnev holding summits and reaching agreements in what seemed to be an annual ritual. In June 1973 the two sides met for a week in Washington, DC, producing the Agreement for the Prevention of Nuclear War. They met again in July 1974 in Moscow, where they signed the Threshold Test Ban Treaty, limiting the size of underground nuclear explosives that both parties could test.

That final summit meeting, however, was marred by a political scandal that would sink the Nixon administration. Two weeks after the signing of SALT I, five men broke into Democratic Party headquarters at the Watergate office complex in Washington, DC. An FBI investigation into the break-in revealed that cash found on the burglars was linked to a slush fund for the Committee for the Re-election of the President. A congressional investigation followed and uncovered secret recordings made by Nixon. After a bitter court battle, the president was forced to turn over the tapes, which revealed that he had been complicit in the cover-up of the Watergate burglaries. Under mounting political pressure and the threat of impeachment, Nixon was forced to resign. In the wake of the largest political scandal of the twentieth century, Vice President Gerald Ford assumed the presidency, with the weight of a pending arms control treaty and US-Soviet détente resting on his shoulders.

Concluding Thoughts

Domestic politics, interest groups, and lobbying play a profound role in even the most sensitive national security issues. A close examination of the politics of arms control in the early 1970s demonstrates the illusions of détente and superpower summitry. Indeed, the decision to pursue arms control and détente for political purposes, with no concern for the consequences of MIRV technology, allowed the arms race to continue into the next decade unabated. The political battles over arms control unleashed the forces that would guide US nuclear diplomacy in the early years of the Reagan era. By the end of the 1970s, the same forces that had lobbied against the ABM Treaty and advocated MIRVs now claimed that the United States was suffering from a "window of vulnerability," necessitating the modernization of American nuclear forces. A new wave of nuclear fear would grip the globe, awakening the peace movement from its decade-long slumber and, subsequently, setting off a new battle in the realm of domestic politics and national security.

Notes

1. Walter LaFeber, *The Deadly Bet: LBJ, Vietnam, and the 1968 Election* (Lanham, MD: Rowman and Littlefield, 2005), 131–33; Larry Berman, *No Peace, No Honor: Nixon, Kissinger, and Betrayal in Vietnam* (New York: Free Press, 2001), 32–35.

2. Jeremi Suri, *Power and Protest: Global Revolution and the Rise of Détente* (Cambridge, MA: Harvard University Press, 2003), 213.

3. Don Irwin, "Nixon Pledges to Seek Arms Curbs, Guard Nation's Strength," *Los Angeles Times,* October 27, 1968, A1; Robert B. Semple Jr., "Nixon Vows Effort to Seek Arms Curb; Stand Seen Eased," *New York Times,* October 27, 1968, 1, 72.

4. Jeremi Suri, *Henry Kissinger and the American Century* (Cambridge, MA: Belknap Press, 2007), 202.

5. R. W. Apple Jr., "Kissinger Named a Key Nixon Aide in Defense Policy," *New York Times,* December 3, 1968, 1; Gerard C. Smith, *Disarming Diplomat: The Memoirs of Gerard C. Smith, Arms Control Negotiator* (Lanham, MD: Madison Books, 1996), 148–49, 164–65; Raymond L. Garthoff, *Détente and Confrontation: American-Soviet Relations from Nixon to Reagan,* rev. ed. (Washington, DC: Brookings Institution Press, 1994), 161; Seymour M. Hersh, *The Price of Power: Kissinger in the Nixon White House* (New York: Summit Books, 1983), 161.

6. Garthoff, *Détente and Confrontation,* 148; Francis J. Gavin, *Nuclear Statecraft: History and Strategy in America's Atomic Age* (Ithaca, NY: Cornell University Press, 2012), 104–5.

7. Richard Smoke, *National Security and the Nuclear Dilemma: An Introduction to the American Experience in the Cold War,* 3rd ed. (New York: McGraw-Hill, 1993), 116–17.

8. Henry A. Kissinger, *White House Years* (Boston: Little, Brown, 1979), 204–5.

9. Paul H. Nitze with Ann M. Smith and Steven L. Rearden, *From Hiroshima to Glasnost: At the Center of Decision—A Memoir* (New York: Grove Weidenfeld, 1989), 294; Thomas A. Halstead, "Lobbying against the ABM, 1967–1970," *Bulletin of the Atomic Scientists* 27, no. 4 (April 1971): 23–28; "A Numb Society: The Real Threat," *SANE World,* June 1969, 1.

10. Ernest J. Yanarella, *The Missile Defense Controversy: Technology in Search of a Mission,* rev. and updated ed. (Lexington: University Press of Kentucky, 2002), 147; Halstead, "Lobbying against the ABM," 26.

11. "Chicago Area Missile Site Is Protested," *Chicago Tribune,* November 25, 1968, F3; E. N. K., "Opposes ABM," *Chicago Tribune,* December 10, 1969, 12; "Citizen Groups Files Suit to Bar Missiles," *Chicago Tribune,* January 18, 1969, 12.

12. Yanarella, *Missile Defense Controversy,* 147; Kelly Moore, *Disrupting Science: Social Movements, American Scientists, and the Politics of the Military, 1945–1975* (Princeton, NJ: Princeton University Press, 2008), 136; Halstead, "Lobbying against the ABM"; "Committee Is Started to Fight ABM System," *Harvard Crimson,* February 9, 1969, http://www.thecrimson.com/article/1969/2/10/committee-is-started-to-fight-abm.

13. Kissinger, *White House Years,* 206–7.

14. Ibid.

15. Robert B. Semple Jr., "Nixon for Limited Missile Plan to Protect U.S. Nuclear Forces," *New York Times,* March 15, 1969, 1, 17; Richard Nixon, *RN: The Memoirs of Richard Nixon* (New York: Grosset and Dunlap, 1978), 416.

16. Jacob Heilbrunn, *They Knew They Were Right: The Rise of the Neocons* (New York: Doubleday, 2008), 121; Desmond Ball, *Politics and Force Levels: The Strategic Missile Program of the Kennedy Administration* (Berkeley: University of California Press, 1981), 39–40.

17. Robert G. Kaufman, *Henry M. Jackson: A Life in Politics* (Seattle: University of Washington Press, 2000), 248, 253.

18. Wolfowitz quoted in ibid., 211.

19. Robert Kleiman, "MIRV and the Offensive Missile Race," *New York Times,* October 9, 1967, 46; Robert Kleiman, "MIRV's First Test and the Missile Freeze," *New York Times,* August 5, 1968, 38; "Delay the MIRV Tests," *New York Times,* August 5, 1968, 38.

20. John Noble Wilford, "A Fateful Step in the Arms Race," *New York Times,* August 18, 1968, E12; David R. Ingles, "Conservative Judgments and Missile Madness," *Bulletin of the Atomic Scientists* 24, no. 5 (May 1968): 6.

21. John W. Finney, "Missile Testing Divides U.S. Aides," *New York Times,* May 22, 1969, 11; Gregg Herken *Cardinal Choices: Presidential Science Advising from the Atomic Bomb to SDI* (Stanford, CA: Stanford University Press, 2000), 167–71; Hersh, *Price of Power,* 147; Nitze, *From Hiroshima to Glasnost,* 198.

22. Biographical information on Paul Doty obtained from his Harvard website: http://belfercenter.ksg.harvard.edu/experts/134/paul_doty.html.

23. Smith, *Disarming Diplomat,* 148–49, 164–65; Hersh, *Price of Power,* 161.

24. "Moratorium on MIRV," *New York Times,* June 12, 1969, 46; "SANE Urges Start of Missile Talks," *SANE World,* February 1969, 2; "MIRV Moratorium Urged," *SANE World,* June 1969, 1; "Senate in Showdown to Curb Arms Race," *SANE World,* April 1970, 1. SANE's call was echoed by the Central Conference of American Rabbis; see "Rabbis Urge Curb on Arms Project," *New York Times,* June 18, 1969, 54.

25. "Senate in Showdown to Curb Arms Race," *SANE World,* April 1970, 1; Edward W. Brooke, *Bridging the Divide: My Life* (New Brunswick, NJ: Rutgers University Press, 2007), 204–5.

26. Brooke, *Bridging the Divide,* 204–5; John Henry Cutler, *Ed Brooke: Biography of a Senator* (New York: Bobbs-Merrill, 1972), 354.

27. Brooke, *Bridging the Divide,* 204–5; Cutler, *Ed Brooke,* 355; Chalmers M. Roberts, "Hill Unit Asks A-Freeze by U.S., Russia," *Washington Post,* March 21, 1970, A1, A7.

28. Cutler, *Ed Brooke,* 356–57.

29. "MIRV Tests Opposed," *New York Times,* June 16, 1969, 94; Herken, *Cardinal Choices,* 171; "Memo: Jack Ruina and George Rathjens to Henry Kissinger, June 2, 1969," in Herken, *Cardinal Choices,* 247; Hersh, *Price of Power,* 151–52.

30. Herken, *Cardinal Choices,* 173–74; Ted Greenwood, *Making the MIRV: A Study of Defense Decision Making* (Cambridge, MA: Ballinger Publishing Company, 1975), 123.

31. Nitze, *From Hiroshima to Glasnost,* 299.

32. Hersh, *Price of Power,* 147–48

33. Nitze, *From Hiroshima to Glasnost,* 304.

34. Memorandum of conversation between Henry A. Kissinger and Anatoly F. Dobrynin, January 9, 1971, in *Foreign Relations of the United States, 1969–1976,* vol. 32, *SALT I,* ed. Erin R. Mahan (Washington, DC: US Government Printing Office, 2010), 385–86 (hereafter cited as *FRUS*).

35. Conversation between Richard Nixon and Henry Kissinger, March 12, 1971, in *The Nixon Tapes, 1971–1972,* ed. Douglas Brinkley and Luke A. Nichter (New York: Houghton Mifflin Harcourt, 2014), 39–42.

36. Conversation between Richard Nixon and Henry Kissinger, March 16, 1971, ibid., 42–45.

37. Conversation among Richard Nixon, Bob Haldeman, and Henry Kissinger, April 23, 1971, ibid., 99.

38. Conversation among Richard Nixon, Bob Haldeman, and Henry Kissinger, April 17, 1971, ibid., 76.

39. Conversation among President Nixon, his deputy national security adviser (Haig), and the assistant to the president (Haldeman), May 6, 1971, in *FRUS,* 32:469, 471.

40. Conversation between Richard Nixon and Henry Kissinger, April 14, 1971, in *Nixon Tapes,* 67–68.

41. Max Frankel, "Compromise Set: Scope and Shape of Possible Nuclear Accord Defined," *New York Times,* May 21, 1972, 1–2; Raymond L. Garthoff, "Negotiating SALT," *Wilson Quarterly* 1, no. 5 (Autumn 1977): 80; "One and a Half Cheers for SALT!" *SANE World,* May 1972, 1.

42. Terry Terriff, *The Nixon Administration and the Making of U.S. Nuclear Strategy* (Ithaca NY: Cornell University Press, 1995), 30; Garthoff, *Détente and Confrontation,* 534–41.

43. Smoke, *National Security and the Nuclear Dilemma,* 153.

44. Anne Hessing Cahn, *Killing Détente: The Right Attacks the CIA* (University Park: Pennsylvania University Press, 1998), 18–19.

45. Memorandum from the President to his deputy national security adviser (Haig), May 20, 1972, in *FRUS,* 32:833–34.

46. Ibid.

47. Kaufman, *Henry M. Jackson,* 254–55; Henry Jackson, "The Senate and the Interim SALT I Agreement," August 11, 1972, in *Henry M. Jackson and World Affairs: Selected Speeches, 1953–1983,* ed. Dorothy Fosdick (Seattle: University of Washington Press, 1990), 140, 143. The two opposing votes were James L. Buckley (C-NY) and James B. Allen (D-AL).

48. John W. Finney, "Senate Approves Pact with Soviets on Missiles, 88–2," *New York Times,* August 4, 1972, 1–2; Cahn, *Killing Détente,* 18; John W. Finney, "A Tango with Two Left Feet: Arms Control," *New York Times,* August 13, 1972, E3; Smoke, *National Security and the Nuclear Dilemma,* 152–54.

49. Associated Press, "Modified SALT Pact Proviso Endorsed by White House," *Chicago Tribune,* August 8, 1972, 21; Cahn, *Killing Détente,* 19–20; Raymond L. Garthoff, *A Journey through the Cold War: A Memoir of Containment and Coexistence* (Washington, DC: Brookings Institute, 2001), 274.

50. Garthoff, *Détente and Confrontation,* 155–56; Smith, *Disarming Diplomat,* 168; Greenwood, *Making the MIRV,* 135.

51. Associated Press, "Soviets May Gain Missile Edge, Defense Chief Says," *Portsmouth Times,* August 18, 1973, 1; Greenwood, *Making the MIRV,* 116, 118.

52. Smith, *Disarming Diplomat,* 164; Hersh, *Price of Power,* 167; Kissinger, *White House Years,* 210–12; Henry A. Kissinger, *Years of Upheaval* (Boston: Little, Brown, 1982), 259–60.

6

"One Picture May Not Be Worth Ten Thousand Words, but the White House Is Betting It's Worth Ten Thousand Votes"

Richard Nixon and Diplomacy as Spectacle

Tizoc Chavez

"An election loss," Richard Nixon told Chinese premier Zhou Enlai, "was really more painful than a physical wound in war. The latter wounds the body—the other wounds the spirit."[1] Having felt the sting of electoral defeat before, Nixon was determined to avoid that fate again in 1972. To achieve victory, he sought to leverage every available resource—whether legal or not. Domestically, this led to abuses like Watergate. Internationally, it shaped his historic trips to China and the Soviet Union.

Driven by a realistic outlook, a perspective he shared with his national security adviser Henry Kissinger, Nixon sought to avoid idealistic policy and focus on what he deemed the national interest. Weakened by Vietnam as other nations grew in strength, the United States was no longer the dominant power it had once been. The bipolarity of the global arena that had existed since the end of World War II was breaking down. With the nation's overwhelming dominance diminished, Nixon and Kissinger sought a way to move forward and stabilize America's global position. The administration thus pursued a policy of détente with the Soviets and rapprochement with China, and it attempted to end the Vietnam War.

But these moves were not made out of desperation. In absolute terms, American power—economic, military, and technological—was still supreme. To stunt the relative decline of US strength, however, Nixon and Kissinger sought new approaches. They saw their various policies and actions as interconnected. The duo believed success in one area would lead to improvement in another. Rapprochement with China would strengthen America's position against the Soviet Union, and détente with the Soviets would enhance America's posture in relation to China. Improved relations with both communist powers would help in Vietnam, and ending the conflict in Southeast Asia would further relations with both nations. Nixon and Kissinger were confident their efforts would enhance America's strategic position and that, as a result, the nation would emerge from this tumultuous period stronger, with its dominance intact.[2]

Yet, as Nixon carried out his geopolitical strategy, domestic considerations were never far from his thoughts. When he traveled to Beijing and Moscow in 1972, part of his goal was to establish a productive working relationship with Soviet and Chinese leaders that would advance his foreign policy agenda. At the same time, however, interacting with his communist counterparts bolstered his reelection bid. It has been said that diplomacy is a type of "theater," and if so, personal diplomacy between world leaders is diplomatic drama at the highest level. Nixon's journeys to meet with Mao Zedong, Zhou Enlai, and Leonid Brezhnev created a spectacle that captivated Americans. China and the Soviet Union became a stage and its leaders props in a theatrical performance in which the president was the star and the audience the American voting public.[3]

Presidents rarely admit the extent to which domestic politics influences their foreign policy. That would appear self-serving and opportunistic. But all presidents are politicians. They want to be held in high public esteem, be reelected, and leave a positive legacy. Domestic political concerns, then, cannot help but creep into a president's calculations. "The president's trip [to China] may not have been politically motivated," noted NBC's Garrick Utley, "but it is politically convenient."[4] Indeed, Nixon used these high-profile summits—and the spectacles they created—not only to further US foreign policy but also for domestic political gain.

With Nixon's poll numbers sliding in 1971 and his reelection prospects endangered, he used foreign affairs to change the narrative. He created a media event and cultivated the image of a world statesman par excellence. This was not a strategy unique to Nixon. As a group, modern presidents have used foreign travel and interactions with world leaders to bolster their domestic position. Such activities have often garnered significant media coverage, allowing White House occupants to look "presidential." Writing in the 1980s, journalist Hedrick Smith noted that the Reagan administration "created a storybook presidency, using the pageantry of presidential travel to hook the networks and captivate the popular imagination. They projected Reagan as the living symbol of nationhood. And there was a payoff for policy: The more Reagan wrapped himself in the flag, the harder it became for mere mortal politicians to challenge him, the more impossible he was to defeat come reelection, the more worthy he seemed of trust and latitude on policy."[5] Nixon was a forerunner to this strategy, and in 1972 he sought to create his own storybook presidency by crafting a diplomatic drama in which he portrayed the world's leading apostle of peace.

Television, Spectacle, and Image Making

"Jack doesn't stand a ghost of a chance," Vice President Richard Nixon boasted to a cheering crowd of up to 140,000 on the eve of Halloween, a little more than a week before the 1960 presidential election.[6] But when the votes were tallied, he had lost one of the closest elections in US history. Senator John F. Kennedy had defeated him by less than 120,000 votes (49.7 to 49.5 percent). For the bitter Nixon, his loss was not so much the fault of his policies or ideas but rather the result of "showbiz politics."[7] The young, charming senator had strategically turned himself into a celebrity and deftly used television and the media to sell his personality. Indeed, Kennedy attracted huge crowds on the campaign trail. In the waning days of the presidential contest, an estimated 500,000 came to see him in New York City. The throngs frequently overran police barricades to get closer to JFK. "Kennedy spoke often," the *Chicago Daily Tribune* reported, "but it was the man and not his words the people seemed interested in."[8]

The image and mystique Kennedy created left an indelible mark on Nixon. When he lost the 1962 contest for governor of California, he ripped into the press for what he saw as its bias against him: "For 16 years

. . . you've had a lot of fun . . . you've had an opportunity to attack me. . . . You won't have Nixon to knock around any more because, gentlemen, this is my last press conference."[9] His loss to Kennedy and failed attempt at the governorship had convinced him that what mattered to the American public was not substance or qualifications but the ability to craft an appealing, glamorous image through the mass media, particularly television.[10]

In television, Nixon saw a tool that might be more easily manipulated than the print media, allowing him to project a favorable image to voters. He was encouraged in this by his chief of staff H. R. Haldeman. Haldeman had previously worked in advertising, so he was already familiar with promoting an agenda and selling an image. In particular, he was an advocate of television. During the 1968 election he advised his boss on new ways to use the medium, stating that the time had come in "political campaigning—its techniques and strategies—to move out of the dark ages and into the brave new world of the omnipresent eye." Once in office, Nixon and Haldeman would spend much time crafting a public relations strategy.[11]

In the second half of the twentieth century, the presidency increasingly became the center of American government, and public focus centered on the individual occupying the White House. "Since the president has become the embodiment of government," presidential scholar Theodore Lowi observed, "it seems perfectly normal for millions upon millions of Americans to concentrate their hopes and fears directly and personally upon him."[12] But even the most competent presidents have found it difficult to meet such expectations. No matter their actions or policies, it is never enough. Thus, according to Bruce Miroff, "presidents turn to gestures of spectacle to satisfy their audience." Spectacles are symbolic events that present "intriguing and often dominating characters not in static poses, but through actions that establish their public identities."[13] These events are centrally concerned with sending signals to the public.

This was Nixon's goal in 1972. His trips to China and the Soviet Union were spectacles on a grand scale that improved his image domestically by presenting himself as a statesman and a peacemaker, which he believed would boost his reelection prospects. Even before 1972 the president's aides were pondering how to leverage image making, spectacle, and foreign affairs for electoral advantage. Early on, the administration was concerned with creating an "aura" and "mystique" around the president, and foreign affairs offered one way to accomplish this.[14] In February 1971 special assistant to the president Dwight Chapin recommended that, over the next twenty months, the administration should spend at least a third of its time emphasizing foreign policy and highlighting Nixon's interactions with foreign leaders. The focus should be on the president as a world leader, his vast knowledge of global issues, the respect shown to him by foreign counterparts, and his image as a statesman. To further these aims, Chapin suggested the administration strive for greater television coverage of state visits.[15]

Chapin saw the media as a tool the administration could exploit "to build [a] Presidential image of capability, strength, leadership, and command," and foreign policy was central to this endeavor.[16] As Nixon told an aide in the fall of 1971, "International affairs is *our* issue," and in 1972 the administration planned to build up the president's image as "Mr. Peace," in the words of Haldeman.[17] He would become the peace candidate by improving relations with China and the Soviet Union, which provided the opportunity for presidential spectacle—"splashy, headline-grabbing, camera-pleasing event[s] that would drive home his international successes" to the American voting public.[18]

Political Benefits of Foreign Travel and Engagement with World Leaders

It is ironic that Nixon, an introverted and socially awkward man, would rely so heavily on foreign travel and personal contact with world leaders to create presidential spectacle. Nixon's fascination with foreign affairs partially explains this, but he also believed that personal contact with world leaders could advance American interests. "I have learned that there is an intangible factor which does affect the relations between nations," Nixon said. "When there is trust between men who are leaders of nations, there is a better chance to settle differences than when there is no trust."[19] However, he realized there were limits to what leader-to-leader diplomacy could achieve.

When Nixon became president in 1969 he already had a wealth of experience engaging world leaders and traveling abroad. As Dwight Eisenhower's vice president, he went overseas seven times, visiting fifty-four countries and meeting numerous heads of state and government. But according to the political opposition, these trips were not merely diplomatic missions. Paul Butler, chairman of the Democratic National Committee, observed that the vice president's travels toward the end of the Eisenhower years were "nothing more than cleverly concealed propaganda campaigns designed to keep him on Page 1 of the newspapers as a preliminary to the 1960 Presidential campaign."[20]

Nixon's most famous journey as vice president came in 1959 when he traveled to the Soviet Union to attend the opening of an American cultural exhibit and hold talks with Soviet leader Nikita Khrushchev. But with the election year less than six months away, Nixon had a personal stake in the outcome of the trip. "Mr. Nixon's trip behind the Iron Curtain has, as everyone knows, been planned and prepared as a triple wager," prominent journalist Walter Lippmann wrote. "It is a flyer in propaganda, a flyer in diplomacy, and a flyer in his own personal presidential politics."[21]

Because Nixon was the highest-ranking American official to visit the Soviet Union since Franklin Roosevelt attended the Yalta Conference in 1945, interest in the trip was immense. Nixon received mostly positive press coverage, and prior to his departure, newspapers wrote approvingly of his extensive preparation and his plans to talk "tough" with Khrushchev. Once he was face-to-face with the Soviet leader, the vice president generated even greater headlines. In what became known as the "Kitchen Debate," the two men engaged in a spirited discussion about the merits of their respective countries' systems of government. The debate was front-page news across the globe.[22] It also became a television event when it was discovered that cameras had recorded sixteen and a half minutes of the clash. The three television networks (ABC, CBS, NBC) promptly aired the footage. As a result of the exchange, influential Republicans such as Senate minority leader Everett Dirksen and numerous political commentators praised Nixon and recognized that the trip had boosted his political fortunes. In the end, though, it was not enough to get him elected president in 1960. His Soviet sojourn showed the electoral limits of personal diplomacy and foreign travel.[23]

Despite losing the election, Nixon acknowledged the appeal of going abroad and meeting with world leaders, as well as the opportunity for image building it provided. After losing his bid for California governor in 1962, he spent the next five years rehabilitating his image, an effort that relied heavily on journeys overseas. During his years in the so-called political wilderness, Nixon was a frequent traveler. In 1967 alone he visited Europe, Asia, Latin America, Africa, and the Middle East, meeting with foreign leaders at each stop. These trips allowed him to portray himself as an experienced statesman with both knowledge and gravitas, which was becoming "increasingly important to voters," according to the *Wall Street Journal.* The paper added: "As part of his effort to develop a less partisan image, Mr. Nixon has minimized his party appearances. Each of his four foreign tours since the first of the year has kept him out of the country two to three weeks. These trips . . . refreshed his acquaintance with crucial foreign policy areas. In the months ahead he will be able to sprinkle his speeches with remarks such as 'when I was in Indonesia last April . . . ' or 'as President de Gaulle told me in June. . . . '"[24]

Given that his travels and meetings with foreign leaders did not lead to victory in 1960, it is unclear how much the statesman image helped in Nixon's 1968 presidential victory. But what is not debatable is that once he became president, he sought to make his mark internationally, and as he moved to reorient American foreign policy, personal diplomacy with heads of government was part of that mission. During his first year in office Nixon told his staff he wanted to communicate with various foreign leaders on a regular basis. "Sometime ago I suggested that I would like to start a practice of writing a letter from time to time to some of the major leaders we have met on our trips abroad or on their visits here," he wrote to Henry Kissinger. "I still think this would be a very good idea. . . . For example, a letter to the Pope, to [Willy] Brandt, perhaps [Georges] Pompideau [*sic*], etc. on various subjects in which they would be interested and which would serve our purposes might be extremely helpful." To that end, White House staff prepared a list of possible leaders for Nixon to correspond with, which he then edited. He was also eager for face-to-face interactions. A month into office he went on a tour of Europe, visiting five countries and the Vatican. Five months later he went to Asia, stopping in six nations and holding state visits in five of them.[25]

Nixon's early trip to Europe was the first by a US president in five and a half years, and it represented an attempt to reset relations after years of complaints over the United States' neglect and questions about its reliability. With almost 200 journalists traveling with the president, however, the visit also proved to be a public relations boon and generated extensive media coverage, most of it positive. Prior to the trip, the State Department had found that opinion in the American press was overwhelmingly favorable, and once the trip began, all three television networks provided "special coverage." NBC's morning show devoted thirty minutes each day to the president's journey, and the station's nightly news show was extended from thirty minutes to an hour.[26]

While there were no agreements or major announcements, Nixon seemed to accomplish his goal of restoring a spirit of cooperation and goodwill. He also showed his skill in cultivating the camera. As one reporter noted, "Nixon proved an adept television performer. He is always aware of cameras and microphones and openly plays to them. His microphone technique is almost flawless." And because of "a kind of circular illogic that a person's merely being on TV makes that person important," the administration was able to use television "to stress to each citizen that Mr. Nixon, elected by a small margin, is now the President of the United States."[27]

Once he returned home, Nixon continued to occupy the media spotlight by giving a nationally televised address. He spoke for five minutes about his European travels before answering reporters' questions for fifty minutes. Nixon's remarks, the longest presidential press conference ever televised to that point, were carried on each of the networks as well as numerous other independent stations. According to one estimate, the president reached as many as 75 million Americans. And most agreed that they witnessed an exceptional performance. Speaking without notes, Nixon handled a total of twenty-six questions with ease and aplomb. The *New York Times* wrote that he was "impressive in scope and grasp . . . it was a *tour de force.*" The *Los Angeles Times* echoed those sentiments: "The American public had seldom been so impressed . . . [Nixon] emerged as a vitally healthy world leader in complete command of the situation."[28] All this positive press had an effect on the American people too. Asked by Gallup how important the trip was for developing good relations between the United States and western Europe, 37 percent of respondents said very important, and 32 percent said fairly important. For a president who placed great emphasis on polling and sought to exploit positive numbers, the results no doubt pleased him.[29]

Overall, the European trip demonstrated two aspects of how Nixon would conduct foreign policy. First, his administration would rely on television—"electronic statecraft"—to get its message across and project an image of leadership. Second, in carrying out foreign policy and electronic statecraft, interactions with foreign leaders would play an important role. "His visits to the West European capitals," one reporter noted, "offered all the proof that is needed that the American people have a new President who relishes personal diplomacy and feels at home abroad."[30] In 1972 this penchant for foreign travel would reach new heights, as Nixon's trips to China and the Soviet Union became grand productions.

Nixon Goes to China

During the first two years of Nixon's presidency, his approval rating hovered in the high fifties and low sixties. It is hard to say with precision what role his early forays into personal diplomacy played, but polls taken as he departed for Europe and about a week after his return showed a six percentage point increase in approval, from 60 to 66 percent. But by June 1971, any boost from the European trip was long gone. Only 48 percent of Americans now approved of Nixon's job performance. Faced with a worsening economic situation as inflation and unemployment rose, the president was becoming increasingly unpopular. His failure to end the Vietnam War and, in fact, his escalation of it into Cambodia and Laos generated widespread protests and spelled trouble for his reelection bid.[31]

To combat the growing economic discontent, Nixon reversed some long-held convictions. He instituted price and wage controls, allowed a floating exchange rate, and stopped the convertibility of dollars to gold. These were all policies he had once opposed, and they upset the global economic order that had been in place since the end of World War II. But he was more concerned about the domestic impact than the international one. These moves were popular at home, and although economic troubles eventually returned, in the short term, the economy improved and boosted Nixon's reelection prospects.[32]

In the realm of foreign policy, he also went against his previous reputation and positions. As a young congressman Nixon had made his name as the coldest of cold warriors. During campaigns for the House and Senate, he attacked his opponents by implying they secretly held radical views or were closet communists. Once in Congress, Nixon rose to fame as a member of the House Un-American Activities Committee (HUAC).

In 1948 he led the HUAC's investigation of Alger Hiss, a former State Department employee accused of being a communist spy. Though Hiss never admitted to espionage, uncovered documents suggested that he was a spy or, at the very least, had contact with communists—something he denied. In the end, Hiss was convicted of perjury, and as a result of the intense media spotlight on the hearings, Nixon became a national figure.

By the time he assumed the presidency, he was calmer and more restrained but was still viewed as staunchly anticommunist. However, a world in flux and the goal of preserving America's global influence required a new approach. Rather than being guided by a reflexive hatred of communism, Nixon and Kissinger's realistic outlook led them to focus on issues of power and security rather than ideological compatibility or moral dilemmas. Thus, they felt that engagement with communist foes in Beijing and Moscow would better serve American interests than continued hostility.

Nixon previewed his thinking on China in a 1967 article in *Foreign Affairs*: "Any American policy toward Asia must come urgently to grips with the reality of China." While recognizing the danger China presented, he argued that the United States needed to differentiate between "long-range and short-range policies" and concentrate on "fashioning short-range programs so as to advance our long-range goals. . . . Taking the long view, we simply cannot afford to leave China forever outside the family of nations."[33] Once in office, Nixon's administration moved in this direction. Months after the inauguration, Secretary of State William Rogers proclaimed that the United States was open to improved relations and would work to make it a reality. This was accompanied by other moves, such as stopping aggressive naval actions regularly conducted near the Chinese coast and easing travel restrictions to China. The administration also sought to establish a secret back channel through intermediaries such as Yahya Khan, the leader of Pakistan.[34]

By the spring of 1971, enough progress had been made through the secret Pakistani back channel that a high-level meeting between American and Chinese officials was considered desirable. Chinese premier Zhou Enlai suggested that a special envoy, or even Nixon himself, should visit Beijing, and the president quickly accepted the proposal. Before he visited, however, he wanted to lay the groundwork with a preliminary meeting between Kissinger and Chinese officials. Nixon insisted that any such gathering had to be covert, and he wanted it clearly "*understood that this first meeting between Dr. Kissinger and high officials of the People's Republic of China be strictly secret.*"[35]

While Nixon would eventually push for as much publicity as possible, at this early stage, such exposure was seen as dangerous. As Kissinger later recalled, if his visit to China had been made public, the administration would have been "caught between those who wanted a catalogue of concessions and others who wanted guarantees of our intransigence."[36] Internationally, other nations that opposed improved US-China relations might have attempted to undermine the visit. Perhaps most importantly, announcing the trip ahead of time would have given domestic opponents time to mobilize. By the early 1970s, the once influential "China lobby" had declined in prominence, but there were still some vocal members who could cause trouble for the president. And while relations with China seemed to be on the upswing, there was no guarantee of success. The administration had no idea what to expect. "It is difficult to recapture now the sense of mutual ignorance of the United States and China in those days," Kissinger remembered. "We had no contact of any sort with the Chinese leadership . . . we had no idea what we would find in Peking [Beijing]."[37] This partially explains why Nixon's later trip captivated the American public. The communist nation was a great mystery. But until he was sure the dramatic diplomatic initiative would pay off, he wanted to keep it secret. The opening to China would become a spectacle, but it would be on the president's terms.

In July 1971 Kissinger left for China. Again relying on Pakistan, he feigned illness while there, and once he was out of the press spotlight he was secretly shuttled into China. He then met extensively with Zhou, discussing relevant issues and details about the president's trip. When the visit was over, Kissinger was jubilant. Despite the difficulties ahead, he was confident that the foundation had been set for Nixon and Chinese leaders "to turn a page in history."[38]

Once Kissinger returned, Nixon told an unsuspecting world on live television about the clandestine trip and revealed that he would visit China the following year. The statement was brief, but it sent shock waves around the globe. The main objective of the China initiative was peace, the president said, and implicitly he conveyed the message that he was the conduit of that peace: "I will undertake what I deeply hope will become a journey for peace, peace not just for our generation but for future generations on this earth we share together."[39]

Nixon's bombshell was guaranteed to dominate the news cycle, but the administration strove to maximize coverage. In conversations with Zhou, Kissinger had pushed for the announcement of Nixon's trip (which occurred simultaneously in China) to be made on July 15, a Thursday evening. This was less than five days after their talks, and Zhou thought this might be too soon, not allowing enough time to fully brief Nixon and prepare for the announcement. Kissinger's mind, however, was on something else. "The weekly news magazines such as *Time* and *Newsweek* are printed on Friday and Saturday," he said, "therefore, if the announcement is made on Thursday night, they can do a better job of reporting it than if it were Friday night." Though this was not a sticking point, he told the Chinese premier that a Thursday announcement would mean better coverage not only in the newsmagazines but also in the Sunday newspapers. "In America they are very big," he said, "they are printed on Friday and Saturday, and therefore if the announcement is Friday evening they wouldn't be able to give any analysis on Sunday."[40] To the Americans' delight, Zhou consented.

Within a month of announcing the trip, Nixon's political fortunes quickly improved. Whereas a June Gallup poll had showed him trailing Edmund Muskie (his presumed Democratic opponent in the 1972 election) 41 to 39 percent, an August poll found him on top 42 to 36 percent. China and the theme of peace were proving to be political winners, and lest anyone try to steal his thunder, Nixon made it clear to the Chinese that he expected them to restrict American political visitors until after his trip. Indeed, he worked to craft the notion that he alone was capable of this dramatic undertaking and understood the issues better than anyone: "No one in this world, I think, knows better than I do, how imperative it is to see that great nations that have enormous differences . . . find ways to . . . talk, get along."[41]

Whether or not Nixon was truly the only one who understood the challenges of rapprochement with China, this is what the White House wanted conveyed to the American voters. Image was key. Deeds were great, but unless they were promoted and shaped into a triumphant narrative, there was little domestic political benefit. "What the people want is the appearance of action," Nixon told his advisers. As Haldeman recorded in his diary, the president wanted to focus not so much on concrete issues but rather on notions of "leadership: boldness, courage, etcetera" and depict "the President as the world leader for peace[,] the biggest leader in the world."[42] Thus, as the Nixon administration made the China trip a grand production, presenting the American public with political and diplomatic theater at the highest level, the focus was more on Nixon himself than on US-China relations. "This country is soon to be flooded with more news from China than will be easily digested," CBS's Eric Sevareid commented, "but it won't really be the story of China. It'll be the story of President Nixon in China."[43]

In crafting Nixon's story and creating a presidential spectacle, the maximization of media coverage, particularly television exposure, was crucial. "For most Americans at home the dramatic journey will be a TV spectacular which the White House obviously wants. One picture may not be worth ten thousand words," Sevareid mused, "but the White House is betting it's worth ten thousand votes."[44] Events were scheduled so they could be televised in prime time back in the United States, and the president was especially anxious about his arrival and departure. As Haldeman recorded in his diary, Nixon was concerned that his arrival "be handled flawlessly since that will be the key picture of the whole trip," and returning home "he definitely does not want to arrive in Washington at noon, but rather at 9:00 at night to make prime time television." The advance team worked out every detail, including the optimal spot to land on the runway to ensure the best angle for photos—and there would be plenty of photos. The administration received more than 2,000 press applications, and Nixon—who favored television over print—personally chose the journalists who would accompany him.[45]

With so many members of the media making the trip, abundant coverage was certain. From his arrival to the lavish opening banquet to his meeting with Chinese leaders and his visit to the Great Wall, Nixon created a spectacle that dominated American media and wreaked havoc on the campaigns of his two primary challengers.[46] In New Hampshire, site of the year's first primary, Nixon dominated print, radio, and especially television. "To his opponents here in New Hampshire it must have seemed as if the president were everywhere," NBC's Doug Kiker reported; he was "the most active candidate in this primary this week even though he was half a world away."[47] Nationally, the story was the same. A Gallup poll taken days after the visit showed that 97 percent of Americans had heard or read about the trip.[48] Whether they regularly paid attention to politics or not, Americans could not escape the president's trip to China.

Nixon no doubt relished the historic nature of his journey to China, but his immediate concern was to influence Americans of the 1970s. If the goal was for Nixon to be the peace candidate, he was well on his way. After the trip, Gallup asked how effective the president's journey to China would be in terms of improving world peace: 50 percent said fairly effective, and 16 percent said very effective.[49]

In the aftermath, the State Department reported, "No other international political event has commanded such overwhelming [media] treatment, much of it instantaneous thanks to satellite relay of live television." Some compared Nixon's journey to the moon landing—both "venture[s] into the unknown." And "like a moon flight," the department noted, "the voyage to China was a media phenomenon, tightly scripted and edited by time and technology, of a new kind scarcely imaginable before the age of television and communications satellites."[50] Having already gone to the diplomatic equivalent of the moon, one might have thought that Nixon would be satisfied. But the peace candidate had another spectacle to perform.

The Moscow Summit

While diplomacy with China was new terrain, dealing with the Soviets was well-trod—if hazardous—ground. The United States had had little to no contact with China for more than two decades, but it frequently communicated with the Soviet Union. For Nixon, it was important that a meeting at the highest level produce tangible results. If he met with Soviet leaders and nothing of substance was accomplished or, even worse, if tensions rose, the public would be disillusioned and his political opponents would pounce. "I am greatly concerned," Nixon told his ambassador to the Soviet Union, "about the adverse effects of a meeting that ends in deadlock even if it is surrounded by agreeable social functions. In this respect, top level meetings between US and Soviet leaders are different from other top level meetings."[51] Whereas a more symbolic encounter lacking in concrete results was acceptable for a China summit, a US-Soviet meeting had to produce something substantial. Thus, to lay the groundwork, Nixon directed Kissinger to engage in back-channel discussions with Soviet ambassador Anatoly Dobrynin.

For the administration, lessening tensions with the Soviets was an important step toward ending the Vietnam War. As relations improved, it was thought the Soviets would aid the United States as it tried to extricate itself from Southeast Asia. There were other issues to discuss as well, such as arms control, but neither side wanted to appear desperate for a summit. In Nixon's first years in office, the Soviets had floated the idea of a meeting multiple times, only to have the administration reject it. In the view of Nixon and Kissinger, the Soviets overestimated the president's desire for a summit, and they tried to extract numerous concessions simply for agreeing to meet.[52] As reelection neared, however, the administration became more eager.

The path to a summit, though, was not smooth. On the critical issue of Vietnam, the Soviets were no help, but the two sides did make some progress on arms control. By the spring of 1971, there was a "conceptual breakthrough" in the Strategic Arms Limitation Talks (SALT), as well as negotiations over antiballistic missile (ABM) systems. Yet they still could not agree on a date for a summit. From the administration's perspective, the Kremlin was dithering. But once news broke of Nixon's planned trip to China, the Soviets quickly agreed to a date for their own summit. Dobrynin tried to persuade Kissinger to have the president visit Moscow before he went to Beijing, but the request was rejected. The visits would take place in the order they were agreed to.[53]

For the Soviets, news of a US-China rapprochement was worrisome. Once allies, the two communist powers were adversaries by the 1970s. And as their monthlong border skirmish in 1969 made evident, the threat of a Sino-Soviet war was real. Kissinger tried to assure Dobrynin that improved American-Chinese relations were not a threat to the Soviet Union, but in reality, the division between the communist rivals served American purposes, as each side worried that the other might develop closer ties to the United States.

Months before the Moscow summit, Nixon told a Soviet official that his talks with Soviet leader Leonid Brezhnev "could be the most important heads-of-government meetings in this century."[54] Though he was guilty of a bit of self-aggrandizement, Nixon and Brezhnev did sign two arms control agreements—an ABM treaty and a SALT accord. A variety of other agreements dealing with environmental protection, medical science and public health, and cooperation in space, science, and technology were also concluded. Perhaps most important was the "Basic Principles" document, which defined relations between the United States and the Soviet Union. For the Soviets, this was particularly significant, as they believed it signaled the Americans now viewed them as equals. Nixon even became the first American president to speak on Soviet television.[55]

Like the trip to China, the president's Moscow visit furthered not only geopolitical goals but domestic ones as well. Shortly before the trip, pollster Louis Harris found that a large part of the president's improved standing with voters was attributable to his initiatives with America's communist foes. "In a period marked by little confidence in political leadership of nearly any stripe," Harris wrote, "Nixon's announcement of journeys to Moscow and Peking [Beijing] met with remarkably high acceptance from the American public." Over 70 percent of Americans approved of the summits, and almost 60 percent believed Nixon was "working for peace in the world."[56]

Upon returning home, Nixon dramatically flew by helicopter from Andrews Air Force Base to the Capitol, where he delivered a thirty-five-minute, nationally televised address to Congress. Only about half the members were present, but Nixon's real audience was the American people. Playing on the theme of peace, he stated that for both the United States and the Soviet Union, there was "an overriding desire to achieve a more stable peace in the world," and having embarked on that course, "history now lays upon us a special obligation to see it through."[57] And clearly the statesman best able to guide America down that path was Nixon.

Both summits, by improving relations with the two major communist powers, furthered the administration's goals of stabilizing the international environment and strengthening America's position in it. At the same time, they were spectacles and personal successes for Nixon. He became the first president to visit Beijing and Moscow—the capitals of America's two major adversaries—and combined with his reputation as a hard-line anticommunist and an American public anxious for peace, these journeys presented the perfect stage for diplomatic stagecraft. Of the two, China was the greater theater—"a technicolor picture story," according to CBS. But the Soviet summit also provided drama. "The pencils raced. The flash bulbs popped. The cameras whirred," reported one journalist as Nixon arrived at the Kremlin, "a moment in time that few soothsayers would have dared to predict was frozen in history." CBS labeled it a "political soap opera." Global headlines also heralded the president, with one Paris paper calling the Soviet trip "another sensation. . . . In fact, Mr. Nixon is in the process of taking his place among the great Presidents of the U.S." In the aftermath of Moscow, the president's popularity rating hit a two-year high, rising from 53 percent two months before the trip to 61 percent, an even greater boost than he saw after China.[58]

Nixon easily won reelection in 1972, beating George McGovern with 60.7 percent of the popular vote and 96.7 percent of electoral votes. Whether foreign policy and Nixon's trips played the decisive role is debatable, but they were prominently highlighted in campaign ads. In one television commercial titled "Passport," the narrator extolled Nixon's numerous trips abroad and meetings with foreign leaders: "President Nixon's travels represent a new foreign policy for the United States, a policy that calls for . . . peaceful negotiations with our enemies, all for a single purpose, world peace. But there are still places to go and friends to be won. That's why we need President Nixon. Now more than ever." Another ad featured a cheery song proclaiming, "Nixon Now." As a woman sang "Reaching out across the sea / making friends where foes used to be / giving hope to humanity," images of Nixon with Mao and Brezhnev flashed across the screen.[59]

It is impossible to know the exact impact of the summits, but the media clearly saw the trips as an attempt to influence public opinion. "The China visit, part diplomacy, part contrived public relations circus, drove up his [Nixon's] popularity several points in the opinion polls," Eric Sevareid noted. Others were convinced the trips were crucial to the president's electoral triumph. Nixon adviser Chuck Colson believed "RN's election is in the hands of Peking [Beijing]." And while the Soviet press criticized the China trip as "little more than a publicity stunt on the part of Mr. Nixon designed to get him reelected," the attitude changed when he went to Moscow. As Brezhnev told Al Haig, the Soviets "were doing everything to help the President get re-elected." But regardless of what was actually on voters' minds as they cast their ballots, the visits to Beijing and Moscow began the process of changing the public's perception of Nixon and led to very visible successes.[60]

The Limits of Image Making

Nixon and Brezhnev would meet again in 1973, this time in the United States. After the drama and major achievements in Moscow, the Soviet leader's visit to the United States was lackluster by comparison and less politically beneficial to the president. "In 1972, your trip to Moscow took place on the crest of your successful China visit and firm stance in Vietnam," the State Department told Nixon. "This year, our allies and the American public will be more prone to subject the results of your meetings with Brezhnev to skeptical examination, searching for signs of weakness on our part."[61] Indeed, by this time, SALT was under attack from conservatives and hard-liners such as Washington senator Henry Jackson. The fact that SALT allowed the Soviets to have a greater number of land-based and submarine-launched missiles was anathema to Cold War hawks. In late 1972 Jackson secured passage of a resolution that required parity in any future arms control agreements. He also worked to hinder détente by holding up a trade agreement with the Soviets unless they allowed unlimited Jewish emigration. Nixon's attempts to negotiate another SALT agreement became increasingly problematic.

But even without dedicated opponents of détente, Nixon was in trouble, as Watergate threatened to destroy his presidency. In mid-1973, with his domestic position crumbling and the congressional investigation of the scandal intensifying, Senator Jackson publicly stated that the upcoming summit with Brezhnev should be postponed. But as Kissinger recalled, that was not an option: "We had no choice except to pretend that our authority was unimpaired . . . we needed to project self-confidence no matter what we felt." Thus, the summit went ahead. The president also had a more "personal motive" for not wanting to postpone, according to Kissinger: "For him to concede that his ability to govern had been impaired would accelerate the assault on his Presidency. He could not bring himself to admit the growing disintegration of what he had striven all his life to achieve."[62]

The summit, however, did nothing to bolster Nixon's approval ratings, and some feared the desperate president would "be under terrible pressure to report new and favorable turns in U.S.-Soviet relations if only to counteract the running horror of the Watergate headlines." At the same time, according to one survey, 78 percent of Americans approved of the summit, and most believed it had furthered the cause of world peace. And the meeting did give Nixon some respite from Watergate. Congressional hearings were postponed for the week, allowing him to once again play the role of statesman.[63]

David Greenberg has written that Nixon's peacemaker image "constituted a key plank in his Watergate defense."[64] So as the scandal reached its peak in 1974, the embattled president embarked on a heavy schedule of foreign travel, visiting Europe, the Middle East, and the Soviet Union again. These trips abroad provided a brief reprieve and gave the beleaguered administration a "noticeable morale boost," reported ABC's Tom Jarriel. Nixon reprised his role as peacemaker and was feted in places like Egypt, where an official told NBC News that his government wanted to give Nixon "the biggest reception any American president ever had, anywhere."[65]

During the president's sojourns his staff played up his relationships with world leaders and stressed how vital those connections were to world peace. Nixon did this as well. While in the Soviet Union he proclaimed in a toast that the lessening of tensions was the result of "a personal relationship that was established between" Brezhnev and himself, and "because of our personal relationship," he said, "there is no question about our will to keep these agreements and to make more."[66] For those listening back home, the not so subtle message was that if Nixon were no longer in power, the country would lose the advantages of his close bond with Brezhnev, which could lead to increased hostilities with the Soviet Union.

But if he hoped such statements would influence the public, he was mistaken. The summit "turned into a pale imitation of the first two," Kissinger recalled. Like the previous year, some believed the whole trip had been designed to distract Americans from Watergate, and critics worried that a weakened president eager for success would make harmful concessions. The trip did produce some minor agreements, and looking back, Kissinger believed it was a beneficial meeting. But given Nixon's previously orchestrated diplomatic spectacles, anything less would almost surely fail to gain the public and media traction he needed to improve his image. And more importantly, Watergate tainted every action the president took.[67]

Brezhnev would be the last foreign leader Nixon met with. A little over a month later he resigned. In the span of two years, he went from the height of his popularity to leaving the presidency in disgrace. It was the use of diplomatic spectacle—foreign travel and interactions with world leaders—that helped Nixon reach the pinnacle of success. But ultimately, the role of statesman and peacemaker could not save him. Presidential spectacles can help domestically, but they cannot work miracles. Just as a president can use diplomacy for domestic gain, domestic troubles can hinder diplomatic effectiveness. "The strategy of the Nixon Administration presupposed a decisive President willing to stake American power to resist Soviet expansionism and ready to negotiate seriously if the Soviets would accept coexistence on this basis," Kissinger recalled. But Nixon's ability to perform the role of bold statesman was "destroyed by our domestic passion play."[68] No amount of foreign travel and personal diplomacy could save the president. Though his administration worked hard to produce diplomatic theater at the highest level and create grand spectacles of summitry, there were limits to what it could achieve domestically, especially when faced with a scandal as toxic as Watergate.

Geopolitical objectives drove Nixon's opening to China and pursuit of détente with the Soviet Union, and he believed that doing so put the United States in a better strategic position, helping to preserve and further America's dominant place in the world order.[69] Diplomacy at the highest level advanced these moves but also presented political opportunities domestically. Nixon's prepresidential career provided him with numerous examples of how television, foreign travel, and engagement with world leaders could boost popularity and enhance a politician's image. Thus, in 1972 he was well aware of how visits to Beijing and Moscow—and the accompanying newspaper and television coverage—could influence the voting public. CBS's Eric Sevareid perhaps came closest to capturing Nixon's need for popular approval, as well as his attempts to use the international sphere to strengthen his domestic position: "This president has never had the solid, unquestioning majority support that . . . Eisenhower enjoyed. Mr. Nixon is a stronger president, but with a weaker mandate, and he requires periodic drama. World affairs provide a much handier stage for it than domestic affairs."[70]

And the drama of the international stage led to images of the president as a bold statesman and peacemaker, which helped shift perceptions and improve Nixon's electoral prospects. As nationally syndicated columnist

William White wrote in the aftermath of the China and Soviet summits, "The loner who always has been Richard Nixon has now toiled upward to his third summit within months—this one the summit of his power and influence and perhaps also of his popularity. . . . Moscow has accomplished what Nixon's withdrawn personality could never accomplish on its own in signaling to the people the slogging, determined, utterly indomitable nature that underlies an outward absence of easy appeal to others."[71]

While Nixon is an extreme example, he is not alone in using foreign travel and interactions with world leaders for domestic political gain. Other modern presidents have also sought to bolster their images as statesmen, with an eye toward generating publicity and improving their domestic standing, and they have planned their international trips "with an eye toward public support."[72] But does it work?

Political scientists have shown that foreign travel and high-level diplomacy with world leaders generally lead to a boost in a president's approval rating. The sizable bounce that Nixon received from his election year summits is rare, however. More common is a small increase that quickly diminishes.[73] But as presidential scholar George Edwards argues, the "greatest source of influence for the president is public approval." And Bruce Miroff notes that the public and the media expect spectacle, and they use such performances to judge a president's leadership.[74] Given the enormous expectations of the Oval Office, presidents take whatever help they can get to enhance their approval ratings, strengthen their political power, boost their reelection prospects, and secure a place in history. Thus, even if the spectacle of foreign travel and personal diplomacy does not pay huge domestic dividends, presidents still attempt to leverage them for personal political gain.

Notes

1. Richard Nixon, *RN: The Memoirs of Richard Nixon* (New York: Grosset and Dunlap, 1978), 573.

2. Fredrik Logevall and Andrew Preston, "The Adventurous Journey of Nixon in the World," in *Nixon in the World: American Foreign Relations, 1969–1977,* ed. Fredrik Logevall and Andrew Preston (New York: Oxford University Press, 2008), 4–8.

3. For this notion of diplomacy as performance, see Raymond Cohen, *Theatre of Power: The Art of Diplomatic Signalling* (London: Longman, 1987); Andreas W.

Daum, *Kennedy in Berlin* (New York: Cambridge University Press, 2008). For Nixon's use of diplomacy for image building and domestic gain, see David Greenberg, "Nixon as Statesman: The Failed Campaign," in Logevall and Preston, *Nixon in the World,* 45–66.

4. NBC Evening News, February 25, 1972, Vanderbilt Television News Archive (hereafter VTNA).

5. Hedrick Smith, *The Power Game: How Washington Works* (New York: Ballantine Books, 1988), 414.

6. Robert T. Hartmann, "'Jack Hasn't Ghost of Chance,' Nixon Asserts," *Los Angeles Times,* October 30, 1960.

7. For the development of "showbiz politics," see Kathryn Cramer Brownell, *Showbiz Politics: Hollywood in American Political Life* (Chapel Hill: University of North Carolina Press, 2014). See also Alan Schroeder, *Celebrity-in-Chief: How Show Business Took over the White House* (Boulder, CO: Westview Press, 2004); Kenneth T. Walsh, *Celebrity in Chief: A History of the Presidents and the Culture of Stardom* (New York: Routledge, 2017).

8. Joseph Hearst, "Kennedy Met by Big Crowds in New York," *Chicago Daily Tribune,* October 28, 1960; Peter Kihss, "City Crowds Hail Kennedy on Tour; He Gibes at Nixon," *New York Times,* October 28, 1960.

9. "Text of Nixon's Press Conference," *Los Angeles Times,* November 8, 1962.

10. Kathryn Cramer Brownell, "The Making of the Celebrity Presidency," in *Recapturing the Oval Office: New Historical Approaches to the American Presidency,* ed. Brian Balogh and Bruce J. Schulman (Ithaca, NY: Cornell University Press, 2015), 172.

11. Haldeman quoted in Nixon, *RN,* 303; Lawrence R. Jacobs and Melinda S. Jackson, "Presidential Leadership and the Threat to Popular Sovereignty," in *Polls and Politics: The Dilemmas of Democracy,* ed. Michael A. Genovese and Matthew J. Streb (Albany: State University of New York Press, 2004), 29–54.

12. Theodore J. Lowi, *The Personal President: Power Invested, Promise Unfulfilled* (Ithaca, NY: Cornell University Press, 1985), 96.

13. Bruce Miroff, "The Presidential Spectacle," in *The Presidency and the Political System,* 10th ed., ed. Michael Nelson (Washington, DC: CQ Press, 2014), 232, 234. On spectacle in politics, see also Murray Edelman, *Constructing the Political Spectacle* (Chicago: University of Chicago Press, 1988).

14. Jacobs and Jackson, "Presidential Leadership," 34.

15. Memorandum from Dwight L. Chapin to H. R. Haldeman, "Schedule Planning," February 1, 1971, Doc. No. CK2349697245, Declassified Documents Reference System, http://tinyurl.galegroup.com/tinyurl/3eQ4U4.

16. Ibid.

17. Nixon quoted in Stephen E. Ambrose, *Nixon: The Triumph of a Politician, 1962–1972,* vol. 2 (New York: Simon and Schuster, 1989), 478; Haldeman quoted in Robert Dallek, *Nixon and Kissinger: Partners in Power* (New York: HarperCollins, 2007), 246.

18. David Greenberg, *Nixon's Shadow: The History of an Image* (New York: W. W. Norton, 2003), 277. For more on the administration's attempt to make Nixon the "Peace Candidate," see Thomas Alan Schwartz, "The Peace Candidate: Richard Nixon, Henry Kissinger, and the Election of 1972," in *US Presidential Elections and Foreign Policy: Candidates, Campaigns, and Global Politics from FDR to Bill Clinton,* ed. Andrew Johnstone and Andrew Priest (Lexington: University Press of Kentucky, 2017), 204–27.

19. "The President's News Conference," March 4, 1969, in *Public Papers of the Presidents of the United States, Richard Nixon: 1969* (Washington, DC: US Government Printing Office, 1971), 180.

20. John C. Baumgartner, *The American Vice Presidency Reconsidered* (Westport, CT: Praeger, 2006), 32, 121; Robert Blanchard, "Butler Sees Nixon's Tours as 'Propaganda,'" *Los Angeles Times,* May 17, 1958.

21. Walter Lippmann, "Nixon in Russia," *Washington Post,* July 28, 1959.

22. For newspaper coverage of Nixon's plans to talk tough, see "Reckoning with His Host, Nixon Is Packing Proverbs," *New York Times,* July 19, 1959; Robert Hartmann, "Nixon Plans Tough Talk in Visit to Moscow," *Los Angeles Times,* July 21, 1959; Roscoe Drummond, "Nixon's New Mission . . . He'll Be Ready for K.'s Arguments," *Washington Post,* July 22, 1959. For "Kitchen Debate" coverage, see Willard Edwards, "Khrushchev, Nixon Debate," *Chicago Daily Tribune,* July 25, 1959; Harrison E. Salisbury, "Nixon and Khrushchev Argue in Public as U.S. Exhibit Opens; Accuse Each Other of Threats," *New York Times,* July 25, 1959. In Britain and France, the debate was front-page news. While the British press was critical of both Nixon's and Khrushchev's behavior, the French commended the vice president. See "British Press Is Critical," *New York Times,* July 26, 1959; "Paris Reaction Is Favorable," *New York Times,* July 26, 1959.

23. Richard F. Shepard, "Debate Goes on TV over Soviet Protest," *New York Times,* July 26, 1959; Jack Gould, "TV: Debate in Moscow: Taped Exchange between Nixon and Khrushchev Personalizes History," *New York Times,* July 27, 1959. There was no shortage of positive assessments of Nixon's trip. For example, see UPI, "Moscow Trip Boosts Nixon, Dirksen Says," *Chicago Daily Tribune,* July 27, 1959; James Reston, "Nixon Visit Assessed," *New York Times,* July 27, 1959; James Reston, "Nixon's Political Coup: His Soviet Tour Viewed as Perfect Way to Open Campaign for U.S. Presidency," *New York Times,* July 30, 1959; Alan L. Otten, "Nixon in Russia," *Wall Street Journal,* July 27, 1959; George E. Sokolsky, "Nixon's Value," *Washington Post,* July 31, 1959.

24. Alan L. Otten, "Nixon's New Course," *Wall Street Journal,* July 24, 1967.

25. Even during the campaign, Nixon made his interest in personal diplomacy and summitry known. See James Reston, "Mr. Nixon Looks beyond the Election Campaign," *New York Times,* September 25, 1968; Ernest Conine, "Nixon Too, Has 'Summit Itch,'" *Los Angeles Times,* November 10, 1968; memorandum from Nixon to Kissinger, November 24, 1969, National Security Council Files (hereafter NSC), Presidential Correspondence, box 759, folder 9, Richard Nixon Presidential

Library, Yorba Linda, CA (hereafter RNL); memorandum from Haldeman to Kissinger, November 7, 1969, with attachment memorandum from Kissinger to Nixon, October 25, 1969, ibid., box 766, folder 3.

26. Memorandum from William Rogers to Nixon, "Subject: Your Trip to Europe—Scope Paper," n.d., NSC, President's Trip Files, box 443, folder 5, RNL; "Trip Tests President's Diplomacy," *Washington Post,* February 23, 1969; "Advance Comment on Pres. Nixon's Trip," Department of State, February 14, 1969, NSC, President's Trip Files, box 444, folder 2, RNL. NBC had a seventy-six-person crew to cover Nixon's journey, and CBS interrupted its normal programming for a midday special report on the trip. See "TV Highlights: The President in Europe," *Washington Post,* February 24, 1969; "President's Tour to Get TV Coverage," *Los Angeles Times,* February 17, 1969; "TV Highlights," *Washington Post,* February 27, 1969.

27. Lawrence Laurent, "Two Looks at Nixon's TV Report," *Washington Post,* March 5, 1969.

28. Don Oberdorfer, "Nixon Reviews World Scene with Deft, Direct Remarks," *Washington Post,* March 5, 1969; Laurent, "Two Looks at Nixon's TV Report"; "Mr. Nixon on Foreign Policy . . . ," *New York Times,* March 6, 1969; "Nixon's Report," *Los Angeles Times,* March 9, 1969.

29. Gallup poll, May 1–6, 1969. All polls accessed from iPOLL Databank, Roper Center for Public Opinion Research, https://ropercenter.cornell.edu. For Nixon's use and manipulation of polls, see Lawrence R. Jacobs and Robert Y. Shapiro, "The Rise of Presidential Polling: The Nixon White House in Historical Perspective," *Public Opinion Quarterly* 59, no. 2 (Summer 1995): 163–95, and "Presidential Manipulation of Polls and Public Opinion: The Nixon Administration and the Pollsters," *Political Science Quarterly* 110, no. 4 (Winter 1995–1996): 519–38.

30. Oberdorfer, "Nixon Reviews World Scene with Deft, Direct Remarks"; Robert J. Donovan, "Nixon's Trip Shows Promise of New Diplomatic Era in West," *Los Angeles Times,* March 2, 1969.

31. Gallup polls, February 20–25, 1969; March 12–17, 1969; June 25–28, 1971.

32. See Luke A. Nichter, *Richard Nixon and Europe: The Reshaping of the Postwar Atlantic* (New York: Cambridge University Press, 2015), 36–102.

33. Richard Nixon, "Asia after Viet Nam," *Foreign Affairs* 46, no. 1 (October 1967): 121.

34. Margaret Macmillan, *Nixon and Mao: The Week that Changed the World* (New York: Random House, 2007), 163–65. For a complete account of Nixon's rapprochement with China, see Chris Tudda, *A Cold War Turning Point: Nixon and China, 1969–1972* (Baton Rouge: Louisiana State University Press, 2012). For the Pakistani back channel, see F. S. Aijazuddin, *From a Head, through a Head, to a Head: The Secret Channel between the US and China through Pakistan* (Karachi: Oxford University Press, 2000).

35. Message from Nixon to Zhou, via Hilaly, May 10, 1971, Doc. 23, National Security Archive (hereafter NSA) Electronic Briefing Book, No. 66, http://nsarchive.gwu.edu/NSAEBB/NSAEBB66/ch-23.pdf (emphasis in original).

36. Henry Kissinger, *White House Years* (Boston: Little Brown, 1979), 725.

37. Ibid.

38. Memorandum from Kissinger to Nixon, "My Talks with Chou En-lai," July 14, 1971, Doc. 144, in *Foreign Relations of the United States* (hereafter *FRUS*), *1969–1976,* vol. 17, *China, 1969–1972* (Washington, DC: US Government Printing Office, 2006), 454.

39. "Remarks to the Nation Announcing Acceptance of an Invitation to Visit the People's Republic of China," July 15, 1971, in *Public Papers of the Presidents of the United States, Richard Nixon: 1971* (Washington, DC: US Government Printing Office, 1972), 820.

40. Memorandum of conversation, Kissinger and Zhou, July 11, 1971, Doc. 38, NSA Electronic Briefing Book, No. 66, http://nsarchive.gwu.edu/NSAEBB/NSAEBB66/ch-38.pdf.

41. William Bundy, *A Tangled Web: The Making of Foreign Policy in the Nixon Presidency* (New York: Hill and Wang, 1998), 240–41; memorandum for the President's File, "Meeting between President, Dr. Kissinger and General Haig," July 1, 1971, Doc. 137, in *FRUS, 1969–1976,* 17:356; Nixon conversation with Barend Biesheuvel, Alexander Haig, and J. William Middendorf, January 26, 1972, tape 656-10, RNL, https://www.nixonlibrary.gov/virtuallibrary/tapeexcerpts/china-656–10b.pdf.

42. H. R. Haldeman Diaries, August 16, 1971, RNL, http://www.nixonlibrary.gov/virtuallibrary/documents/haldeman-diaries/37-hrhd-audiotape-ac12b-19710816-pa.pdf.

43. CBS Evening News, February 11, 1972, VTNA.

44. Ibid.

45. H. R. Haldeman, *The Haldeman Diaries: Inside the Nixon White House* (New York: G. P. Putnam's, 1994), 412; Macmillan, *Nixon and Mao,* 51, 152; Haldeman Diaries, February 15, 1971, RNL, https://www.nixonlibrary.gov/virtuallibrary/documents/haldeman-diaries/37-hrhd-audiocassette-ac19a-19720215-pa.pdf.

46. All three networks carried Nixon's arrival live. ABC's coverage was fifty minutes, CBS's a little over an hour, and NBC almost an hour and a half. See ABC Special for Sunday, February 20, 1972; CBS Special for Sunday, February 20, 1972; NBC Special for Sunday, February 20, 1972, VTNA.

47. NBC Evening News, February 25, 1972, VTNA.

48. Gallup poll, March 3–5, 1972.

49. Ibid.

50. US Information Agency, "Foreign Media Treatment of President Nixon's Visit to China: Summary as of February 28, 1972," NSC, President's Trip Files, box 501, folder 3, RNL.

51. Memorandum from Kissinger to Jacob D. Beam, "Instructions for Your Oral Presentation to Kosygin," March 26, 1969, NSC, Presidential Correspondence, box 765, folder 7, RNL.

52. Gordon R. Weihmiller, *U.S.-Soviet Summits: An Account of East-West Diplo-*

macy at the Top, 1955–1985 (Lanham, MD: University Press of America, 1986), 54–57.

53. Kissinger, *White House Years,* 731; Editorial Note, Doc. 94, in *FRUS, 1969–1976,* vol. 1, *Foundations of Foreign Policy, 1969–1972* (Washington, DC: US Government Printing Office, 2003), 327–29.

54. Memorandum for the President's File, "The President's Meeting with Soviet Minister of Agriculture Vladmir Matskevich," December 9, 1971, Doc. 23, in *FRUS, 1969–1976,* vol. 14, *Soviet Union, October 1971–May1972* (Washington, DC: US Government Printing Office, 2006), 71.

55. Weihmiller, *U.S.-Soviet Summits,* 65, 142; Theodore Shabad, "Nixon Talks on TV to Soviet People and Hails Accord," *New York Times,* May 29, 1972.

56. Louis Harris, "Summit Vital to Nixon," *Chicago Tribune,* May 18, 1972.

57. Bernard Gwertzman, "Nixon Flies Home and Tells Nation of Summit Gain," *New York Times,* June 2, 1972.

58. CBS Evening News, May 22, 1972, VTNA; Louise Hutchinson, "Red Carpet for Nixons; U.S. Flag over Kremlin," *Chicago Tribune,* May 23, 1972; memorandum from Henry Loomis to Alexander Haig, October 13, 1971, NSC, President's Trip Files, box 474, folder 1, RNL; George Gallup, "Nixon Popularity Hits 2-Year Peak on Soviet Trip," *Washington Post,* June 4, 1972.

59. Committee to Re-elect the President, "Passport" and "Nixon Now," 1972, Museum of the Moving Image, The Living Room Candidate: Presidential Campaign Commercials 1952–2012, www.livingroomcandidate.org/commercials/1972/passport; www.livingroomcandidate.org/commercials/1972/nixon-now.

60. CBS Evening News, February 29, 1972, VTNA; Colson quoted in George C. Herring, *From Colony to Superpower: U.S. Foreign Relations since 1776* (New York: Oxford University Press, 2008), 791; transcript of telephone conversation between Nixon and Haig, April 21, 1972, Doc. 137, in *FRUS, 1969–1972,* 14:512.

61. Memorandum from Kenneth Rush to Nixon, "Brezhnev Visit to the United States," June 12, 1973, NSC, VIP Visits, box 939, folder 5, RNL.

62. Henry Kissinger, *Years of Upheaval* (Boston: Little Brown, 1982), 289.

63. John Chamberlain, "Nixon's Dilemma in Brezhnev Talks," *Chicago Tribune,* June 16, 1973; Louis Harris, "Majority See Summit as Breakthru," *Chicago Tribune,* June 23, 1973.

64. Greenberg, *Nixon's Shadow,* 280.

65. ABC Evening News, June 18, 1974, VTNA; NBC Evening News, June 11, 1974, VTNA.

66. Greenberg, *Nixon's Shadow,* 282; Robert G. Kaiser and Peter Osnos, "Soviets Greet Nixon Warmly: Nixon Cites Ties with Soviet Leader," *Washington Post,* June 28, 1974. Interestingly, in the official Russian translation of Nixon's toast, the word "personal" was dropped, leading some to believe that the Soviets tried to distance themselves from Nixon's claims of close ties. See John Herbers, "Tass Deletion of a Word in Nixon Speech Disputed," *New York Times,* June 29, 1974.

67. Kissinger, *Years of Upheaval,* 300, 1177; Aldo Beckman, "It's Perils v. Promises in Moscow," *Chicago Tribune,* June 23, 1974.

68. Kissinger, *Years of Upheaval,* 300.

69. For the impact of these summits on Cold War competition, see Yafeng Xia and Chris Tudda, "Beijing, 1972," and James Cameron, "Moscow 1972," in *Transcending the Cold War: Summits, Statecraft, and the Dissolution of Bipolarity in Europe, 1970–1990,* ed. Kristina Spohr and David Reynolds (New York: Oxford University Press, 2016), 43–66, 67–91.

70. CBS Evening News, March 10, 1972, VTNA.

71. William S. White, "A Personal Triumph for the President," *Chicago Tribune,* June 11, 1972.

72. Samuel Kernell, *Going Public: New Strategies of Presidential Leadership,* 4th ed. (Washington, DC: CQ Press, 2007), 125–28; Paul Brace and Barbara Hinckley, "Presidential Activities from Truman through Reagan: Timing and Impact," *Journal of Politics* 55, no. 2 (May 1993): 387.

73. For example, see Elmer Plischke, "The President's Image as Diplomat in Chief," *Review of Politics* 47, no. 4 (October 1985): 544–65; Robert E. Darcy and Alvin Richman, "Presidential Travel and Public Opinion," *Presidential Studies Quarterly* 18, no. 1 (Winter 1988): 85–90; Dennis M. Simon and Charles W. Ostrom Jr., "The Impact of Televised Speeches and Foreign Travel on Presidential Approval," *Public Opinion Quarterly* 53, no. 1 (Spring 1989): 58–82; Agnes Simon, "The Political and Economic Consequences of the Summit Diplomatic Activity of the U.S. President" (PhD diss., University of Missouri, 2012).

74. George C. Edwards III, *The Public Presidency: The Pursuit of Popular Support* (New York: St. Martin's Press, 1983), 1; Miroff, "Presidential Spectacle," 255.

7

Creating an Ethnic Lobby

Ronald Reagan, Jorge Mas Canosa, and the Birth of the Cuban American National Foundation

Hideaki Kami

No serious analysis of US-Cuban relations during the late Cold War can ignore the role played by the Cuban American National Foundation (CANF). Born in July 1981, CANF consisted of directors, trustees, and other contributors who opposed the Cuban government in Havana. Under the strong leadership of Jorge Mas Canosa, the foundation quickly gained political prominence in Washington. CANF contributed to the 1985 start-up of Radio Martí, as well as the 1990 establishment of TV Martí, providing US-sponsored programming for Cuba. The foundation also became a driving force behind the 1992 enactment of the Cuban Democracy Act, which not only tightened the US economic embargo on the island but also stipulated US assistance to a "post-Castro Cuba." Even after the end of the Cold War, CANF stood for some years at the forefront of the anti-Castro movement in the United States.

Although CANF received much attention from contemporary mass media, its scholarly analysis remains scarce. Political scientists, international relations scholars, and diplomatic historians have identified Cuban Americans' political influence on US policy toward Cuba, yet few have explored the complex relationship between the US government and the Cuban American community. Without access to the substantial volume of primary sources in Washington and Miami, researchers have not uncovered the stories of the foundation from a historical standpoint.[1] Nor have studies of the Cuban American community examined the historical records to trace the development of the foundation's power network. The study of Cuban migration to the United States is plentiful, yet CANF has not undergone historical scrutiny mainly because of the lack of materials.[2]

One should also note that CANF received scathing criticism not only in Cuba but also in the United States. Especially in the 1990s, US newspapers and magazines repeated numerous episodes of Mas Canosa's "bullying" character, his alleged ambition to be president of Cuba, and CANF's confrontations with "left-leaning" US academics and newspapers. For example, the foundation publicly accused the *Miami Herald* of being a mouthpiece for Fidel Castro, prompting CANF supporters to make bomb threats against *Herald* executives and to vandalize the newspaper's vending machines.[3] According to the human rights organization Americas Watch, these activities constituted significant human rights violations for which CANF was mainly responsible.[4] Although the foundation blamed Havana's "defamation campaign" for this increasingly critical portrayal of its activities, the image of intolerance has persisted for decades.[5] In revolutionary Cuba CANF was considered a terrorist-mafia organization, especially due to its alleged plots against Fidel Castro.[6]

Given these political disputes, it is not surprising that existing studies disagree on many issues, including the origins of CANF. Two nonprofessional historians recruited personally by Mas Canosa have presented generally sympathetic accounts of the foundation's history. Their official descriptions emphasize Miami Cubans' desire to continue their battle against Castro and claim that the foundation's creation was inspired by their passion, sacrifices, and unwavering devotion to their "cause." Lamentably, these books cite no internal sources to corroborate their arguments. Critics of CANF have given negative descriptions of Mas Canosa and his followers, even though they rely mainly on newspaper articles and contemporary interviews. The critics assert that the Reagan administration gave birth to the foundation in its pursuit of foreign policy goals in Latin America. By casting the foundation as a by-product of Reagan's foreign policy, they downplay Miami Cubans' agency.[7]

Based on a diverse range of newly available sources, this essay reexamines the origins of CANF from a historical perspective. Rather than entering a polemical debate, it treats CANF as an important case study of ethnic groups and US foreign policy, a topic that should attract additional scholarly attention as an important segment of US politics and diplomacy.[8] In particular, this study outlines key dynamics in the creation of the foundation and its support network that proved pivotal in expanding their influence in Washington. The major focus of this research is on the early years (1980–1982), not the development of CANF's activities thereafter. By exploring the foundation's origins, this analysis provides a rare inside look into an ethnic organization that played an important role in the making of US foreign policy during the late Cold War. By underscoring Miami Cubans' agency, it reveals the intimate relationship between domestic politics and foreign policy, a major feature of US policy toward Cuba for a long time.[9]

This essay confirms existing studies that claim that the Reagan presidency strongly incentivized Mas Canosa and his followers to create the foundation in July 1981. Yet it also highlights the highly independent nature of Miami Cubans' political activities. Alarmed by the US pursuit of coexistence with communist countries, Mas Canosa and his friends began to explore ways to stem the seemingly inevitable shift toward US-Cuban rapprochement since the mid-1970s. Far from being puppets of the Reagan administration, these counterrevolutionary actors looked to Reagan as a tool to promote their own cause, rather than serve the interests of Washington. The Reagan administration and CANF often engaged in power struggles, despite their shared anticommunist mind-set. In this regard, the study emphasizes the fact that the foundation benefited from the generous support of fellow Cuban Americans, key congressional members, and a Jewish lobby in creating an independent power base that would sustain its activities for years.

Anti-Castro Politics, 1959–1992

Since the 1959 Cuban revolution, more than a million Cubans have left their homeland. The reasons for their departure were diverse, according to Thomas D. Boswell and James R. Curtis. "Certainly a desire to escape the socialistic regime imposed by Castro was, and still is, a powerful migrational catalyst," they wrote in 1983. "Yet, the promise of refuge and political exile, the lure of economic opportunity, the quest for family reunification, and a desire for personal and religious freedom have also been important factors."[10] As such, the Cuban emigration included people with varying socioeconomic and political backgrounds. Many eventually settled in Miami, where they found jobs, capital, friends, and a warm climate. As historian María Cristina García explains, "Miami had become Havana USA: the border town between Cuba and the United States."[11] Because many of these Cubans harbored strong hostility toward revolutionary leader Fidel Castro, Miami also became the capital of the anti-Castro movement in the United States.[12]

Over the years, the United States sponsored and exploited the anti-Castro movement in Miami. As US relations with revolutionary Cuba deteriorated, President Dwight Eisenhower concocted a plot to bring about a regime change. On April 17, 1961, President John F. Kennedy implemented this plan, which used counterrevolutionary Cuban fighters headed toward the Bay of Pigs. The failure of this invasion not only cemented Castro's rule over the island but also convinced Moscow to deepen its commitment to the defense of Havana. Whereas the Kennedy administration was willing to resort to anything short of a direct US invasion to topple the Castro regime, the Soviet Union deployed nuclear weapons to protect its Caribbean ally and paved the way for the 1962 missile crisis. In return for Moscow's removal of the missiles from the island, Washington essentially pledged that it would not invade Cuba again.[13]

Yet, even after the most dangerous crisis of the Cold War, counterrevolutionary Cubans in Miami kept fighting against Castro. Their military operations attacked ships headed to Cuban ports and provoked vocal protests from Cuba, the Soviet Union, and third-party countries. The growing international pressure was so embarrassing that the US government decided to phase out its involvement with the Cuban counterrevolution.[14] Thereafter, numerous anti-Castro organizations sprang up, pledged to invade Cuba, and disappointed their supporters. In the 1970s anti-Castro politics fell into disarray. As the US government began to explore a modus vivendi with Cuba in the context of US-Soviet détente, dozens of anti-Castro groups unleashed international terrorist campaigns that were beyond anybody's control. Washington's attempts at dialogue with

Havana went nowhere, but these developments forced anti-Castro activists to reconsider their strategies.

US-Cuban tensions reached another peak in the early 1980s. President Ronald Reagan focused on Central America and the Caribbean, identified Cuba as the source of regional turmoil, and pursued a hostile policy toward the island. The president not only assisted the Nicaraguan contras and the Salvadoran government but also invaded Grenada, a close ally of Castro's Cuba. It was around this time that CANF emerged as a political force and expanded its political activities in Washington. Unlike previous paramilitary groups trying to topple the Cuban government by force, the foundation chose Washington as a major battleground and searched for ways to influence US policy toward Cuba. This change in strategy proved effective. CANF took credit for Congress's 1983 approval of the establishment of Radio Martí under the Voice of America. This momentous achievement was followed by other accomplishments, such as the 1990 setup of TV Martí and the 1992 enactment of the Cuban Democracy Act.

Former US officials readily affirmed CANF's influence. US policy toward Cuba "has been hijacked by the Cuban American community certainly in the years since the end of the Cold War," lamented Stephen Bosworth, deputy assistant secretary of state for the Western Hemisphere from 1981 to 1983. "It's very difficult to construct a rationale for continuing to try to isolate the country particularly when we have failed. . . . I attribute all of this basically to the power, influence and money of the Cuban American community."[15] Some scholars remain skeptical of claims about CANF's actual strength, highlighting its ideological similarities with the Reagan and Bush administrations.[16] Yet Myles Frechette, Cuban desk officer for the State Department from 1979 to 1982, dismissed this point. "CANF was very powerful," he said.[17] Robert Gelbard, deputy assistant secretary of state for the Western Hemisphere from 1991 to 1993, reacted in a similar manner. "Their power was very big," he said. "CANF was an overwhelmingly influential Cuban group in Miami."[18]

Jorge Mas Canosa and the Idea of a Lobby

At the center of CANF was Jorge Mas Canosa, the first chairman of the foundation. Born in Santiago de Cuba in 1939, Mas Canosa was outspoken and politically active at an early age. In 1956 he criticized Fulgencio

Batista during a radio broadcast and was exiled to the United States. After a brief return following the revolution, he left Cuba again in opposition to Fidel Castro. In April 1961 he joined the Bay of Pigs invasion, although he never landed on the island. After his brief service with the US military, Mas Canosa continued to participate in anti-Castro organizations such as the Representación Cubana del Exilio (RECE). Meanwhile, he used his RECE connections to get a job with Iglesias y Torres, a construction company on the verge of bankruptcy. He later obtained loans to purchase the company, promptly renamed it Church and Tower, and became its president.[19]

Mas Canosa held a leadership position in RECE, which was most active in the mid-1960s and early 1970s. Originally sponsored by José Pepin Bosch of Bacardi, the largest privately held spirits company in the world, RECE aspired to be an umbrella group for anti-Castro Cubans abroad. The group raised funds, lobbied Latin American governments for support, and financed the paramilitary operations of other groups that conducted raids against the island. But by the mid-1970s, as the US government explored the idea of normalizing relations with Cuba, these violent activities proved not only impractical but also ineffective in stopping the momentum to break Cuba's isolation. RECE probed for ways to influence the US government, whose traditional hostility toward Cuba could no longer be taken for granted. The first attempt occurred in December 1974, when the organization invited Senator Harry F. Byrd of Virginia to Miami Senior High School. Three thousand Miami Cubans joined Byrd to underscore their opposition to US-Cuba normalization.[20]

Mas Canosa felt compelled to upgrade these incipient lobbying efforts during the late 1970s, when President Jimmy Carter stepped up attempts to normalize diplomatic relations with Cuba. The president intensified crackdowns on militants who were still trying to topple the Cuban government by force. Carter also addressed human rights issues—such as the release of political prisoners and the reunification of Cuban families—as one of the principal US objectives in Cuba. He proposed a dialogue to achieve these ends. Fidel Castro responded to this request, and Havana drastically changed its policy toward Cuban emigration. For the first time since the revolution, Castro hosted *diálogo,* a dialogue with Cuban nationals abroad. The Cuban leader released more than 3,600 prisoners, including those who had participated in the Bay of Pigs and CIA operations to overthrow his regime, and he permitted more than 100,000 Cubans to travel abroad to visit their families for the first time in twenty years.[21]

Castro's willingness to address humanitarian issues was a source of much chagrin for Mas Canosa. "Talk with Castro . . . is politically absurd," he wrote, and he urged his readers not to succumb to "emotional impulse" and not to "fall into Castro's ploy."[22] When many ignored this warning and traveled to Cuba anyway, Mas Canosa grudgingly admitted that the *diálogo* was Castro's victory and his defeat.[23] Mas Canosa could not be too callous about the plight of prisoners, whom he considered patriots. He signed up as a member of the Vuelos de la Dignidad (Flights with Dignity), a group that offered flight assistance to bring released Cuban prisoners to Florida. Even those who still intensely opposed talks with Castro supported his release of prisoners.

Mas Canosa sensed that Carter and Castro had been working to neutralize opposition to the idea of US-Cuba normalization among Miami Cubans. Havana kept inviting US senators and representatives to observe revolutionary achievements and encouraging them to speak favorably about the improvement in US-Cuba relations. Washington had already lifted the ban on American tourists to the island and had agreed with Havana on fishing, maritime boundaries, and the opening of interest sections in the two capitals. But nothing was more significant than Washington-Havana collaboration on the departure and entrance of ex-prisoners. For Mas Canosa and his supporters, it appeared that Washington had exploited human rights issues—something nobody could contest—to justify US communication with Cuba. According to Pepé Hernández, a CANF founding member and its longtime president, this move was alarming, since it would further marginalize their voice. The creation of a new ethnic lobby in Washington was their solution to this fundamental problem.[24]

Alfredo Durán, chair of the Florida Democratic Party and a close ally of Carter, confirmed this story. Durán initially sought to bridge differences of opinion between US officials and anti-Castro hard-liners by asking Carter to consider the views of Miami Cubans before devising US policy. Yet when Carter administration officials tried to persuade anti-Castro hard-liners to support dialogue as a way to solve human rights issues, Mas Canosa and others refused to talk with Castro, whom they regarded as an inveterate enemy.[25] Mas Canosa later invited Durán to his group's discussion of a plan to create a lobby in Washington, probably to broaden support for his idea of expanding the Cuban American presence in US politics. But the two men went their separate ways before long. "He never listened to me," Durán said of Mas Canosa, "or anybody." A decade later, Durán played a role in establishing the Cuban Committee for Democracy, a CANF rival. Nevertheless, during an interview with this author, Durán affirmed that CANF was Mas Canosa's idea, and he pointed out that the discussion took place even before Reagan launched his 1980 presidential campaign.[26]

Mariel, Reagan, and the American Israel Public Affairs Committee

Ronald Reagan was an ideal presidential candidate for anti-Castro Cubans searching for an ally in Washington. Reagan repeated his hard stance against Cuba, and the Republican Party platform not only denounced the "takeover" by Marxist-Leninists in Cuba, Nicaragua, and elsewhere but also claimed that "Castro's totalitarian Cuba, financed, directed, and supplied by the Soviet Union, aggressively trains, arms, and supports forces of warfare and revolution" in Latin America.[27] Many anti-Castro activists and organizations liked this gung-ho language, and so did ordinary American voters of Cuban origin. Reagan received more than 90 percent of Miami Cubans' votes in both the 1980 and 1984 presidential elections.[28]

The rise of Reagan presented an ideal opportunity for Mas Canosa's group to gain a foothold in Washington. Indeed, many scholars look at the timing of political change in Washington and Miami and conclude that the formation of CANF must have resulted from the new administration's initiative. In his award-winning book, Cuban scholar Jesús Arboleya claims that CIA director William Casey created the foundation to make public opinion more receptive to Reagan's policy in Latin America by carrying out public diplomacy both inside and outside the United States.[29] Political scientists Patrick J. Haney and Walt Vanderbush assert that Richard Allen, Reagan's first national security adviser, weighed the potential importance of anticommunist Cuban exiles and "encouraged" Mas Canosa, Carlos Salmán, and Raúl Masvidal to form a lobby.[30] Sociologist María de los Angeles Torres takes a similar view, claiming that the foundation's first meeting took place at the National Security Council office in Washington.[31]

But a distinction should be made between "encouragement" and "creation." The idea of forming a Cuban American lobby in Washington already existed in Miami. Anti-Castro activists like Mas Canosa perceived Carter as hopelessly weak and unbelievably naïve in his dealings with the Cuban government. They claimed that Carter yielded too often to Castro, who had exploited the US-Cuban dialogue to cement his rule on the island and marginalize his foes abroad.[32] In addition, Miami Cubans' aspirations to broaden their political presence in Washington increased after the Mariel boatlift of 1980, in which nearly 125,000 Cubans flooded South Florida. Mas Canosa and his followers were convinced that Carter had mismanaged the migration crisis to allow Castro to embarrass the United States—and the Cuban American community in Miami. Sensational reports about criminals and "undesirable" migrants entering the United States during the boatlift undermined the image of Cuban Americans in the rest of the world. For some, restoring a positive Cuban American image was the main reason for participating in Mas Canosa's project.[33]

According to Pepé Hernández, the meeting with Richard Allen was Mas Canosa's idea, not Allen's. Carlos Salmán, a founding member of CANF and head of the 1980 Reagan-Bush campaign in Dade County (Miami), had direct access to Allen, who was one of Reagan's top nationwide campaign organizers. At the same time, Mas Canosa's group looked beyond Reagan Republicans for assistance. Among the group's initial members were several Cuban American Democrats such as Alfredo Durán and Raúl Masvidal. They were close to Democratic senators Ted Kennedy and John Glenn, two major political figures who opposed Reagan. José Ruiz Rodríguez, another CANF founding member and president of the Florida Fruit and Vegetable Association, invited his Jewish friend Barney Barnett to join the circle. Barnett was a Republican lobbyist active in pro-Israel causes. He was also a former national president of the United Jewish Appeal, an umbrella philanthropic group aiding the Jewish community abroad.[34]

In particular, Miami Cubans benefited from their access to Jewish lobbyists' experiences in Washington. Barnett apparently liked the new project, and he introduced the group to Tom Dine, executive director of the American Israel Public Affairs Committee (AIPAC). In early 1981

AIPAC set up the orientation seminars for CANF directors in a hotel in West Palm Beach, Florida, and taught them how to build an effective organization, how to gain tax-exempt status, and how to lobby the US government.[35] Dine liked Cuban Americans. "They were the young yuppies, straight out of the American melting pot," he recalled years later. Dine advised these Cubans to build political support for their cause regardless of party or ideological affiliations.[36] Dine probably kept in touch with Mas Canosa, and he later sent a copy of AIPAC's bylaws to Mas Canosa through Barnett, asking whether the CANF chairman wanted to see him while he was in southern Florida.[37] Aside from connecting the Cubans to AIPAC, Barnett played another important role: he gave CANF its name.[38]

Mas Canosa later called Barnett "our teacher" and a "master in politics." According to Mas Canosa, Barnett "knew every important person in Washington" and "taught us how to operate and get into the political system in this country."[39] So why did Barnett step in to assist Mas Canosa's group? Particularly noteworthy is his close attention to the link between Cuba and the Palestine Liberation Organization (PLO), which became a growing concern among the pro-Israel lobby. In a memorandum dated August 5, 1983, for example, the Conference of Presidents of Major American Jewish Organizations warned about Cuba's role in the expansion of PLO influence in Latin America. "Castro had begun as a supporter of Israel," the memo stated, "but by 1966 the Cuban leader was already making the PLO a factor in Latin American revolutionary activities." The danger of Cuban cooperation with the PLO was growing. The Salvadoran and Nicaraguan revolutionaries—allied with the revolutionary government in Cuba—expressed "solidarity with the Palestinian people." These Latin Americans denounced Israel as "racist" and encouraged "terroristic" activities.[40]

Many reporters and policy analysts took note of this seemingly threatening trend in the Western Hemisphere. "Since being introduced to the region by Castro," the authors of *White House Digest* noted, "the PLO has developed ties with revolutionary groups in nearly half the countries in the [Latin American] region."[41] Curiously, Barnett read all these reports and forwarded many of them to Mas Canosa.[42] By drawing his attention to these materials, Barnett was probably trying to persuade Mas Canosa that they were on the same side of the related Cold War battle. As long as Cuba was allied with the PLO, Cuba was Israel's enemy. If so, anti-Castro activists were enemies of the enemy or, more simply, friends. According to his son Charles, Barney Barnett became active in Cuban issues because he thought Cuban émigrés were much like "the Jews in Israel, against totalitarianism and for freedom."[43]

Barnett made some interesting comments about CANF during a telephone interview with the *New York Times.* "They [CANF directors] came to understand," he said, "that you have to support the people who support your issues." He was probably hinting about the CANF-AIPAC collaboration, designed to attack Cuban-PLO ties in US politics and beyond. Not surprisingly, Barnett had a high opinion of Mas Canosa, characterizing him as a strong and capable leader. He believed Mas Canosa had managed to bring "exiles who couldn't agree on anything in the past . . . along a moderate road."[44]

The Birth of CANF and Its Lobby

CANF was born on July 6, 1981, as a nonprofit Florida corporation. The purpose of the foundation was "to advise, educate, and otherwise inform the public of the advantages of a democratic form of government and the threat by communistic forms of government in the Western Hemisphere, such as those represented by the country of Cuba."[45] Its members supported this purpose through their annual fees. The directors contributed $10,000 per year, organized fund-raising campaigns, and solicited financial contributions from Cuban American companies in Miami. The bylaws established the Board of Directors and gave it the authority to control and manage the foundation's business affairs.

On July 15 Jorge Mas Canosa, Raúl Masvidal, and Carlos Salmán met in an office in Miami, where they elected Mas Canosa chairman. They also approved a list of seventeen directors, including Carlos Benitez, Luis Botifoll, Tony Costa, Oscar Fernández, Feliciano Foyo, Jorge L. Garrido, Felix Granados, Francisco "Pepé" Hernández, Alberto J. Mariño, Miguel Angel Martínez, Domingo R. Moreira, Carlos Pérez, José Luis Rodríguez, and Diego R. Suárez.[46] These wealthy Miami Cubans had achieved economic success in one generation and now wanted to use their resources to strengthen their fight against the Cuban revolution. The foundation's executive director in Washington was Frank Calzón, a Cuban American activist and lobbyist for human rights in Cuba. CANF members worked to "Americanize" anti-Castro politics. Washington, rather than Cuba, would have to be their main battleground for the time being.

CANF's confidential internal records dated August 11, 1981, tell part of the story of the group's first activities. On July 30, with the help of columnist Jack Anderson, the foundation placed a message from Armando Valladares, a well-known Cuban political prisoner, in the *Washington Post*. "An appalling message has been smuggled to me from the confines of Fidel Castro's political prison system, an anguished account of torture experienced by Cuban poet Armando Valladares." The columnist added, "It is the first personal word I've received from him in two years." A week later, Anderson again relied on CANF to write another Cuba-related column entitled "Castro's Power Boosted by Two Strange Crashes." Anderson suspected that Castro was involved in two plane crashes that had killed Panamanian strongman Omar Torrijos and Ecuadoran president Jaime Roldos.[47]

Aside from these negative media campaigns against the Cuban leader, the same CANF document referenced the foundation's incipient lobbying in the US Congress. In particular, the foundation worked to broaden congressional support for a resolution proposed by Senators Harry Byrd and Ernest Hollings, which condemned US participation in the Inter-Parliamentary Union Conference at Havana in September. The anti-Castro activists tried to enlist some House members to adopt a similar resolution, and they contacted all foreign policy staffs for the congressional members who had expressed an interest in visiting Cuba, seeking a chance to meet with them.[48] In the end, Congress sent delegations to Havana, as it had for all previous meetings.

In the following months, CANF enlarged its bipartisan support on Capitol Hill. Those who were already hostile to Fidel Castro, such as Senator Jesse Helms, were natural allies for the foundation, although they did not always focus on Cuba. In this regard, members of the Florida delegation who had a strong political interest in securing the votes of Miami's Cuban Americans were particularly important. Despite his liberal stance on domestic matters, Dante Fascell, a Democratic congressman representing Miami, was mindful of his constituency, especially with regard to Cuba. Fascell was an influential member of the House Committee on Foreign Affairs from 1983 until his retirement in 1993.

Even more remarkable was the role of Paula Hawkins, a first-time Florida senator elected in 1980. Mas Canosa supported her campaign and later kept in touch with Hawkins.[49] When the foundation emerged, Mas Canosa convinced her to participate on its Advisory Committee.[50] Among all US politicians, Hawkins proved most eager to promote Mas Canosa. For example, she wrote numerous letters in support for his candidacy for a governmental post, especially when the Reagan administration announced its setup of the Presidential Commission on Broadcasting to Cuba, a special advisory board to undertake preparations for Radio Martí.[51] When Mas Canosa was selected as a board member, Hawkins lobbied the Immigration and Naturalization Service and the FBI to speed up the naturalization process so that Mas Canosa could become a US citizen at the earliest possible date.[52]

Outside Florida, the foundation sought to overcome negative stereotypes of Cuban Americans as terrorists and drug traffickers, images reinforced by newspaper reports about the Mariel boatlift.[53] To compete with the Cuban government in Havana, the foundation invited members of Congress—along with their families—to Miami, where they enjoyed lavish fund-raising events and comfortable stays in the winter. These efforts appeared to bear fruit. For instance, Senator Howard Metzenbaum, one of those with a negative opinion of Miami Cubans prior to his visit, expressed his appreciation for Mas Canosa's hosting of a fund-raising event. "The warmth of your hospitality, your beautiful home, and the fabulous food made for an unforgettable evening," the senator noted. Mas Canosa's generosity and that of his friends "meant a great deal *particularly* in these last few weeks [prior to the 1982 midterm elections]."[54]

CANF directors often lobbied themselves rather than hiring professional lobbyists. "I don't look at them as typical lobbyists," said a favorably impressed aide for a US congressman. "They are doing it out of an emotional and personal imperative that is diametrically opposed to 99 percent of the lobbyists in Washington." Such comments imply that even if the volume of CANF's financial contributions was relatively small, personal encounters and interactions added value to its lobbying efforts.[55] The effect was immeasurable. After all, every politician wants to be able to say that his or her actions were motivated by pleas from the people rather than the power of money.

CANF's Political Power

The Reagan administration was receptive to the growth of CANF's power in Washington. As many scholars note, CANF undoubtedly benefited from its ideological compatibility with the Reagan administration's foreign policy in the Caribbean and Central America. To spur domestic support for his unpopular foreign policy in the region, the president signed National Security Decision Directive 77 to embark on a public relations campaign inside and outside the United States. The foundation's "educational" activities fell within this foreign policy framework.[56] CANF published numerous essays and books written by conservative politicians and academics, including Lord Hugh Thomas, Paul Hollander, Susan Kaufman Purcell, Mark Falcoff, and Jeane Kirkpatrick, then US ambassador to the United Nations. The foundation distributed these published materials to more than 2,000 professors across the United States for free.[57] At one point, Reagan himself praised CANF for providing "an antidote to the big lie of Castro's Cuba." According to the president, CANF reminded Americans that Cuba was "little more than a surrogate for a faraway totalitarian power which threatens the vital interests of the United States and undermines the stability of the hemisphere."[58]

The Reagan administration also counted on information supplied by CANF to condemn Cuba on the international stage. For example, in his June 1982 cable to US embassies in London, Paris, Madrid, Bonn, and Zurich, Secretary of State Alexander Haig asked US diplomats to assist the foundation in lobbying their host governments. "It is U.S. policy to undermine Cuban credit-worthiness," Haig wrote. "One means to do so is to call attention to the severe hard currency problems that [the Cuban] economy is suffering." In particular, Haig wanted the diplomats to work with CANF. "A private group, the Cuban American National Foundation, has completed a study of the Cuban debt crisis and plans to travel in September to address cities to discuss their findings with appropriate interlocutors." The State Department had already created a preliminary list of contacts for the diplomats, chiefly individuals working for the press and the banks.[59] The extent to which foreign governments responded to this type of lobbying is unclear. Yet it is undeniable that the Reagan administration took advantage of the rise of CANF both at home and abroad.

CANF was not the Reagan administration's puppet, however. Despite the commonality of interests, CANF often exerted inordinate pressure on the administration. Particularly telling was the January 1982 incident involving Andrés Rodríguez Hernández, a Cuban stowaway found on a Panamanian vessel in Miami. Although Rodríguez applied for asylum in the United States, the Justice Department immediately repatriated him to Cuba, making him the first Cuban in decades who had been refused admission to the United States.[60] Why did this happen? The State Department had confirmed with the Cuban government that Rodríguez would not be harshly treated if he were sent back to Cuba. Since the Cuban government had accepted him as a deportee, it was impossible for Rodríguez to establish a "well-founded fear of persecution based on race, religion, nationality, membership of a particular social group, or political opinion"—a necessary condition for the granting of asylum under the Refugee Act of 1980. Havana was well aware of the symbolic importance of this deportation. Cuban authorities not only dropped illegal exit charges against Rodríguez but also allowed the *Miami Herald* to interview him and his family in Havana.[61]

Yet as so often happened, Havana's satisfaction meant Miami's resentment. The deportation of Rodríguez instigated a riot in Miami, as 5,000 angry demonstrators clashed with police officers. To deal with the crisis, the city of Miami established a blue-ribbon commission whose members included Jorge Mas Canosa, and the commission issued a resolution condemning the deportation instead of the demonstration.[62] Angry Miami Cubans also met with White House chief of staff James A. Baker III to convey "the unprecedented rise of anti-Reagan sentiment."[63] Attorney General William French Smith defended the deportation as "consistent" with US "policy of discouraging mass migrations to the United States, like the Mariel boatlift."[64] But the White House relented, and national security adviser William Clark reported that no one, including stowaways, would be returned to Cuba.[65] The White House did something else: it blocked Myles Frechette, the State Department's Cuban desk officer (whom Mas Canosa blamed for the deportation) from becoming chief of the US interests section in Havana and later from becoming deputy assistant secretary of state for inter-American affairs. In his talks with the Canadian ambassador in Washington, Frechette himself confirmed that his appointment as deputy assistant secretary had been canceled due to White House pressure.[66] Frechette ended up going to Cameroon as ambassador.

Kenneth Skoug, Frechette's successor as Cuban desk officer, wondered why Miami Cubans blamed Frechette for this incident. In fact, the government records show that it was not the Cuban Desk Office but the Bureau of Human Rights and Humanitarian Affairs that assisted the Justice Department on this case.[67] According to Frechette, he tried to stop the deportation, but the Immigration and Naturalization Service refused to listen to him.[68] It is possible that Mas Canosa used this incident to oust an unfriendly bureaucrat from an important State Department post related to Cuban affairs. In an August 1981 letter to Senator Hawkins, Mas Canosa urged her to prevent Johns Hopkins University from inviting "a high level mission" from Cuba for a September symposium. "WE MUST STOP THIS," Mas Canosa wrote. "It is an offense to the Cuban American community." He then blamed Frechette for not blocking this event, calling it "one more reason to push for the replacement" of the Cuban desk officer.[69] In another letter to Hawkins, Mas Canosa called Frechette "an enthusiastic spokesman of the weak and permissive policy of the Carter administration towards the Castro regime."[70]

Indeed, Mas Canosa's advocacy for Frechette's removal reached the latter's ears prior to Rodríguez's deportation. When asked by this author about Reagan's relationship with Mas Canosa, Frechette noted that Mas Canosa was a big contributor to the Reagan campaign and had good access to the president. Certainly, the Reagan–Mas Canosa ties were often exaggerated. According to Frechette, Reagan listened to what Mas Canosa had to say, responded politely, and then forgot much of what had been said. But "Carter offended Miami Cubans," Frechette observed, "and the last thing Reagan wanted to do was to follow Carter's steps." The former Cuban desk officer added that Reagan "counted on their votes in Florida."[71]

Reagan was mindful of his 1984 reelection campaign, as indicated by his participation in a Cuban "Independence Day" ceremony in Miami on May 20, 1983. The event was sponsored by CANF and became the biggest public relations success for Reagan Republicans in South Florida. Reagan made a highly emotional speech before the Cuban American audience. "Now is the time to act reasonably and decisively," he argued, "to avert a crisis and prevent other people from suffering the same fate as your brothers and sisters in Cuba." Referring to congressional opposition to his foreign policy in Latin America, the president emphasized the urgency of defending the region from aggression by "the Soviet-Cuban-Nicaraguan axis."[72] Reagan's audience interrupted this hawkish speech thirty-two times with standing ovations. Outside the auditorium he was welcomed by "up to 70,000 flag-waving fans" along the route of his motorcade. "Superstar Wows Little Havana," said the headline in the *Miami Herald*.[73]

This response no doubt pleased Reagan, who intended to win Florida, a strategically important swing state in US presidential elections, in 1984. "Off to Miami to address the Cuban American [National] Foundation," the president scribbled in his diary. "It was a thrilling experience. I was told there were 50,000 outside the hall hearing me, as well as the 3 or 4,000 in the hall." Reagan continued, "I couldn't count the standing ovations. All their businesses had closed for the occasion and the streets were lined with people cheering and applauding."[74] Financial contributions, shared anti-Castro ideology, and reelection strategies incentivized the Reagan administration's outreach to CANF. By appealing directly to the US president, the foundation grew politically powerful.

Established in July 1981, the Cuban American National Foundation could trace its lineage directly from the Cuban counterrevolutionary tradition in Miami. Since the early years of the Cuban revolution, Jorge Mas Canosa and his followers engaged in the battle against Fidel Castro and his regime in Cuba. Although their military operations failed to topple the Cuban government, they continued to be politically active. Much like other counterrevolutionary forces throughout Latin America, these anticommunist activists looked to US-Cuban rapprochement in the 1970s with alarm and felt obliged to contest US policy toward Cuba. They thought that, without their participation in US politics, US-Cuban rapprochement was inevitable and just around the corner. By undermining the popular image of Cuban Americans, the Mariel boatlift also motivated their pursuit of greater representation of their political opinions in Washington.

A Cuban American political lobby would have emerged in the early 1980s with or without a Reagan presidency, although the latter was a critical factor in the foundation's quick rise to power. Reagan Republicans did not create the foundation, but they encouraged Miami Cubans to enter US politics in pursuit of their aim to topple the Cuban government. As he engaged in the Cold War in Latin America, Reagan welcomed this mobilization because he believed his administration's foreign policy and the Cuban American community's interests were harmonious, especially in terms of garnering domestic support for the contra war in Central America and attacking Cuba's economy. Reagan also liked to think that his popularity among Miami Cubans would translate into more votes for the Republican Party in Florida.

CANF nonetheless remained essentially independent because of its ability to expand its support network beyond Reagan Republicans. Fellow anti-Castro Cubans gave funds to the foundation's cause, and members of Congress came to its assistance out of political necessity and personal obligation. The foundation also relied on Jewish lobbyists to establish a strong organizational structure and to learn lobbying techniques. CANF was ready to exert pressure on the Reagan administration if necessary, as seen in the immediate aftermath of the January 1982 deportation of Andrés Rodríguez Hernández. The foundation joined Washington's internal battle in favor of a hard-line Cuban policy and successfully replaced the State Department's Cuban desk officer. By combining the rising economic strength of Cuban Americans with decades-long counterrevolutionary goals, CANF managed to increase its power. Whether it would come close to toppling the Castro regime was another question.

Notes

The University of Miami's Cuban Heritage Collection (CHC) Graduate Fellowship, funded by the Goizueta Foundation, provided support for my research in Miami. I am especially grateful to María Estorino, then CHC chair, and Gladys Gómez-Rossie, who assisted my research even outside the CHC. I am also grateful to archivist Matthew Angles for allowing me to examine unprocessed files at the Cuban American National Foundation Archive. Note that the numbers of record groups and names of folders may change in the near future; the untitled boxes are cited as such.

1. See, for example, Damián Fernández, "From Little Havana to Washington, D.C.: Cuban-Americans and U.S. Foreign Policy," in *Ethnic Groups and U.S. Foreign Policy,* ed. Mohammed E. Ahrari (Westport, CT: Greenwood Press, 1987); Morris Morley and Chris McGillion, *Unfinished Business: America and Cuba after the Cold War, 1989–2001* (Cambridge: Cambridge University Press, 2002); Pat-

rick J. Haney and Walt Vanderbush, *The Cuban Embargo: The Domestic Politics of an American Foreign Policy* (Pittsburgh: University of Pittsburgh Press, 2005); Lars Schoultz, *That Infernal Little Cuban Republic: The United States and the Cuban Revolution* (Chapel Hill: University of North Carolina Press, 2009).

2. One major study of Miami Cuban history is María Cristina García, *Havana USA: Cuban Exiles and Cuban Americans in South Florida, 1959–1994* (Berkeley: University of California Press, 1996). See also María de los Angeles Torres, *In the Land of Mirrors: Cuban Exile Politics in the United States* (Ann Arbor: University of Michigan Press, 1999); Gerald E. Poyo, *Cuban Catholics in the United States, 1960–1980: Exile and Integration* (Notre Dame, IN: University of Notre Dame Press, 2007).

3. See, for example, *Economist,* March 28, 1992, A24; *Miami Herald* (hereafter *MH*), October 11, 1992, 21A; *Time,* October 26, 1992, 56–57; *New York Times,* October 29, 1992, 18A; Gaeton Fonzi, "Who Is Jorge Mas Canosa?" *Esquire,* January 1993, 86–89, 119. See also the work by journalist Ann Louise Bardach, *Cuba Confidential: Love and Vengeance in Miami and Havana* (New York: Vintage, 2002).

4. Americas Watch, *Dangerous Dialogue: Attacks on Freedom of Expression in Miami's Cuban Exile Community,* August 1992.

5. For Mas Canosa's belief in Havana's shadow, see minutes of the board meeting, December 13, 1991, box 1.04, CANF Archive. At one board meeting, Mas Canosa commented that the US media was not only supportive of Fidel Castro but also "unwilling to admit" that the foundation was "right about Cuba." Minutes of the board meeting, November 20, 1992, 6, box 1.04, CANF Archive.

6. See, for example, Ramón Sánchez-Parodi, *Cuba-USA: diez tiempos de una relación* (Havana: Editorial de Ciencias Sociales, 2012), 194–200.

7. For works by supporters, see Álvaro Vargas Llosa, *El exilio indomable: historia de la disidencia cubana en el destierro* (Madrid: Espasa, 1998); Nestor Suárez Feliú, *El Rescate de una Nación* (Miami: Fundación Nacional Cubano Americana, 1997). For critical views, see Torres, *In the Land of Mirrors;* Jesús Arboleya, *The Cuban Counterrevolution,* trans. Rafael Betancourt (Athens: Ohio University Center for International Studies, 2000), 222–26; Jesús Arboleya, *Cuba y los cubanoamericanos: El fenómeno migratorio cubano* (Havana: Fondo Editorial Casa de las Ámericas, 2013), 178–79.

8. See, for example, Jussi Hanhimäki, "Global Visions and Parochial Politics: The Persistent Dilemma of the 'American Century,'" *Diplomatic History* 27, no. 4 (September 2003): 423–47.

9. For a larger picture of Cuban American roles in US-Cuba relations, see Hideaki Kami, *Diplomacy Meets Migration: U.S. Relations with Cuba during the Cold War* (New York: Cambridge University Press, forthcoming).

10. Thomas D. Boswell and James R. Curtis, *The Cuban-American Experience: Culture, Images, and Perspectives* (Totowa, NJ: Rowman and Allanheld, 1983), 1.

11. García, *Havana USA,* 118.

12. For the broader context of Cuban American politics, see Hideaki Kami,

"Ethnic Community, Party Politics, and the Cold War: The Political Ascendancy of Miami Cubans, 1980–2000," *Japanese Journal of American Studies* 23 (2012): 185–208.

13. Alexander Fursenko and Timothy Naftali, *"One Hell of a Gamble": Khrushchev, Castro, and Kennedy, 1958–1964* (New York: Norton, 1997), x; Michael Dobbs, *One Minute to Midnight: Kennedy, Khrushchev, and Castro on the Brink of Nuclear War* (New York: Knopf, 2008). In 1970 the US government confirmed its noninvasion pledge during a mini-crisis over a Soviet submarine base in Cienfuegos.

14. Don Bohning, *The Castro Obsession: U.S. Covert Operations against Cuba, 1959–1965* (Washington, DC: Potomac, 2005), chap. 13.

15. Stephen Bosworth, interview, 64, Foreign Affairs Oral History Project, Association for Diplomatic Studies and Training, Library of Congress.

16. See, for example, Haney and Vanderbush, *Cuban Embargo,* 99–100.

17. Myles Frechette, interview with author, Washington, DC, July 18, 2014.

18. Robert Gelbard, interview with author, Washington, DC, June 30, 2015.

19. "Jorge Mas Canosa," in *Encyclopedia of Cuban–United States Relations*, ed. Thomas M. Leonard (Jefferson, NC: McFarland, 2010), e-book (accessed October 25, 2014); *Los Angeles Times Magazine,* May 3, 1992, 22–23. For a far more critical portrait, see, for example, Arboleya, *Cuban Counterrevolution,* 228–31.

20. *Diario Las Américas* (Spanish-language newspaper in Miami), December 17, 1974, 1, 8.

21. Kami, *Diplomacy Meets Migration,* chap. 3.

22. *Diario Las Américas,* September 14, 1978, in "Jorge Mas Canosa," 1:333–34.

23. RECE, Mensaje, December 1978, ibid., 338–40.

24. Pepé Hernández, interview with author, Miami, May 7, 2014.

25. See Pastor to Brzezinski, October 8, 1977, NLC-24-11-4-3-6; Pastor to Brzezinski, October 26, 1977, NLC-24-11-4-2-8, Jimmy Carter Library, Atlanta, GA.

26. Alfredo Durán, interview with author, Miami, November 14, 2013. Pepé Hernández confirmed Durán's presence at the initial meetings. Hernández, interview with author, May 7, 2014.

27. Republican Party Platform of 1980, July 15, 1980, American Presidency Project.

28. Kami, "Ethnic Community," 191–93.

29. Arboleya, *Cuba y los cubanoamericanos,* 178–79.

30. Patrick J. Haney and Walt Vanderbush, "The Role of Ethnic Interest Groups in U.S. Foreign Policy: The Case of the Cuban American National Foundation," *International Studies Quarterly* 43 (1999): 348.

31. Torres, *In the Land of Mirrors,* 115. The first meeting in fact took place in Miami.

32. Pepé Hernández, interview, Luis J. Botifoll Oral History Project, Cuban Heritage Collection, University of Miami.

33. Ibid. For Mas Canosa's reaction to the Mariel boatlift, see RECE, Men-

sage, June 1980, in "Jorge Mas Canosa," 1:359–60. See also Durán, interview with author, November 14, 2013.

34. Hernández, interview with author, May 7, 2014. Allen claimed that he encouraged Mas Canosa to adapt the Jewish lobbying model. Cited in Andrew Cockburn, "Secretary of Nothing," *Harper's Magazine,* December 2013, https://harpers.org/archive/2013/12/secretary-of-nothing/3/ (accessed July 9, 2017).

35. Hernández, interview with author, May 7, 2014.

36. Quoted in *MH,* August 11, 1986, 1A.

37. Cited in Dine to Mas Canosa, November 3, 1982, "Old Docs" folder, box 4, CANF Archive.

38. Hernández, interview with author, May 7, 2014. See also Vargas Llosa, *El exilio indomable,* 121.

39. Quoted in *MH,* December 12, 1987, 3C.

40. Conference of Presidents of Major American Jewish Organizations, "Middle East Memo: Brotherhood of Terrorism," August 5, 1983, "AIPAC" folder, box 6.04, CANF Archive.

41. "PLO in Central America," *White House Digest,* July 20, 1983, 3, "AIPAC" folder, box 6.04, CANF Archive.

42. Karen Payne, "Central American Jews Fear PLO Ties," *Miami News,* June 13, 1983; Wolf Blitzer, "The Link with Latin America," *Jerusalem Post* (international edition), June 19–25, 1983, 4; Richard Araujo, "The Sandinista War on Human Rights," July 19, 1983, *Heritage Foundation Backgrounder,* all in "AIPAC" folder, box 6.04, CANF Archive.

43. Quoted in *MH,* December 12, 1987, 3C.

44. Quoted in *New York Times,* July 12, 1986, 6.

45. Articles of incorporation, July 6, 1981, and bylaws of CANF, "Incorporation and By-Laws" folder, box 1.04, CANF Archive.

46. Minutes of the board meeting, July 15, 1981, "Minutes, 1981–1985" folder, box 1.04, CANF Archive.

47. Informe de actividades recientes, August 11, 1981, "Old Docs" folder, box 4, CANF Archive. See also Jack Anderson, "Message from Valladares," *Washington Post,* July 30, 1981, B19; Jack Anderson, "Castro's Power Boosted by Two Strange Crashes," *Washington Post,* August 11, 1981, C15.

48. Informe de actividades recientes, August 11, 1981.

49. Mas Canosa to Hawkins, October 29, 1980, "Cuba/Jorge Mas" folder, box 1, series 7, Paula Hawkins Papers, Winter Park Public Library, Winter Park, FL.

50. Hawkins to Mas Canosa, June 9, 1981, "Old Docs" folder, box 4, CANF Archive.

51. Hawkins to Allen, September 25, 1981, "Cuba—Radio Broadcasting/Radio Martí (2)" folder; Hawkins to Allen, October 23, 1981, "Cuba—Radio Broadcasting/Radio Martí (1)" folder, box 90125, Roger Fontaine Files, Ronald Reagan Library, Simi Valley, CA.

52. Hawkins to John Gossart, November 18, 1981, and Hawkins to Bill Garvey, November 20, 1982, "Cuba/Jorge Mas" folder, box 1, series 7, Hawkins Papers.

53. Hernández, interview, in "Jorge Mas Canosa," 2:1473–74; Vargas Llosa, *El exilio indomable,* 130.

54. Metzenbaum to Mas Canosa, October 12, 1982, "Old Docs" folder, box 4, CANF Archive (emphasis added); Hernández, interview, in "Jorge Mas Canosa," 2:1473–74.

55. *MH,* August 11, 1986, 1A.

56. Haney and Vanderbush, *Cuban Embargo,* chaps. 2–3.

57. Suárez, *El Rescate,* 145.

58. Video address to CANF, May 20, 1983, in *Reagan on Cuba* (Miami: CANF, 1986), 32–33.

59. Haig to US embassies in London, Paris, Madrid, Bonn, and Zurich, June 25, 1982, State Department Records released through Freedom of Information Act, in author's possession.

60. Chronology in Alan C. Nelson (acting commissioner of Immigration and Naturalization Service) to William French Smith, January 22, 1982, "Immigration: Cubans/Haitians" folder, OA11593, Michael Uhlman Files, Reagan Library; memo for William P. Clark, "Repatriation of Cuban Stowaway," January 29, 1982, "Cuba (1/23/1982–2/1/1982)" folder, box 29, NSC-ES-CF, Reagan Library.

61. *MH,* January 21, 1982, A1; Canadian embassy in Havana to Ottawa, January 27, 1982, vol. 22007, 20-Cuba-1-3-USA, pt. 6, RG 25: Department of External Affairs, Library and Archive of Canada.

62. City of Miami, "Blue Ribbon Committee Report on Miami Cuban Demonstration of January 16, 1982," July 28, 1982.

63. Elizabeth H. Dole to Baker, January 21, 1982, "Immigration: Cubans/Haitians" folder, OA11593, Michael Uhlman Files, Reagan Library.

64. Craig Fuller to William French Smith, January 28, 1982, and Smith to Fuller, February 5, 1982, "Immigration Policy: Cubans and Haitians" folder, box 10, James W. Cicconi Files, Reagan Library.

65. Clark to Reagan, January 30, 1982, Declassified Documents Reference System.

66. Canadian embassy in Havana to Ottawa, November 3, 1982, vol. 22004, 20-Cuba-1-3-USA, pt. 7, RG 25, Library and Archive of Canada.

67. Kenneth Skoug, interview, 148, Foreign Affairs Oral History Project, Association for Diplomatic Studies and Training, Library of Congress; chronology in Nelson to Smith, January 22, 1982.

68. Frechette, interview with author, July 28, 2014.

69. Mas Canosa to Hawkins, August 21, 1981, "Cuba/Jorge Mas" folder, box 1, series 7, Hawkins Papers.

70. Mas Canosa to Hawkins, September 25, 1981, "Radio Marti Correspondence" folder, box 1.06, CANF Archive.

71. Frechette, interview with author, July 28, 2014.

72. Speech by Reagan, May 20, 1983, American Presidency Project.

73. *MH,* May 21, 1983, 1A, 9A.

74. Ronald Reagan, *The Reagan Diaries Unabridged,* ed. Douglas Brinkley (New York: HarperCollins, 2009), 1:228 (entry for May 20, 1983).

8

Forging Consensus on Vietnamese Reeducation Camp Detainees

The Families of Vietnamese Political Prisoners Association and US-Vietnam Normalization

Amanda C. Demmer

In early June 1992 Dr. Lewis M. Stern, the Department of Defense's country director for Indochina, Thailand, and Burma, wrote to Mrs. Khuc Minh Tho to request information about detainees held in Vietnamese reeducation camps.[1] Stern explained that the US government was contacting Tho, a Vietnamese American who had arrived in the United States as a refugee, because "there are few who know as much about this issue as you."[2] Tho served as president of the Families of Vietnamese Political Prisoners Association (FVPPA), a nongovernmental organization dedicated to securing the release of reeducation camp prisoners and their resettlement abroad. Although they rarely made headlines, the reeducation camp issue in general and FVPPA's efforts in particular played a significant role in US-Vietnam relations after 1975.

Scholars have long documented the ability of domestic political forces and nonstate actors to influence US policymaking during the Vietnam War.[3] Most histories of the conflict, however, end in 1973 with the Paris Peace Accords and the withdrawal of American military forces or in 1975 with the fall of Saigon. Among the relatively small number of historians who study post-1975 US-Vietnam relations, there is a strong consensus that nongovernmental actors continued to play a powerful, sometimes definitive role in US policymaking.[4] More specifically, scholars have highlighted the role of two powerful groups. The first and most prominent is the prisoner of war–missing in action (POW-MIA) lobby, spearheaded by the National League of Families of American Prisoners and Missing in Southeast Asia. Scholars such as Bruce Franklin and Michael Allen have demonstrated the many reasons it is appropriate to consider the league one of the "most formidable interest groups in wartime and postwar Washington."[5] They agree that the league's pervasive influence and insistence that US policymakers provide a "full accounting" of missing American servicemen actively forestalled normalization for decades.[6] The second influential group cited by historians is a powerful conglomeration of American corporations—loosely referred to as the "business lobby"—that added a strong voice in favor of normalization in the late 1980s and early 1990s.

Vietnamese Americans, this essay argues, also played a substantive role in US-Vietnam normalization.[7] While it is often tempting to equate "domestic politics" with election cycle–related demands and pressures, scholars have long demonstrated the need for a much broader understanding that includes, among other things, migrant groups' "immigrant foreign relations," or efforts to influence US policy toward their homelands.[8] Vietnamese studies is a robust field that has uncovered a great deal about Vietnamese Americans' resettlement and Americanization experiences, but we still have much to learn about their homeland politics.[9] This essay contributes to that larger goal by demonstrating how the Virginia-based Families of Vietnamese Political Prisoners Association influenced US policy toward reeducation camp detainees.

Washington announced special initiatives calling for the detainees' release and pledging to resettle former prisoners and their close family members in 1984, 1988, 1989, 1991, and 1996. The United States' consistent, long-term commitment to these individuals was far from inevitable. Indeed, given Americans' eagerness to wash their hands of Vietnam after 1975, the national preoccupation with missing American servicemen, and the highly visible plight of refugees who escaped Vietnam by sea, colloquially known as "boat people," it is a wonder that US policymakers paid more than lip service to reeducation camp prisoners. In the cold calculus of public perception and bottom lines, a major American commitment to reeducation camp detainees seemed to offer little upside, yet US policymakers made their release and resettlement a constant feature of the approach to US-Vietnam relations during the normalization period. While there are always multiple factors at work, FVPPA deserves a large share of the credit for making reeducation camp prisoners an American priority.

Scholars are beginning to document FVPPA's importance. Frances Martin's 2015 master's thesis is a valuable contribution to our understanding of FVPPA's internal workings and external advocacy.[10] Sam Vong's forthcoming article adds to Martin's analysis by examining FVPPA through "the prism of Vietnamese women's activism."[11] This essay expands on these works by demonstrating that FVPPA played a vital role not only in advocacy and resettlement but also in elevating the issue to a pillar of US normalization policy. By playing a key role in what human rights scholars call the "politics of information," and by embodying and consolidating connections between reeducation camp prisoners and long-standing family reunification precedents in US immigration law, FVPPA left an indelible imprint on the nation's foreign policy.[12]

Precedents and Challenges

The "support group of wives and family members" that eventually became the Families of Vietnamese Political Prisoners Association began meeting in 1977, the same year Jimmy Carter took the presidential oath of office.[13] As Vong details, in its early years the association functioned primarily as a "self-help group" for women whose "husbands, brothers, and sons" were in reeducation camps. The group worked primarily at the local level and met in the Virginia home of its future president Khuc Minh Tho. Tho lost her first husband, who fought for South Vietnam, to the war; her second husband was incarcerated in a reeducation camp. When Saigon fell, Tho was in the Philippines, where she worked in the South Vietnamese embassy. This position helped her gain knowledge of the bureaucratic workings of government, which would serve her well in years to come. In the late 1970s, however, Tho and her associates avoided overt political activism, fearing it would prompt Hanoi to retaliate against their loved ones.[14]

Although international observers were aware that reeducation camps existed in post-1975 Vietnam, definitive information remained elusive throughout the normalization period and is unavailable even today, as Vietnamese records on the camps remain closed. Quality information was especially scarce during the Carter administration because, as a Congressional Research Service report explained, "statistics are often unavailable and the Vietnamese Government carefully controls any outside observation."[15] This lack of information suited many Americans, who were eager to turn their attention elsewhere after years of seeing the Vietnam War dominate the news cycle. For the few that remained interested and invested in Indochina, the brutality and tragedy of genocide in Cambodia and the massive surge in boat people drew the most international attention. Finally, it is likely that Vietnam's reeducation policy seemed mild to those who expected that US government warnings of a "bloodbath" would come true. The existence of reeducation camps and the lives of those detained therein thus remained underreported, overshadowed, and unable to inspire the sympathy necessary for external intervention in the late 1970s.[16]

Slowly, however, a clearer picture of the Hanoi's reeducation system emerged. What is generally understood is that the Socialist Republic of Vietnam (SRV) ordered significant numbers of citizens of the former South Vietnam—perhaps more than 1 million—to report for "reeducation" that would take approximately ten to thirty days.[17] While Hanoi released half of these individuals within three months, the government expanded the program's time frame, keeping detainees "until their political loyalty is insured . . . or for a maximum period of 3 years."[18] The SRV, however, did not release the last detainees until 1992, and former members of the South Vietnamese military—that is, former American allies—accounted for the majority of those with the longest sentences. The elaborate reeducation camp system included more than 100 different detention facilities. Although there were undoubtedly differences, conditions at each of the camps involved armed guards, barely subsistence rations, harsh physical labor, mandatory "confessions," nonexistent medical care, and little if any family visitation.[19] Human rights activists later estimated that the annual mortality rate among reeducation detainees was 10 to 15 percent from 1975 to 1979.[20] As time went on, the camps regularly drew comparisons to concentration camps and gulags.[21]

The Carter administration knew of the camps' existence but did not press Hanoi on the issue. This is not to say that the president ignored Vietnam; on the contrary, many expected Carter to quickly normalize relations with Hanoi. As a February 1977 National Security Council memo put it: "obviously, we must seek to normalize relations with Vietnam."[22] During the early stages of normalization talks, Carter emphasized the importance of normalization without preconditions, that is, immediate normalization without any concomitant concessions or demands.[23] Given this stance, the administration decided—despite its embrace of human rights rhetoric—to leave "more difficult, time-consuming bilateral issues" such as reeducation camp prisoners to be resolved *after* normalization.[24]

The initial optimism that surrounded official normalization talks in the early Carter years proved unfounded. A series of international and regional shifts—including the US tilt toward China, the Vietnamese invasion of Cambodia, the outpouring of boat people, and the SRV-Soviet alliance—prompted the Carter administration to put official normalization negotiations on hold and then suspend them indefinitely.[25] Subsequent US policymakers adopted Carter's position and refused to resume formal normalization talks until Vietnamese troops withdrew from Cambodia and Hanoi provided a "full accounting" of missing American servicemen.

The United States did not publicly announce its willingness to resettle former reeducation camp prisoners until 1984. In the meantime, nongovernmental advocates lobbied to secure and then maintain an American commitment to reeducation camp detainees. From 1977 to 1984, FVPPA strategically consolidated its contacts with members of the Indochinese diaspora and with allies still living in Vietnam, securing an effective transnational information flow that one newspaper dubbed the "Vietnamese grapevine."[26] FVPPA also reached out to human rights organizations and US policymakers, especially State Department officials.[27] Once Ronald Reagan replaced Carter as commander in chief, more established organizations took note of the reeducation camp prisoners' plight and lobbied the White House and Congress to respond.

Foremost among these advocates was Ginetta Sagan's California-based Aurora Foundation. In 1983 the Aurora Foundation published *Violations of Human Rights in the Socialist Republic of Vietnam, April 30, 1975–April 30, 1983,* which contained a forty-six-page chapter on Hanoi's reeducation camp policy. That chapter used the testimony of former detainees who had fled Vietnam to expose the horror of daily life in the camps, and the report garnered a great deal of attention. Elliot Abrams, the assistant secretary of state for human rights and humanitarian affairs, congratulated Sagan on the publication. "I want . . . to tell you how important I think the report is," Abrams wrote in a June 1983 letter. "It has been getting wide distribution, and is really a landmark: no one will ever again be able to claim that he did not know."[28] The US Committee for Refugees, another human rights organization, also called on the administration to take action, as did members of Congress.[29]

In September 1984 Reagan responded. In testimony before Congress, Secretary of State George P. Shultz announced that the administration intended to create a special migration program for former reeducation camp detainees and their "close family members" through a preexisting multilateral initiative called the Orderly Departure Program (ODP). The ODP had started in 1979 as part the international community's response to the boat people and aimed to provide migrants a safe alternative to clandestine flight for "family reunification and humanitarian cases."[30]

While Reagan echoed this humanitarian rhetoric, the administration also clearly saw an opportunity to use this issue to serve larger geopolitical ends. Reagan's rebranding of the Vietnam War as a "noble cause" in 1980 is well known.[31] Yen Le Espirtu and Heather Marie Stur demonstrate the extent to which the White House used refugees both as retroactive "evidence of the appropriateness of U.S. actions in Vietnam" and as "part of a larger American effort to rehabilitate its image of itself as a benevolent power."[32] Given these policy goals, it was no coincidence that Reagan announced new policies for POW-MIAs, reeducation detainees, and Amerasians—the children of American servicemen and Vietnamese women—at the end of his first term. Embracing these issues reflected the administration's willingness, even eagerness, to publicly criticize Hanoi's internal policies.

US policymakers therefore employed a very specific definition of "humanitarian" when crafting policy toward Hanoi after 1975. US officials in Congress, the State Department, and the White House equated "humanitarian" with those issues that involved family reunification: POW-MIAs, reeducation camp prisoners, Amerasians, and, more broadly, emigration through the ODP.[33] It is important to note that this framing was not inevitable and omitted many unresolved issues from the Vietnam War that could have fallen under the "humanitarian" umbrella, such as the lasting effects of Agent Orange, to name only one example. The advocacy of nonstate actors such as the National League of Families of American Prisoners and Missing in Southeast Asia and FVPPA therefore helped popularize and legitimize a family reunification–based definition of "humanitarian." Although US officials insisted that the release and resettlement of reeducation camp prisoners were, like other humanitarian issues, separate from political concerns, they also insisted that Hanoi address humanitarian issues *before* the two sides moved forward with formal political and economic relations, thereby adding to the political significance of these purportedly nonpolitical issues. Ultimately, in the absence of official ties, humanitarian issues became the basis of ongoing US-Vietnam relations.

The United States could not unilaterally impose its desired policies, however. The ODP required US-Vietnamese cooperation through multilateral channels, and a special program for former reeducation detainees would require even more direct, bilateral policies. Despite initial offers to comply, Hanoi consistently rebuffed US efforts to create a separate detainee subprogram, likely viewing this as an uninvited intrusion into its internal affairs.[34] It was during this impasse that FVPPA solidified its place as a potent force in US domestic politics and contributed to changes in the nation's normalization policy.

FVPPA Becomes a Major Force

Shultz's public pledge to support the creation of a special program for reeducation prisoners within the ODP marked a key turning point for FVPPA.[35] The following month, the association received official nonprofit corporation status and increased its lobbying efforts dramatically. On September 15, four days after Shultz's testimony, Tho wrote identical letters to President Reagan and Secretary of State Shultz expressing FVPPA's gratitude and offering its services. "With our capability, our devotion and our tract [*sic*] record," she explained, "our association endeavors to be a clearing house for the political prisoners and their family members . . . to ensure family reunification."[36] FVPPA certainly made good on this promise, as American policymakers would soon attest.

Shultz's and Reagan's responses to the September 15 letter demonstrate the limits—but also the potential—of FVPPA's power in 1984. Shultz responded four days later and emphasized that the State Department shared FVPPA's concerns. "I can assure you," Shultz promised, "that this government is ready to do its part for those who have suffered so much for their support of the cause of freedom in Vietnam."[37] FVPPA did not hear from the White House until October 16, a month later, and Linas Kojelis, the associate director of the Office of Public Liaison, incorrectly addressed the letter to "Mr. Tho."[38] Although it was beginning to make connections and solidify its position as an important lobbying force, FVPPA did not demand the attention the White House consistently awarded to the National League of Families.[39] The league's director Ann Mills Griffiths, for example, occupied a permanent seat on the official POW-MIA Interagency Group; this gave her access to US officials and classified documents, garnering sufficient influence to earn the nickname "the fourth branch of government."[40] Although FVPPA never attained the league's visibility, it achieved similar policy successes, despite starting from a much weaker position.

FVPPA enhanced its stature on the domestic political scene by wielding the language of family and developing and maintaining close relationships with key US officials. The association's emphasis on family relationships and family reunification served multiple functions. First, it vividly captured the organization's primary goal: to secure family reunification through the release and resettlement of political prisoners. Second, FVPPA framed itself—in both name and practice—in ways that highlighted familial relationships and gave the association an emotionally poignant way to sell its cause. As Martin notes, "by calling them brothers, sons, and fathers, Khuc gave them an identity, rather than allowing them to remain abstract ideas like 'prisoner' or 'refugee.'"[41] This emphasis helped transcend any potential cultural barriers that separated newly arrived Vietnamese refugees and the American officials whose support FVPPA needed to achieve its goals. Family reunification rhetoric fell on especially receptive ears in the 1980s, thanks to the Reagan administration's emphasis on a return to "family values."[42]

FVPPA's focus on family reunification also echoed decades of American immigration law. As immigration historian Roger Daniels notes, "family reunification" had been "a cornerstone of American immigration policy since 1921."[43] Family reunification's place in US immigration policy grew dramatically during World War II and the early Cold War, especially with regard to migrants from Asia, thanks to special provisions for military brides and international adoption.[44] The 1952 McCarran-Walter Act and the landmark 1965 Hart-Cellar Act codified this trend even further by earmarking family reunification as a preference category that superseded national and hemispheric limits.[45] The association shrewdly tied these precedents to the specific issue of reeducation detainees and, through its consistent personal advocacy on behalf of "husbands, brothers, and sons," gave a human face to an abstract concept.

Rather than simply lobby US officials, FVPPA developed close, mutually beneficial relationships with key figures in Congress, the National Security Council, and the State Department.[46] One noteworthy example is FVPPA's relationship with Robert F. Funseth, senior deputy assistant secretary of state for the Bureau of Refugee Affairs and the primary negotiator with the SRV on the reeducation issue throughout the 1980s. In Tho's words, Funseth and his staff "continuously kept us appraised [*sic*] of . . . information that would not have been otherwise available to us."[47]

FVPPA also returned the favor. Under the ODP, Vietnam had to approve individuals for departure by issuing exit permits and then allowing UN officials to interview potential migrants in Ho Chi Minh City. These requirements gave the SRV considerable power. Hanoi refused to publish reeducation detainees' names, which meant that US officials were unable to advocate for exit permits on behalf of specific individuals. Accurate information was so rare that international observers regularly disputed the camps' total population. For example, by Vietnam's own admission, 16,000 people remained incarcerated in 1985; yet two years later, an Aurora Foundation publication estimated that reeducation detainees numbered "at least 25,000."[48] FVPPA filled this information gap and provided the US government with reliable information on specific cases. In 1985 alone, when there were only 150 FVPPA members, the association received approximately "5,000 dossiers requesting their intervention on behalf of prisoners" and would receive "three to four times" that number by 1991.[49] FVPPA, then, is a prime example of what Margaret E. Keck and Kathryn Sikkink describe as "nontraditional international actors . . . mobiliz[ing] information strategically" to persuade and pressure traditional state actors by tapping into transitional networks.[50]

FVPPA established itself as a vital link in the release and resettlement process. As Martin has shown, FVPPA provided US officials with constantly updated lists of those still held in reeducation facilities and also sent out regular (bilingual) newsletters informing Vietnamese families about the many procedural changes and new forms that accompanied shifts in official interviewing procedures.[51] By providing the US government *and* Vietnamese families with scarce, accurate information, FVPPA performed a valuable and difficult function in a complex international process and exerted an influence that far eclipsed its modest membership and limited financial resources.

In addition to acting out of a compelling personal desire to be reunited with their loved ones, FVPPA members made many strategic decisions that helped the association solidify its position as an organization of national importance. FVPPA keenly understood that it was not operating in a cultural or political vacuum. The year after Shultz's announcement of the expansion of the ODP program, *Rambo*: *First Blood Part II* appeared in theaters. As Edwin Martini explains, the film's "shameless propagandizing of the POW/MIA myth"—the idea that Hanoi was holding live American POWs against their will—set off a wave of "'Rambomania' in the summer of 1985," and the film "became a new reference point in American culture."[52]

FVPPA appropriated this POW-MIA rhetoric to serve its own ends.[53] In a series of letters to officials in the White House, Congress, and the State Department, FVPPA emphasized that it was fighting the same fight as the National League of Families: "We share the same pain and sufferings as the wives and children of American POWs," FVPPA informed Secretary of State Shultz in September 1985, and "in a sense, our husbands and fathers are POWs too."[54] When writing to Congressman Gerald B. H. Solomon, chairman of the POW-MIA Task Force, Tho introduced the organization by explaining, "we are . . . the Vietnamese version of The National League of Families of POWs in more modest proportions," and she argued that Vietnamese political prisoners "are POWs in the truest sense. The United States can in good conscience close the books on the war *only* when all of the American POWs will be released—and the Vietnamese POWs also."[55] As FVPPA put it in an August 1986 letter to President Reagan, "we understand America's concern for her MIA's; we think it important to speak out for our husbands, brothers, and sons as well. Please do not forget them!"[56] POW-MIA rhetoric, which was both culturally powerful and a significant basis of US policy, helped FVPPA consolidate official backing by speaking to American officials in a language they understood. Moreover, whereas MIA advocates demanding the return of live American POWs challenged US policymakers with a request that "could never be satisfied," FVPPA presented them with a solvable problem.[57]

FVPPA thus personified and consolidated the connection among reeducation camp detainees, family reunification, humanitarian language, and the nation's Indochina policy. This potent combination earned the association widespread bipartisan support. As it achieved greater recognition within the corridors of power, FVPPA used POW-MIA rhetoric less and less, reflecting that it no longer needed to justify itself in reference to another cause; the release and resettlement of reeducation camp prisoners could stand on its own merits.

As proof, one need only look at the guest list for FVPPA's first annual reception on Capitol Hill in April 1987. Robert Funseth, Senator Bob Dole (R-KA), Senator Ted Kennedy (D-MA), and Representative Stephen J. Solarz (D-NY) all attended and gave speeches in support of FVPPA's cause to an audience of over 300 members of Congress, State Department officials, administration representatives, and Vietnamese Americans. "It isn't often you find Senator Dole and I together speaking alike in support of issues," Kennedy explained, "but this is certainly one that brings all Americans together." He continued, "All of us Americans put a very strong emphasis on families" and noted that familial ties are the "bedrock of our strength."[58] Senator Dole, a longtime and vociferous supporter of POW-MIA accounting, echoed FVPPA's equating of reeducation detainees and American POWs: "We have a responsibility," he argued, "whether they're in reeducation camps, or are POWs, or MIAs. It is a responsibility we share and one that we will not forget."[59]

Dole and Kennedy backed their words with action. The very next day they cosponsored a resolution, along with Claiborne Pell (D-RI), chairman of the Senate Foreign Relations Committee, "calling for the release of political prisoners by the government of Vietnam." As Dole explained, the resolution urged the SRV to release the prisoners and "expedite all family reunification cases still outstanding."[60] When introducing the resolution, Kennedy noted that it was intended "to focus renewed attention on one of the utmost urgent humanitarian issues in the aftermath of the Vietnam War—the continued plight of political prisoners in Vietnam and the problem of family reunification."[61] As Dole argued, it "is totally nonpolitical; certainly, in our political terms in the Senate, it is totally nonpartisan. All Senators ought to support it."[62] And they did; the Senate passed Resolution 205, the first of many resolutions on this issue, unanimously.[63]

US policy toward Vietnam during the Reagan administration thus involved a specific merging of larger trends in American law and thought. Crucially, the particular mix of ideas was not preordained, and FVPPA's brand of advocacy helped crystalize and catalyze the links among human rights, family reunification, and refugee law in a way that had wide bipartisan appeal. Thus, as Barbara Keys has demonstrated, human rights rhetoric appealed to both those on the Left *and* those on the Right—to those who wished to replace the shattered Cold War consensus with a human rights–based foreign policy and those who saw human rights as justification for continuing the nation's decades-long fight against communism.[64] Although US officials who supported FVPPA often did so for different or even opposing reasons, the association had clearly garnered bipartisan support by Reagan's second term.

The powerful, though not universal, consensus that coalesced around the reeducation issue in the late 1980s coincided with Vietnam's increased willingness to cooperate with the United States. The change in Hanoi's stance on the reeducation camp issue and other humanitarian concerns resulted from events outside of American control. The rise of a new generation of Vietnamese leaders, dire economic straits in Vietnam, and political shifts within the Soviet Union all prompted Hanoi to covet outside economic assistance.[65] The Vietnamese sought an end to the American embargo and, perhaps more importantly, an inflow of investment from international bodies such as the International Monetary Fund and the World Bank, which would not lend to Vietnam without American acquiescence.

In February 1987 the Reagan administration attempted to capitalize on these shifting political winds by appointing General John Vessey Jr., former chairman of the Joint Chiefs of Staff, as a "personal emissary" to Vietnam.[66] Before his departure, legislators discussed the desirability and goals of Vessey's mission at length. There was very little debate. Every senator who took the floor the day before Vessey's departure spoke favorably about his "humanitarian" trip and defined the mission's scope in the same way—that is, as involving issues of family reunification, including reeducation camp prisoners.[67] Senator Pell, for example, took special care to elaborate on the political prisoner issue, mentioning FVPPA by name and describing Hanoi's reeducation policy as a "black mark on the image that Vietnam seeks to present to the rest of the world."[68] The same day, Pell and Kennedy sent Vessey a personal letter, stating their hope that his mission would be "the basis for progress" on the emigration of former reeducation detainees and other "humanitarian problems."[69] Senators John McCain (R-AZ) and Mark Hatfield (R-OR) were among the notable Republican legislators to make the same argument. FVPPA's ability to forge a bipartisan consensus on the reeducation camp issue, even as the nation continued to vociferously debate the Vietnam War's legacy, "lessons," and memory, was a testament to the association's persistence, information-gathering network, and strategic appropriation of the language of family.

Vessey's mission brought tangible, if modest, results. The following month Hanoi released 480 prisoners who were "military and civilian personnel of the toppled South Vietnamese regime," and in February 1988 Vice Minister Phan Quang announced the release of 1,104 additional detainees.[70] However, the difference between physical release from a reeducation camp and resettlement in the United States remained vast. Logistical, bureaucratic, financial, and legal obstacles made the transition from the former to the latter a time-consuming, difficult undertaking. Given these realities, FVPPA barely took time to celebrate the releases before writing to its friends in Congress and requesting "a resolution for an expeditious processing of all released prisoners for resettlement in the U.S."[71] FVPPA's allies in the State Department and Congress echoed FVPPA's emphasis and made similar appeals.[72]

Despite the absence of formal diplomatic relations, in July 1988 an American delegation traveled to Hanoi to discuss the emigration of former reeducation camp detainees and their families.[73] Although the two nations had been discussing the issue for years in multilateral forums and in bilateral meetings, the July 1988 summit marked the first time the United States and Vietnam engaged in bilateral talks for the sole purpose of addressing reeducation camp prisoners. The talks led to an agreement in principle and a pledge to meet the following year to continue the discussions.

In the interim, the SRV ambassador to the United Nations "requested to set up a meeting" with Tho "to discuss issues and concerns we have regarding the political prisoners."[74] On April 14 Tho met with the SRV ambassador in New York.[75] The ambassador's desire to meet with the president of FVPPA demonstrates that Hanoi recognized the association's importance to the American stance on the issue. Although Tho, unlike the National League of Families' Griffiths, never accompanied Funseth on his trips to Geneva and Hanoi, this meeting suggests that Hanoi saw the parity between the two organizations and tried to address them both.

In July1989, after another round of negotiations in Hanoi, the United States and Vietnam signed a bilateral agreement. A joint statement explained that the accord "provided for the resettlement in the United States of released reeducation center detainees and their close family members who wish to emigrate to the United States."[76] The rhetorical division between "humanitarian" and "political" issues, then, served contradictory purposes in rhetoric and reality. While this framing helped the United States impose unilateral demands and criticize the SRV, the actual implementation of humanitarian policies helped thaw US-Vietnam relations by creating personal, institutional, and governmental ties. Indeed, as Gaston J. Sigur, the assistant secretary of East Asian and Pacific affairs, explained in July 1988, thanks to cooperation on humanitarian issues, "the United States has more contact with the Vietnamese on operational and policy levels than any other Western nation, including those which maintain diplomatic relations."[77]

FVPPA celebrated the 1989 bilateral agreement at its annual dinner on August 5, 1989. Funseth provided the keynote address and expressed his hope that the 1989 accord "will come to be seen as a historic and humanitarian agreement."[78] When explaining the "history of the negotiations," Funseth told the audience, "*first and foremost,* your steadfast support encouraged me to persist in these negotiations until we reached our goal."[79] "This Association," Funseth continued, "has provided an important service for families who are trying to bring their relatives to the United States from Vietnam. They maintain files on some 10,000 people in Vietnam, including about 7,000 reeducation center detainees" and their family members.[80] As Funseth explained, "Mrs. Khuc Minh Tho and her friends meet with my staff every week in the evening to review individual cases."[81] According to Martin, Funseth found FVPPA's contributions so valuable that he gave Tho the pen he used to sign the agreement.[82] Finally,

Funseth characterized the 1989 agreement as the culmination of seven years of "U.S. diplomatic actions using all available channels . . . bilateral, multilateral, and private non-governmental."[83] This "intensive seven-year U.S. diplomatic effort," he said, should be seen, along with negotiations on the POW-MIA issue, as part of the US-SRV normalization process.[84]

US-Vietnam Normalization

The personal and institutional ties that led to implementation of the 1989 accord—and the years of negotiations it took to reach that milestone—helped lay the foundation for "normal" relations between the former adversaries. During the George H. W. Bush years, these trends accelerated. Once the fall of the Berlin Wall removed barriers to greater cooperation with communist regimes, domestic calls for normalization gained significant momentum, especially as a formidable bloc of US businesses aligned in the US-Vietnam Trade Council. This coalition clamored for access to an untapped Vietnamese market with a preexisting appetite for American goods.[85] Nongovernmental organizations dedicated to Indochina issues and human rights organizations also called for an end to the embargo and normalization as a way to gain greater access to the populations they wished to assist.

FVPPA also joined the conversation. In December 1990 Tho explained in identical letters to Assistant Secretary of State Richard Solomon and President Bush, "as U.S. citizens . . . it is our hope that the Department of State will also include the Vietnamese political prisoners in the process toward full diplomatic relations with Vietnam."[86] FVPPA sent many additional letters making this same point throughout early 1991, lamenting that Vietnamese Americans "have been waiting nearly 16 years to be reunited with our loved ones."[87] In January, for example, Tho secured a meeting with Solomon even as American boots were on the ground in the Persian Gulf. "In the discussion about the normalization with Vietnam, we the association would like to request the State Department to include three main conditions concerning the political prisoners for the discussions," FVPPA's agenda for the meeting explained. The association's "three main conditions" were: "1. Immediately release . . . all political prisoners. 2. Promptly permit released political prisoners to migrate to countries of their choice. 3. Respect the human rights of those who choose to remain in Vietnam."[88] Although FVPPA's records do not contain minutes of this meeting, later events suggest that this request found receptive ears.

In April 1991 the United States offered Vietnam a "Roadmap to U.S.-S.R.V. Normalization."[89] Both contemporaries and scholars recognized this as a major initiative, signaling a change in American tone if not official policy and indicating that normalization would be forthcoming. The "Roadmap" enumerated specific steps each nation had to take before they could move from phase to phase, ultimately culminating in formal economic and diplomatic relations. Although the document's contents were classified, the press knew the "Roadmap" emphasized the two conditions US officials had been demanding since the 1970s: resolution of the Cambodian conflict and a "full accounting" of POWs and MIAs.

The "Roadmap" also included provisions relating to Vietnamese reeducation camp detainees. Phase I required the SRV to "release . . . those remaining Vietnamese detainees eligible for the ODP reeducation resettlement program and permit their departure if they so desire" before the two nations could move to phase II.[90] In other words, the SRV would be required to meet FVPPA's longtime goals. The first page of the document also informed the SRV that "the pace and scope of the normalization process will be directly influenced by your government's degree of cooperation on the POW/MIA and other humanitarian issues." By this point, "other humanitarian issues" had become shorthand for family reunification, including the reeducation camp detainees' release and resettlement.[91] The "Roadmap" thus framed progress on the release and resettlement of reeducation detainees as both an explicit benchmark and a general standard the SRV had to meet before the United States would normalize relations.

On April 9, the same day Solomon delivered the "Roadmap" to the Vietnamese, FVPPA had a meeting with State Department officials.[92] FVPPA's records do not contain minutes of the meeting, and the State Department records that would shed light on it remain closed. I suspect, however, that if Tho did not know about the reeducation camp prisoners' inclusion in the "Roadmap" prior to that meeting, State Department officials informed her that day. FVPPA's impassioned if polite requests to have reeducation detainees included in the official steps toward US-SRV normalization stopped abruptly in April 1991, a likely sign that Tho knew there was no need for continued lobbying. The most persuasive evidence, however, is that Tho announced in June that FVPPA "will be closing . . . in January 1992."[93] Given Tho's tenacity and consistent advocacy, it seems highly unlikely that the organization would suddenly close its doors without assurances from the US government that its objectives would be enshrined in formal US policy.

This conclusion, however, inspires other questions. If Tho knew about the reeducation camp detainees' inclusion in the "Roadmap," why did the FVPPA not mention this significant step? Indeed, its absolute silence on the contents of the "Roadmap" stands in sharp contrast to its vociferous celebration and publication of the 1989 bilateral agreement, the arrival of the first former political prisoners in the United States, and all other major milestones. Given these facts, and the continued classification of official records, it seems likely that the State Department gave FVPPA verbal assurances of the political prisoners' inclusion in the official normalization process but also requested that it not make such linkages public. This sequence of events would explain both the dramatic shift in the focus of FVPPA's lobbying efforts and its subsequent silence. This approach would have enabled US officials to focus publicly on the two issues they had emphasized since 1978—Cambodia and POW-MIAs—while privately resolving an issue that had become a significant item on the national agenda in the mid-1980s. Moreover, the relative US silence on the reeducation camp issue's inclusion in the "Roadmap" permitted Hanoi to save face and not appear to be giving in to any meddling in its internal policy.

Despite Tho's announcement about the association's imminent closure date, FVPPA remained operational until 1999. In many ways, FVPPA was a victim of its own success. Both Vietnamese families and US officials continued to turn to FVPPA for information and assistance.[94] In April 1992, for example, Kenneth Quinn, deputy assistant secretary at the Bureau of East Asian and Pacific Affairs, wrote to Tho, "the information and insights you continue to share with us have been of invaluable assistance as we work to encourage Vietnam to release all political prisoners."[95]

On June 4, 1992, the SRV released the last of the prisoners.[96] The State Department news ticker, which an official sent to Tho, noted that "the release of all former officials sent for re-education when South Vietnam fell under communist rule in 1975 was one of the three conditions set by the United States for lifting its economic embargo and establishing diplomatic relations with Hanoi."[97] In July FVPPA hosted its annual reunion picnic, and Robert Funseth, Thomas Raezer (Department of State), Dr. Lewis M. Stern (Department of Defense), and Dr. Nguyen Van Hanh (deputy director, Office of Resettlement for Refugees, Department of Health and Human Services) all gave speeches to an audience of US officials and Vietnamese American community members—including former reeducation detainees.[98] In his speech, Dr. Nguyen commended FVPPA "for all its efforts, over many years, to effect the release of the former political prisoners." He observed, "Throughout my decades of work with refugees in California and the nation, I must say that I have encountered only a few such groups as yours. Your dedication, volunteerism, and efforts, the financial burden you have taken upon yourselves, and your time spent on behalf of the former political prisoners are worthy of more than any words I can express."[99] By all accounts, US officials and Vietnamese Americans had a wonderful time celebrating the realization of their joint objectives.

The same could not be said for the National League of Families' annual meeting that took place two days earlier. President Bush not only attended the meeting but also gave the keynote address. Almost as soon as the president began speaking, however, a group of attendees broke into a chant of "No more lies! Tell the truth!"[100] When the crowd interrupted him a second time, the president, "his jaw tightening and finger wagging, exploded at them: 'Would you please shut up and sit down!'"[101] The contrast with the FVPPA gathering could not have been sharper. Although the league still had the political clout to warrant a presidential visit, Bush's 1992 keynote address marked the last time a sitting American president attended a league meeting.[102] While FVPPA and US officials worked collaboratively and productively toward a common cause, the league lost control over its members, who still wanted the impossible: the return of live American POWs.

FVPPA's Continued Influence

Resettlement and family reunification proceeded apace during the Clinton years. By August 1993, nearly 72,000 former detainees and their families had immigrated to the United States.[103] A year later, that number had swelled to over 100,000, and by November 1995, the total exceeded 200,000.[104] It was in this context of major progress on the reeducation detainee issue, Cambodia, and a "full accounting" of POW-MIAs that the United States lifted the economic embargo in February 1994 and President Bill Clinton announced in July 1995 that relations between the United States and Vietnam were "normalized."[105]

Imminent normalization, however, both accelerated and challenged family reunification. In December 1994 the Bureau for Population, Refugees, and Migration at the Department of State and the Immigration and Naturalization Service (INS) announced that in order to combat fraud and in anticipation of normalization, US-SRV migration procedures would be altered to conform to worldwide standards.[106] The most significant consequence of this change, at least for FVPPA, was that unmarried children over the age of twenty-one were no longer eligible for resettlement.

FVPPA was incensed that, without warning, the United States was reneging on a significant aspect of its long-standing commitment to family reunification. Tho immediately contacted her friends in high places, among them Senator John McCain and Eric Schwartz, director of human rights, refugees, and humanitarian affairs at the National Security Council and a longtime friend of FVPPA since his days as a member of Congressman Solarz's staff. "I must be candid in telling you," Tho wrote in nearly identical letters to the two men, "that I find this decision arbitrary, illogical, unfair and contrary to the spirit of the admissions program. . . . What is the logic of excluding this group, at this stage when most of the children from the Vietnam era of the former political prisoners are over 21 years of age? What is the fairness in disadvantaging those families who have waited for their turn in the processing queue?"[107] McCain shared Tho's confusion and wrote to the State Department three days later, reminding it of "our obligation to these families" and suggesting that "Mrs. Tho raises some very important questions . . . I would appreciate your responses."[108] Schwartz also responded right away, meeting with FVPPA on January 19 and facilitating a meeting between FVPPA and Phyllis Coven, INS director for the Office of International Affairs, on January 23.[109] Coven told FVPPA that "the decision was not reversible," but she did "offer the possibility that exceptions could be made for hardship cases."[110]

Coven, it turns out, underestimated the power of FVPPA and its allies. They were able to delay the policy shift's effective date, "given the fact that the Orderly Departure Program (ODP) suddenly implemented the policy eligibility change without consultation."[111] Throughout 1995 and 1996 FVPPA continued to meet with INS officials, correspond with McCain and Schwartz, and reach out to other trusted allies, including Senator Kennedy, in an effort to reinstate US policy to reflect "its original purpose of resettlement of the former political prisoners and their families as family units."[112] In July 1996 McCain offered amendment 5064 to the foreign operations appropriations bill (HR 3540)—also known as the "McCain amendment"—which proposed to reestablish the eligibility of former prisoners' unmarried children older than twenty-one. The Senate passed the bill in August, and President Clinton signed it into law in October.[113]

Knowledgeable individuals largely credited FVPPA for the McCain amendment's success. On October 1, 1986, Shep Lowman, director of international refugee affairs at the powerful US Catholic Conference and former deputy assistant secretary in the State Department's Bureau of Refugee Programs, wrote to Tho to express his "congratulations on your work on the McCain Amendment." "The McCain language," Lowman noted with satisfaction, "was one of the last pieces needed to bring the Vietnamese refugee program to an honorable and compassionate end." "This was the most effective advocacy efforts by the Vietnamese American community that I have ever seen and your efforts were the key ones," Lowman applauded. "It was a good show, Tho, and thousands of families have been helped to reunify."[114] As Martin details, FVPPA made similar efforts on behalf of reeducation camp detainees' widows and orphans, demonstrating its determination to "preserve the family unit."[115]

Domestic groups played an instrumental role in the US-SRV normalization process. FVPPA never acquired the cultural omnipresence, financial resources, or public recognition achieved by the National League of Families of American Prisoners and Missing in Southeast Asia. Yet, like the league, FVPPA negotiated the complex politics of Washington and secured important alliances with key US officials that elevated its cause to a top objective of American foreign policy. In so doing, FVPPA exerted a significant, if focused, influence over US normalization policy. When there is an absence of formal diplomatic relations, when states are deprived of the physical and bureaucratic presence they normally possess in other countries, this seems to create the space for organizations like FVPPA and the National League of Families to wield considerable influence. FVPPA certainly seized that opportunity, but its success also depended in large part on cultural trends, legal precedents, and geopolitical agendas outside of its control.

Within these constraints, however, FVPPA illustrates the ability of nonstate actors to carve out niches of influence and mobilize information in ways that develop coalitions, often among unlikely allies. FVPPA's advocacy provided the information and the human insistence that prompted US policymakers to adopt the release and resettlement of reeducation camp detainees as a major US policy objective. While other actors and organizations mattered, FVPPA played a definitive role during multiple administrations. Incorporating the voices of Vietnamese Americans into our historical understanding, then, not only adds new elements to the old narrative but also changes the story itself by demonstrating the importance of domestic, transnational, and international forces in the shaping of US normalization policy.

A generous US response to reeducation camp detainees' plight served contradictory purposes, perhaps even simultaneously. US officials could use the detainees' incarceration and their families' suffering as an example of the rightness of the American cause in Vietnam and US benevolence thereafter. Yet the 1989 emigration program required far more than a simple allocation of funds and admission quotas, although both were certainly important. Successful negotiation and implementation of resettlement programs required extensive US-SRV cooperation. The intensive, seven-year effort that Robert Funseth described, and continued cooperation thereafter, helped lessen tensions between Washington and Hanoi and laid the groundwork for more normal ties. In the absence of formal relations, humanitarian issues served as the basis for ongoing US-Vietnam relations.

Notes

1. Lewis M. Stern, Country Director for Indochina, Thailand, and Burma, OASD/ISA/EAP, to Tho, June 1992, Families of Vietnamese Political Prisoners Association Collection (hereafter FVPPAC), box 130, folder 6, Vietnam Center and Archive, Lubbock, TX (hereafter VCA).

2. Ibid.

3. For a sampling of this literature, see Francis M. Bator, "No Good Choices:

LBJ and the Vietnam/Great Society Connection," *Diplomatic History* 32, no. 3 (June 2008): 309–70; Andrew L. Johns, *Vietnam's Second Front: Domestic Politics, the Republican Party and the War* (Lexington: University Press of Kentucky, 2010); Ken Hughes, *Fatal Politics: The Nixon Tapes, the Vietnam War and the Casualties of Re-election* (Charlottesville: University of Virginia Press, 2015).

4. Lewis M. Stern, *Defense Relations between the United States and Vietnam: The Process of Normalization, 1977–2003* (Jefferson, NC: McFarland, 2005); Edwin A. Martini, *Invisible Enemies: The American War and Vietnam, 1975–2000* (Amherst: University of Massachusetts Press, 2007); Michael J. Allen *Until the Last Man Comes Home: POWs, MIAs, and the Unending Vietnam War* (Chapel Hill: University of North Carolina Press, 2009).

5. Allen, *Until the Last Man Comes Home,* 4.

6. Bruce H. Franklin, *M.I.A. or Mythmaking in America* (New Brunswick, NJ: Rutgers University Press, 1993); Jussi M. Hanhimaki, "Global Visions and Parochial Politics: The Persistent Dilemma of the 'American Century,'" *Diplomatic History* 27, no. 4 (September 2003): 426.

7. On the value of this methodology, see Meredith Oyen, *The Diplomacy of Migration: Transnational Lives and the Making of U.S.-Chinese Relations in the Cold War* (Ithaca, NY: Cornell University Press, 2015).

8. Donna R. Gabaccia, *Foreign Relations: American Immigration in Global Perspective* (Princeton, NJ: Princeton University Press, 2012), 1. On the importance of homeland politics, see Melvin Small, *Democracy and Diplomacy: The Impact of Domestic Politics in U.S. Foreign Policy, 1789–1994* (Baltimore: Johns Hopkins University Press, 1996); Kieu-Linh Caroline Valverde, *Transnationalizing Viet Nam: Community, Culture, and Politics in the Diaspora* (Philadelphia: Temple University Press, 2012).

9. For a sampling of this literature, see Thuy Vo Dang, "The Cultural Work of Anticommunism in the San Diego Vietnamese American Community," *Amerasia Journal* 31, no. 2 (2005): 65–86; Sucheng Chan, *The Vietnamese American 1.5 Generation Stories of War, Revolution, Flight, and New Beginnings* (Philadelphia: Temple University Press, 2006); Linda Trinh Vo, "Constructing a Vietnamese American Community: Economic and Political Transformation in Little Saigon, Orange County," *Amerasia Journal* 34 (2008): 85–109; Karin Aguilar-San Juan, *Little Saigons: Staying Vietnamese in America* (Minneapolis: University of Minnesota Press, 2009); Nhi T. Lieu, *The American Dream in Vietnamese: Fantasy, Desire, and Community in Vietnamese American Popular Culture* (Minneapolis: University of Minnesota Press, 2011); Yen Le Espiritu, *Body Counts: The Vietnam War and Militarized Refuge(es)* (Oakland: University of California Press, 2014).

10. Frances P. Martin, "'Freed Vietnamese Have Her to Thank': Khuc Minh Tho, the FVPPA, and the Use of Grassroots Diplomacy in the Release, Immigration, and Resettlement of Vietnamese Re-education Camp Prisoners, 1977–2011" (MA thesis, Texas Tech University, 2015).

11. Sam Vong, "'Compassion Gave Us a Special Superpower': Vietnamese Women Leaders, Reeducation Camps, and the Politics of Family Reunification,

1977–1991," *Journal of Women's History,* forthcoming. I follow Vong by using "Tho" instead of the surname "Khuc" throughout, in conformity with Vietnamese usage.

12. Kenneth Cmiel, "The Emergence of Human Rights Politics in the United States," *Journal of American History* 86, no. 3 (December 1999): 1232–33.

13. FVPPA to President Ronald Reagan, September 15, 1984, FVPPAC, box 127, folder 6, VCA.

14. See Vong, "Compassion Gave Us a Special Superpower."

15. "Human Rights Conditions in Selected Countries and the U.S. Response," July 25, 1978, prepared for the Subcommittee on International Organizations of the Committee on International Relations, US House of Representatives, by the Foreign Affairs and National Defense Division, Congressional Research Service, Library of Congress.

16. Amnesty International (but not Amnesty International USA) and Humanities International stood as exceptions to this general trend. See, for example, "Amnesty International Report 1977," AI International Secretariat, January 1, 1977, index no. POL 10/006/1977, 227–32, https://www.amnesty.org/en/documents/p0110/006/1977/en/.

17. Letter from 13 congressmen to President Reagan, August 10, 1984, FVPPAC, box 136, folder 28, VCA; Edward P. Metzer, *Reeducation in Postwar Vietnam: Personal Postscripts to Peace* (College Station: Texas A&M University Press, 2001), xii–xiii; Ginetta Sagan and Stephen Denney, *Report on the Violations of Human Rights in the Socialist Republic of Vietnam, April 1975–December 1988* (Atherton, CA: Aurora Foundation, 1989), 40.

18. Sagan and Denney, *Report on Violations of Human Rights,* 21; "The Status of Human Rights in Selected Countries and the U.S. Response," July 25, 1977, prepared for the Subcommittee on International Organizations of the Committee on International Relations, US House of Representatives, by the Foreign Affairs and National Defense Division, Congressional Research Service, Library of Congress.

19. Sagan and Denny, *Report on Violations of Human Rights,* 21; Martin, "Freed Vietnamese Have Her to Thank," 18–20.

20. Ginetta Sagan, "Introduction" to 1989 publication, Ginetta Sagan Papers, box 205, Hoover Institution Archives, Stanford, CA.

21. Nguyen Van Canh with Earle Cooper, *Vietnam under Communism, 1975–1982* (Stanford, CA: Hoover Institution Press, 1983), 222–24; letter from 13 congressmen to Reagan, August 10, 1984; FVPPA to Secretary of State George P. Shultz, September 10, 1984, FVPPAC box 127, folder 6, VCA; FVPPA to General Westmoreland, June 13, 1994, ibid., box 136, folder 10B; Sagan and Denney, *Report on Violations of Human Rights,* 56–57.

22. Memorandum from Mike Armacost to Zbigniew Brzezinski, "U.S. Policy toward Vietnam: Some Wider Aspects of the Problem," February 4, 1977, "Vietnam, 1/77–12/78" folder, box 85, Zbigniew Brzezinski Material—Country Files (NSA 6), Office of the National Security Advisor, Jimmy Carter Presidential Library, Atlanta, GA.

23. Memorandum from Mike Armacost to Zbigniew Brzezinski, "U.S.-S.R.V. Negotiations in Paris," April 12, 1977, ibid.

24. Memorandum from Richard Holbrooke to the Secretary, "U.S.-SRV Negotiations," April 25, 1977, ibid.

25. Steven Hurst, *The Carter Administration and Vietnam* (Houndmills, UK: Macmillan, 1996); Cecile Menetrey-Monchau, *American-Vietnamese Relations in the Wake of War* (Jefferson, NC: McFarland, 2006). See also Kenton Clymer, *The United States and Cambodia, 1969–2000* (London: Routledge Curzon, 2004); Sheldon Neuringer, *The Carter Administration, Human Rights, and the Agony of Cambodia* (Lewiston, NY: Edwin Mellen Press, 1993).

26. Dennis Rockstroh, "A Few Work to Keep Issue Alive," *San Jose Mercury News,* October 11, 1987.

27. Martin, "Freed Vietnamese Have Her to Thank," 9.

28. Elliot Abrams to Ginetta Sagan, June 6, 1983, Sagan Papers, box 305, Hoover Institution Archives.

29. Letter from 13 congressmen to Reagan, August 10, 1984; Roger P. Winter to President Reagan, July 23, 1984, C0172 Vietnam (15000-249999) WHORM: Subject File, Ronald Reagan Library, Simi Valley, CA.

30. Judith Kumin, "Orderly Departure from Vietnam: A Humanitarian Alternative?" (PhD diss., Fletcher School of Law and Diplomacy, Tufts University, 1987), 5.

31. Ronald Reagan, "Peace: Restoring the Margin of Safety," presented at the Veterans of Foreign Wars Convention, Chicago, August 18, 1980, https://reaganlibrary.archives.gov/archives/reference/8.18.80.html; http://www.presidency.ucsb.edu/ws/index.php?pid=40495.

32. Espiritu, *Body Coun*ts, 2; Heather Marie Stur, "'Hiding behind the Humanitarian Label': Refugees, Repatriates, and the Rebuilding of America's Benevolent Image after the Vietnam War," *Diplomatic History* 39, no. 2 (April 2015): 224. The best books on US refugee policy during the Cold War are Gil Loescher and John A. Scanlan, *Calculated Kindness: Refugees and America's Half-Open Door, 1945 to the Present* (New York: Free Press, 1986), and Carl J. Bon Tempo, *Americans at the Gate: The United States and Refugees during the Cold War* (Princeton, NJ: Princeton University Press, 2008).

33. For the administration's consistent expression of this policy, see National Security Council (NSC) Message Center, "USG Vietnam/Kampuchea Policy: Talking Points," March 1982, folder "Vietnam May 1980–1982 (3 of 4)," RAC box 13, Richard T. Childress files, Reagan Library; "Trip to Vietnam, Laos and Thailand, Richard Childress, Director of Political-Military Affairs, NSC, Ann Mills Griffiths, Executive Director, National League of Families," folder "POW/MIA: U.S.-Vietnam Negotiations (2 of 6)," RAC box 16, ibid.; "Codel Murkowski: Meeting with Vietnamese Foreign Minister Nguyen Co Thach: January 18, 1986," White House Situation Room, folder "POW/MIA: U.S.-Vietnam Negotiations (3 of 6)," ibid.; confidential memo to Secretary of State and Defense, Acting Director of CIA, Chairman of the Joint Chiefs of Staff and Director of the NSA, "Support for Presi-

dential Envoy," May 4, 1987, folder "POW/MIA Special Mission 1987 [1984–1988] (2)," ibid.; NSC Memorandum of Conversation, "Meeting with the Vietnamese to Discuss the Vessey Initiative," October 10, 1988, folder "POW/MIA: U.S.-Vietnam Negotiations (6 of 6)," ibid.

34. On previous SRV offers, see NSC Message Center, "Vietnamese 'Offer' to Release Re-education Camp Detainees," July 1982, Confidential, folder "Vietnam May 1980–1982 (2 of 4)," RAC box 13, Childress files, Reagan Library; "A Chronology of Vietnamese and American Statements on Release of 'Re-education Camp' Inmates," FVPPAC, box 137, folder 14, VCA.

35. Martin, "Freed Vietnamese Have Her to Thank," 22.

36. FVPPA to Secretary of State Shultz, September 15, 1984, FVPPAC, box 127, folder 5, VCA.

37. Secretary of State Shultz to FVPPA, September 19, 1984, ibid.

38. Linas Kojelis to FVPPA, October 16, 1984, ibid.

39. Perhaps nothing better symbolizes the White House's consistent attentiveness to the National League of Families than the fact that siting American presidents gave the keynote address at its annual meeting nine times. See Allen, *Until the Last Man Comes Home,* 279.

40. Ibid., 234.

41. Martin, "Freed Vietnamese Have Her to Thank," 24.

42. Vong's forthcoming "Compassion Gave Us a Special Superpower" is very attentive to these themes.

43. Roger Daniels, *Guarding the Golden Door: American Immigration Policy and Immigrants since 1882* (New York: Hill and Wang, 2004), 224.

44. Erica Lee, *The Making of Asian America: A History* (New York: Simon and Schuster, 2015), 264–70; Arrisa Oh, *To Save the Children of Korea: The Cold War Origins of International Adoption* (Stanford, CA: Stanford University Press, 2015).

45. Lee, *Making of Asian America,* 270–71, 286; Daniels, *Guarding the Golden Door,* 136.

46. Martin discusses these relationships in detail in "Freed Vietnamese Have Her to Thank," 27–36.

47. FVPPA to Funseth, November 8, 1985, FVPPAC, box 127, folder 18, VCA.

48. Press release, "Amnesty International Urges Release or Trial for Thousands in Viet Nam," April 20, 1985, Sagan Papers, box 301, Hoover Institution Archives; Aurora Foundation, "Summary of the Current Conditions in the Re-education Camps of the Socialist Republic of Vietnam," January 1987, ibid., box 70.

49. For 1985 membership data, see "Report to the Secretary," FVPPA Newsletter, special issue, April 30, 1985, FVPPAC, box 149, folder 20, VCA. For 1991 data, see "Annual Awards Address Delivered by Mrs. Khuc Minh Tho, President, Families of Political Prisoners Association at the 'Unity and Reunion Dinner,'" July 27, 1991, ibid., box 135, folder 26B.

50. Margaret E. Keck and Kathryn Sikkink, *Activists beyond Borders: Advocacy Networks in International Politics* (Ithaca, NY: Cornell University Press, 1988), ix.

51. Martin, "Freed Vietnamese Have Her to Thank," 26.

52. Martini, *Invisible Enemies,* 129, 126,128. Vong, "Compassion Gave Us a Special Superpower," also discussions this point.

53. Martin, "Freed Vietnamese Have Her to Thank," 21–24. Scholars suggest that nongovernmental advocates focused on Amerasian immigration made similar connections. See Jana K. Lipman, "'The Face Is the Road Map': Vietnamese Amerasians in U.S. Political and Popular Culture, 1980–1988," *Journal of Asian American Studies* 14, no. 1 (2011): 44; Sabrina Thomas, "The Value of Dust: Policy, Citizenship, and Vietnam's Amerasian Children" (PhD diss., Arizona State University, 2015), 154.

54. FVPPA to Secretary of State Shultz, August 26, 1985, FVPPAC, box 127, folder 15, VCA.

55. Tho to Congressman Gerald B. H. Solomon, Chairman, POW/MIA Task Force, December 4, 1985, ibid., folder 19; Jeremy Tinker, counsel for the Subcommittee on Immigration and Refugee Policy of the Senate Judiciary Committee, made this same argument in "The Vietnamese Left Stranded Merit Consideration: Political Prisoners; Relatives," *New York Times,* January 27, 1986, A27.

56. Tho to President Ronald Reagan, August 23, 1986, FVPPAC, box 127, folder 23, VCA.

57. Allen, *Until the Last Man Comes Home,* 206.

58. Remarks by Senator Ted Kennedy at the FVPPA reception at the Senate, April 30, 1987, FVPPAC, box 134, folder 9, VCA.

59. Remarks by Senator Bob Dole at the FVPPA reception at the Senate, April 30, 1987, ibid.

60. *Congressional Record*—S5816, May 1, 1987, ibid., box 134, folder 10.

61. Ibid., S5815.

62. Ibid., S5816.

63. Memorandum, "S. Res 205 Political Prisoners in Vietnam," May 7, 1987, C0172 Vietnam (40000-514999), WHORM: Subject File, Reagan Library.

64. Barbara Keys, *Reclaiming American Virtue: The Human Rights Revolution of the 1970s* (Cambridge, MA: Harvard University Press, 2014). Keys devotes chapter 4 to liberal and chapter 45 to conservative uses of human rights. For the conservative embrace of human rights, see also Carl J. Bon Tempo, "From the Center-Right: Freedom House and Human Rights in the 1970s and 1980s," in *The Human Rights Revolution: An International History*, ed. Akira Iriye, Petra Goedde, and William I. Hitchcock (Oxford: Oxford University Press, 2012), 223–44.

65. NSC Secretariat, "Vietnamese Policy as Described at the Sixth Party Congress," January 1987, folder "Vietnam 1986–1987 (2 of 3)," RAC box 13, Childress files, Reagan Library; Huynh Kim Khanh, "Vietnam's Reforms: Renewal or Dearth," *Indochina Issues 84,* September 1988, Indochina Project, Sagan Papers, box 309, Hoover Institution Archives; Allen E. Goodman. "Dateline Hanoi: Recognition at Last," *Foreign Policy* 100 (1995): 146.

66. NSC secret memorandum from Richard Childress to Frank C. Carlucci,

"Emissary to Hanoi" [Vessey appointment], February 5, 1987, folder "POW/ MIA Special Mission 1987 [1984–1988] (1)," RAC box 16, Childress files, Reagan Library. Allen calls Vessey's appointment a "major breakthrough" (*Until the Last Man Comes Home,* 257).

67. *Congressional Record*—Senate, July 28, 1987, S10728.

68. Ibid., S10729.

69. Senators Claiborne Pell and Edward M. Kennedy to General Vessey, July 27, 1987, FVPPAC, box 127, folder 39, VCA.

70. Rockstroh, "A Few Work to Keep Issue Alive"; "VNA Announces Release of Former Officials," February 11, 1988, Sagan Papers, box 68, Hoover Institution Archives.

71. Template letter, February 10, 1988, FVPPAC, box 128, folder 2, VCA. See also Tho to the Honorable Rudy Boschwitz, United States Senate, April 27, 1988, ibid., folder 4.

72. Senator Boschwitz to President Reagan, February 25, 1988, Refugees and Immigrants folder, Legislative Assistant files, box 31, Rudy Boschwitz Papers, Minnesota Historical Society Archives, St. Paul.

73. FVPPAC, box 151, folder 4, VCA.

74. The Honorable Robert L. Funseth, Senior Deputy Assistant Secretary, Bureau for Refugee Programs, Department of State, March 27, 1989, ibid., box 128, folder 15.

75. For the meeting with Funseth, see "A Report of Activities," ibid., box 137, folder 43A; The Honorable Nguyen Van Linh, General Secretary of the Vietnamese Communist Party, Socialist Republic of Vietnam, c/o Mr. Ambassador, Permanent Representative at the United Nations of the Socialist Republic of Vietnam, April 19, 1989, ibid., box 128, folder 16A.

76. "Joint Statement," ibid., box 134, folder 32B; Martin, "Freed Vietnamese Have Her to Thank," 38.

77. Gaston J. Sigur, Assistant Secretary of East Asian and Pacific Affairs, Current Policy Issue No. 1098, "Review of U.S.-Vietnam Issues," given before the Subcommittee on East Asian and Pacific Affairs of the House Foreign Affairs Committee, July 28, 1988, FVPPAC, box 149, folder 62, VCA. See also "Defense Draft Testimony on H. Con. Res. 271 . . . ," Dr. Karl Jackson, July 25, 1988, C0172 Vietnam (560000-599999), WHORM: Subject File, Reagan Library.

78. Robert L. Funseth, "Hope and Challenge: Report on the 1989 Hanoi Negotiations for the Resettlement of the Vietnamese Reeducation Center Detainees," August 5, 1989, FVPPAC, box 134, folder 32B, VCA.

79. Ibid., emphasis in original. Martin calls the agreement a "major victory for the FVPPA" ("Freed Vietnamese Have Her to Thank," 38).

80. Funseth, "Hope and Challenge."

81. Ibid. For Tho's description of the number of cases, see "Annual Awards Address Delivered by Mrs. Khuc Minh Tho," July 27, 1991.

82. Martin, "Freed Vietnamese Have Her to Thank," 38.

83. Robert L. Funseth, FVPPAC, box 135, folders 1–3, VCA.

84. Robert L. Funseth, "Humanitarian Endeavor: Emigration from Vietnam," given before the Subcommittee on Asian and Pacific Affairs and the Subcommittee on International Economic Policy and Trade, Committee of Foreign Affairs, House of Representatives, November 17, 1989, ibid., folder 5.

85. Although some companies were undoubtedly less enthusiastic about the Vietnamese market than others, those that supported normalization formed a formidable lobby. The combination of the "petroleum, construction, telecommunications and consulting" industries, among others, ensured that their voices would be heard, as reported by Barbara Crosette, "Companies Press U.S. on Vietnam," *New York Times,* February 10, 1992, D2. Pro-business calls for normalization were widely reported in national newspapers. See, for example, Gregg Hitt, "U.S. Firms Push Bush Administration to End Ban on Trade with Vietnam," *Wall Street Journal,* April 3, 1990, A17; Samuel A. Stern, "We're Losing out in Vietnam: Letter to the Editor," *Wall Street Journal,* December 6, 1990, A19; Karl Schoenberger, "Door into Vietnam: U.S. Companies Test Limits of Trade Embargo," *Los Angeles Times,* August 30, 1992; Barbara Crosette, "Bush Is Pressured on Vietnam Embargo," *New York Times,* March 31, 1992.

86. FVPPA to Richard Solomon, Assistant Secretary, Department of State, December 7, 1990, FVPPAC, box 129, folder 12, VCA. On December 12, 1990, FVPPA sent the same letter to President George Bush.

87. Ibid.

88. "Agenda for Meeting with Mr. Richard Solomon, Assistant Secretary, U.S. State Department to Discuss Issues Concerning Political Prisoners," January 9, 1991, FVPPAC, box 137, folder 74, VCA.

89. "Roadmap to U.S.-S.R.V. Normalization," April 9, 1991, OSS 91-2128, box 61, Declassified Files, Record Group 46, Records of the United States Senate, Records of the Senate Committee on POW/MIA Affairs, 102nd Congress, 1991–1993, National Archives, Washington, DC.

90. Ibid., 5.

91. Ibid., 1.

92. "Department of State Meeting Agenda," April 9, 1991, FVPPAC, box 129, folder 22, VCA.

93. Tho to Mr. and Mrs. Robert L. Funseth, June 14, 1991, ibid., folder 18A.

94. For example, in May 1992 the Department of Defense wrote to FVPPA requesting that it be added to the association's mailing list. Dr. Lewis M. Stern, Country Director for Indochina, Thailand, and Burma, Office of the Assistant Secretary of Defense, to FVPPA, May 17, 1992, ibid., box 130, folder 4.

95. Kenneth Quinn, Deputy Assistant Secretary, Bureau of East Asian and Pacific Affairs, to Tho, April 8, 1992, ibid.

96. John Kerry to H. E. Vo Van Kiet, Prime Minister, S.R.V., April 15, 1992, ibid.; Department of State News Ticker, from Frank Light to Khuc Minh Tho, June 4, 1992, ibid., folder 6.

97. Department of State News Ticker, June 4, 1992.

98. Annual Reunion Picnic, July 26, 1992, FVPPAC, box 130, folder 7, VCA.

99. Annual Reunion Picnic, speech of Nguyen Van Hanh, PhD, Deputy Director, Office of Refugee Resettlement, July 26, 1992, ibid.

100. Allen, *Until the Last Man Comes Home,* 279.

101. Ibid., 280.

102. Ibid., 279.

103. Dewey Pendergrass, Chief, Overseas Operations Office of Admissions, Bureau of Refugee Programs, Department of State, to Khuc Minh Tho, August 13, 1993, FVPPAC, box 38, folder 24, VCA; letter template, November 15, 1995, ibid., box 131, folder 11A.

104. Robert Funseth, "Reflect and Rejoice," remarks at "A Dinner to Celebrate Freedom," sponsored by FVPPA, May 20, 1994, ibid., box 36, folder 9A.

105. William J. Clinton, "Remarks Announcing the Normalization of Diplomatic Relations with Vietnam," July 11, 1995, http://www.presidency.ucsb.edu/ws/?pid=51605.

106. Theresa L. Rusch, Office of Admissions, Bureau of Population, Refugees, and Migration Director, to Tho, December 6, 1994, FVPPAC, box 130, folder 36, VCA.

107. Tho to Eric Schwartz, Director, Human Rights, Refugees, and Humanitarian Affairs, National Security Council, January 6, 1995, ibid., box 131, folder 1A; Tho to Senator John McCain, January 9, 1995, ibid.

108. Senator John McCain to Phyllis E. Oakley, Assistant Secretary of State for the Bureau of Population, Refugees, and Migration, January 12, 1995, ibid.

109. FVPPA to Schwartz, January 26, 1993, ibid. Agendas for both meetings were included in the same folder.

110. Ibid.

111. FVPPA to John McCain, December 14, 1995, ibid., folder 12.

112. FVPPA to Edward M. Kennedy, May 6, 1996, ibid., folder 17A. On this process, see Martin, "Freed Vietnamese Have Her to Thank," 60–62.

113. See FVPPA to John McCain, August 5, 1996, and FVPPA Robert Funseth, August 9, 1996, FVPPAC, box 131, folder 3, VCA. For Martin's analysis of the McCain amendment, see "Freed Vietnamese Have Her to Thank," 59–61.

114. Shep Lowman, Director, International Refugee Affairs, United States Catholic Conference Migration and Refugee Services, to Tho, October 1, 1986, FVPPAC, box 132, folder 5B, VCA.

115. Martin, "Freed Vietnamese Have Her to Thank," 57, 62.

9

The Congressional Human Rights Caucus and the Plight of the Refuseniks

Rasmus Sinding Søndergaard

When Congressman John Porter (R-IL) returned from a trip to the Soviet Union in September 1982, he was a man with a mission. Porter had met more than forty Jewish families who had been denied permission to emigrate.[1] Moved by this encounter, Porter felt compelled to do something to alleviate their struggle. His solution was to establish a caucus to draw attention to the cause of these Soviet Jews—the so-called refuseniks.[2] Rather than devoting the caucus solely to the cause of the refuseniks, Porter widened its scope to include a number of similar causes under the umbrella of human rights, naming his group the Congressional Human Rights Caucus (CHRC).

This essay investigates the establishment of the CHRC and its advocacy for the refuseniks.[3] It examines how a congressional assertion on human rights in 1981 led the Reagan administration to reevaluate its stance. It then traces the formation of the CHRC and its initiatives on behalf of the refuseniks. Next it assesses the CHRC's contribution to US policy on the refusenik issue as US-Soviet relations improved over the second half of the 1980s. As this essay demonstrates, the CHRC contributed to the ongoing institutionalization of human rights concerns in American foreign policy.

In addition, this essay contributes to our understanding of the underexposed role of Congress in American foreign policy. Although this topic has not always received the recognition it deserves, diplomatic historians are beginning to pay more attention to Congress's contributions to US foreign policy during the Cold War.[4] This newfound interest is part of a larger trend that examines the intersection of domestic politics and foreign policy.[5] Like most congressional caucuses, the CHRC remains a largely unexamined element in congressional politics.[6] In focusing on the CHRC, this essay contributes to the growing body of historical scholarship that assesses the role of human rights in American foreign policy.[7] This scholarship has largely concentrated on the 1970s, but as archives have been declassified, historians have started to move into the 1980s.[8] In addition to exploring the role of human rights in a broad conception of US foreign policy, a few articles have specifically analyzed the role of Congress in relation to US human rights policy.[9]

The idea that the United States should support human rights through its foreign policy reflects the assumption that America's external relations should reflect its domestic politics and values. Politicians continuously refer to America's political tradition of democracy and respect for individual rights when they articulate US human rights policy. Concern for human rights has been cast as part of an American political tradition spanning the ideals of the founding fathers, Woodrow Wilson's declaration to "make the world safe for democracy," and Franklin Delano Roosevelt's "Four Freedoms." As noted by Joseph Nye and Richard Cooper, "Neither politics nor morality stops at the water's edge. . . . Given the nature of American political culture, there will always be a demand for moral expression in foreign policy."[10] Since the mid-1970s, human rights have been the dominant expression of this demand.

Like previous moral expressions in US foreign policy, human rights policy from the 1970s onward has been the result of more than pure idealism. Sometimes, when human rights were only a minor concern, policymakers have invoked them as window dressing to give legitimacy to foreign policy. Strategic foreign policy concerns and domestic political interests have often trumped human rights or compromised the consistency and evenhandedness of America's commitment to human rights. The rivalry between the executive and legislative branches may be the most influential aspect of domestic politics when it comes to human rights policy. The centrality of this executive-legislative struggle became particularly evident during the Reagan administration.

Ronald Reagan's presidency marked the pinnacle of a conservative ascendancy that included the rise of the New Right and the first Republican Senate majority since 1955.[11] This shift toward the right also affected US human rights policy. Jimmy Carter had promoted a human rights–based foreign policy that, despite some disagreements, generally enjoyed the support of a Democratically controlled Congress. Reagan entered the White House determined to replace Carter's human rights policy with a foreign policy based on "peace through strength." Whereas Carter had sought to break with the Cold War dichotomy, Reagan escalated the struggle with the Soviet Union in an attempt to roll back communism, guided by the so-called Reagan Doctrine.[12]

As Reagan moved to downgrade the role of human rights in US foreign policy, Congress retained and reinforced its position as the most significant proponent of human rights in American foreign relations. Throughout the 1980s Congress strengthened its existing human rights institutions and created new ones such as the CHRC. One of the issues that attracted the greatest political and public attention during that decade was the struggle of the refuseniks. It became a dominant issue because it united human rights advocates and anticommunists on both the Left and the Right and received the support of American Jewish groups and human rights–related nongovernmental organizations (NGOs). Over the course of the 1980s, the refuseniks became a vital component in East-West diplomacy, and they remained the core focus of the CHRC's human rights advocacy. Staff member Elizabeth Schrayer recalled that Congressman Porter initially preferred a caucus focused solely on the refuseniks, but "I convinced John Porter that the caucus should be a general human rights caucus with a broader focus than simply refuseniks."[13]

Congress Stands up for Human Rights

The broad political support for the refuseniks did not readily translate into broad support for a human rights–based foreign policy. By the early 1980s, human rights had become a highly polarizing issue in American politics. When Carter, the most prominent human rights advocate to date, left the White House in January 1981, he was immensely unpopular, and contemporary observers viewed his attempt to implement a human rights–based foreign policy as generally unsuccessful. His successor went out of his way to distance himself from Carter and human rights. This was evident in the Reagan administration's early proclamation that the fight against "international terrorism will now take the place of human rights."[14] According to Elliott Abrams, who would serve as assistant secretary for human rights from 1981 to 1985, the administration's initial approach to human rights was, "'This is no good . . . throw it out!' And this is pretty much what the Administration started with."[15] Carter's willingness to criticize the human rights policies of allies and adversaries alike was both practically and ideologically incompatible with Reagan's conservative internationalism, which sought to strengthen US support for repressive allies to roll back communism.

The new view of human rights in the White House affected US policy from day one. Whereas Carter had made a point of distancing himself from foreign leaders guilty of human rights abuses, Reagan did not shun leaders from countries with dismal human rights records.[16] On February 2, 1981, less than two weeks after taking office, Reagan warmly welcomed South Korean president Chun Doo Hwan to the White House, despite loud protests over his regime's human rights transgressions.[17] Documents show that although the administration was concerned about the perception that it was uncritical of human rights violations, its desire to strengthen security relations with South Korea took precedence.[18] Chun was only one of several foreign leaders with abysmal human rights records that Reagan welcomed to the White House. The diminished priority ascribed to human rights was also evident in the restructuring of the foreign policy bureaucracy, which included a diminished role for the State Department's Human Rights Bureau.[19]

Congress, however, was not willing to accept a downgrading of human rights, and along with the wider human rights community, it strongly protested the new course set by the White House. This was evident when the Senate Foreign Relations Committee rejected Reagan's nomination of Ernest Lefever to head the Human Rights Bureau. Lefever had been a fierce critic of Carter's human rights policy, arguing that the United States should not promote human rights abroad. In a 1977 letter to the Carter administration, Lefever proclaimed, "The consistent and single-marked invocation of the 'human rights standard' in making United States foreign policy decisions serves neither our interests nor the cause of freedom."[20]

The Senate Foreign Relations Committee's confirmation hearing became a full-scale attack on Lefever and the Reagan administration's disregard for human rights as a component of US foreign policy. Several senators, including the committee's chairman, moderate Republican Charles Percy of Illinois, rose to defend human rights. The long-serving Democratic whip of the Senate, Alan Cranston of California, attacked Lefever for wanting to abolish human rights constraints on foreign assistance, advocating for close relations with the South African apartheid regime, and being blind to human rights violations of right-wing dictatorships.[21] The hearing ended with the committee rejecting the nomination by a comfortable thirteen-to-four vote in June 1981. The rejection of Lefever illustrated the executive and legislative branches' divide over human rights, but it also highlighted that bipartisan cooperation on human rights was possible. Of the nine Republican senators on the committee, five voted with their Democratic colleagues to reject the nomination. The opposition to Lefever also manifested itself outside Capitol Hill, where the Ad Hoc Committee of the Human Rights Community, consisting of sixty organizations and individuals, immediately condemned the nomination.[22] A *New York Times* editorial on May 24 decried the Reagan administration's "shameful squirming on human rights" and deemed Lefever an "unworthy nominee."[23]

The amount of public attention paid to the nomination of a relatively minor official was highly unusual, and so was the committee's decision to reject the nomination. That the nominee of an immensely popular Republican president was rejected by a Senate committee with a Republican majority made the situation even more spectacular. The implications were clear. Congress's message to the new president was that it was unwilling to sell off human rights. This boosted the still nascent human rights community and helped increase its importance.

The Reagan Turnaround

Congressional opposition made it clear to the Reagan administration that the failure to address human rights concerns would come at great political cost. This realization, along with an opportunistic decision to utilize human rights for propaganda purposes in the Cold War, led the Reagan administration to reevaluate its stance on human rights. It became apparent to Reagan's advisers that if the administration was perceived as indifferent to human rights, it could jeopardize popular support for the president's general foreign policy. The administration therefore went back to the drawing board and sought to develop a robust human rights policy within its overall foreign policy strategy that could win over the critics. In late July 1981 Charles Fairbanks Jr. circulated a draft paper on human rights among a number of senior officials in the State Department. The paper opened with these words: "Within the Department there is a widespread feeling that we need a more definite human rights policy after the delays caused by Dr. Lefever's nomination process." It then stated, "Congress is now troubling us at hearings in a way that we could avoid with a fuller determination of policy. . . . Human rights is now the main area of assault by the Left on the new Administration's foreign policy."[24]

In October 1981 the administration leaked a high-level internal State Department memorandum drafted by Elliott Abrams that called for a renewed commitment to human rights.[25] The memorandum, partially reprinted in the *New York Times* a week later, recognized the utility of a more active human rights policy, arguing that such an approach would help counter Congress and other domestic critics and serve as a useful ideological weapon against the Soviet Union.[26] The introduction to the State Department's *Country Reports on Human Rights Practices for 1981,* submitted to Congress in February 1982, repeated the new approach to human rights.[27]

In direct response to congressional criticism, the Reagan administration executed a turnaround on human rights, moving from rejected to adaption.[28] The administration developed a "two-track human rights policy." The first track consisted of speaking out against human rights violations, and the second track focused on promoting democracy, which the administration deemed the best institution to secure human rights.[29] In practice, however, the promotion of democracy became almost synonymous with fighting communism, and the administration overwhelmingly directed its human rights criticism toward communist countries. This priority was heavily influenced by the so-called Kirkpatrick Doctrine, conceived by Reagan's ambassador to the United Nations Jeane Kirkpatrick. The Kirkpatrick Doctrine made a distinction between authoritarian governments capable of democratizing and totalitarian (i.e., communist) regimes for which there was no hope of reform.[30] The conclusion was that the former were preferable to the latter, and the United States ought to support friendly authoritarians and direct its criticism against communist countries. Adapting human rights to the Kirkpatrick Doctrine, the administration co-opted the concept into its overall foreign policy strategy.

Establishing the Congressional Human Rights Caucus

Given the political climate and the fact that human rights was such a hotly debated issue, Porter aimed to make his caucus as bipartisan as possible. To this end, he asked Tom Lantos (D-CA) to cochair the CHRC with him. Lantos was already involved in human rights issues as a member of the House Foreign Affairs Committee and its Subcommittee on Human Rights, and his background as a Jewish Holocaust survivor meant that he was deeply committed to the refusenik cause. Before going further, Lantos and Porter secured the approval of existing congressional human rights institutions, such as the Helsinki Commission. According to the commission's chief of staff at the time, R. Spencer Oliver, "the two groups were in-sync on all policy issues."[31] The Helsinki Commission, formed in 1976, was the leading congressional body on human rights issues in the Soviet Union and eastern Europe. Its prime task was monitoring compliance with the provisions of the Helsinki Final Act of 1975, to which the United States, the Soviet Union, and most European states were signatories. The Helsinki Final Act was an attempt to improve East-West relations through cooperation on security, trade, and culture.[32] It also included a commitment to respect basic human rights, a clause that human rights advocates used to criticize the Soviet Union's abysmal human rights record.

The bipartisan nature of the CHRC meant that it preferred human rights issues that both conservatives and liberals could get behind. By extension, the CHRC largely avoided controversial cases such as US policy toward Central America and Southeast Asia. Similarly, the CHRC did not seriously protest South African apartheid until the issue had garnered broad congressional and public interest. Instead, the CHRC devoted considerable time to protesting the persecution of religious minorities such as the Baha'i, Tibetans, and refuseniks.[33] Bipartisanship was also evident in the CHRC's approach to drafting members. According to Elizabeth Schrayer, "the strategy was to get people from both ideological wings on board to convince other members of Congress that it was 'safe' to join."[34] The early membership of ideological outliers such as liberal Democrat Barney Frank of Massachusetts and conservative Republican Henry Hyde of Illinois helped achieve this goal. The CHRC's avoidance of controversial issues facilitated this broad ideological membership and allowed participants to demonstrate support for human rights in the abstract, with a very low risk of offending constituents.

After its formal establishment in the spring of 1983, the CHRC set up a three-tier structure consisting of cochairs Lantos and Porter, an Executive Committee, and general members. The CHRC grew quickly, and by 1985 it had 150 members, making it one of the largest congressional caucuses.[35] By 1988, the CHRC included most of the House leadership, including the chairs of ten full committees, three of whom served on the CHRC Executive Committee.[36] Despite the wide membership, the CHRC was run by its founders. Both Porter and Lantos designated staffers to work for the CHRC, and they paid higher membership fees than the regular members.[37] The CHRC soon began to generate interest in its selected human rights issues by disseminating information on Capitol Hill. A key vehicle was a regular newsletter covering all human rights activity in Congress, such as pending legislation, hearings, letters, and petitions.[38] The CHRC also created a computer tracking system that maintained a record of all congressional human rights actions. Using this tracking system, members of Congress could obtain information about any specific human rights issue, as well as access a list of their own actions on human rights issues.[39] By 1986, this system contained almost 2,000 human rights cases, many of them involving refuseniks.[40] The CHRC also held its own briefings, organized letter-writing campaigns, compiled reports, gave press conferences, and staged various events to draw attention to human rights issues.

In the early years, the CHRC focused primarily on mobilizing and coordinating congressional and public support in collaboration with other congressional actors. Gradually, the CHRC also developed a close collaboration with human rights NGOs. On the issue of refuseniks, American Jewish groups such as the Union of Councils for Soviet Jewry (UCSJ) and the National Conference for Soviet Jewry (NCSJ) became its most important partners. A few months after the formation of the CHRC, the Chicago branch of the NCSJ declared, "The Congressional Human Rights

Caucus is critically important now for marshaling attention to this issue," and Paul Meek, executive director of the UCSJ, added, "There is nothing else like it in Congress."[41] The collaboration was mutually beneficial: the NGOs supplied the CHRC with essential information, and the caucus offered the NGOs a way to transmit their viewpoints to policymakers. For instance, on August 9, 1988, the UCSJ briefed the CHRC on antisemitism in the Soviet Union.[42]

CHRC members also engaged in extensive correspondence with dissidents throughout the world, including refuseniks, learning about their grievances and concerns. The most committed CHRC members became deeply involved with the refuseniks they contacted, establishing ongoing relationships that both parties characterized as friendships—for instance, Porter and refusenik Boris Prudinsky.[43] The CHRC archives contain numerous letters from refuseniks expressing gratitude for CHRC members' advocacy. "I want to bow before you on behalf of many and many people who have escaped the tenuous clutches of the KGB," refusenik Yakov Galperin wrote to Lantos a few months after immigrating to the United States.[44]

As the CHRC's visibility grew, American citizens increasingly contacted the caucus to express their views as well. In this way, the CHRC became a link between NGOs, foreign dissidents, and American citizens concerned with human rights on one side and American policymakers and foreign leaders on the other side.

The Caucus Joins the Refuseniks' Struggle

By the time the CHRC took up the refuseniks' cause in 1983, the issue had already become a core component of Cold War diplomacy. Yet, despite the surge in advocacy and public support for the refuseniks, diminishing numbers were being allowed to leave, leading to gridlock and a virtual halt in emigration.[45] US policymakers needed Soviet cooperation to secure progress on emigration, and the Soviet Union categorically refused to discuss the topic, arguing that human rights issues were internal matters.

Soviet Jews had been seeking to leave the Soviet Union in large numbers since the 1960s, but Soviet authorities severely restricted their emigration. The number of Jews allowed to leave varied greatly over the years, in response to the state of US-Soviet relations. During the heyday of détente in the early 1970s, Brezhnev loosened restrictions on emigration as part of negotiations with the Nixon administration, hoping to ensure the Senate's ratification of treaties on arms control and trade. Passage of the Jackson-Vanik amendment in 1974, which denied most-favored-nation status to communist countries that restricted emigration, contributed to the derailing of this superpower détente. The Nixon administration was unsuccessful in stopping the amendment, and it so infuriated the Soviet Union that Moscow reacted by virtually freezing Jewish emigration.[46] After the signing of SALT II in 1978, the Soviets again loosened emigration restrictions in the hope of persuading the Senate to ratify the treaty, and Jewish emigration rose to a high of 51,320 in 1979. That same year, however, US-Soviet relations plummeted when the Soviets invaded Afghanistan in December, and relations further deteriorated with the crackdown against pro-democracy forces in Poland in October 1980. As a result, the number of Jews emigrating from the Soviet Union dropped dramatically, reaching a historic low of only 896 in 1984.[47]

It is important to note that not all Soviet Jews wanted to leave the Soviet Union, and the ones who actively sought to do so represented a minority. Some Soviet Jews chose to stay, fighting antisemitism and trying to improve conditions in the Soviet Union. Another sizable part of the Soviet Jewish community tried to tone down their Jewishness and avoid the attention of Soviet authorities, hoping to live their lives quietly.[48] The exact size of the various groups is hard to determine, and estimates are imprecise and contested. In 1983 the official Soviet statistics claimed there were 1.3 million Jews in the Soviet Union, but Western governments and NGOs estimated that the number was significantly higher. According to the NCSJ, roughly 300,000 individuals were awaiting exit visas in 1983, among them approximately 10,000 refuseniks (defined as Jews whose applications had been rejected at least twice).[49] Refuseniks were thus only a small fraction of the Soviet Jewish population, but they became the main focus of American policy toward Soviet Jews.[50]

The CHRC strengthened existing congressional efforts on behalf of the refuseniks by adding another voice to the choir and systematizing congressional advocacy through its computerized tracking system and increased coordination of activities. In collaboration with the Helsinki Commission and other members of Congress, CHRC members sent letters about the refuseniks to both the Soviets and the Reagan administration.[51] Moreover, they introduced legislation in relevant committees, calling on the Soviet Union to release jailed refuseniks, and they urged Reagan to push the Soviets on Jewish emigration.[52] The CHRC then worked to coordinate and maximize the effect of such initiatives, using its newsletters and internal congressional letters to lobby members of Congress for signatures and votes.[53] The CHRC thus played an important mobilizing role for the refusenik cause on Capitol Hill.

New Initiatives: Expanding the Human Rights Community on Capitol Hill

The CHRC also created a number of new initiatives to draw more attention to the cause of the refuseniks. In 1983 Porter, Lantos, and Executive Committee member Gus Yatron (D-PA) cosponsored the formation of the International Parliamentary Group for Human Rights in the Soviet Union (IPG).[54] The IPG consisted of parliamentarians from the United States, Canada, and western European countries who worked to coordinate the efforts of their legislative bodies to increase public awareness of Soviet human rights violations.[55] By 1987, the IPG encompassed more than 600 parliamentarians, and it had formed standing human rights committees in a number of national parliaments, as well as coordinating legislative efforts and arranging trips to the Soviet Union to discuss human rights.[56]

In 1985 the CHRC launched the Congressional Spouses Committee of 21, consisting of wives of congressmen. Each of them adopted a high-profile refusenik to increase attention to their struggle.[57] The idea came from refuseniks in Moscow, who told Annette Lantos (wife of Tom) that they feared the West would forget about them.[58] The members of the Committee of 21 sought to prevent this by taking advantage of their status as both the spouses of prominent politicians and ordinary citizens. The former gave them access to media coverage and meetings with Soviet officials, while the latter allowed them to speak candidly as ordinary citizens who did not represent the US government. As Annette Lantos explained in a 1986 *New York Times* article, "Every time we go there, we name these people to the [Soviet] authorities. We don't let them forget."[59]

Lantos and Porter also set up the Congressional Human Rights Foundation (CHRF) in 1985 as a "private sector initiative operating parallel to the CHRC," according to former CHRF president David L. Phillips.[60] The purpose of the CHRF mirrored that of the CHRC, seeking to "assure that human rights are fully considered in the development of United States foreign policy."[61] The CHRF raised money for activities such as international conferences, fact-finding missions, and cultural events, as well as offering strategic planning for human rights NGOs.

Enter Gorbachev: A Way out for the Refuseniks?

As the CHRC was launching these new initiatives, changes inside the Soviet Union indicated that US-Soviet relations might be about to change. In March 1985 Mikhail Gorbachev became the fourth leader of the Soviet Union in less than two and a half years. Gorbachev wanted to reinvigorate the ailing Soviet economy and minimize the widening military gap, and to achieve this, he needed to halt the expensive arms race and promote collaboration on trade and technology with the West. He realized that such collaboration required an improvement in East-West relations, which in turn required addressing Western concerns about human rights.

American human rights advocates within and outside government saw the rise of Gorbachev as an opportunity to push for concessions on Jewish emigration. At first, however, it seemed that Gorbachev's rise to power would not lead to significant changes for Jews in the Soviet Union. It was not until late 1986, when Gorbachev launched his reform agenda of glasnost and perestroika, that a potential relaxation on emigration seemed possible.

In May 1985 CHRC leaders and the IPG participated in the Ottawa Human Rights Experts Meeting, under the auspices of the Conference on Security and Cooperation in Europe (CSCE), established by the Helsinki Final Act. The meeting represented the first East-West gathering devoted solely to the discussion of human rights issues. The leaders of the CHRC used the opportunity to press the issue of Jewish emigration directly with the Soviets. The meeting, however, was largely a failure, as the participants' positions differed too much for them to agree on a concluding document. Deeply disappointed, Porter later stressed that political and economic cooperation was invariably linked to progress on human rights: "If we find the human rights basket empty," he proclaimed, "then the Soviet Union ought to expect to find the political and economic benefits baskets empty as well."[62] The IPG also expressed disappointment over the outcome but concluded that the value of the CSCE as a forum to hold the Soviet Union accountable to world public opinion was unquestionable.[63] The dialogue at Ottawa failed to deliver, but it was a dialogue nonetheless. Even failed exchanges on human rights helped position Jewish emigration as an important component of the dialogue on improving East-West relations. The very existence of an experts' meeting on human rights within the CSCE context helped solidify human rights as a legitimate topic for discussion.[64]

In November of that year, Reagan and Gorbachev met in Geneva—the first face-to-face meeting between an American president and a Soviet general secretary in more than six years. Like other congressional advocates for the refuseniks, the CHRC maximized its efforts around such US-Soviet summits in the second half of the 1980s. Days before the Geneva summit in 1985, the CHRC held a press conference on the steps of the Capitol with Avital Shcharansky, wife of famed author and refusenik Natan Shcharansky. Together they called on the Soviets to release her husband. They also sent a letter to Secretary of State George Shultz, urging him to bring up Shcharansky during the summit.[65] This practice continued throughout the 1980s as the CHRC lobbied American and Soviet leaders before summits in Reykjavik in 1986, Washington in 1987, and Moscow in 1988.

Potential implications for domestic politics motivated the Reagan administration to step up its efforts on behalf of the refuseniks. An internal White House memo about a meeting with leaders of the American Jewish community days before the Reykjavik summit expressed concern that Reagan was losing the support of the Soviet Jewry movement and stressed that this could result in "very serious political consequences."[66] The next day the White House released a statement by Reagan that emphasized his commitment to discussing human rights and Jewish emigration at Reykjavik.[67] Statements like these reflected Reagan's increasing willingness to raise human rights concerns with Gorbachev. The combined advocacy of American Jewish NGOs and Congress helped draw Reagan's attention to the domestic costs of not doing enough for the refuseniks.[68]

Reagan also took advantage of congressional concerns over Jewish emigration in his negotiations with Gorbachev. At Geneva, Reagan explained to Gorbachev that if he allowed refuseniks and divided families to leave the Soviet Union, it would be much easier to attain congressional approval for cooperation on other issues, such as trade. Gorbachev dismissed the argument and accused Reagan of using Congress as a pretext for gaining concessions on human rights. However, this did not discourage Reagan from raising the argument again at Reykjavik the following year.[69] Reagan thereby sought to use the divided powers of the American political system as leverage in foreign diplomacy. In other words, congressional advocacy for Soviet Jewry became an instrument that Reagan used to elicit concessions from Gorbachev. This move would not have been possible without the outspoken congressional advocacy on behalf of the refuseniks.

Real Progress, or "House Cleaning" before Closing Time?

By the mid-1980s, the most prominent refuseniks had become household names in the United States, lending great public attention to their cause. When the Soviets suddenly released Natan Shcharansky from prison in February 1986 and allowed him to travel to Israel, it became an international media event. Senate minority leader Robert Byrd (D-WV) described the release as "a reward for millions in one man's freedom."[70] Human rights advocates and the Jewish emigration movement celebrated the release as a much-needed victory. When Shcharansky visited the United States later that year, he received a welcome worthy of a head of state, meeting Reagan in the White House and receiving a Congressional Gold Medal.[71] Again, the CHRC was at the forefront of congressional action, with caucus leaders sponsoring the legislation that awarded Shcharansky the medal.[72] Speaking at the annual Prayer Vigil on Capitol Hill that year—another CHRC initiative—Porter cautioned against complacency and urged his colleagues to use the release of Shcharansky as motivation to "re-double" their efforts.[73]

As it turned out, Shcharansky's was the first of a number of high-profile releases. A year later, the Soviets had allowed most refusenik leaders to emigrate, including almost every refusenik adopted by the Committee of 21.[74] The CHRC celebrated the breakthrough but realized that these releases did not translate into any significant improvements in Soviet emigration policy, and in fact, they posed a challenge to the cause. Gorbachev had released the leaders in an attempt to silence Western criticism and appease the refuseniks at home, but he had not increased the general level of Jewish emigration, which remained as low as 914 in 1986.[75] The releases thus risked drawing Western attention away from the cause of the refuseniks, without any real improvements in Jewish emigration policy. The CHRC did what it could to highlight this risk. Before the beginning of the CSCE's Vienna meeting in November 1986, the CHRC sent Secretary of State Shultz a letter that warned against believing that Soviet performance had fundamentally improved.[76] The letter also contained a set of recommendations by the IPG, urging the linkage of progress on security and economy and human rights.[77]

Emigration numbers finally started to increase in 1987, amidst general human rights improvements in the Soviet Union, such as greater tolerance for demonstrations and the release of several political prisoners. However, the CHRC remained skeptical about Soviet intentions. At the outset of the meeting in Vienna on November 4, 1986, the Soviet Union had shocked everyone by proposing to host a conference on "human contacts" in Moscow. In the year that followed, the Soviets continued to show progress.[78] Still, the CHRC was not convinced. In June 1987 Porter noted that the increase in Jewish emigration was modest, with 2,030 Jews allowed to leave the Soviet Union in the first five months of 1987.[79] However, a few months later he called the emigration process "a frustrating struggle against a mindless bureaucracy," and he maintained that the emigration requests of approximately 11,000 refuseniks had been denied, while as many as 375,000 Jews wanted to leave but had not yet applied for visas.[80] In August the CHRC circulated a report on Capitol Hill that interpreted the recent rise in emigration as "house cleaning" before the Soviets shut the door, pointing out that the Jews who had been allowed to leave were almost exclusively known refuseniks from American lists.[81] The report warned that once Moscow had released the high-profile refuseniks who were obstructing improved relations with the United States, the thousands of Jews still in the Soviet Union would be left to suffer in silence. The report also attested to the continued discrimination against these Jews in the Soviet Union. The following month Shcharansky expressed the same concern about Soviet intentions to Shultz, prior to a meeting with Reagan.[82]

In some ways, conditions for Jews still living in the Soviet Union actually worsened amidst the general human rights improvements. The CHRC drew attention to this by hosting a number of congressional briefings with NGOs during 1988 that testified to a rise in antisemitism.[83] The worsening economic crisis and the greater freedom to form civil society groups under Gorbachev's reforms paved the way for stronger, more organized antisemitism from private groups. In August the CHRC organized a news conference on the issue and subsequently spearheaded a letter to Gorbachev urging him to intervene. At the news conference, Lantos said that Gorbachev should not "move back on glasnost," but he must recognize that "openness is not a license to perpetrate racial and religious persecution, possibly leading to pogroms."[84] In October the CHRC followed up with another letter to Gorbachev signed by 170 members of Congress protesting the activities of the most influential of the antisemitic groups, Paymat.[85] The CHRC thus drew attention to the negative side effects of glasnost and the considerable room for improvement on Jewish emigration.

The CHRC continued to press its point as Gorbachev and Reagan met once again in Moscow in May 1988. On the eve of the summit, the CHRC cochairs wrote to both Reagan and Gorbachev, urging them to solve the issue of Jewish emigration.[86] After the summit, CHRC members met with Richard Schifter, the assistant secretary of state for human rights and humanitarian affairs, to discuss the outcome of the summit and the future course of US human rights policy toward the Soviet Union.[87] Earlier in the year, CHRC leaders had raised their concerns with officials of the Soviet Foreign Ministry and Supreme Soviet during a visit to Moscow, where they also visited thirty-five refuseniks.[88] The CHRC thus kept pressure on both the Reagan administration and the Soviets to remember the refuseniks, even as US-Soviet relations were rapidly improving.

In the end, the general human rights improvements in Soviet society were reflected in Jewish emigration numbers. In 1989 no fewer than 71,000 Jews left the Soviet Union. In its *Country Report on Human Rights Practices* for that same year, the State Department reported that the Soviet Union had "witnessed a remarkable opening up of the political process and improvements in human rights practices."[89] As the Cold War ended and the Soviet Union fell apart, a staggering 570,000 Soviet Jews seized the moment and left between 1990 and 1993.[90]

The Ongoing Institutionalization of Human Rights

The CHRC made an important contribution to congressional advocacy for the refuseniks, which, according to the research of other historians, forced the Reagan administration to give the issue greater priority.[91] This advocacy provided Reagan with broad political support to push the issue in negotiations with Gorbachev.[92] Most important, it allowed Reagan to use congressional opinion as leverage in negotiations with the Soviet leader. To be sure, congressional advocacy was only one factor leading to change in Soviet Jewish emigration policy. Arguably, Reagan's interest in using the refuseniks as a tool of Cold War diplomacy, the election of Gorbachev, and the Helsinki process were all more decisive. Still, the CHRC and wider congressional advocacy played an important role in keeping the issue on the US-Soviet agenda. The successful release of individual refuseniks targeted by the CHRC's advocacy before the increase in general emigration suggests that this advocacy mattered.

Even so, the refuseniks' impact on the CHRC was probably far greater than its impact on them. Porter's encounter with refusenik families in 1982 laid the groundwork for his commitment to human rights and the establishment of the CHRC. The refusenik issue helped consolidate the CHRC as the largest forum for human rights issues in Congress. Ten years after emerging from a single congressman's encounter with refusenik families, the CHRC was an established part of the congressional infrastructure, encompassing half of all House members.[93] The CHRC fostered bipartisan collaboration on human rights issues and helped systematize congressional human rights policy through its computer tracking system, newsletters, and briefings. It launched new initiatives such as the IPG, the Committee of 21, and the CHRF, greatly expanding the number of human rights bodies in Congress. Moreover, it fostered closer collaboration between Congress and NGOs by providing the latter with another avenue to reach legislators. The CHRC set roots in Congress that allowed it to outlive both its founders and the refusenik issue, thereby contributing to the institutionalization of human rights in American foreign policy. In 2008 the CHRC became the first caucus ever elevated to the status of a commission.[94] The refusenik cause was instrumental in this achievement, as it was the motivator for both the CHRC's establishment and its expansion throughout the 1980s.

Notes

1. *Human Rights: Hearing before the Committee on Foreign Relations, United States Senate, Ninety-Eighth Congress, First Session, on the Promotion and Protection of Human Rights in Eastern Europe and the Soviet Union, Chicago, Ill., November 9, 1983* (Washington, DC: US Government Printing Office, 1984), 149.

2. Also known as congressional member organizations (CMOs), a caucus is a group of members of Congress united in the pursuit of common legislative objectives. See Susan Webb Hammond, *Congressional Caucuses in National Policy Making* (Baltimore: Johns Hopkins University Press, 1998).

3. I am grateful to the Lantos Foundation for granting me exclusive access to the previously unstudied archive of Congressman Tom Lantos (D-CA), whose papers cover the work of the CHRC.

4. The key work remains Robert David Johnson, *Congress and the Cold War* (New York: Cambridge University Press, 2006).

5. Andrew Johnstone, "Before the Water's Edge: Domestic Politics and U.S. Foreign Relations," *Passport: The Newsletter of the SHAFR* 45, no. 3 (2015); Melvin Small, *Democracy and Diplomacy: The Impact of Domestic Politics on U.S. Foreign Policy, 1789–1994* (Baltimore: Johns Hopkins University Press, 1996); Campbell Craig and Fredrik Logevall, *America's Cold War: The Politics of Insecurity* (Cambridge, MA: Belknap Press of Harvard University Press, 2009); Julian E. Zelizer, *Arsenal of Democracy: The Politics of National Security—From World War II to the War on Terrorism* (New York: Basic Books, 2010).

6. The only publication on the CHRC is James M. McCormick and Neil J. Mitchell, "Commitments, Transnational Interests, and Congress," *Political Research Quarterly* 60, no. 4 (2007): 579–92.

7. For a review of this scholarship, see Sarah B. Snyder, "Human Rights and U.S. Foreign Relations: A Historiographical Review," *Passport: The Newsletter of the SHAFR* 44 (2013). Key works include Samuel Moyn, *The Last Utopia: Human Rights in History* (Cambridge, MA: Belknap Press of Harvard University Press, 2010); Barbara J. Keys, *Reclaiming American Virtue: The Human Rights Revolution of the 1970s* (Cambridge, MA: Harvard University Press, 2014).

8. Christian Philip Peterson, "'Confronting' Moscow: The Reagan Administration, Human Rights, and the Final Act," *Historian* 74, no. 1 (2012): 57–86; Sarah B. Snyder, *Human Rights Activism and the End of the Cold War: A Transnational History of the Helsinki Network* (New York: Cambridge University Press, 2011); Christian Philip Peterson, *Globalizing Human Rights: Private Citizens, the Soviet Union, and the West* (New York: Routledge, 2012); Carl J. Bon Tempo, "From the Center-Right: Freedom House and Human Rights in the 1970s and 1980s," in *The Human Rights Revolution: An International History,* ed. Petra Goedde and William Hitchcock (New York: Oxford University Press, 2012).

9. Barbara J. Keys, "Congress, Kissinger, and the Origins of Human Rights Diplomacy," *Diplomatic History* 34, no. 5 (2010): 823–51; Sarah B. Snyder, "'A Call for U.S. Leadership': Congressional Activism on Human Rights," *Diplomatic History* 37, no. 2 (2013): 372–97; "The Defeat of Ernest Lefever's Nomination: Keeping Human Rights on the United States Foreign Policy Agenda," in *Challenging U.S. Foreign Policy: America and the World,* ed. Bevan Sewell and Scott Lucas (Basingstoke, UK: Palgrave Macmillan UK, 2011).

10. Joseph S. Nye and Richard N. Cooper, "Ethics and Foreign Policy," in

Global Dilemmas, ed. Samuel P. Huntington, Joseph S. Nye, and Richard N. Cooper (Cambridge, MA, and Lanham, MD: Center for International Affairs, University Press of America, 1985), 23, 41.

11. For more on the New Right and the conservative ascendancy, see Michael Schaller, *Right Turn: American Life in the Reagan-Bush Era, 1980–1992* (New York: Oxford University Press, 2007), 27–48.

12. Zelizer, *Arsenal of Democracy,* 300–301; Charles Krauthammer, "The Reagan Doctrine," *Time,* April 1, 1985.

13. Elizabeth Schrayer, congressional staffer for John Porter (1980–1982), interview by the author, 2015.

14. Quoted in Peterson, *Globalizing Human Rights,* 108.

15. Quoted in Hauke Hartmann, "US Human Rights Policy under Carter and Reagan, 1977–1981," *Human Rights Quarterly* 23, no. 2 (2001): 424.

16. It is important to note that Carter was also inconsistent in his intent to distance the United States from oppressive dictators. For instance, Carter hosted the shah of Iran on November 15, 1977. Reagan, however, found such intentions to be misplaced.

17. See editorial, "Wrong Turns on Human Rights," *New York Times,* February 6, 1981.

18. Memorandum of Conversation, Subject: Summary of the President's Meeting with President Chun Doo Hwan of the Republic of Korea, February 2, 1981, 11:20–12:05 p.m., Cabinet Room, with cover memorandum, Richard V. Allen to President Reagan, February 6, 1981, Subject: Your Meeting with President Chun of Korea, National Security Archive, http://nsarchive.gwu.edu/NSAEBB/NSAEBB306/doc05.pdf (accessed June 19, 2017).

19. Edwin S. Maynard, "The Bureaucracy and Implementation of US Human Rights Policy," *Human Rights Quarterly* 11, no. 2 (1989): 182.

20. Ernest W. Lefever, *Morality and Foreign Policy: A Symposium on President Carter's Stance* (Washington, DC: Ethics and Public Policy Center, Georgetown University, 1977).

21. *Nomination of Ernest W. Lefever: Hearings before the Committee on Foreign Relations, United States Senate, Ninety-Seventh Congress, First Session, on Nomination of Ernest W. Lefever, to Be Assistant Secretary of State for Human Rights and Humanitarian Affairs, May 18, 19, June 4, and 5, 1981* (Washington, DC: US Government Printing Office, 1981), 4.

22. Charles Mohr, "Coalition Assails Reagan's Choice for State Dept. Human Rights Job," *New York Times,* February 25, 1981.

23. Editorial, "Semantic Antics over Human Rights," *New York Times,* May 24, 1981.

24. Memo, Charles Fairbanks to EUR, S/P, HA, July 29, 1981, box 1, 006R, Carnes Lord files, Ronald Reagan Presidential Library, Simi Valley, CA (hereafter RPL).

25. Maynard, "Bureaucracy and Implementation of US Human Rights Policy," 183.

26. Barbara Crossette, "Strong U.S. Human Rights Policy Urged in Memo Approved by Haig," *New York Times,* November 5, 1981.

27. US Congress, House Committee on Foreign Affairs, Subcommittee on Human Rights and International Organizations, *Review of State Department Country Reports on Human Rights Practices for 1981: Hearing before the Subcommittee on Human Rights and International Organizations of the Committee on Foreign Affairs, House of Representatives, Ninety-Seventh Congress, Second Session, April 28, 1982* (Washington, DC: US Government Printing Office, 1982).

28. Tamar Jacoby, "The Reagan Turnaround on Human Rights," *Foreign Affairs* 64, no. 5 (1986): 1066–86.

29. US Department of State, *Country Reports on Human Rights Practices for 1983* (Washington, DC: US Government Printing Office, 1984), 5; Peterson, *Globalizing Human Rights,* 113.

30. Jeane J. Kirkpatrick, "Dictatorships and Double Standards," *Commentary,* November 1979, 34–45.

31. R. Spencer Oliver, chief of staff, Helsinki Commission (1976–1985), interview by the author, July 8, 2014.

32. For more on the CSCE, the Helsinki Final Act, and the Helsinki Commission, see Snyder, *Human Rights Activism and the End of the Cold War.*

33. The priorities of the CHRC exemplify the degree to which the issue of human rights, despite its supposed universality, is constantly interpreted and adapted to fit specific political agendas.

34. Schrayer interview.

35. The Congressional Human Rights Caucus, Tom Lantos Papers (hereafter TLP), BANC MSS 2008/121, carton 102, folder 21, Bancroft Library, University of California, Berkeley.

36. The three CHRC Executive Committee members were Dante Fascell (D-FL) of the Foreign Affairs Committee, Peter Rodino (D-NJ) of the Judiciary Committee, and Les Aspin (D-WI) of the Armed Services Committee. Congressional Human Rights Foundation, Statement of Purpose (description of CHRC), TLP, carton 113, folder 21.

37. As of January 1, 1986, the fees were as follows: cochairs, $10,000; executive members, $1,000; basic members, $250. Letter to Committee on House Administration, TLP, carton 112, folder 18.

38. CHRC Newsletter, November 1983, TLP, carton 111, folder 34.

39. CHRC Newsletter, April 30, 1984, TLP, carton 102, folder 19.

40. CHRC Newsletter, April 1986, TLP, carton 102, folder 19.

41. Chicago Conference on Soviet Jewry: News, June 13, 1983, National Conference on Soviet Jewry records, I-181A, box 292, folder 6, American Jewish Historical Society, New York, NY, and Boston, MA.

42. Statement of the UCSJ to the CHRC, August 9, 1988, Union of Councils for Soviet Jewry, records, I-410A, box 66, folder 14, American Jewish Historical Society.

43. Correspondence between John Porter and Boris Prudinsky, 1983–1986, TLP, carton 103, folder 19.

44. Yakov Galperin to Tom Lantos, July 30, 1987, TLP, carton 106, folder 8.

45. The total number Jews allowed to leave in 1983 was 1,315, down from 51,320 in 1979. Fred A. Lazin, *The Struggle for Soviet Jewry in American Politics: Israel versus the American Jewish Establishment* (Lanham, MD: Lexington Books, 2005), 309.

46. Justin Vaïsse, *Neoconservatism: The Biography of a Movement* (Cambridge, MA: Belknap Press of Harvard University Press, 2010), 114–18; Keys, *Reclaiming American Virtue,* 124; Daniel Sargent, A *Superpower Transformed: The Remaking of American Foreign Relations in the 1970s* (Oxford: Oxford University Press, 2015), 212–14.

47. Commission on Security and Cooperation in Europe, *Implementation of the Helsinki Accords: Hearing before the Commission on Security and Cooperation in Europe, One Hundredth Congress, First Session, Glasnost: The Soviet Policy of "Openness," March 4, 1987* (Washington, DC: US Government Printing Office, 1987), 82.

48. George Perkovich, "Soviet Jewry and American Foreign Policy," World Policy Journal 5, no. 3 (1988), 435–467: 444.

49. *Soviet Jewry Hearing and Markup before the Subcommittee on Human Rights and International Organizations of the Committee on Foreign Affairs and the Commission on Security and Cooperation in Europe, House of Representatives, Ninety-Eighth Congress, First Session, on H. Con. Res. 63, June 23 and 28, 1983* (Washington, DC: US Government Printing Office, 1984), 33–35.

50. This focus was partly the result of American Jewish groups and human rights NGOs drawing attention to the refuseniks. Furthermore, it was arguably more likely that the United States could persuade the Soviet Union to allow thousands to leave than to liberalize the entire Soviet society and secure the religious freedom and other rights of millions.

51. The first letter-writing campaign resulted in more than 150 letters. CHRC Newsletter, August 1986, TLP, carton 102, folder 19. As an example, see Congress to Chernenko, March 1, 1984, ibid., folder 36.

52. H. Con. Res. 34 (100th Congress), introduced by CHRC executive member Dante Fascell and passed unanimously in the House on March 31, 1987; H. Res. 455 (100th Congress), introduced by CHRC executive member Gus Yatron and passed unanimously by the House on May 24, 1988.

53. CHRC Newsletter, March 1987, TLP, carton 102, folder 19.

54. CHRC Newsletter, November 1983, TLP, carton 111, folder 34.

55. CSCE Human Rights Expert Meeting, Ottawa—IPG Report, June 1985, Jack Kemp Papers, carton 130, folder 12, Manuscript Division, Library of Congress, Washington, DC.

56. Report, *IPG Call to Conscience,* December 3, 1987, ID #548208, HU, WHORM: Subject File, RPL.

57. CHRC Summary of Activities, 1985, TLP, carton 111, folder 34.

58. CHRC Newsletter, June 1985, TLP, carton 102, folder 19.

59. "Wives' Group: 'Not Just John Q. Citizens,'" *New York Times,* February 21, 1986.

60. David L. Phillips, president, Congressional Human Rights Foundation (1988–1995), interview by the author, July 30, 2015.

61. Congressional Human Rights Foundation, Statement of Purpose, TLP, carton 113, folder 21.

62. CHRC Newsletter, September 9, 1985, TLP, carton 102, folder 19.

63. CSCE Human Rights Expert Meeting, Ottawa—IPG Report, June 1985.

64. Sarah B. Snyder has similarly argued for the overlooked importance of the CSCE expert meetings at Ottawa and elsewhere between 1984 and 1986. See Sarah B. Snyder, "The Foundation for Vienna: A Reassessment of the CSCE in the Mid-1980s," *Cold War History* 10, no. 4 (2010): 503–4.

65. CHRC press release and letter, January 3, 1985, TLP, carton 107, folder 11.

66. Memo from Mari Maseng and Rodney McDaniel to Frederick Ryan, October 6, 1986, ID#440961, C0165, WHORM: Subject File, RPL.

67. The White House, Office of the Press Secretary, October 7, 1986, series I, box 47, Anthony Dolan files, RPL.

68. Peterson, "'Confronting' Moscow" 76. Moreover, Reagan felt he was now in a better position to coerce Soviet concessions on human rights than he had been previously.

69. Jack F. Matlock, *Reagan and Gorbachev: How the Cold War Ended,* 1st ed. (New York: Random House, 2004), 161, 218.

70. 132 *Congressional Record,* 99th Cong., 2nd sess., 2134 (February 18, 1986).

71. Gal Beckerman, *When They Come for Us, We'll Be Gone: The Epic Struggle to Save Soviet Jewry* (Boston: Houghton Mifflin Harcourt, 2010), 505.

72. H.R. 4186 (99th Congress), introduced by CHRC executive member Benjamin Gilman and passed in the House on May 12, 1986; testimony of John Porter presented to Committee of Banking, May 1, 1986, TLP, carton 107, folder 10.

73. News—John Porter, TLP, carton 110, folder 10.

74. CHRC Newsletter, March 1987, TLP, carton 111, folder 20.

75. US Department of State, *Country Reports on Human Rights Practices for 1986* (Washington, DC: US Government Printing Office, 1987), 1066.

76. CHRC to George Shultz, TLP, carton 110, folder 17.

77. CHRC to George Shultz: IPG Recommendations for the Vienna Review Conference, ibid.

78. US Department of State, *Country Reports on Human Rights Practices for 1987* (Washington, DC: US Government Printing Office, 1988), 1045–55.

79. Porter, extended remarks to *Congressional Record,* July 8, 1987, TLP, carton 102, folder 35.

80. Congressman Porter's report, October 28, 1987, TLP, carton 106, folder 01.

81. Letter with report, CHRC to Peter Rodino, August 12, 1987, Peter W. Rodino Jr. Archives, box POL-010, folder 1, Seton Hall University School of Law, Newark, NJ.

82. Memo: Meeting with Natan and Avital Shcharanskiy, September 21, 1987, ID #506980, C0165, WHORM: Subject File, RPL.

83. CHRC Annual Report, 1988, TLP, carton 111, folder 34.

84. "Members of Congress Ask Gorbachev to Investigate Latest Anti-Semitism," Jewish Telegraphic Agency, August 10, 1988.

85. CHRC Newsletter, October 1988, TLP, carton 102, folder 19.

86. CHRC to Gorbachev, May 24, 1988, TLP, carton 110, folder 17; CHRC Annual Report, 1988.

87. CHRC Annual Report, 1988.

88. CHRC Newsletter, April 1988, TLP, carton 102, folder 19.

89. US Department of State, *Country Reports on Human Rights Practices for 1989* (Washington, DC: US Government Printing Office, 1990), 1274.

90. Beckerman, *When They Come for Us, We'll Be Gone,* 528.

91. Snyder, *Human Rights Activism and the End of the Cold War;* Peterson, *Globalizing Human Rights.*

92. Ronald Reagan, *An American Life* (New York: Simon and Schuster, 1990), 705; *Religious Persecution in the Soviet Union. Part I—Soviet Jewry. Hearing before the Subcommittees on Europe and the Middle East and on Human Rights and International Organizations of the Committee on Foreign Affairs, House of Representatives, Ninety-Ninth Congress, First Session, September 11, 1985* (Washington, DC: US Government Printing Office, 1985), 89; Matlock, *Reagan and Gorbachev,* 161, 218.

93. CHRC brochure, 1992, TLP, carton 102, folder 21.

94. H. Res. 1451, "Tom Lantos Human Rights Commission Establishment Resolution," September 24, 2008, http://tlhrc.house.gov/about.asp.

10

Peace through Austerity

The Reagan Defense Buildup in the "Age of Inequality"

Michael Brenes

In response to what he believed had been a decade of neglect toward America's military, President Ronald Reagan raised defense spending 35 percent during his presidency (1981–1989). To Reagan, no deficit was too large if it prevented a nuclear attack by the Soviet Union. Much of the defense spending under Reagan went toward research and development of expensive projects such as the Strategic Defense Initiative (SDI) and Cold War interventions in Central America and elsewhere in the developing world. Like all other Cold War presidents before him, Reagan relied on American military might to deter potential threats from communist countries. He rejected the policy of containment as insufficient to deter communist aggression. New international threats from the Soviet Union and its allies seemingly demanded a return to the arms and technology race, as communism once again appeared to be marching toward the West. Reagan responded to the new international context of the Cold War with a mission to "roll back" communism by placing the United States in a position of military dominance over the Soviet Union.[1]

But the domestic consequences of the Reagan defense buildup disproportionately enhanced the fortunes of wealthy Americans to the detriment of the working class and defense workers of color. High-tech areas in the western United States benefited the most from investment in the missile defense shield. But SDI remained an experimental and untested program, which meant that most of the jobs went to skilled engineers, mathematicians, and physicists. Unlike the production of current defense products—which required a manufacturing base—Reagan's weapons systems were developmental and required no major investment in industry. With an eye toward defeating the Soviets in a race for military predominance, Reagan's defense policy involved primarily investment in new programs, not the production of preexisting weapons of war, which resulted in a net loss of jobs for many unskilled workers who produced and manufactured armaments in the Rust Belt. As historian Judith Stein has written, Reagan's economic policies promoted "nontradable sectors like real estate, financial services, and defense," which resulted in "hobbling tradable manufacturing and agriculture," economic sectors that were occupied predominantly by working-class Americans. Reagan's defense policy thereby exacerbated the problems of deindustrialization, enhancing the fortunes of the skilled workforce and promoting a shift to what Stein has called the "Age of Inequality."[2]

In connecting the militarization of Cold War foreign policy to the rise of income inequality and austerity policies in the 1980s, this essay argues that Reagan's defense policies furthered economic and racial inequality in the United States. I pay particular attention to the appropriations for SDI and how defense contracts for the program were inequitably distributed in the United States. I examine the creation and funding of SDI in a domestic context as I analyze the Reagan defense buildup within the uneven regional landscape of American capitalism and the role it played in electoral politics during the 1980s and 1990s.[3]

When the political economy of the Cold War (like the overall economy) confronted tepid economic growth rates and stagnant wages brought on by globalization, deindustrialization, and a weakened labor force during the Carter and Reagan administrations, residents of "Cold War communities" faced a perfect storm: job losses that coincided with higher costs of living.[4] Communities reliant on the Department of Defense for employment were therefore more willing to support proposals that lowered federal taxes and reduced government influence in the regulation of local economies, while also campaigning for additional federal defense contracts to keep those local economies afloat. The unequal distribution of contracts and disproportionate investment in Cold War communities within the "Gun Belt" during the Reagan years meant that companies that profited the least from the defense buildup merged with bigger defense companies or drastically downsized, leading to unemployment on some scale.[5]

This essay suggests that Reagan's defense buildup mattered for its domestic outcomes as well as its international impact. While conceived within the international context of the Cold War, the Reagan defense buildup was also an extension of the administration's domestic policies. Reagan, his advisers, and like-minded congressional Democrats and Republicans saw the defense economy as an antidote to unemployment and stagnation in a postindustrial age, as the defense buildup provided jobs to many unemployed Americans. In allocating defense contracts to localities and districts dependent on Cold War military spending, Republicans in Congress and the Reagan administration embraced government spending to ameliorate and stimulate employment. In his speeches on SDI and the defense buildup, Reagan promoted the missile defense system as a check to Soviet power, but he also frequently touted the economic growth and good-paying jobs SDI brought to Americans.[6]

But the defense workers who benefited financially from SDI did not think highly of the federal government. When Reagan left office in 1989, residents of Cold War communities throughout the country ultimately felt that the federal government had failed them in some capacity—despite being employed by it. As the country experienced wage stagnation and low overall growth relative to past decades, defense workers demanded lower taxes, reduced government regulation, and, at the same time, higher defense spending. This was not a partisan message. Both Democrats and Republicans from defense communities wanted more monies from the Pentagon, but they wanted the government to stay out of their lives in other areas. Americans' close relationship with the military economy and Cold War foreign policy therefore revealed an interesting and sorely overlooked contradiction about voters who identified as liberal or conservative, Democrat or Republican. In terms of federal benefits, they wanted less—*and more.*

In making such demands, Cold War Americans echoed long-standing paradoxical dynamics between the federal government and the public. Indeed, historian Gary Gerstle claims that Americans' association with the federal government is concurrently marked by "liberty and coercion." Since 1776, Americans have exchanged freedom from government influence for the miscellaneous benefits government has provided. Whether it be isolated agrarians accepting federal farm subsidies, racist southerners mouthing "states' rights" while being employed by a New Deal job program, or corporate executives in the 1970s demanding less government regulation while making sure they received tax breaks to move their companies to cheaper locales, Americans have excelled at accommodating mantras of self-reliance with an ever-larger federal state. As they relate to areas reliant on defense production in the latter years of the Cold War, these perceptions of government enabled and justified wider economic inequality in the United States, deepening the political chasms between Americans and compelling electoral change.[7]

The results exacerbated economic inequality in long-standing sites of defense manufacturing in the Northeast. When the Cold War ended, drastic cutbacks in defense ensued. Defense spending was reduced by more than $100 billion after Reagan's presidency. As a percentage of gross domestic product, defense spending declined by more than half from 1987 to 2000. And the defense jobs lost to peace were not replaced by better ones. As in other regions distressed by plant closures, the service economy often replaced the defense economy. Demilitarization therefore had the greatest effect on working-class defense employees, as many found themselves displaced or underemployed after 1991. Skilled workers had more mobility and better opportunities than their working-class counterparts. Liberals and antinuclear activists (both inside and outside the Democratic Party) tried to sell defense conversion to ameliorate the employment situation, but there were few buyers. Defense companies were resistant to conversion to peacetime projects for fear of losing profits (and future defense contracts), and their workers feared being dislocated or unemployed in the transition to nondefense work—before being laid off.

When President Ronald Reagan took office in 1981, he sincerely feared that the Soviet Union would outpace the United States in military strength. The Soviet Union had invaded Afghanistan in 1979, increased defense production in the 1980s, and reemerged as an ongoing existential threat. Reagan was also determined in his belief that the Soviet Union was an "evil empire" that responded only to military power.[8] For Reagan, the only counter to Soviet aggression was American might. During the

1980s the United States' expenditures on national defense in "peacetime" matched what it had spent during the initial years of the Vietnam War. Much of this money went for research and development of programs such as the Strategic Defense Initiative. Conceived by Reagan in 1983, SDI was designed to intercept Soviet missiles in the event of a nuclear war. It relied on a system of satellites to deploy lasers in such an event, leading critics of the program to dub it "Star Wars," after the popular 1977 movie directed by George Lucas. For the detractors of Reagan's defense programs, *Star Wars* (the movie) seemed just as fantastical as the proposal for SDI—the technology to develop SDI would take untold amounts of money and potentially decades of research.

Moreover, SDI was a source of contention when Reagan met with Soviet premier Mikhail Gorbachev in October 1986 at Reykjavik, Iceland, to discuss the reduction of nuclear weapons. Gorbachev was ready to eliminate much of the Soviet Union's arsenal of ballistic missiles. But before agreeing to universal cuts in nuclear weapons, he demanded that Reagan relegate SDI to a nonactive stage of research and development. The Soviets viewed SDI as an offensive (not defensive) program and were suspicious that it would provide the United States with a first-strike capability. But Reagan would not change his position on the missile defense shield, declaring SDI nonnegotiable. Reagan's intransigence over SDI stalled the talks at Reykjavik and postponed diplomatic agreements between the two nations for several months. Gorbachev would eventually relent one year later—having been convinced that SDI was not feasible. Gorbachev's decision (and Reagan's willingness to work with him) reduced tensions between the United States and the Soviet Union. Although Reagan modified his opinions over time, even as he pursued negotiations with Gorbachev during his second term, Reagan still argued that military strength was fundamental to protecting the nation from external threats.[9]

More than furthering the interests of US foreign policy, SDI was indicative of how federal defense spending would function under a president managing a postindustrial economy. From SDI's inception, the major winners were the nation's defense contractors (and their employees), which waged bidding wars to build components of the missile defense shield. SDI was a boon to defense companies that had seen lean times in the 1970s due to post-Vietnam criticism of the military-industrial complex and the policy of détente between the two superpowers. During the years of détente under the Nixon and Ford administrations, defense spending was cut in half as a percentage of total budget outlays after 1968. The entire defense economy was sorely in need of a stimulus, and SDI provided one.

Two regions received most of the federal funds for SDI: suburban Denver and the suburbs of Washington, DC. The major contractor for SDI was Martin Marietta, located in Waterton, Colorado, about half an hour south of Denver. Waterton was, in essence, Martin Marietta, and vice versa. Before the federal government directed the aerospace and defense industry's expansion into Colorado, places like Waterton had been sparsely populated towns with no driving economic force, but America's mission to fight communism through massive defense spending reinvented the landscape.[10] National regulations stipulated that defense factories had to be built in isolated regions away from population centers. This spurred suburban construction to accommodate the influx of defense employees, creating high-tech Cold War defense communities populated by wealthy engineers and scientists.[11]

This was also the case in Colorado Springs, about an hour south of Waterton. Before the twentieth century, Colorado Springs had been a railroad and mining town, but the Great Depression hit it hard. To raise the city's fortunes, a group of local residents tried to attract the military. These boosters included restaurateur and Chamber of Commerce member Joe Reich, gold processor Charles Tutt, and a hardware store owner, plumber, dentist, and banker. The city had dry, flat land for airstrips, cheap land for base construction, and an economically desperate population willing to accommodate the military on any terms. In 1942 the US Army built Camp Carson and Peterson Army Air Base in Colorado Springs, and after the war the city remained a vital military outpost, particularly for the US Air Force. Colorado Springs became the testing ground for new radar, communications, and aerospace technologies, all of which required a highly educated workforce. By 1985, the total population of military-related personnel was 61,437—double the entire population of Colorado Springs at the outset of World War II. The Cold War created affluence from deprivation.[12]

Reagan's Cold War also created wealth in the DC suburbs. SDI expanded the network of high-tech firms in Bethesda, Maryland, and

Arlington, Virginia. Rather than working in factories, though, the designers of these new weapons occupied skyscrapers and college campuses, since the companies that received funds under SDI were not asked to produce anything tangible. Their research was stored in computers; there was no hardware to be packed and shipped to military installations around the world. As in Colorado Springs, SDI funds that flowed into these areas generated higher incomes for already prosperous physicists and mathematicians. SDI essentially made the wealthy even wealthier.[13] The political by-product of high-tech investment in places like Bethesda and Colorado Springs was that it engendered a large bloc of Republican-leaning voters who were pro-military but concerned that federal taxes on the wealthy would erode the security of their government-funded jobs.[14]

Indeed, SDI had a significant role in shaping the political culture as the missile defense system became a political issue, particularly in Colorado. The 1986 Senate race between Republican Ken Kramer and Democrat Tim Wirth best captured SDI's influence on American electoral politics. Prior to running for the Senate, Kramer served in the House representing the Fifth District, which included Colorado Springs. For the most part, Kramer was an antigovernment conservative who promised to both reduce the size of government and create defense jobs in his district, and he used SDI to bolster his image as a job creator. He boasted to reporters about bringing defense jobs to Colorado Springs, including 8,000 jobs from SDI, at a time when the rest of the region was suffering from significant unemployment. Wirth, his Democratic challenger, was opposed to SDI but did not want to say so publicly. Wirth recognized the salience of SDI in the state, and he did not want his campaign to center on his opposition to the program. As his campaign manager said, "there are a lot of livelihoods riding on S.D.I., and we don't want to seem anti-job."[15]

With Election Day nearing, Reagan appeared at a rally for Kramer, praising his stance on SDI. Kramer's supporters cheered while anti-SDI demonstrators confronted Reagan with signs that read, "Keep Star Wars in the Movie Theaters."[16] SDI was, Reagan said, "America's insurance policy to protect us from accidents or some madman who might come along, as a Hitler did or a Qadhafi, or just in case the Soviets don't keep their side of a bargain." Linking antigovernment rhetoric to the local and international context of the Cold War, Reagan went on to say that Kramer "has proven crucial in our efforts to cut your taxes and get big government off your backs," and he was "central in our efforts to rebuild the nation's defenses." Reagan called Kramer an early and "strong supporter of our Strategic Defense Initiative. And he helped convince the administration to put the major research center that will be the brains of SDI right here in Colorado." Kramer understood that "our Strategic Defense Initiative will open the door to a new technological age. Just as America's space program created new jobs and industries, SDI could open whole new fields of technology and industry, providing jobs for thousands, as Ken said, right here in Colorado and improving the quality of life in America and around the world." Reagan also took the opportunity to offer vague comparisons between himself and John F. Kennedy, implying that SDI was like the Apollo space program, in that both would provide new jobs and innovations to better the lives of Coloradoans and people throughout the world.[17]

Even with Reagan's endorsement, Kramer lost the election. The jobs SDI brought to Colorado Springs could not make up for employment losses in other areas of the state. But Reagan continued to turn to Coloradoans employed by SDI to promote his economic and defense policies. Approximately a year after Kramer's defeat, Reagan visited the Denver headquarters of Martin Marietta on November 24, 1987, to launch a public relations event for SDI. The National Security Council (NSC) prepared drafts of Reagan's speech to 2,000 Martin Marietta employees, telling the president to make it clear that SDI is "strengthening deterrence" and to downplay arms control while highlighting Soviet efforts to build their own version of SDI. According to American intelligence estimates, the Soviets had spent $200 billion "on strategic defense programs over the last 10 years, roughly what they've spent on offense," versus America's $10 billion. Reagan should emphasize this point to the workers, the NSC suggested. After Reagan toured the Martin Marietta facility and received updates on the Zenith Star (a program to develop chemical lasers to be emitted from space), he took the podium and told the scientists and engineers, "You are laboring to develop a defensive system that will change history. Once you've completed your work, the world will never be the same."[18]

Colorado was not the only state where the international Cold War informed local politics. Defense communities in the Northeast and Midwest suffered significantly from cuts in the military in the 1970s, but they did not share in the spoils of SDI. Areas such as Long Island, New York, and southeastern Connecticut, focusing on aircraft and heavy industry, had little to offer SDI. Places like Brookhaven National Laboratory in Suffolk County, Long Island, received monies to research the effects of radiation on semiconductors intended for use in the missile defense shield, but no weapons were produced. As a result, major Long Island defense firms such as Fairchild Industries in Nassau County (which had its origins in World War II) and Grumman Aerospace in Suffolk County suffered. Grumman's future was in doubt almost as soon as Reagan launched his defense buildup. Indeed, Republican representatives Barber Conable Jr. and Jack Kemp wrote to Reagan in 1981, asking him to prevent Grumman's acquisition by LTV Corporation, as they feared the buyout would "lead to the liquidation of Grumman operations and the resultant loss of hundreds of jobs in New York." The full weight of federal regulations and laws, including antitrust laws and federal statutes regarding defense contracting, would be impediments to any deal, Kemp implied. The preservation of Grumman would "insure the wellbeing of our national defense industrial base" and prevent disastrous "consequences for Grumman employees and shareholders, for New York aerospace workers and the state economy." LTV dropped its takeover bid in November 1981, but Grumman continued to struggle until merging with Northrop in 1994. By the late 1980s, as major military electronics and defense companies were bought out or went bankrupt, Wall Street predicted that the "takeover trend" would continue into the near future.[19]

The collapse of the Berlin Wall and the demise of global communism made the regional separation between the winners and losers in Reagan's defense buildup more acute. By 1987, Fairchild's financial portfolio was so poor that when the company did not win a contract to manufacture the T-46A jet, executives laid off 2,500 employees. Because of the lobbying efforts of Senator Bob Dole (R-KS), the T-46A contract went to Cessna Manufacturing Company in Wichita, Kansas, sealing the fate of Fairchild. By the end of the year, Fairchild closed its doors. The loss of Fairchild was a loss for all of Nassau County. It meant declining profits for the company's various subcontractors and the suppliers of Fairchild's equipment; it even led to the closing of restaurants that had supplied the workers with lunch and coffee.[20]

Democrat Thomas Downey, who had represented Suffolk County in the House of Representatives since 1975, felt compelled to save Fairchild. Elected as one of the "Watergate babies" in 1974, Downey was a leading voice against SDI and Reagan's foreign policy in Central America in the House (as well as a supporter of arms control and the nuclear freeze movement). Though he opposed Reagan's defense buildup, Downey felt obligated to support the Cold War interests in his district, and he rushed to protect Fairchild and the jobs it provided. Downey pronounced Fairchild's collapse "a human tragedy of the first order." He went on to say that Long Island was not just losing "manufacturing jobs—jewels in any economy—but we also stand to lose the jobs of all the contractors, vendors, and others who have depended on the factory." The answer, according to Downey, was more defense spending. Much like his Democratic colleagues who represented Cold War communities, Downey fought for defense funds to ensure the survival of his district, even while arguing that the underlying foreign policy was wrong. Downey later admitted his "hypocrisy" toward defense spending, but like many antimilitarist congressional representatives of the 1970s, Downey had to confront the reality of the military-industrial complex and the demands it placed on citizens who depended on it.[21]

While defense cuts led to unemployment across class lines, workers of color were especially hurt by the downturn in defense production. Since World War II, defense jobs had served as tickets to the middle class for African Americans. Long Island defense contractors were notorious for discriminating against African Americans in their hiring practices, but the jobs available to blacks (mostly in manufacturing) still paid more than the national hourly average. Blacks also utilized the armed forces to achieve social mobility, accounting for 20.6 percent of the men and women in the military by 1992. In addition to the decline in defense manufacturing, capital flight played a role in the predicament of black defense workers. When defense contractors sent manufacturing jobs to white suburbs in Mid-Atlantic states such as Pennsylvania or to the South to take advantage of cheaper labor and overhead costs, black communities saw more layoffs and greater segregation from white communities.[22]

As white Long Islanders decried the Berlin Wall's collapse and the diminution of the defense industry, black civil rights leaders responded with mixed results. Black businessman and entrepreneur Bruce Llewelyn ruffled feathers when he accused the Cold War economy of enfranchising whites over blacks. In criticizing America's inattention to "schools, health care and physical plants" to serve a larger defense budget, Llewellyn said, "Defense spending is the white people's welfare program." He observed, "It's nice to be able to say that instead of going to the welfare office to get my check, I go to Grumman to get my check."[23] Llewellyn had sufficient evidence to make his point. Again, although the defense industry offered blacks access to good-paying jobs, blacks made up only a fraction of the defense workforce. Since 1941 and for twenty-five years thereafter, the defense industry employed one out of every ten workers on Long Island, yet blacks made up less than 4 percent of the workforce for the first eighteen years. Out of 50,000 workers, black employees numbered only about 1,900 up until 1960. Of those blacks who found work in the defense industry, many had long commutes because they were unable to find housing, having been redlined for decades.[24] Housing segregation was rampant on Long Island, and blacks were barred from the suburbs, compounding the problem of finding employment at one of the defense contractors in the area.

Llewellyn implicitly invoked this history while questioning the international and strategic need for an apparatus that increased class and racial disparities. But white Grumman workers were having none of it. Llewellyn's comments provoked an angry response from Grumman employee A. Roger Yackel from Huntington, who claimed that "Grumman has a fully integrated work force." The diversity and democracy in the workforce ensured that "Grumman is nonunion," since its workers "are rated on a merit system, not on longevity." Yackel ended his comments by rhetorically asking whether Llewellyn "has seen a welfare program that produced a lunar module, a first line of defense aircraft or postal trucks." In Yackel's' view, Grumman sustained economic growth in Long Island and throughout the country—while preserving national security.

But while Grumman employees like Yackel were quick to defend the company—and, by default, the government that kept the company afloat—they were critical of government involvement in their lives. The lack of high-paying, stable jobs made tax rates, public school spending, and other aspects of local government a growing concern among residents of Long Island. The absence of "affordable housing" and the "cost of public education" were now high on the list of concerns among business leaders and residents.[25] Suburban Long Island's crippling reliance on the

Cold War economy led its residents to search for solutions to the downsizing of the defense industry, with few answers. Frustrated and angry, Long Islanders felt burdened by high taxes and an increased cost of living. Though dependent on the federal government for employment, they also felt abandoned by it.

The antigovernment discontent inspired a tax revolt by the late 1980s. The Long Island tax revolt manifested itself in a variety of curious ways. County politicians—both Democrats and Republicans—riffed on George H. W. Bush's pledge of "read my lips—no new taxes." Local primary elections grew heated as the fate of school budgets lay in the balance; bills were introduced to enact property tax caps. The tax revolt also spread antigovernment messages that belied the reality behind the rhetoric. James L. Larocca, president of the Long Island Association, argued that one out of every ten residents of Long Island worked for the government, making it "the biggest employer." According to Larocca, the time of Long Island governments "operating like big urban machines rather than as conservative suburban bodies" was over.[26]

Long Islanders' discontent was evident in Thomas Downey's narrow defeat in 1992 by Republican Rick Lazio. Only six percentage points separated the candidates. Unemployment in Suffolk County was one of the major campaign issues, as was Downey's liberalism. Lazio criticized Downey's "tax and spend" policies and his detachment from local issues. Downey defended his record of supporting Long Island's defense economy, which included obtaining federal funds for the F-14 fighter jet built by Grumman, but he had difficulty escaping blame for the region's downturn. He also had trouble convincing voters that his call for defense cuts did not include Long Island. Downey offered circuitous statements on the subject of defense spending, saying, "I think there should be less defense money spent, but what is spent should go to Long Island." Downey also touted his work to achieve defense conversion on Long Island, but voters saw his willingness to "spend money to diversify our defense industry" as more of a liability than a service.[27]

With Republicans like Lazio now in charge, the primary solution to the financial problems of former defense communities was to reduce their governmental burden. Poor economic conditions in (now former) Cold War communities like Nassau and Suffolk Counties made proposals to cut taxes and reduce the size of government attractive. Indeed, Nassau

County Executive Thomas Gulotta (a Republican) pleaded with state officials to alleviate the county's spending obligations; he asked Governor Mario Cuomo not to "shift more of the burden onto the shoulders of local government, our taxpayers, and our home owners." To Americans in defense communities, state and federal officials had seemingly abandoned them after the Cold War, leaving them at the mercy of the unemployment line and impersonal market forces. Long Island defense workers argued that the federal government should have intervened to keep their communities afloat.[28]

But dramatic cutbacks in military spending also turned defense workers and their political representatives into citizen-lobbyists for the Cold War. The new era of international relations after 1989 led to a crisis in the economic and political fortunes of many Americans, who then fought to maintain the structure of the national security state beyond the Cold War. The local constituents of the Cold War wanted to retain militarization as a distinct feature of American foreign policy, as they argued that the federal government had a commitment to their financial well-being. Having made them reliant on the military-industrial complex, the federal government could not discard them and their communities when the international environment did not align with the interests of Cold War workers.

Cold War communities in the areas hit hardest by the end of the East-West conflict called on the federal government to help "veterans of the cold war." Workers at United Nuclear Corporation Naval Products in Montville, Connecticut, formed the Save Our State (SOS) committee to lobby the federal government, asking "federal officials to help find Government contracts to replace the defense work at UNC and other Connecticut companies." Republican representative (and later governor) John G. Rowland worked with UNC employees to get them another contract after they lost one to build a navy reactor to Babcox & Wilcox, based in Lynchburg, Virginia. Rowland appeared to be weary of the impact of global peace on the workers in his state, noting that unemployment was "the other side of the peace dividend." Efforts by UNC workers to save their jobs were to no avail, as the plant closed in 1991.[29]

Grassroots activists based in Connecticut realized the potential problems of scaling back the defense economy. The end of the Cold War made the push for conversion to nondefense work a primary issue for the anti–

Cold War Left and nuclear freeze activists. After its initial defeat in Congress in 1983, the freeze campaign did not retreat; it regrouped to deal with the social effects of the Cold War in local areas. The fall of the eastern bloc of Soviet states provided momentum for antinuclear activists to challenge the need for a national security state. Instead of protesting in the streets of New York City, the nuclear freeze movement reformed to sever the cord between defense monies and Cold War communities. Conversion was the way to disarmament, and congressional representatives should not be "held hostage to continue the arms race as a condition of supplying jobs and money to their constituencies."[30] Nuclear freeze activists and antimilitarist liberals worked together to create conversion programs to reemploy workers in the name of peace, but they sought to do so by enfranchising the marketplace. Kevin Bean, chairman of the Economic Conversion Task Force of the Connecticut Campaign for a US-USSR Nuclear Arms Freeze, rightly stated that once highly skilled defense workers were laid off, they were often forced to take jobs in the low-wage service sector. "Low-paying service jobs are the only alternatives for many laid-off defense workers whose skills are mismatched with the limited number of civilian jobs that would pay comparable to their previous jobs in defense facilities." Jobs in defense were inherently unstable, Bean said, and companies needed to stop going from contract to contract to survive. The "permanent war economy," he said, hindered the nation's productivity, interfered in the market economy, and was inefficient in creating jobs compared with the private sector. Globalization and outsourcing contributed to the problem too, as defense dollars earmarked for Connecticut went "right back out to out-of-state subsidiaries, vendors in the Sun Belt or the third world and coproduction setups overseas in order to cash in on cheaper labor, tax breaks, and to widen Congressional influence."[31] Bean therefore grounded defense conversion in the rhetoric of economic efficiency and antistatism particular to the era of neoliberalism.[32] If the market did not have to compete with the federally subsidized defense sector, there would be more jobs available for Connecticut residents.

Joining the Connecticut Campaign for a US-USSR Nuclear Arms Freeze in fighting for defense conversion was the Coalition to Stop the Trident. Formed in 1977 to prevent construction of the Trident missile submarine by the Electric Boat Company, based in Groton, Connecticut, the Coalition to Stop the Trident started out with good intentions. The group isolated general issues of concern to workers and activists, such as "health hazards, child care, workers control, [and] full employment," and it encouraged collaborative meetings with workers outside of a political context, including "picnics, parties and house meetings." In addition to these outreach efforts, the coalition spoke to workers directly, telling them it should not be "working people who pay for militarism, especially in the form of inflation," and assuring them that the coalition wanted to see their wages go further "at the grocery check out." The group emphasized that although it did not want workers to lose their jobs, the "men and women now working on the Trident and other weapons have skills which can be used in a peace economy." The coalition also noted that blue-collar workers lose the most in a defense economy, since "compared with other products, the manufacture of complex weapons systems requires small numbers of highly trained technicians; all the money goes for raw materials and sophisticated equipment, *not* large numbers of jobs."[33]

The Coalition to Stop the Trident was marred by debates over purpose, strategy, and leadership, and it ultimately folded in 1989. But as its life extended into the 1980s, it decided to tackle a hodgepodge of issues, some unrelated to the Trident. Tactics included advocating for protesters who shut down the stock exchange, showing antinuclear documentary films, and supporting general antinuclear protests. The group's focus was on civil disobedience and demonstrations, a worthy and necessary activity, but one carried out without consideration for defense workers' everyday lives in Connecticut. Holding a "die-in" did not resonate with workers concerned about their paychecks and the cost of living. Most importantly, the group had no coherent, concrete proposal for defense conversion. When layoffs inevitably came to Electric Boat employees, the coalition was unprepared to offer any policies to lessen the effects of those job losses. Three thousand white-collar workers, predominantly "designers, draftsmen, and clerical personnel," were laid off at Electric Boat, and the Pentagon found that most of them managed to find employment, albeit in other industries and other parts of the country. The white-collar drain from Electric Boat concerned the coalition and members of the Democratic Party, including Connecticut representative Christopher Dodd, who advocated for diversification of the defense industry. But like the Coalition to Stop the Trident, he had no defense conversion plan to sell to Connecticut voters.[34]

The Left therefore had no satisfactory answer for workers concerned about the decline in defense jobs in the Gun Belt. Without an adequate response from the Left, voters turned to the Right. As was the case in Colorado, when the Cold War enriched defense communities that already leaned Republican, it made voters there more dependent on the national security structure. Despite their antigovernment posture, the government had been good to them. Defense contracts had increased their income and wealth. Yet they were suspicious of the government in other areas—namely, tax policies (and social policies) that infringed on the health of their financial portfolios. Government was an unwelcome presence in all nondefense matters. But in traditionally Democratic states like New York and Connecticut, defense communities had a similar perception of government. These Democratic-leaning states therefore felt betrayed by the government, but at the same time they looked for help in the form of more defense contracts, tax cuts, and government subsidies.

With the demise of defense manufacturing in Long Island and southeastern Connecticut, job prospects (and good wages) for working-class Americans decreased. The end of the Cold War essentially eliminated high-paying defense jobs and replaced them with low-wage service jobs. And Long Island never fully recovered from the peace dividend. The area became a haven for wealthy vacationers and commuters to Manhattan, but the local economy was typical of that of many postindustrial towns. Long Island was touted by the *Wall Street Journal* as an "unlikely jobs engine," and after the Great Recession of 2008, the paper acknowledged that half of the 30,000 jobs created there "were in low-wage industries like retail and restaurants" that catered to tourists. The high-paying "manufacturing and defense industry jobs that once defined the island aren't likely to return after being trimmed during the most recent recession." Indeed, Northrop Grumman's Long Island workforce was only 550 in 2013, down from 13,000 in 1991.[35]

The remilitarization of the Cold War during the 1980s widened economic inequality in defense communities to the benefit of educated, skilled, upper-class Americans. In the suburban enclaves of Denver and Washington, DC, defense spending enriched already wealthy areas. To these Americans, defense projects such as SDI were like expansive jobs programs; they functioned more as public works agencies than a deterrent to nuclear war. In retrospect, SDI employed the educated and affluent to build an overwrought missile defense system, even though such programs had no feasible application in the current foreign policy environment. But in the Northeast and Midwest, regions heavily invested in aircraft production, the Cold War put many Americans out of work by the 1980s. With nothing to produce, defense factories shut their doors, and workers were sent to the unemployment line. In the final analysis, Reagan's Cold War reinforced class and regional tensions, steering federal benefits to an overwhelmingly white and upper-class set of elites, to the detriment of the blue-collar defense workforce—a process that was fateful in remaking American political culture on a local and national scale.

Notes

1. On the Reagan defense buildup, see Frances Fitzgerald, *Way out There in the Blue: Reagan, Star Wars, and the End of the Cold War* (New York: Simon and Schuster, 2000); Daniel Wirls, *Buildup: The Politics of Defense in the Reagan Era* (Ithaca, NY: Cornell University Press, 1992).

2. Judith Stein, *Pivotal Decade: How the United States Traded Factories for Finance in the Seventies* (New Haven, CT: Yale University Press, 2010), 268. See also Thomas Piketty, *Capital in the Twenty-First Century*, trans. Arthur Goldhammer (Cambridge, MA: Belknap Press of Harvard University Press, 2014). Diplomatic historians have just begun to incorporate the new history of capitalism into studies of US foreign relations. See Daniel J. Sargent, *A Superpower Transformed: The Remaking of American Foreign Relations in the 1970s* (New York: Oxford University Press, 2015).

3. On uneven capital development, see David Harvey, *Spaces of Global Capitalism: A Theory of Uneven Geographic Development* (New York: Verso Books, 2006).

4. Ann Markusen calls these areas "Cold War communities" due to their reliance and, indeed, dependence on Cold War military spending for economic growth and local employment. Ann Markusen, "Cold War Workers, Cold War Communities," in *Rethinking Cold War Culture*, ed. Peter J. Kuznick and James Gilbert (Washington, DC: Smithsonian Institution Press, 2001), 35–60.

5. Ann Markusen, Peter Hall, Scott Campbell, and Sabina Deitrick, *The Rise of the Gunbelt: The Military Remapping of Industrial Politics* (New York: Oxford University Press, 1991). The "Gun Belt" is defined in geographic terms as the region that stretches from New England through the Sun Belt and up to the Northwest; it is the premier site of defense production in the United States. Areas in the Gun Belt have disproportionately benefited from defense spending, which in turn has shaped and distinguished the political, cultural, and economic makeup of local communities.

6. See Peter Trubowitz, *Defining the National Interest: Conflict and Change in American Foreign Policy* (Chicago: University of Chicago Press, 1998), chap. 4.

7. Gary Gerstle, *Liberty and Coercion: The Paradox of American Government from the Founding to the Present* (Princeton, NJ: Princeton University Press, 2015). For more on the relationship between the national security state and public attitudes toward government, see James Sparrow, *Warfare State: World War II Americans and the Age of Big-Government* (New York: Oxford University Press, 2011); Gretchen Heefner, *The Missile Next Door: The Minuteman in the American Heartland* (Cambridge, MA: Harvard University Press, 2012).

8. Ronald Reagan, "Remarks at the Annual Convention of the National Association of Evangelicals, in Orlando, Florida, March 8, 1983," in *Public Papers of the Presidents, Ronald Reagan, 1981–1989,* http://www.presidency.ucsb.edu/ws/index.php?pid=41023&st=evil+empire&st1=.

9. Presidential Remarks: Budget Event Monday November 30, 1987, box 30, Presidential Handwriting File Series III: Presidential Speeches 11/24/87–2/1/88, Ronald Reagan Presidential Library (hereafter RRPL); James Mann, *The Rebellion of Ronald Reagan: A History of the End of the Cold War* (New York: Penguin, 2009), 45–46. For Soviet attitudes toward SDI, see Peter J. Westwick, "Space Strike Weapons and the Soviet Response to SDI," *Diplomatic History* 32, no. 5 (November 2008): 955–79.

10. Due to the Reagan defense buildup, by the end of the third quarter of 1987, Martin Marietta had net sales of $4.75 billion, net earnings of $202 million, and capital assets of $535 million; it employed 11,397 people in its Astronautics Group, 1,638 in its Information and Communications Systems, and 1,700 in Data Systems—a total of 14,735 employees. Other components of the corporation included its Astronautics Group in Colorado; Electronics and Missiles Group in Orlando, Florida; Information Systems Group based in Bethesda; Manned Space Systems in New Orleans; and operations located at Vandenberg Air Force Base in California and Cape Canaveral. The figures on Martin Marietta are from "General Information," Denver SDI 11/24/1987 (5) folder, box 355, White House Office of Speechwriting: Research Office, 1981–1989, RRPL. Total property taxes collected in Colorado in 1987 amounted to approximately $2.1 billion; Martin Marietta's share came to 0.0361 percent—a significant amount from one employer. See "Colorado Property Values and Tax Trends, 1987–2006," http://www.centerfortaxpolicy.org/reports/Colorado_Property_Values_and_Tax%20_Trends.pdf.

11. Joshua B. Freeman, *American Empire: The Rise of a Global Power, the Democratic Revolution at Home, 1945–2000* (New York: Viking, 2012), 127.

12. Markusen et al., *Rise of the Gunbelt,* 176.

13. On the relationship between the Cold War military-industrial complex and the expansion of the educated, white middle class, see Lisa McGirr, *Suburban Warriors: The Origins of the New American Right* (Princeton, NJ: Princeton University Press, 2000); Darren Dochuk, *From Bible Belt to Sunbelt: Plain Folk Religion, Grassroots Politics, and the Rise of Evangelical Conservatism* (New York: W. W. Norton, 2010).

14. On the role of Cold War defense spending in the political economy of Wash-

ington, DC, suburbs, see Markusen et al., *Rise of the Gunbelt;* Andrew Friedman, *Covert Capital: Landscapes of Denial and the Making of U.S. Empire in the Suburbs of Northern Virginia* (Berkeley: University of California Press, 2013).

15. "Senate Nominee Pushes 'Star Wars' in Colorado," *New York Times,* October 15, 1986.

16. "Reagan Asserts 'Star Wars' Plan Will Create Jobs and Better Life," *New York Times,* October 31, 1986.

17. Ronald Reagan, "Remarks at a Senate Campaign Rally for Representative Ken Kramer in Colorado Springs, Colorado, October 3, 1986," in *Public Papers of the Presidents of the United States: Ronald Reagan, 1981–1989,* http://www.presidency.ucsb.edu/ws/?pid=36370.

18. Memorandum from James Hooley to Howard H. Baker Jr., November 19, 1987, folder Denver SDI 11/24/1987 (3), box 355, White House Office of Speechwriting, RRPL; address on SDI/INF Martin Marietta Plant, Denver, Colorado, November 24, 1986, folder 603, box 30, Series III Presidential Speeches, Presidential Handwriting file, RRPL; drafts of speech to Martin Marietta employees for November 24, 1987, folder Denver SDI 11/24/1987 (2), box 355, White House Office of Speechwriting, RRPL.

19. Barber B. Conable Jr. and Jack Kemp to Ronald Reagan, October 5, 1981, folder 5, box 122, Jack Kemp Papers, Library of Congress, Washington, DC; "LTV Ends Its Bid for Grumman," *New York Times,* November 17, 1981; "Military Issues: 'Fallen Angels,'" *New York Times,* September 15, 1987.

20. "2,500 to Lose Jobs in L.I. Plant as U.S. Ends Jet Contract," *New York Times,* March 14, 1987.

21. On Downey and defense spending, see Robert David Johnson, *Congress and the Cold War* (New York: Cambridge University Press, 2005), chap. 7. On Downey's "hypocrisy," see Johnson, *Congress and the Cold War,* 233; "2,500 to Lose Jobs in L.I. Plant."

22. "Cuts in Arms Spending: No Help for the Economy," *New York Times,* August 12, 1992.

23. "Defense Spending: Whose Welfare?" *New York Times,* July 17, 1988; "Helping Blacks Get Ahead," *New York Times,* June 26, 1988.

24. Timothy G. Keogh, "Suburbs in Black and White: Race, the Decline of Industry, and Suburban Social Policy in Long Island, New York" (PhD diss., City University of New York, 2016), chap. 3, pp. 9–10 (copy in author's possession).

25. "Learning to Adapt without Defense," *New York Times,* December 21, 1991; "L.I. Growth Years over, Looking beyond Defense," *New York Times,* August 13, 1989.

26. "Tax Revolt Builds on L.I.," *New York Times,* April 16, 1989; "To Quell Revolt, Halpin Pledges No Tax Increase," *New York Times,* July 2, 1989.

27. *Statistics of the Presidential and Congressional Election of November 3, 1992* (Washington, DC: US Government Printing Office, 1993), 51, 55, http://clerk.house.gov/member_info/electionInfo/1992election.pdf; "Lazio Ends Downey's

Tenure," *New York Times,* November 4, 1992; "Green and Downey Lose as New York State Delegation Changes Dramatically," *New York Times,* November 4, 1992; "Long Island Needs Military Spending," *New York Times,* May 21, 1989; "Downey Is Facing His Toughest Challenge," *New York Times*, October 11, 1992.

28. "Higher Taxes, Dire Prospects," *New York Times,* February 5, 1989.

29. "As Layoffs Loom, Defense Workers Mount a Battle for Jobs," *New York Times,* June 3, 1990.

30. "Arms Makers Get Aid on Diversifying," *New York Times,* March 6, 1988.

31. "State's Defense Jobs Are Not that Secure," *New York Times,* June 23, 1985.

32. On neoliberalism, see David Harvey, *A Brief History of Neoliberalism* (New York: Oxford University Press, 2005).

33. "Trident/Conversion Campaign Goals and Strategies, 6/79," Coalition to Stop the Trident Records, series I, box 2, folder 29, Manuscripts and Archives, Yale University Library, New Haven, CT; coalition leaflet, "Peace Conversion and the Trident Conversion Campaign," ibid., folder 24.

34. The Coalition to Stop the Trident vigorously debated defense conversion, wrote proposals for defense conversion, and collaborated with other organizations on the issue, but it never put defense conversion at the top of its agenda. See "Minutes of the Trident Conversion Campaign Meeting, 9/10/79," Coalition to Stop the Trident Records, series I, box 2, folder 32; "Study Shows Many Laid off at EB Found New Jobs," ibid., box 5, folder 102.

35. "Long Island Is an Unlikely Jobs Engine," *Wall Street Journal,* May 16, 2013, http://online.wsj.com/article/SB10001424127887324082604578487262418389512.html.

11

The Domestic Politics of Superpower Rapprochement

Foreign Policy and the 1984 Presidential Election

Simon Miles

Looking back on 1984, the reelection of Ronald Reagan and George H. W. Bush appears to have been all but certain. But in fact, the Republican victory over the Democratic ticket of Walter Mondale and Geraldine Ferraro—winning 58.8 percent of the popular vote as well as 525 electoral votes to Mondale's 13—put paid to considerable political uncertainty leading up to the election. Domestic economic woes continued to plague the Reagan administration, earning excoriations from the *New York Times* and the *Wall Street Journal*.[1] On foreign policy matters, negative public opinion of Reagan's conduct of the Cold War, especially in Latin America, also imperiled his bid for reelection.[2] But when voters went to the polls on November 6, 1984, these concerns amounted to naught.

Today, Reagan's public image is dominated by the triumphalist narrative of US victory in the Cold War. While many historians have debunked this assertion, the end of the Cold War continues to loom large in assessments of Reagan's presidency—and above all his foreign policy.[3] In 1984, however, the Cold War seemed far from won, and Mondale's bid for the White House gave voice to the concerns of many regarding the role of the United States in the world. This essay examines how the Mondale campaign used foreign policy to attack the Reagan administration. It focuses on four areas of contention: high military expenditures, failure to make progress on arms control, poor relations with the Soviet Union, and the abandonment of core principles in US foreign policy, including alliances and human rights. It then examines Reagan's policy shift toward the Soviet Union, announced on January 16, 1984, in a speech to US and European audiences in which Reagan publicly affirmed his intention to improve US-Soviet relations. Finally, it analyzes Mondale's attempts to turn Reagan's new willingness to engage in dialogue with the Kremlin against the president.

Reagan's apparent change of course has spawned a variety of explanations. In her pathbreaking book on the subject, Beth Fischer argues that the crises of 1983—particularly the Soviet downing of Korean Airlines flight 007 and the deployment of US intermediate-range nuclear forces to Europe—led Reagan to reevaluate how his administration prosecuted the Cold War. Reagan's fear of the catastrophic consequences of a misstep, Fischer concludes, led him to soften his tone and make overtures toward the Kremlin—what she terms the "Reagan reversal."[4] James Mann does not dispute the importance of these crises but highlights the role of electoral politics, suggesting that Reagan's concerns about his reelection prospects led to this change of course.[5] James Graham Wilson stresses the importance of Reagan's own understanding of the Soviet Union, particularly his coming to terms with Soviet leaders' perception of a US threat. Reagan hoped that through direct, personal diplomacy he could allay these fears and persuade the Soviet Union to moderate its policies while also moderating his own.[6] All three of these prominent interpretations (and many others) focus on the role of the individual—Reagan—which cannot be discounted, but less so on the structural constraints and changing nature of the world in which he operated.

This essay identifies Reagan's change in tone as being squarely rooted in the balance of power between the United States and the Soviet Union. As early as the 1980 election campaign, Reagan made his desire for greater dialogue with the Soviet Union clear, but perceived US weakness when he entered the White House on January 20, 1981, retarded these efforts. By 1984, however, the United States enjoyed a position of strategic superiority to the Soviet Union, and Reagan and his national security team knew it.[7] This emboldened the president to expand contacts with the Soviet Union, the very thing Mondale had attacked him for failing to do.

Mondale's Case against Reagan

Mondale's 1984 campaign may have been unsuccessful, but it was far from unserious. Planning began almost immediately after he and Carter lost in 1980. In fact, Mondale and his aides began crafting a stump speech at the time of Reagan's inauguration. From the outset, the Mondale campaign worked to separate the candidate from his political past: "Carter, inflation, Iran, . . . 'Big Spender' [at home], Mr. Busing, opponent of military spending, [and] leader of the opposition to the space shuttle." Casting Mondale as a viable commander in chief posed a "special problem," given the sense of weakness associated with Carter. Public sentiment favored arms control and rapprochement with the Soviet Union, and people associated Mondale with these issues, but he still needed to establish his national security bona fides.[8]

"The solution," Mondale's aides concluded, "is neither to abandon your vigorous commitment to arms control and peace nor to try to sound like a hawk, which you are not."[9] Mondale would govern with a steady hand, unlike Reagan and his "radical economic policy" of skyrocketing interest rates, "radical social policy" leading to widening income inequality and cuts to social services, and "foreign policy which radically departs from the bipartisan policies of the past."[10] In short, Mondale sought to paint Reagan as a dangerous choice to lead the United States—a choice that threatened the nation's security and future—just as Carter had, also unsuccessfully, in 1980.

Mondale and his team also set about developing a visibility strategy for the former vice president intended to overcome his association with Carter and the far left of the political spectrum. Mondale planned to defend the Carter administration's policies only when explicitly called upon to do so, for example. He would avoid references to his vice presidential record, making nebulous assertions regarding his experience rather than underscoring his association with Carter's White House. Mondale planned to sell himself as the smarter, surer option for the White House. As one of his aides put it, Mondale was "the only living former president or vice president who's neither a criminal nor a nincompoop."[11]

Throughout Reagan's first term, Mondale critiqued the administration's high military spending. In a time of growing income inequality, Reagan had "bought every big ticket weapon in the candy store."[12] But Mondale undercut his own line of attack in the hopes of bolstering his national security credentials, pledging to increase US defense spending to a level higher than in any earlier peacetime budget—and higher than at the Vietnam War's peak.[13] Mondale criticized Reagan's own defense buildup as both wasteful and ill-considered. "Reagan's near-trillion dollar defense expenditure," the campaign asserted, "is not producing near a trillion dollars' worth of defense. . . . This is not security, it's [a] house of cards that will tumble down on our children, leaving them with neither military nor economic security." The Democrats found considerable evidence to support this line of attack. Both administration officials and military leaders publicly conceded the decline in US readiness, despite the buildup.[14] Many of these expenditures seemed wasteful. The MX missile, for example, cost a great deal, but the silos across the Midwest where it would be based could not be sufficiently hardened to survive a Soviet first strike.[15] Mismanagement in the procurement process led to the purchase of working aircraft to be cannibalized for spare parts (so-called hangar queens), instead of buying those parts individually.[16] Mondale therefore pledged to increase the defense budget, but also to make smarter choices.[17] He proposed the smaller, more survivable Midgetman missile over the MX, the nascent stealth bomber over the B-1, and realistic strategic defenses coupled with successful arms control negotiations instead of Reagan's fanciful Strategic Defense Initiative (SDI).[18]

Arms control figured prominently in Mondale's attacks. He charged that Reagan, by failing to make progress with the Soviets, had made the world a more dangerous place. "The highest responsibility of a president," Mondale told a Chicago audience, "is to get those godawful weapons under control."[19] He cast himself as the first presidential candidate to be outspoken in favor of the nuclear freeze movement, seeing clear public support for new, intensified arms control negotiations. He went on to condemn Reagan's characterization of the freeze movement as "the dupes of Moscow."[20] It only made sense to put limitations on a contest that neither side could win, Mondale insisted.[21] "Arms control [was] not a gift to the Soviets."[22]

Mondale argued that his twenty years of experience with the arms control portfolio (both in the Senate and as vice president) made him uniquely capable of bringing such agreements to fruition.[23] He hoped to "point towards sanity" in the conduct of US foreign relations, committing his prospective administration to curbing the nuclear arms race.[24] Reagan, by contrast, espoused "the fallacy of American weakness, . . . the fallacy that arms control is weakness, . . . [and] the fallacy that we can win an arms race, and that we should try to."[25] Mondale's campaign went even further: the foreign policy of the first Reagan administration betrayed the US foreign policy tradition of (allegedly) always seeking peace.[26] All six of Reagan's predecessors, regardless of party, had concluded agreements with their counterparts in the Kremlin. Reagan's policies, in comparison, had destabilized the situation.[27] "Nuclear arms control is not a partisan issue," Mondale insisted. "Whatever divides us, survival is not on that list."[28]

Instead of investing in costly and allegedly destabilizing nuclear weapons, Mondale promised to shift the focus of US defense policy to conventional capabilities.[29] Doing so, the Mondale campaign argued, would be an important step in and of itself toward decelerating the arms race.[30] Mondale also pledged to end the inchoate arms race in outer space, allegedly triggered by SDI. As president, Mondale promised to focus on ending the arms race on earth rather than starting a second one in the heavens. He decried "Reagan's fantasy that space weapons can protect Americans . . . [as] a cruel hoax."[31] He stressed that SDI would destabilize the Cold War and undermine the existing Anti-Ballistic Missile Treaty. At a time when Washington's objective should be to conclude more arms control agreements with the Soviet Union, the United States "should be purer than Caesar's wife."[32]

Mondale made his full case against SDI in Cleveland on April 24, 1984. He outlined the reasons why he opposed (and the general public should oppose) Reagan's "Star Wars fantasy." SDI opened a new, dangerous front of superpower competition, adding a defensive arms race to the ongoing offensive one, and an extraterrestrial arms race to the terrestrial one. Building such a program would cost hundreds of billions of dollars at a time when Washington should be devoting its resources to reducing income inequality at home. And SDI would not necessarily guarantee protection for the United States: Mondale insisted that sophisticated Soviet antisatellite weapons could disable it. To little end, therefore, Reagan's plan would upend mutually assured destruction, on which Cold War stability rested. SDI would also create a rift with US allies. Washington's NATO partners opposed the program, believing it would undermine the US nuclear security guarantee to Europe. Overall, Mondale argued, the United States should focus on reducing, not increasing, the number of weapons in the world. All this assumed, however, that SDI would come to fruition, and Mondale claimed it rested on outlandish, flawed scientific premises.[33] It would "put a hair trigger on the nuclear balance and a premium on striking first in a crisis . . . [and] hand over to a computer the decision to make the first hostile act of nuclear war."[34] He presented an alternative: a plan "to stop the heavens from being militarized," beginning with a unilateral, temporary moratorium on the testing of antisatellite weapons, which Mondale anticipated would lead to a verifiable ban. His plan also included a temporary moratorium on the development and deployment of all weapons in space, which he similarly hoped would lead to a treaty with the Soviet Union.[35]

Relations with the Soviet Union lay at the heart of Mondale's campaign, foreign policy–wise: "we have opposing interests, and we have the power to destroy each other."[36] "On the day I am inaugurated," Mondale pledged, "I will tell the Soviet leader, meet me in Geneva within six months to negotiate a mutual, verifiable nuclear freeze."[37] Mondale also proposed annual summits between the superpowers going forward.[38] After all, he argued, the United States met with the G-7 countries on an annual basis, why not do the same with the Soviet Union?[39] (Not until ten months after his second inauguration did Reagan start meeting with his Soviet counterpart on an annual basis.) Negotiations between Washington and Moscow, Mondale charged, had achieved nothing because Reagan viewed negotiations—and foreign policy in general—as a public relations exercise rather than a means of finding common ground.[40]

Mondale rejected the idea of putting blind faith in the Kremlin, but he insisted that Reagan's failure to meet with his Soviet counterparts constituted a crucial failure to ensure US security.[41] As he told a New York audience, "we do not believe that Andropov is the chairman of the Moscow branch of the United Way."[42] But John F. Kennedy, the campaign argued, had been able to move forward from the Cuban Missile Crisis to the Limited Test Ban Treaty by unilaterally declaring a halt to US atmospheric testing and challenging the Soviets to respond in kind, which they did.[43] Meanwhile, "Reagan has wasted three and one half precious years in the illusion that an arms race leads to arms control. He's dead wrong. He's proved that an arms race leads to an arms race."[44] Whereas his predecessors had relied on a two-track approach of deterrence and negotiation, Reagan's seemingly singular focus on deterrence only made the world a more dangerous place.[45] Moscow noted this position with approval, echoing Mondale's criticism that Reagan had failed to meet with his Soviet counterparts and applauding its centrality in the Democratic platform.[46]

As part of his effort to be perceived as the presidential candidate who could improve US-Soviet relations, Mondale met with Soviet foreign minister Andrei Gromyko when the latter visited the United States in September 1984. The Mondale campaign hoped to demonstrate that its candidate would be a tough negotiator if elected, but also that "serious, businesslike" negotiations between the superpowers were necessary.[47] To Gromyko, Mondale conveyed his belief that US-Soviet relations had reached a "fateful moment." He explained that the superpower relationship must be the top priority of both nations and referenced his public commitment to annual summits in that context. He underscored his commitment to arms control negotiations, particularly with respect to space-based weapons.[48] After the meeting, the Soviet media broadcast Mondale's views and expressed the hope that they would be realized (i.e., that Mondale would be elected).[49]

Mondale saw improving superpower relations as the key to achieving a host of other US foreign policy goals. In eastern Europe, the campaign argued, increased tensions stemming from Reagan's foreign policy hampered the full implementation of the Helsinki Accords and thereby improvements in the quality of life of those living in the region. A general climate of global tension led Moscow to increase the pressure on eastern European states and demand strict ideological conformity, ending the process of a gradual drifting away from Moscow, which so many had hoped for (and seen evidence of).[50] Mondale believed that decreasing tensions would create a "window of opportunity" to capitalize on these governments' desire for freedom and stronger ties to the West through trade and contacts.[51] Elsewhere, Mondale pledged to shift the focus of US policy in Latin America from military engagement to negotiation, reducing the military forces in the region on both sides, while continuing to give US allies "legitimate security assistance."[52] Reagan, by comparison, saw Latin American conflicts only through the lens of the Cold War.[53] The

Mondale campaign also alleged that the United States had abandoned its leadership role in pushing for peace in the Middle East, an effort in which Mondale himself had played a crucial role as vice president.[54]

Reagan's worldview, according to Mondale, lacked any subtlety and cast the world in the black-and-white terms of East-West competition. "When the globe is a tinderbox," Mondale argued, "we need a president who knows what he's doing."[55] But Reagan failed to understand the core problem of US foreign policy, Mondale charged: the world did not doubt US power; the world recognized the enormity of that power but doubted the Reagan administration's responsible stewardship of it. For instance, the presence of US nuclear missiles in Europe caused more widespread discontent and fear among European youth than did the Soviet missiles pointed at their own homes.[56]

Mondale accused Reagan of abandoning two fundamental aspects of US foreign policy: working with Washington's allies and championing human rights. In the first case, Reagan embraced a "go-it-alone policy" that weakened the Western alliance and undermined US interests. The Mondale campaign pledged to work more closely with US allies and to convince them to shoulder more of the burden in NATO and similar organizations.[57] In that regard, Mondale charged that Reagan and his foreign policy advisers "have allowed our Alliance to grow flabby." US allies consistently failed to increase their defense expenditures, leading to a dangerous overreliance on US nuclear weapons to deter Soviet aggression in Europe.[58] Mondale laid the blame squarely on Reagan and his leadership. The allies were not the problem; the administration's failure to consult them was. Regarding the 1983 invasion of Grenada, for example, the United States' failure to consult with its NATO allies—particularly the United Kingdom and Canada, both members of the Commonwealth to which Grenada also belonged, and ostensibly key US partners—put considerable strain on Washington's relationships.[59]

In short, Mondale charged that Reagan caused US allies to "doubt the wisdom of [US] leadership." Mondale touted his own experience as an internationalist in foreign policy terms, pledging to strengthen US relationships around the world, as the challenges of the 1980s demanded a multilateral approach.[60] According to his advisers, as a new generation of voters and policymakers matured, the global memory of World War II faded. Washington could no longer assume that ties of sentiment would survive into the future, especially as transatlantic economic competition intensified. Leaders and voters would have to be persuaded anew that US power would be used responsibly.[61] Adopting a more cooperative posture toward the Soviet Union would, Mondale argued, strengthen NATO by building support for US leadership, as would a serious and successful effort at arms control.[62] Instead, the Reagan administration had intensified the arms race and appeared to entertain the notion of fighting and winning a limited nuclear war. This eroded allies' confidence and scared Europeans into believing that the United States, like the Soviet Union, posed a significant threat to world peace.[63]

Mondale also argued that the United States had forfeited its global leadership role regarding human rights. The Reagan administration had downplayed or ignored human rights abuses in right-wing dictatorships while simultaneously using human rights as a propaganda tool against left-wing regimes. Clearly, Mondale had not broken with Carter's policies entirely.[64] "Promoting American values has been a tactic and not a principle," Mondale charged, which discredited the US cause in the world.[65] The campaign publicized the candidate's letter to Chernenko condemning the Soviet Union for its treatment of dissident Andrei Sakharov and his wife Elena Bonner. In it, Mondale urged the Politburo to free the couple and allow them to travel abroad to obtain medical care and reunite with their family—a one-way trip, to be sure. "Such action is a simple matter of justice and human decency," Mondale wrote. "And it is important to all of us who hope for improved relations between our two countries."[66]

Understanding Reagan's New Tack

The Mondale campaign's four-pronged criticism began to coalesce shortly after Reagan took office, as Mondale started planning for the next election four years away. A great deal, however, changed over the course of those years. Aggressive rhetoric toward the Soviet Union characterized the Reagan administration's first-term foreign policy. Two speeches exemplify this aggressively anti-Soviet rhetoric, both of which were given chiefly at the behest of Reagan's subordinates, not on the president's own initiative.[67] On June 8, 1982, Reagan gave a speech before the British Parliament was intended to highlight the dangers of "appeasement in the face of coercion" and "the decay of the Soviet experiment." The president exhorted the West to launch "a crusade for freedom" to roll back Soviet influence across the globe and "leave Marxism and Leninism on the ash heap of history."[68] Reagan's address to the National Association of Evangelicals on March 8, 1983, was similarly anti-Soviet in tenor, climaxing with his now famous (or infamous) reference to the Soviet Union as an "evil empire."[69]

On January 16, 1984, however, Reagan gave a speech pledging to build a "constructive and realistic working relationship with the Soviet Union." Reagan attributed this change in tone, which occurred on the eve of the Stockholm disarmament talks, to the United States' increased defense spending since the 1970s—"years when the United States seemed filled with self-doubt and neglected its defenses." This recovery made both the United States and the world safer, and US credibility was now beyond question. However, Reagan went on, the United States' "working relationship with the Soviet Union [was] not what it must be." He proposed that the two superpowers come together to discuss areas of concern and examine concrete actions to reduce the chances of conflict. Reagan also pledged to work with the Kremlin on reducing global levels of nuclear weapons. Although Reagan and his administration objected to the Soviet system and did not shy away from saying so, he insisted that their "commitment to dialogue [was] firm and unshakeable. . . . We seek genuine cooperation. We seek progress for peace. Cooperation begins with communication."[70] The White House timed the speech to take place in the late morning to maximize news coverage across Europe and in the Soviet Union, its target audience, and the administration tellingly titled the speech "Address to the Nation and Other Countries on United States–Soviet Relations."[71]

The importance of improving relations with the Soviet Union had long figured in Reagan's approach to foreign policy, even if bellicose rhetoric and the military buildup overshadowed it during his first term. Since the 1980 campaign, Reagan had sought to highlight his "strategy for peace" and recognized the danger of being seen as a "saber rattler" or a "button pusher" by the public.[72] Reagan's main foreign policy address in 1980, after all, had been titled "A Strategy of Peace for the '80s." In it, he bemoaned Carter's mischaracterization of his foreign policy as overly bellicose and attempted to reassure voters, "not as a candidate for the presidency, but as a citizen, a parent, [and] a grandparent . . . who shares with you the deep and abiding hope for peace," of his suitability to lead the United States.[73] Personally, Reagan advocated for US overtures to the

Soviet Union guided by "a sober, cautious approach to international reality," structured on the principle of reciprocity. His advisers even recommended that Reagan pledge to visit Moscow early in his first term.[74]

Reagan held strong views on the dangers of nuclear weapons and wanted to eliminate them.[75] In the aftermath of World War II—when he was a registered Democrat—he endorsed the Baruch plan for the internationalization of atomic weapons and planned a rally in Hollywood to support it.[76] Reagan believed that the path to peace with the Soviet Union lay in verifiable agreements to reduce nuclear arsenals.[77] Even as he changed parties, Reagan continued to worry that the unchecked spread of nuclear weapons could lead to Armageddon. Cinematographic depictions of nuclear disasters in *War Games, The Day the Earth Stood Still,* and especially *The Day After* "left [Reagan] greatly depressed."[78] After the turbulence of 1983—including the downing of Korean Airlines flight 007 and the invasion of Grenada—superpower rapprochement seemed all the more imperative.[79]

Reagan's assertions regarding the upturn in US power were genuine, and they best explain his administration's newfound emphasis on negotiating with the Kremlin. At the beginning of Reagan's tenure, the available intelligence painted a grim picture of US power vis-à-vis the Soviet Union. Economically, the United States faced a troubling situation that had brought down Carter, and it became the main preoccupation during Reagan's first term.[80] Looking back at Soviet behavior since Brezhnev had come to power in 1964, the CIA characterized the era as one of steady military buildup and the Kremlin's "increased use of military instruments for political ends." Under Brezhnev, the Soviet military had increased its strategic nuclear arsenal sixfold, giving Moscow quantitative (if not qualitative) superiority and an assured retaliatory capability. The Warsaw Pact's battlefield nuclear capabilities had also increased by a factor of three, reducing the credibility of NATO nuclear forces as a counterweight to the numerically superior Warsaw Pact conventional forces. Soviet defense spending had nearly doubled in real terms, and military manpower had increased by one-third; furthermore, the military research and development establishment had doubled in size, promising to perpetuate the Soviet challenge to the United States.[81]

A 1981 national intelligence estimate concluded that in Europe, "the Soviet goal is clear-cut force superiority—conventional, nuclear, and chemical—with which to fight and win a short war." Going forward, the

Soviet military would likely emphasize qualitative improvements to their already superior quantitative strength.[82] US observers identified a new Soviet willingness since the mid-1970s to challenge the West in the Third World, such as in Angola, Ethiopia, and Afghanistan. This more assertive Soviet behavior, they predicted, would continue as long as the Kremlin perceived Western strength to be in decline. Soviet leaders would be more prepared and more willing to confront the United States directly.[83]

By 1984, the United States' position relative to the Soviet Union had, in the view of Reagan and his national security team, improved. Reagan's national security adviser William Clark made the case for a renewed US engagement with the world, particularly with the Soviet Union:

> It was your view . . . of the state of our relations at the end of the [1970s] that the Soviets may well have considered us a nation in decline and that before we could have any realistic hope of getting them to bargain seriously with us toward the resolution of the many problems between us, we had to make clear that we reversed that trend. . . . Toward that end you set out to restore our defenses, to reassure our allies, to solve our economic problems back home and in sum, to show by action that we were coming back and had to be taken seriously. At the end of two years it seems to me that you have succeeded and that there is a very solid basis for concluding that the Soviets may be reconciled to the fact that by the end of the decade we will have passed them again.[84]

US intelligence echoed Clark's conclusions. The Soviet military found itself bogged down in Afghanistan, failing to win hearts and minds there while losing the support of its own troops.[85] In general, "Soviet forces deployed abroad are thinly spread, . . . vulnerable, and lack offensive punch."[86] Meanwhile, Soviet economic problems, which had been clear to US policymakers from the beginning of Reagan's first term, only worsened. The Eleventh Five-Year Plan for 1981–1985 demonstrated to US analysts that the Soviet leadership lacked either the means or the will to meet these economic challenges.[87] The decline in quality of life led to serious popular discontent, which manifested in the streets as strikes and demonstrations. "We're on the march," Clark concluded, "and [the Soviet Union] knows it."[88]

Reagan's address on January 16, 1984, highlighted this newfound confidence in US power while glossing over the administration's earlier dialogue with the Soviet Union. In fact, as the election approached, Reagan confided that a commitment to "quiet diplomacy" had guided his administration's handling of US-Soviet relations.[89] He wrote to friend and California real estate developer Paul Trousdale that the United States had engaged in "more contact with the Soviets than anyone is aware of" during his first term.[90] This contact began early and under inauspicious circumstances. On the afternoon of March 30, 1981, as Reagan departed the Washington Hilton, John Hinckley Jr. attempted to assassinate the president in a bizarre bid for the affections of actress Jodie Foster. (He failed on both counts.) While recovering, Reagan wrote to Brezhnev to announce the end of the US grain embargo, which he had opposed from the outset. He also implored Brezhnev to take steps to relax Cold War tensions and "act upon [his] pledge to help foster peace."[91]

Reagan began this "quiet diplomacy" in earnest through a back channel in divided Germany. Under the terms of the settlement regarding Berlin, the US ambassador to West Germany and the Soviet ambassador to East Germany met regularly to discuss the city's peculiar situation. Typically, these meetings focused on administrative and logistical matters, such as air and land traffic. But at their first meeting on October 18, 1981, US ambassador Arthur F. Burns told his Soviet counterpart Petr Abrasimov that a "new team" had taken charge of US foreign policy and hoped to turn over a new leaf in US-Soviet relations. He had been instructed by President Reagan to use this forum not only to deal with issues relating to Berlin but also to resolve larger problems in superpower relations. Abrasimov responded in kind, sharing his hope that the recent talks between US Secretary of State Alexander Haig and his Soviet counterpart Andrei Gromyko represented a first step in reinvigorated US-Soviet talks.[92] At the second Burns-Abrasimov meeting on November 24, 1981, the two had a "substantive and frank" discussion of US-Soviet relations and possible means of reducing nuclear arsenals. Abrasimov conveyed his government's desire to engage in constructive negotiations with the United States, and Burns suggested that the Reagan administration was open to any initiatives toward this end.[93] These conversations contain remarkable insights, such as Burns's likening of Reagan's occasionally hostile rhetoric regarding the Soviet Union "to parents getting carried away by anger and using insulting language towards their own children."[94] The Cold War did not end at a conference table in Berlin, but the ongoing dialogue between the two ambassadors provided a forum for them to speak frankly about superpower relations and international stability, devoid of the need for posturing. These interactions helped counteract the pernicious images that abounded in Washington and Moscow of the other side as innately hostile and intractably warlike.

Another episode of "quiet diplomacy" dealt with the Siberian Seven—the Vaschenko and Chmykhalov families, who had fled Siberia and taken refuge in the US embassy in Moscow after the Soviet government refused to let them emigrate so they could practice their Pentecostal faith.[95] For Reagan, this episode came to personify the issue of human rights in the Soviet Union, and he grew increasingly frustrated by the Kremlin's refusal "to face reality or to show normal human feelings."[96] Reagan and George Shultz, who replaced Haig as secretary of state on July 16, 1982, found a solution through another back channel. Max Kampelman, the US representative at the Conference on Security and Cooperation in Europe (CSCE) in Madrid, began meeting with his Soviet counterparts to discuss the state of the superpower relationship with increasing specificity. Kampelman informed his Soviet interlocutor Sergei Kondrashev, a member of the Soviet CSCE delegation and a KGB general, that Washington hoped to see "significant gestures" as a sign of the Kremlin's commitment to improved relations. Kondrashev later announced to Kampelman that the Soviet Union would allow the Siberian Seven and their relatives to emigrate.[97] Shultz then invited Soviet ambassador Anatoly Dobrynin to the State Department and quickly (and without warning) spirited him to the White House to meet with Reagan, where they came to a final understanding: Moscow would allow the Vaschenko and Chmykhalov families to emigrate, and Reagan pledged not to make political hay "by undue publicity, by claims of credit for ourselves, or by 'crowing.'"[98] To Reagan and his advisers, this success demonstrated that they could do business with the Soviet Union.[99]

Punishing Inconsistency

Reagan had spent three years in office publicly espousing a strong anti-Soviet worldview. His "quiet diplomacy" initiatives remained unknown to most voters because, as Reagan put it, "you can't talk about it afterward or then you can't do it again."[100] Thus, to the general public, Reagan's January 16, 1984, speech marked a sharp change of course in US foreign policy toward the Soviet Union. Reagan's new policy appeared strikingly similar to the one proposed by Mondale. "President Reagan has been nagged by his handlers to wash out his mouth when he talks about the Soviets," Mary McGrory opined in the *Washington Post;* "he was performing a campaign chore." Public opinion polls in 1983 predicted that Reagan would lose to Mondale in the upcoming election, largely due to his belligerent foreign policy.[101] Reagan and his advisers expected that a softer tone would help. Nancy Reagan played an important role behind the scenes, encouraging her husband not to allow himself to be portrayed as a reckless warmonger.[102] But political calculus alone did not bring about the so-called Reagan reversal: it was the public debut of Reagan's long-held desire to negotiate with the Soviet Union and his new confidence that the United States could secure advantageous agreements in so doing.

Nevertheless, the administration's new tone gave the Mondale campaign an opening to attack Reagan. In Mondale's last public speech before January 16, he criticized the president's national security policy along the familiar lines of overspending, failing to make progress on arms control, engaging in excessive anti-Soviet rhetoric (and doing so excessively), and abandoning core US values.[103] After Reagan's speech, Mondale scoffed, "Mr. Reagan has started talking about talking to the Soviets. But at three minutes to midnight, it's past time to talk about talking—it's time to start talking." Tellingly, Mondale paid much more attention to foreign policy than in his usual stump speeches, emphasizing his plan for regular US-Soviet summit meetings and a mutual, verifiable nuclear freeze followed by a reduction in both superpowers' nuclear arsenals. Thereafter, even when talking about domestic issues, in an effort to undermine Reagan's new pacific tone, Mondale made frequent reference to the lingering threat of nuclear Armageddon, made worse by Reagan's handling of foreign policy.[104]

Mondale went on to contrast Reagan's new rhetoric with his earlier belligerence, asserting that the administration wanted to gloss over past foreign policy missteps with a new communications strategy that did not reflect Reagan's own views. "What does Mr. Reagan really believe," Mondale asked an audience at George Washington University, "what he says when he knows the camera's on, or when he thinks the microphone's off?"[105] Reagan had not only behaved cynically, Mondale charged; his shifting stance belied incompetence in foreign policymaking. His administration "has not achieved a single, significant foreign policy success," and it was now resorting to the foreign policy of the Democrats.[106]

In effect, Mondale worked to mobilize the electorate to punish Reagan for changing course, even though the president had actually shifted (publicly) toward Mondale's preferred handling of US-Soviet relations.[107] Reagan's January 16, 1984, speech received widespread public acclaim, as the president moved closer to mainstream global public opinion regarding US-Soviet relations. Could a political rival exploit the well-received speech and change the narrative—and thus alter the potential consequences? Mondale certainly tried: "In the last few days, we've heard a soothing new tone from Mr. Reagan, and we welcome it. For four years, he sounded like Ronald Reagan. This last week, he's tried to sound like Walter Mondale. . . . This presidential sea-change raises a crucial question: which Reagan would be president if he's re-elected? Which Reagan are we to believe? How do we know?"[108]

There is no evidence that Mondale's efforts succeeded. Reagan made the case that only he could steer a foreign policy course for the 1980s that balanced defense and deterrence—unlike the outdated, 1970s-inspired thinking of the Democratic candidate.[109] His campaign platform focused on the United States' reliability as an ally. He emphasized the achievements of the preceding four years: expanding relations with the People's Republic of China, promoting democracy, and investing in US national security. On US-Soviet relations, Reagan summed up his record with reference to the infamous Carter-Brezhnev kiss in Vienna: "I've avoided the kiss and I've avoided any more Afghanistans."[110]

At the polls on November 6, Ronald Reagan ran on his record; in many respects, the election was a referendum on his policies, and it vindicated the president.[111] Mondale's campaign failed to score points on foreign policy, despite its clear line of attack regarding the administration's approach.[112] Mondale attempted to make political hay of Reagan's January 16, 1984, speech on US-Soviet relations, which brought the president's foreign policy rhetoric closer to Mondale's own. However, the Democratic candidate's efforts to manufacture costs for Reagan's inconsistency, like his campaign, amounted to little. The US public proved to be open to greater cooperation with and softening rhetoric toward the Soviet Union, but in the highly tense atmosphere of the "Second Cold War," Mondale's attacks on Reagan's past aggressiveness proved counterproductive. Just as (perhaps) only Nixon could have gone to China, it took a president with a long history of anti-Soviet statements but an equally long-held, albeit quiet, desire to see superpower relations improve to steer the Cold War toward a peaceful conclusion.

Notes

1. Wright memorandum, "The Second Half," January 13, 1983, PREM 19/1405, National Archives of the United Kingdom (NAUK), Kew, United Kingdom.

2. Lou Cannon, *President Reagan: The Role of a Lifetime* (New York: Simon and Schuster, 1991), 508.

3. Kyle Longley, Jeremy D. Mayer, Michael Schaller, and John W. Sloane, *Deconstructing Reagan: Conservative Mythology and America's Fortieth President* (Armonk, NY: M. E. Sharpe, 2007).

4. Beth A. Fischer, *The Reagan Reversal: Foreign Policy and the End of the Cold War* (Columbia: University of Missouri Press, 1997), 141–43.

5. James Mann, *The Rebellion of Ronald Reagan: A History of the End of the Cold War* (New York: Viking, 2009), 78–81.

6. James Graham Wilson, *The Triumph of Improvisation: Gorbachev's Adaptability, Reagan's Engagements, and the End of the Cold War* (Ithaca, NY: Cornell University Press, 2014), 81–86.

7. Clark to Reagan, "Proposed Speech on US-Soviet Relations," August 23, 1983, Jack F. Matlock Files (JFMF), box 41, "US-USSR Relations Jul.–Aug. 1983 2" folder, Ronald Reagan Presidential Library (RRPL), Simi Valley, CA.

8. Aronson to Mondale, December 29, 1981, Walter F. Mondale Papers (WFMP), loc. 146.L.10.1B, "Aronson, Bernie" folder, Minnesota Historical Society (MHS), St. Paul.

9. Ibid.

10. "Walter F. Mondale Stump Speech," WFMP, loc. 153.L.2.8F, "Stump Speech" folder, MHS.

11. Isaacs to Mondale, "Visibility Strategy," April 26, 1981, WFMP, loc. 153.L.2.7B, "Visibility Strategy" folder, MHS.

12. Mondale radio address, August 12, 1984, WFMP, loc. 148.J.17.10F, "Mondale/Ferraro Issue Papers Book" folder, MHS.

13. Galston to Mondale, "Preparation for the Brinkley Show," September 14, 1983, WFMP, loc. 153.J.1.9B, "Correspondence 1983–1984" folder, MHS; "Debate Materials," 1984, WFMP, loc. 146.L.9.1B, "Briefing Book Part 2-I" folder, MHS.

14. "Debate Materials," 1984.

15. Berman to Galston, August 29, 1983, WFMP, loc. 146.L.9.7B, "MX Missile Letter" folder, MHS.

16. Mondale radio address, August 12, 1984.

17. "Debate Materials," 1984.

18. "The Mondale Budget Program," September 12, 1984, WFMP, loc. 153.J.9.1B, "Budget, Deficit, Tax Plan" folder, MHS.

19. Mondale remarks, Chicago Council on Foreign Relations, Chicago, March 14, 1984, WFMP, loc. 146.L.9.7B, "Platform Briefing Materials Book" folder, MHS.

20. Mondale remarks, National Press Club, Washington, DC, March 9, 1982, WFMP, loc. 153.J.1.10F, "Nuclear Freeze Package" folder, MHS.

21. McGowan to Doyle, April 15, 1982, WFMP, loc. 153.L.2.7B, "McGowan" folder, MHS.

22. Mondale remarks, Coalition for a Democratic Majority, Washington, DC, November 19, 1983, WFMP, loc. 153.J.1.10F, "Nuclear Freeze Package" folder, MHS.

23. Mondale remarks, Northern California World Affairs Council, San Francisco, May 15, 1984, WFMP, loc. 146.L.9.7B, "Platform Briefing Materials Book" folder, MHS.

24. Mondale remarks, St. Paul, MN, February 21, 1983, WFMP, loc. P2804, folder 2. MHS.

25. Mondale remarks, American Newspaper Publishers Association, New York, NY, April 26, 1983, WFMP, loc. 148.J.17.10F, "Q&A Notebook" folder, MHS.

26. Mondale remarks, American Legion, Salt Lake City, UT, September 5, 1984, WFMP, loc. 148.J.17.10F, "Mondale/Ferraro Issue Papers Book" folder, MHS.

27. "Debate Materials," 1984.

28. Mondale remarks, Iowa State University, Ames, February 23, 1983, WFMP, loc. 148.J.17.10F, "Q&A Notebook" folder, MHS.

29. "Debate Materials," 1984.

30. Ibid.

31. Mondale remarks, George Washington University, Washington, DC, September 25, 1984, WFMP, loc. 148.J.17.10F, "Mondale/Ferraro Issue Papers Book" folder, MHS.

32. "Debate Materials," 1984.

33. Mondale remarks, Case Western Reserve University, Cleveland, OH, April 24, 1984, WFMP, loc. 146.L.9.7B, "Platform Briefing Materials Book" folder, MHS.

34. "Defense—Star Wars," 1984, WFMP, loc. 146.L.9.1B, "Foreign Policy Briefing Book" folder, MHS.

35. Mondale remarks, Case Western Reserve University, April 24, 1984.

36. "Debate Materials," 1984.

37. Mondale remarks, George Washington University, September 25, 1984.

38. "Debate Materials," 1984; "Meeting of Walter F. Mondale with Representa-

tives of Arms Control Groups," January 23, 1984, WFMP, loc. 153.I.20.7B, "Arms Control Group Response" folder, MHS.

39. Mondale remarks, Bryn Mawr College, Philadelphia, April 7, 1984, WFMP, loc. P2804, folder 4, MHS; "Debate Materials," 1984.

40. "Debate Materials," 1984.

41. Mondale remarks, Iowa State University, February 23, 1983.

42. Mondale remarks, American Newspaper Publishers Association, April 26, 1983.

43. Mondale remarks, American Legion, Salt Lake City, September 5, 1984.

44. "Fact Sheet on Arms Control," May 1984, WFMP, loc. 146.L.9.7B, "Platform Briefing Materials Book" folder, MHS.

45. "Debate Materials," 1984.

46. Institut SShA i Kanady Rossiiskoi Akademii Nauk memorandum, "Osnovnye temy predvybornoĭ bor'by v SShA i vozmozhnye meropriiatiia sovetskoĭ propagandy," March 22, 1985, fond 2021, opis 2, delo 3, Arkhiv Rossiiskoii Akademii Nauk, Moscow, Russian Federation.

47. Mondale radio address, September 16, 1984, WFMP, loc. 148.J.17.10F, "Mondale/Ferraro Issue Papers Book" folder, MHS.

48. Mondale remarks, New York, NY, September 27, 1984, WFMP, loc. 148.J.17.10F, "Mondale/Ferraro Issue Papers Book" folder, MHS.

49. Foreign Broadcast Information Service memorandum, "Soviet Treatment of the US Election Campaign (15 September–12 October 1984)," JFMF, box 7, "Signals Oct.–Dec. 1984 1" folder, RRPL.

50. "Debate Materials," 1984.

51. "Eastern Europe," 1984, WFMP, loc. 146.L.9.1B, "Foreign Policy Briefing Book" folder, MHS; "Debate Materials," 1984.

52. "Debate Materials," 1984.

53. Mondale remarks, American Society of Newspaper Editors, Washington, DC, May 10, 1984, WFMP, loc. 148.J.17.10F, "Mondale/Ferraro Issue Papers Book" folder, MHS.

54. "Debate Materials," 1984.

55. Mondale remarks, National Press Club, Washington, DC, January 3, 1984, WFMP, loc. 146.L.9.7B, "Platform Briefing Materials Book" folder, MHS.

56. Mondale remarks, Coalition for a Democratic Majority, November 19, 1983.

57. "Debate Materials," 1984.

58. Mondale remarks, American Legion, Salt Lake City, September 5, 1984.

59. Mondale remarks, Coalition for a Democratic Majority, November 19, 1983.

60. Mondale remarks, Chicago Council on Foreign Relations, March 14, 1984.

61. Aronson to Johnson, August 24, 1982, WFMP, loc. 146.L.10.1B, "Aronson, Bernie" folder, MHS.

62. "Debate Materials," 1984.

63. "NATO," 1984, WFMP, loc. 146.L.9.1B, "Foreign Policy Briefing Book" folder, MHS.

64. "Debate Materials," 1984.

65. Mondale remarks, Chicago Council on Foreign Relations, March 14, 1984.

66. Mondale to Chernenko, May 19, 1984, WFMP, loc. 146.L.9.6F, "Mondale Telegram to Chernenko" folder, MHS.

67. Robert M. Gates, *From the Shadows: The Ultimate Insider's Story of Five Presidents and How They Won the Cold War* (New York: Simon and Schuster, 1996), 263.

68. Reagan remarks, Parliament of the United Kingdom, London, June 8, 1982, in *Public Papers of the Presidents of the United States: Ronald Reagan, 1982,* vol. 1, ed. Wilma Green, Katherine Melody, and Kenneth Payne (Washington, DC: Government Printing Office, 1983), 742–48.

69. Reagan remarks, Annual Convention of the National Association of Evangelicals, Orlando, FL, March 8, 1983, in *Public Papers of the Presidents of the United States: Ronald Reagan, 1983,* vol. 1, ed. Maxine Hill and Thomas Kevan (Washington, DC: Government Printing Office, 1984), 359–64.

70. Reagan remarks, Washington, DC, January 16, 1984, in *Public Papers of the Presidents: Ronald Reagan, 1984,* vol. 1, ed. Wilma Green (Washington, DC: Government Printing Office, 1985), 40–44.

71. Reagan diary entry, January 6, 1984, in *The Reagan Diaries,* vol. 1, ed. Douglas Brinkley (New York: HarperCollins, 2007), 305.

72. Allen memorandum, "The 'Strategy for Peace' Theme," August 25, 978, James Mann Papers, box 51, Hoover Institution Archive (HIA), Stanford, CA.

73. Reagan televised remarks, October 19, 1980, Alexander M. Haig Papers, box 131, folder 8, Library of Congress, Washington, DC.

74. Furniss to Iklé and Allen, "Suggested Guidelines for Captive Nations Statements," Fred C. Iklé Papers, box 14, "Soviet Union" folder, HIA; Rostow memorandum, "Soviet-American Relations (Other than Arms Control Problems)," December 8, 1980, William J. Casey Papers, box 300, "US-Soviet Relations" folder, HIA.

75. Cannon, *President Reagan,* 281.

76. Paul Lettow, *Ronald Reagan and His Quest to Abolish Nuclear Weapons* (New York: Random House, 2005), 3–4.

77. Reagan to Landers, May 20, 1982, in *Reagan: A Life in Letters,* ed. Kiron Skinner, Annelise Anderson, and Martin Anderson (New York: Free Press, 2003), 406.

78. Reagan diary entry, October 10, 1983, in *Reagan Diaries,* 1:273.

79. Jeremi Suri, "Explaining the End of the Cold War: A New Historical Consensus?" *Journal of Cold War Studies* 4, no. 4 (2002): 63.

80. Wilson, *Triumph of Improvisation,* 38–42.

81. CIA memorandum, "The Development of Soviet Military Power: Trends since 1965 and Prospects for the 1980s," April 1981, Record Group (RG) 263, Princeton University Conference (PUC), box 12, folder 21977, National Archives and Records Administration (NARA), College Park, MD.

82. National Intelligence Estimate (NIE) no. 11-14-81, "Warsaw Pact Forces Opposite NATO," July 7, 1981, RG 263, NIE, box 18, folder 51, NARA.

83. NIE no. 11-4-78, "Soviet Goals and Expectations in the Global Power Arena," July 7, 1981, RG 263, NIE, box 6, folder 44, NARA.

84. Clark to Reagan, "The Prospects for Progress in US-Soviet Relations," February 4, 1983, William P. Clark Files (WPCF), box 8, "US-Soviet Relations Papers 2" folder, RRPL.

85. CIA memorandum, "The Soviet Invasion of Afghanistan: Five Years After," May 19, 1985, RG 263, PUC, box 14, folder 22228, NARA.

86. NIE no. 11-6-84, "Soviet Global Military Reach," November 1984, RG 263, NIE, box 18, folder 59, NARA.

87. CIA memorandum, "USSR: Goals of the 11th Five-Year Plan Unattainable," January 1981, RG 263, PUC, box 14, folder 22219, NARA.

88. Clark to Reagan, "The Prospects for Progress in US-Soviet Relations," February 4, 1983.

89. Reagan to Vaschenko, October 11, 1984, in *Reagan: A Life in Letters,* 380.

90. Reagan to Trousdale, May 23, 1983, ibid., 408–9.

91. Reagan to Brezhnev, April 24, 1981, Executive Secretariat–National Security Council, Head of State File, box 38, "Brezhnev 8190204, 8190205" folder, RRPL.

92. Burns-Abrasimov memorandum of conversation, October 19, 1981, DY 30/IV 2/2.035/67, Stiftung Archiv der Parteien und Massenorganisationen der Deutschen Demokratischen Republik (SAPMO), Berlin, Germany. Burns, the former chair of the Council of Economic Advisors (1953–1956) and of the Federal Reserve (1970–1978), had advised Reagan extensively, mostly on economic matters, during the 1980 campaign. See Reagan to Burns, February 14, 1981, Arthur F. Burns Papers, box 3, "Reagan to Burns" folder, David M. Rubenstein Rare Book and Manuscript Library, Duke University, Durham, NC.

93. Burns-Abrasimov memorandum of conversation, November 24, 1981, SAPMO, DY 30/IV 2/2.035/67.

94. Burns-Kochemasov memorandum of conversation, September 23, 1983, SAPMO, DY 30/IV 2/2.035/67.

95. Shultz to Reagan, "Next Steps in US-Soviet Relations," March 16, 1983, JFMF, box 41, "US-USSR Relations Mar. 1983" folder, RRPL; Haig to Reagan, "Meeting with Dobrynin," April 3, 1981, Richard E. Pipes Files (REPF), box 9, "03/26/1981–03/30/1981" folder, RRPL.

96. Arthur Hartman oral history, November 3, 1989, Don Oberdorfer Papers (DOP), box 2, folder 16, Seeley G. Mudd Manuscript Library (MML), Princeton University, Princeton, NJ; Clark to Reagan, "Brezhnev's Answer to Your Letter in Support of the Pentecostalists in Embassy Moscow," January 26, 1982, REPF, box 12, "01/26/1982–01/31/1982" folder, RRPL.

97. Kampelman-Kondrashev memorandum of conversation, May 5, 1983, Max M. Kampelman Papers, loc. 151.C.5.2F, "Department of State Staff Correspondence, 1980–1983" folder, MHS.

98. George Shultz oral history, July 11, 1989, DOP, box 3, folder 2, MML; Jack F. Matlock, *Reagan and Gorbachev: How the Cold War Ended* (New York: Random House, 2004), 54–59.

99. Meeting record, April 6, 1983, WPCF, box 8, "US-Soviet Relations Papers 4" folder, RRPL.

100. Reagan to Koehler, July 9, 1981, in *Reagan: A Life in Letters,* 375.

101. Fischer, *Reagan Reversal,* 51–57.

102. Cannon, *President Reagan,* 508–9.

103. Mondale remarks, New Hampshire National Security Committee, Manchester, January 12, 1984, WFMP, loc. 153.I.20.7B, "New Hampshire National Security Committee" folder, MHS.

104. Mondale remarks, Maycrest College, Davenport, IA, January 18, 1984, WFMP, loc. 153.I.20.7B, "Iowa" folder, MHS.

105. Mondale remarks, George Washington University, Washington, DC, September 25, 1984, WFMP, loc. 148.J.17.10F, "Mondale/Ferraro Issue Papers Book" folder, MHS.

106. Mondale radio address, August 12, 1984, WFMP, loc. 148.J.17.10F, "Mondale/Ferraro Issue Papers Book" folder, MHS; Mondale remarks, National Press Club, Washington, DC, January 3, 1984, WFMP, loc. 146.L.9.7B, "Platform Briefing Materials Book" folder, MHS; Mondale remarks, New Brunswick, NJ, October 1, 1984, WFMP, loc. 148.J.17.10F, "Mondale/Ferraro Issue Papers Book" folder, MHS.

107. This punishment at the hands of the electorate for "backing down" is known as the audience costs mechanism. Generally, it addresses the question of how states make their preferences known, especially during times of crisis, and why threats matter. Voters' ability to punish leaders for failing to implement their earlier threats creates additional incentives for leaders to stand firm. If a government will pay an electoral price (i.e., be voted out of power) for backing down, the theory dictates, its foreign interlocutors will take its commitments more seriously. This is the equivalent of a participant in a game of Chicken finding some way to toss his or her steering wheel out the car window in view of the oncoming challenger. The body of literature holds that this is especially the case in democracies, since their citizens know more about foreign policy and leaders are accountable to an electorate. This is the basic argument of James Fearon, "Domestic Political Audiences and the Escalation of International Disputes," *American Political Science Review* 88, no. 3 (1994): 577–79. For a skeptic's take, see Marc Trachtenberg, "Kennedy, Vietnam, and Audience Costs," *H-Diplo/ISSF Forum* 3 (2014): 6–42.

108. Mondale remarks, New Brunswick, NJ, October 1, 1984.

109. McFarlane to Casey, October 10, 1984, Robert C. McFarlane Files, box 4, "Soviet Union Sensitive File 1984" folder, RRPL.

110. McFarlane to Darman, October 10, 1984, ibid.

111. Wright to Howe, "The 1984 US Presidential Election: Why Reagan Won," November 7, 1984, PREM 19/1405, NAUK.

112. Wright to Howe, "1984 US Presidential Election Result: What Will Reagan Do?" November 6, 1982, ibid.

Conclusion

Politics, Diplomacy, and the State of the Field

Mitchell B. Lerner

In August 2016 two prominent historians—Fredrik Logevall from Harvard and Kenneth Osgood from Colorado School of Mines—penned an editorial for the *New York Times* that lamented the decline of political history as a scholarly field.[1] Universities' commitment to political history—along with its "cousins" military and diplomatic history—had been waning in recent decades, they noted, as evidenced by the dwindling numbers of faculty, graduate students, and new jobs dedicated to the field. This was a fairly recent development. As they explained: "Political history—a specialization in elections and elected officials, policy and policy making, parties and party politics—was once a dominant, if not the dominant, pursuit of American historians." But a number of forces—the public's increased hostility toward elite policymakers after the Vietnam War, the growing demand for a greater focus on grassroots social movements in the wake of the civil rights and other reform movements, and the expanding educational opportunities available after Great Society reforms opened the doors of the profession to those from traditionally neglected backgrounds—helped turn the field away from this top-down approach focusing on structures and policymaking elite and more toward social approaches emphasizing the voices and influence of those outside the traditional ranks of power. The potential consequences for the nation's future seemed dire to Logevall and Osgood. Since fewer classes on political history were being offered, fewer students were being exposed to this critical aspect of their nation's past, and Americans were thus becoming ill equipped to understand their own political environment. "What was once a central part of the historical profession," they lamented, "a vital part of this country's continuing democratic discussion, is disappearing."

The editorial sparked an explosive response from the American public, many of whom agreed with the authors. "This is exactly why younger Americans have little idea of what came before, or how their own government works," wrote one commentator. "It's pretty sad, and it leads to election cycles like the one we have today."[2] Academics were less sympathetic. Political history was not dead, most insisted. The field had simply moved beyond the narrow focus at the core of Logevall and Osgood's definition and embraced newer methodologies, more diverse subjects, and more nuanced approaches that presented a fuller picture of what it meant to be political. "In the last twenty-five years," argued a historian at Claremont McKenna College:

> The field of political history has been reenergized by drawing on the insights and methodologies of other subfields and disciplines such as social history, intellectual history, cultural studies, urban studies, and law. Historians working outside of traditional political history and engaged in the study of race, gender, class and sexuality, the environment, religion, the transnational flow of ideas, peoples and goods, business and the economy, and culture have offered new explorations and insights into topics such as state power and control, citizenship and political movements and subjectivity. Recent scholarly projects and modes of inquiry like study of the carceral state and the history of American capitalism are expanding understandings of political history and political economy. The fact that Logevall and Osgood did not recognize such works in their piece and marginalize them in their own definition of political history, nevertheless, does suggest that scholars committed to this more expansive approach and those who adopt a more traditional and institutionally-based approach are not always in conversation with another.[3]

Others agreed. "The search for politics," concluded a graduate student at City University of New York, "moved out of the state house and into the streets, the fields, the parlor, and even the bedroom. . . . More historians than ever are writing about politics—if not on the terms laid out by Logevall and Osgood."[4]

This broader definition of the field did not sit well with all its practitioners. Some, even before the Logevall-Osgood piece appeared, claimed that these "newer" approaches were defining themselves against a straw man, and even in its infancy, American political history was broader and more diverse than was now being remembered; the "new" approaches were thus less new than their advocates liked to claim.[5] Others dismissed the intellectual underpinnings of the more recent approaches, arguing that they ignored the fact that the political system's centrality was readily acknowledged by the denizens of the very societies in question. The newer approaches, wrote Gertrude Himmelfarb, thus asked "questions of the past which the past did not ask of itself," sought answers where "the evidence is sparse and unreliable," and reached conclusions that were "necessarily speculative, subjective, and dubious."[6] This debate had long flown under the public radar, playing out largely in academic conferences and journals. The *New York Times* op-ed, however, brought the tensions into the public eye and boosted long-simmering grievances to a boil.

In fact, both sides have a point. The "old" political history, with its focus on elections, political parties, and the legislative process, has indeed fallen from favor. Between 1975 and 2015, the percentage of political historians in the profession remained roughly constant, while the number of specialists in religion increased 147 percent, specialists in race and ethnicity increased 220 percent, and historians of women and gender increased 797 percent.[7] Signs suggest that such trends will continue. The tentative results of a survey conducted by Logevall and Osgood after their piece appeared in the *New York Times* found that of almost 7,000 job openings in the field over the last decade, only 1 percent of the advertisements for tenure-track assistant professors listed either US political history or US constitutional history as the preferred area of specialization.[8] Yet, if we move beyond the definition offered by those authors, it appears that the field is as vibrant as ever. Political (as well as diplomatic and military) history has adapted and evolved, embracing and incorporating newer approaches and techniques and reaching new heights in terms of both quality scholarship and academic prominence. A new generation of scholars has penned hundreds of books (and landed any number of tenure-track jobs) that skillfully address political topics and advance our knowledge of American political and diplomatic history, even though their focus might be thousands of miles from Washington, DC.[9] Civil rights efforts, union activism, environmental concerns, class divisions, regional values, nongovernmental organizations, and so much more lie at the heart of these new studies, reminding us that, as Tip O'Neill famously said, "all politics is local." This generation of political historians might not have written about elections, but they certainly wrote about the factors that shape them and the larger sociopolitical milieu in which they occur. To paraphrase Mark Twain, the field's death has been greatly exaggerated, depending on how it is defined.

The eleven essays here speak to the vitality and diversity of the field, in terms of both their unifying themes and their disparate methodological approaches. On the larger level, the works share a desire to bring together the political and the international. Some, like David Prentice's study of how Melvin Laird's views on the Vietnam War evolved in ways that remained true to his core convictions yet advanced the political interests of himself and his party, focus on the international consequences of domestic politics. "Laird's political calculations sharpened his militant rhetoric," Prentice concludes, "providing a blueprint for how to play politics with foreign policy." Henry Maar similarly links domestic politics with major international events, rooting Richard Nixon's arms limitation talks in a changing public mood that forced him to take action to placate the electorate, even though he had little commitment to those reforms. Others reverse this approach and ask how specific events overseas reshaped American politics. Daniel Hummel, for example, demonstrates how changing international conditions in the Middle East helped remake domestic political coalitions, and Rasmus Søndergaard links the growth of the influential Congressional Human Rights Caucus to the plight of the Soviet refuseniks. Regardless of the specifics of the argument, however, the historians whose works are collected here find a synergy between the foreign and the domestic that reflects the profession's growing interest in globalization, transnationalism, and the international world.

At the same time, these essays reflect the growing methodological diversity that has transformed the field over the past decades. Washington, DC, is obviously a central location for many of the stories, but it is just one of many. In this volume, the reader is taken from Vietnam to Colorado to Miami to find the impetus for, and track the consequences of, political activity. Christopher Foss shows us how the politics of Washington State was just as important to understanding the political and economic story of the West Coast as the politics of Washington, DC. Presidential elections are, of course, critical factors in shaping political events, as demonstrated in Tizoc Chavez's argument that Nixon's trips to China and the USSR were shaped in part by the president's desire to "use foreign affairs to change the narrative" of the impending 1972 election. Yet, one is equally struck by the influence of less structural forces such as religious revivals, defense industry lobbyists, and human rights concerns. Amanda Demmer, for example, brings together humanitarian interests, migration studies, and Vietnamese voices in her chronicle of the emergence of the Families of Vietnamese Political Prisoners Association and its impact on American postwar policy toward Vietnam. And while the actual politics of governing is a topic of many of the essays, the authors move beyond traditional concerns about process and impact to discuss larger questions about American identity and values. The State Department's Office of Public Affairs may have played an important role in Harry Truman's foreign policy, Autumn Lass suggests, but she is more interested in understanding how its proponents squared the office's propagandistic functions with American traditions.

Although there is great variety among the essays collected here in terms of topic and approach, a number of central themes emerge, some of which hint at new and exciting directions for the future. Perhaps the most obvious connection among the essays, and one that reflects larger trends in the discipline overall, is the impact nonelites can have on the shaping of foreign policy. Gone are the days (if they ever actually existed) of political and diplomatic historians studying elite policymakers in isolation, as if they were unconstrained in their policymaking by the larger environment surrounding them. In these pages, Jorge Mas Canosa—a Cuban American immigrant who had worked as a milkman and a shoe salesman—forces the Justice Department to reverse its policy on Cuban refugees, and Khuc Minh Tho—a Vietnamese immigrant who did not arrive in the United States until 1975—helps override an Immigration and Naturalization Service decision to change the age requirements for Vietnamese immigrants. In other cases, specific popular movements sparked long-standing structural changes that outlasted the very issues that created them, as Søndergaard demonstrates in his story of the creation of the Congressional Human Rights Caucus. And in still others, a demanding public forced political leaders to embrace positions that were completely antithetical to their own views; Nixon may not have had much interest in limiting the arms race or supporting anti-nuclear activism, but he was compelled to take actions that at least brought the issue into the political dialogue because of grassroots movements.

A second common theme is the correlation between political language and changing social values, as numerous authors note the extent to which political lobbying groups or, in some cases, politicians themselves consciously sought––generally with some success––to use specific language and create specific images that resonated with the sociopolitical views of the American public at the time. Many of these essays—including Hummel's study of how Jewish groups won over evangelicals, Hideaki Kami's examination of how the Cuban American National Foundation helped redefine Cuban Americans as "ordinary" Americans, Lass's examination of how the Office of Public Affairs shaped propaganda pamphlets based on the rhetoric of "freedom," and Simon Miles's examination of the language used by Walter Mondale in his effort to redefine Ronald Reagan in the 1984 presidential election—demonstrate how specific words and phrases were tailored to match the public's core beliefs and values. Framing itself "in ways that highlighted familial relationships," concludes Demmer in her study of the Families of Vietnamese Political Prisoners Association, "gave the association an emotionally poignant way to sell its cause. . . . Family reunification rhetoric fell on especially receptive ears in the 1980s, thanks to the Reagan administration's emphasis on a return to 'family values.'" In today's era of increasing political polarization, attributable at least in part to new forms of communication rooted in the social media explosion and increasingly sophisticated methods of political communication developed over the last few decades, the importance of studies of political rhetoric and societal values seems obvious.

The importance of place, particularly its local context, in shaping political values and thus directing lager policy stands out in some of these essays as well. Until recently, historians generally ignored the impact of regional forces and local values on the modern political system—perhaps a reflection of the embrace of a "consensus" school of American development. "To many scholars," wrote one prominent Western historian, "regional history is where one goes for a nap."[10] And yet the last decade has seen the stirrings of a new interest in the connection between place and policy, with a spate of books, articles, and roundtables devoted to the topic.[11] Region, explained one prominent historian, is "by far the most salient" influence on the "expression of power in American politics."[12] The contributors to this volume seem to agree. Foss's essay is perhaps the most overt, as the linkage between politician and state clearly emerges as the dominant theme in both Senator Henry Jackson's political career and the evolution of Washington State itself. But place (Miami) matters to Kami's story of Cuban lobbyists, and place (Colorado Springs, Bethesda, and Long Island, among others) matters to Michael Brenes's essay on the political economy of the Cold War. Place (Wisconsin) also matters to the "less ideological midwestern Republicans" whom Prentice finds at the heart of Laird's politics and foreign policy. The Cold War shaped the West, just as it shaped the South and the Midwest, through its military and defense investments in the region and its reinforcement, and sometimes redefinition, of regional conceptions of honor, individualism, and militarism.[13] In turn, the people of those regions organized, lobbied, and voted to advance their own perceived interests in accordance with the value system and traditions of the areas that had molded them. Political history, Foss correctly shows us, "is much richer when considering the intersection of domestic politics, regional interests, and US foreign policy."

Foss's words apply to this volume as a whole. Despite their differences, the contributors have managed to find a place at the intersection of diplomatic and political history, where they have brought a wide range of methodological approaches that merges the best of the old and new and makes the field richer overall. Elections, presidents, and laws are still central to the story, but so are ethnic groups, religion, economic development, human rights, and so much more. The authors have embraced the charge of Logevall and Osgood to "remind us of our political past," while incorporating into that reminder a broad and inclusive perspective that reflects the complexity and diversity of the stories themselves. Former national security adviser Anthony Lake once remarked that the intersection of domestic politics and foreign policy was rarely acknowledged by policymakers but always present; it was "like sex to the Victorians: Nobody talks about it, but it's on everybody's mind."[14] The essays here point toward a future relationship between these fields, where their intersection is not only in the back of everybody's minds but at the forefront of the profession as well.

Notes

1. Fredrik Logevall and Kenneth Osgood, "The End of Political History," *New York Times,* August 29, 2016, A17.

2. See the comments section at http://www.nytimes.com/2016/08/29/opinion/why-did-we-stop-teaching-political-history.html.

3. Lily Geismer quoted in http://www.processhistory.org/state-of-political-history/.

4. Roy Rogers quoted in https://earlyamericanists.com/2016/09/09/the-strange-death-of-political-history/.

5. See, for example, Mark Leff, "Revisioning U.S. Political History," *American Historical Review,* June 1995.

6. Gertrude Himmelfarb, *The New History and the Old* (Cambridge, MA: Harvard University Press, 2004), 48.

7. "The Rise and Decline of History Specializations over the Past 40 Years," *Perspectives on History,* December 2015.

8. Fredrik Logevall and Kenneth Osgood, "US Political History: Alive and Well?" *Perspectives on History,* January 2017.

9. A comprehensive list of such works would be far too long to include here, but there are many good examples. Alice Echols, *Hot Stuff* (New York: Norton, 2010), shows how music both reflects and shapes political activism; Erik Loomis, *Empire of Timber* (Cambridge: Cambridge University Press, 2015), redefines our understanding of labor politics by bringing environmental history into the discussion; Meg Jacobs, *Pocketbook Politics* (Princeton, NJ: Princeton University Press, 2007), puts the question of daily living standards into the heart of national politics; Gretchen Heefner, *The Missile Next Door* (Cambridge, MA: Harvard University Press, 2012), demonstrates how the Cold War transformed the lives and values of rural Americans in the Plains states; Timothy Stewart-Winter, *Queer Clout* (Philadelphia: University of Pennsylvania Press, 2015), tracks the increasing political power of the LGBTQ movement; Ronald Takaki, *Double Victory* (Boston: Back Bay, 2001), offers a broad look at the important role played by American minorities during World War II and the impact on subsequent political reform; Hajimu Masuda, *Cold War Crucible* (Cambridge, MA: Harvard University Press, 2015), traces the powerful impact of the Korean War on popular opinion across the globe and the consequences for traditional political structures; Bethany Moreton, *To Serve God and Wal-Mart* (Cambridge, MA: Harvard University Press, 2009), connects evangelical Christianity with capitalism, culture, and globalization to explore political change at home and abroad; Lizbeth Cohen, *A Consumer's Republic* (Cambridge, MA: Harvard University Press, 2003), connects America's consumer mentality with social and political reform; Thomas Borstelmann, *The Cold War and the Color Line* (Cambridge, MA: Harvard University Press, 2003), brilliantly ties together politics, race, and American foreign policy; and Christina Klein, *Cold War Orientalism* (Berkeley: University

of California Press, 2003), merges popular culture, racial perceptions, and foreign policy in East Asia.

10. Patricia Nelson Limerick, "Region and Reason," in *All over the Map: Rethinking American Regions,* ed. Edward L. Ayers, Patricia Nelson Limerick, Stephen Nissenbaum, and Peter S. Onuf (Baltimore: Johns Hopkins University Press, 1995), 84.

11. See, for example, the roundtable "Special Forum: Domestic Regionalism and U.S. Foreign Relations," *Diplomatic History,* June 2012.

12. Ed Ayers quoted in William Leuchtenberg, *The White House Looks South* (Baton Rouge: Louisiana State University Press, 2007), 347.

13. See, for example, Bruce J. Schulman, *From Cotton Belt to Sunbelt* (Durham, NC: Duke University Press, 1994); Ann Markusen, Peter Hall, Scott Campbell, and Sabina Deitrick, *The Rise of the Gunbelt* (New York: Oxford University Press, 1991); Dewey Grantham, *The South in Modern America* (Fayetteville: University of Arkansas Press, 2001); Joseph A. Fry, *Dixie Looks Abroad* (Baton Rouge: Louisiana State University Press, 2002); Leuchtenberg, *The White House Looks South;* Heefner, *Missile Next Door.*

14. Anthony Lake, *Six Nightmares* (Boston: Little, Brown, 2000), 260.

Acknowledgments

This project originated as part of the 2015 Summer Institute sponsored by the Society for Historians of American Foreign Relations (SHAFR), which we codirected. One of our goals was to provide a group of emerging young scholars with an opportunity to showcase their research about the nexus of domestic politics and foreign policy. This book represents the culmination of that goal, and we could not be more thrilled with the results. We look forward to continuing our professional and personal relationships with them in the years to come.

We want to sincerely thank SHAFR for creating and supporting the Summer Institute, both financially and institutionally. We also wish to express our gratitude to the Mershon Center for International Security Studies at The Ohio State University for its support of the Institute. Moreover, we acknowledge the invaluable contributions and involvement of friends and colleagues Peter Hahn, Robert "KC" Johnson, Sean Kay, Ken Osgood, Rachel Osgood, Marc Selverstone, and Molly Wood, and we especially thank Amanda Bundy for her yeoman's work in keeping everything organized in the face of our inefficiencies.

Over the past three years, we have been fortunate to work with a number of talented young historians as this anthology evolved. The contributors to this volume—Michael Brenes, Tizoc Chavez, Amanda Demmer, Christopher Foss, Daniel Hummel, Hideaki Kami, Autumn Lass, Henry Maar, Simon Miles, David Prentice, and Rasmus Søndergaard—have been great to work with, and they are responsible for the success of this collection. We express our heartfelt gratitude to all of them for their exceptional efforts in helping to make this book a reality.

Our sincere thanks also go out to the team at the University Press of Kentucky (UPK), especially Melissa Hammer, for guiding the book through the entire process. We also want to thank Steve Wrinn, former director of UPK (and now director of the University of Notre Dame Press), for his presentation on academic publishing during the Summer Institute and his early and enthusiastic support of this project. Thanks as well to the general editors of the Studies in Conflict, Diplomacy, and Peace series—George Herring and Kathryn Statler—for their confidence in the project and for including it in their terrific series.

We also thank the anonymous reviewers for their careful reading of earlier versions of the manuscript. Their cogent comments and insightful suggestions improved the volume, and we appreciate their contributions to the final book.

Contributors

Michael Brenes is senior archivist for American diplomacy and lecturer in history at Yale University. He is the author of *Power Politics: The Militarization of the Cold War and the Remaking of American Democracy,* which is forthcoming from Cornell University Press. He is currently writing a biography of Hubert H. Humphrey.

Tizoc Chavez is visiting assistant professor of political science at Vanderbilt University. His research focuses on the personal diplomacy of US presidents. He is currently working on a book titled *At the Highest Level: Personal Diplomacy and the American Presidency.* He received his PhD in history from Vanderbilt University.

Amanda C. Demmer is visiting assistant professor at Boston College. She is currently completing a book that explores the role of refugee politics in postwar US-Vietnam relations entitled *Moving On: Migrants and the Last Chapter of the Vietnam War.* She has received fellowships from the Clements Center for National Security, the Society of Historians for American Foreign Relations, the Gerald R. Ford Presidential Library, and the Hoover Institution, among others.

Christopher Foss is a visiting lecturer in history at the University of Portland, Willamette University, and Tokyo International University of America. He received his PhD in US foreign relations history from the University of Colorado at Boulder in 2016. His research has been published in *Passport: The Society for Historians of American Foreign Relations Review, History Teacher,* and *Oregon Historical Quarterly,* and he is currently working on a book exploring the links between international relations and economic growth in the post–World War II Pacific Northwest.

Daniel G. Hummel is Robert M. Kingdon fellow at the Institute for Research in the Humanities at the University of Wisconsin–Madison. He is completing his first book, *A Covenant of the Mind: American Evangelicals, Israel, and the Construction of a Special Relationship,* which is under contract with the University of Pennsylvania Press. His research on religion and foreign affairs has appeared in *Religion & American Culture, Marginalia, War on the Rocks,* and *First Things.*

Andrew L. Johns is associate professor of history at Brigham Young University and the David M. Kennedy Center for International Studies. He is the author of *Vietnam's Second Front: Domestic Politics, the Republican Party, and the War* (2010) and the editor of four books, including *A Companion to Ronald Reagan* (2015) and *Diplomatic Games: Sport, Statecraft, and International Relations since 1945* (2014). He serves as editor of *Passport: The Society for Historians of American Foreign Relations Review;* is general editor of the Studies in Conflict, Diplomacy, and Peace series, published by the University Press of Kentucky; and was elected president of the Pacific Coast Branch of the American Historical Association for 2018–2019.

Hideaki Kami is assistant professor in the Department of English (US History) at Kanagawa University in Yokohama, Japan. His forthcoming book *Diplomacy Meets Migration: U.S. Relations with Cuba during the Cold War* will be published by Cambridge University Press.

Autumn Lass is assistant professor of history at Wayland Baptist University in Plainview, Texas, where she teaches US foreign relations, military history, world history, and twentieth-century US history. A specialist in US foreign relations and Cold War propaganda, her current research project is titled "Far from Being Propaganda: The Office of Public Affairs, Truth-Telling, and Domestic Propaganda during the Truman Administration." She completed her PhD at Texas Tech University.

Mitchell B. Lerner is associate professor of history and director of the Institute for Korea Studies at The Ohio State University. He is the author of *The Pueblo Incident: A Spy Ship and the Failure of American Foreign Policy* (2002) and the editor of *Looking Back at LBJ* (2005) and *A Companion to Lyndon B. Johnson* (2012). He has been a fellow at the University of Virginia's Miller Center of Public Affairs, served on the governing council of the Society for Historians of American Foreign Relations, and held the Mary Ball Washington Distinguished Fulbright Chair at University College, Dublin.

Henry R. Maar III is a modern US historian with interests in the Cold War, social movements, and foreign policy. He received his PhD in history from the University of California, Santa Barbara in 2015. His research has received the support of the American Institute of Physics, the Cushwa Center at the University of Notre Dame, the University of California Institute of Global Conflict and Cooperation, and the Center for the Study of the United States and the Cold War at New York University, where he was the Agnese N. Haury postdoctoral fellow. He is currently finishing a manuscript on the nuclear weapons freeze campaign of the 1980s.

Simon Miles is assistant professor in the Sanford School of Public Policy at Duke University. His current book project explores the causes of the end of the Cold War, using recently declassified archival materials from both sides of the Iron Curtain. He completed his PhD in history at the University of Texas at Austin.

David L. Prentice received his PhD from Ohio University. He is an award-winning instructor at the Osher Lifelong Learning Institute at Oklahoma State University. He is currently revising a book manuscript on the domestic origins and international ramifications of America's exit strategy from Vietnam, tentatively titled *Ending America's Vietnam War.* His article "Choosing 'the Long Road': Henry Kissinger, Melvin Laird, Vietnamization, and the War over Nixon's Vietnam Strategy" was recently published in *Diplomatic History.*

Rasmus Sinding Søndergaard is a postdoctoral fellow at Georgetown University. He holds a PhD in American history from the University of Southern Denmark and has been a visiting scholar at the University of California–Berkeley. His publications include "Bill Clinton's 'Democratic Enlargement' and the Securitisation of Democracy Promotion," *Diplomacy & Statecraft* (2015), and "The Domestic Politics of U.S. Human Rights Policy," *Passport: The Society for Historians of American Foreign*

Relations Review (2016). He is currently working on a book on the role of human rights in US foreign policy during the 1980s.

Index

Studies in Conflict, Diplomacy, and Peace

Series Editors: George C. Herring, Andrew L. Johns, and Kathryn C. Statler

This series focuses on key moments of conflict, diplomacy, and peace from the eighteenth century to the present to explore their wider significance in the development of U.S. foreign relations. The series editors welcome new research in the form of original monographs, interpretive studies, biographies, and anthologies from historians, political scientists, journalists, and policymakers. A primary goal of the series is to examine the United States' engagement with the world, its evolving role in the international arena, and the ways in which the state, nonstate actors, individuals, and ideas have shaped and continue to influence history, both at home and abroad.

Books in the Series

Truman, Congress, and Korea: The Politics of America's First Undeclared War
Larry Blomstedt
The Gulf: The Bush Presidencies and the Middle East
Michael F. Cairo
Reagan and the World: Leadership and National Security, 1981–1989
Edited by Bradley Lynn Coleman and Kyle Longley
American Justice in Taiwan: The 1957 Riots and Cold War Foreign Policy
Stephen G. Craft

Diplomatic Games: Sport, Statecraft, and International Relations since 1945
Edited by Heather L. Dichter and Andrew L. Johns
Nothing Less Than War: A New History of America's Entry into World War I
Justus D. Doenecke
Aid under Fire: Nation Building and the Vietnam War
Jessica Elkind
Enemies to Allies: Cold War Germany and American Memory
Brian C. Etheridge
Grounded: The Case for Abolishing the United States Air Force
Robert M. Farley
The American South and the Vietnam War: Belligerence, Protest, and Agony in Dixie
Joseph A. Fry
Obama at War: Congress and the Imperial Presidency
Ryan C. Hendrickson
US Presidential Elections and Foreign Policy: Candidates, Campaigns, and Global Politics from FDR to Bill Clinton
Edited by Andrew Johnstone and Andrew Priest
The Cold War at Home and Abroad: Domestic Politics and US Foreign Policy since 1945
Edited by Andrew L. Johns and Mitchell B. Lerner
Paving the Way for Reagan: The Influence of Conservative Media on US Foreign Policy
Lawrence R. Jurdem
The Conversion of Senator Arthur H. Vandenberg: From Isolation to International Engagement
Lawrence S. Kaplan
Harold Stassen: Eisenhower, the Cold War, and the Pursuit of Nuclear Disarmament
Lawrence S. Kaplan
Nixon's Back Channel to Moscow: Confidential Diplomacy and Détente
Richard A. Moss
Peacemakers: American Leadership and the End of Genocide in the Balkans
James W. Pardew
The Currents of War: A New History of American-Japanese Relations, 1899–1941
Sidney Pash
Eisenhower and Cambodia: Diplomacy, Covert Action, and the Origins of the Second Indochina War
William J. Rust
So Much to Lose: John F. Kennedy and American Policy in Laos
William J. Rust
Foreign Policy at the Periphery: The Shifting Margins of US International Relations since World War II
Edited by Bevan Sewell and Maria Ryan
Lincoln Gordon: Architect of Cold War Foreign Policy
Bruce L. R. Smith
Thomas C. Mann: President Johnson, the Cold War, and the Restructuring of Latin American Foreign Policy
Thomas Tunstall Allcock